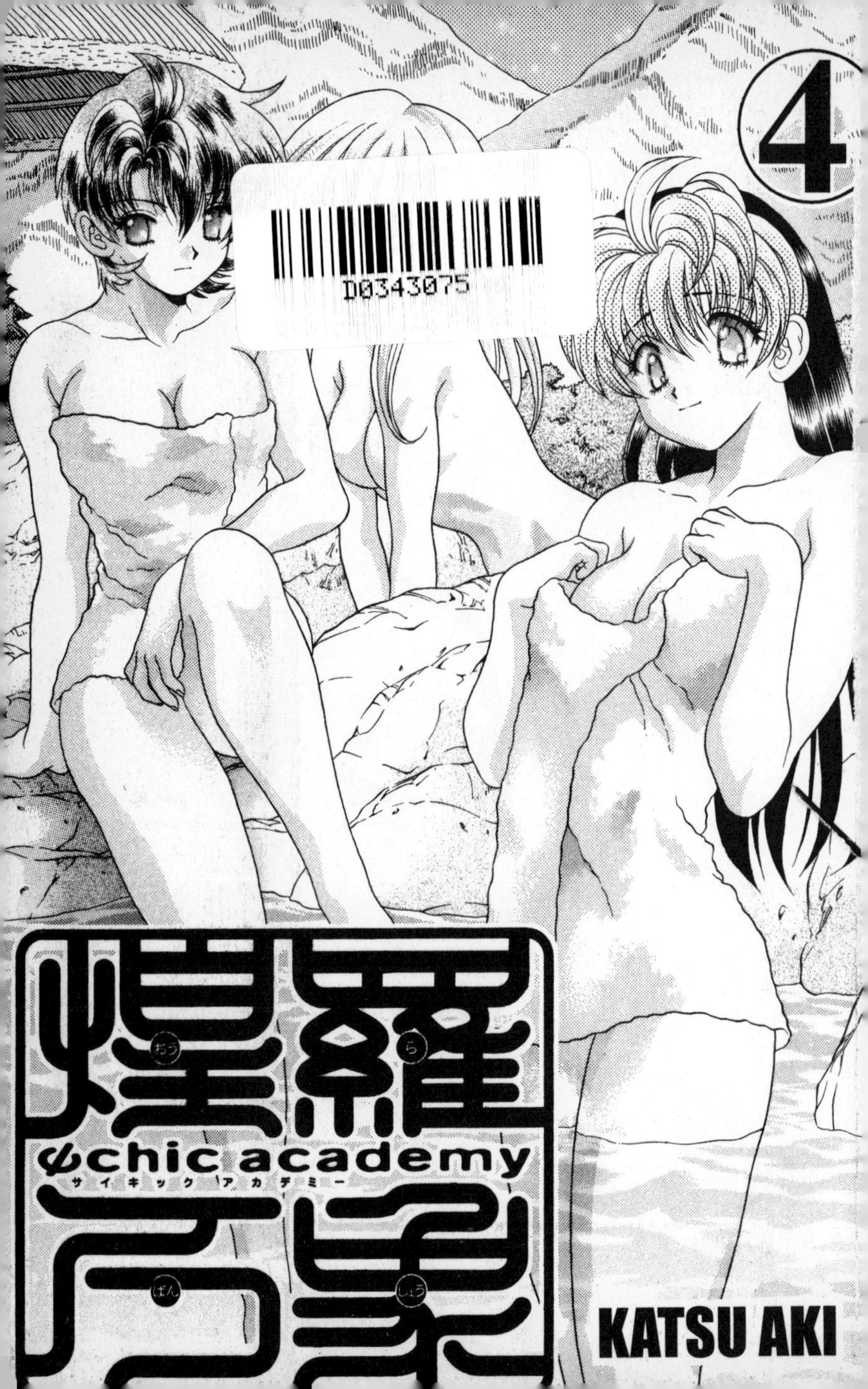
4
煌羅万象
おう ら ばん しょう
ψchic academy
サイキックアカデミー
KATSU AKI

PSYCHIC ACADEMY

VOLUME 4

By
Katsu Aki

TOKYOPOP®

HAMBURG // LONDON // LOS ANGELES // TOKYO

Psychic Academy Vol. 4

created by Katsu Aki

Translation - Jan Scott Frazier
English Adaptation - Nathan Johnson
Associate Editor - Wendy Hunter
Retouch and Lettering - Eric Botero
Production Artist - Louis Csontos
Cover Design - Anna Kernbaum

Editor - Luis Reyes
Digital Imaging Manager - Chris Buford
Pre-Press Manager - Antonio DePietro
Production Managers - Jennifer Miller and Mutsumi Miyazaki
Art Director - Matt Alford
Managing Editor - Jill Freshney
VP of Production - Ron Klamert
President and C.O.O. - John Parker
Publisher and C.E.O. - Stuart Levy

A  Manga

TOKYOPOP Inc.
5900 Wilshire Blvd. Suite 2000
Los Angeles, CA 90036

E-mail: info@TOKYOPOP.com
Come visit us online at www.TOKYOPOP.com

ISBN: 1-59182-624-1

First TOKYOPOP printing: September 2004
10 9 8 7 6 5 4 3 2 1
Printed in the USA

Story Thus Far...

In the near future, the discovery of psychic abilities has run congruously with the threat of evil forces. Luckily one man, Zerodyme Kyupura Pa Azalraku Vairu Rua Darogu, employing his incredible psychic power, has defeated the Dark Overlord and earned the venerable title, "Vanquisher of the Dark Overlord." The world is safe, but not complacent. Now, children who demonstrate a proclivity for psychic powers are separated from the common herd and placed in specialty schools designed to help them enhance their unique abilities. Of course, this separation has aroused suspicion and distrust among "normal" humans.

Ai Shimoi was perfectly happy NOT being so gifted. However, pressured by his parents, and with a filial reputation thrust upon him by his brother, the aforementioned Vanquisher of the Dark Overlord, Ai enrolled in the Psychic Academy. His life at the Academy has been a difficult one, dealing as he is with new powers, a new school and, perhaps worst of all, the onset of adolescence. Luckily he has the support of his old friend Sahra, his roommate Telda, the stern but caring Mew and a strange bunny, Master Boo, who vows to train the young buck in the psychic arts. And as luck would have it, his brother teaches at the school.

Now, he's acing his exams, he's making plenty of friends and his brother is keeping an eye on him—for better or for worse. Nothing really seems to be going that badly... except for the spike in anti-psychic violence, a movement that may very well have its roots within the Psychic Academy itself. And, of course, Ai is torn between his love for Sahra—to whom he has confessed his love, and from whom he has received the same—and his inexplicable connection to Mew, for whom any expression of love or affection is absolute torture.

CONTENTS

煌羅万象
chic academy

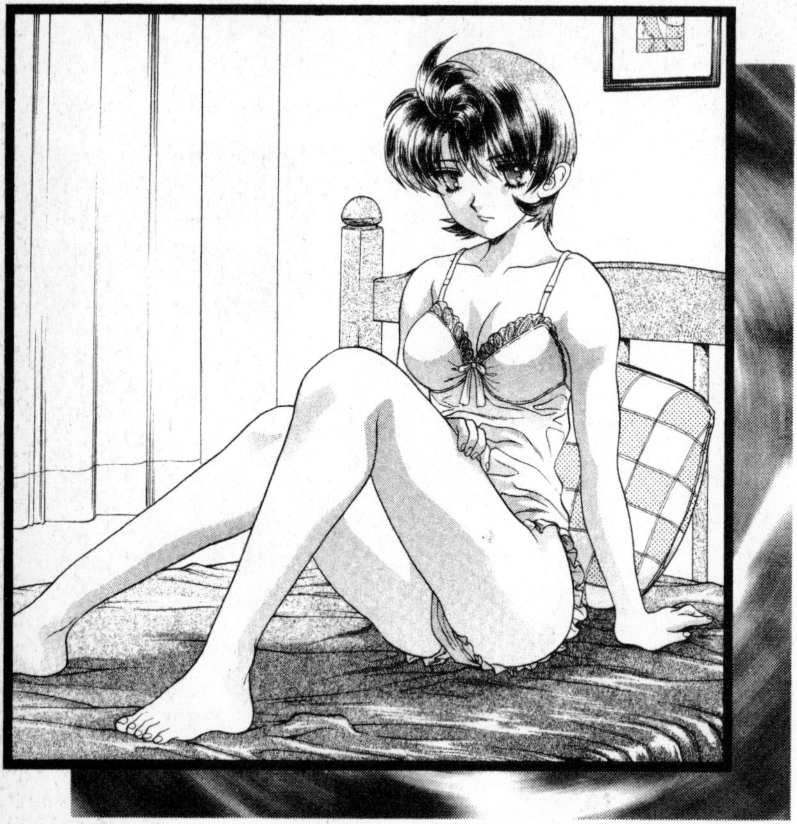

Chapter 11: Shadowed Friends and Masked Enemies

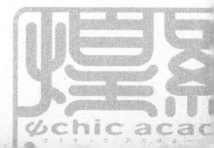

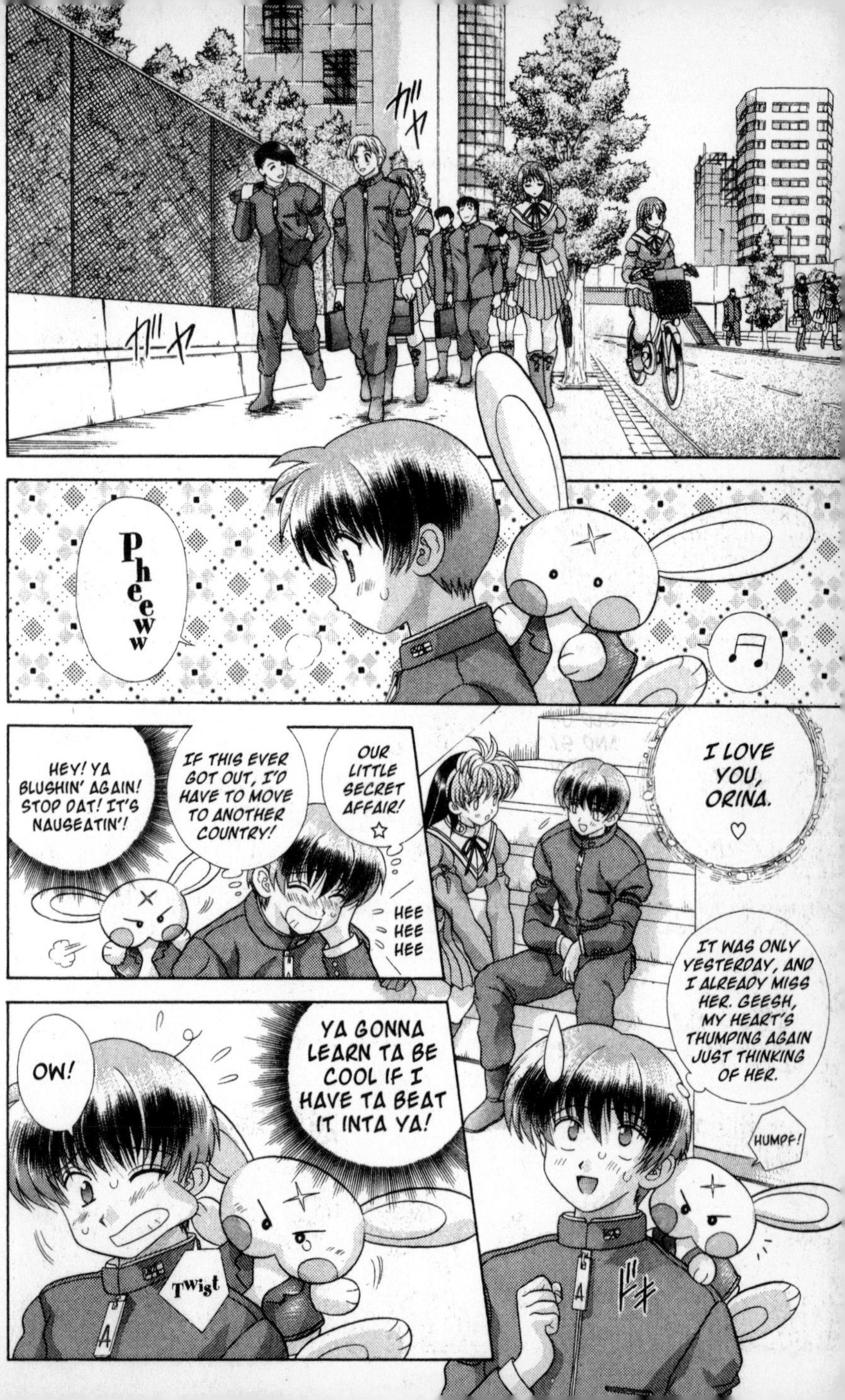
ガヤ
ガヤ
Pheeww
♫
I LOVE YOU, ORINA. ♡
IT WAS ONLY YESTERDAY, AND I ALREADY MISS HER. GEESH, MY HEART'S THUMPING AGAIN JUST THINKING OF HER.
HUMPF!
ドキ
OUR LITTLE SECRET AFFAIR! ☆
IF THIS EVER GOT OUT, I'D HAVE TO MOVE TO ANOTHER COUNTRY!
HEY! YA BLUSHIN' AGAIN! STOP DAT! IT'S NAUSEATIN'!
HEE HEE HEE
YA GONNA LEARN TA BE COOL IF I HAVE TA BEAT IT INTA YA!
OW!
TWist

Blackboard: Congratulations, Baby Ai - Sahra, Love love!
Under Umbrella: Ai, Sahra
Under Face: From Zero

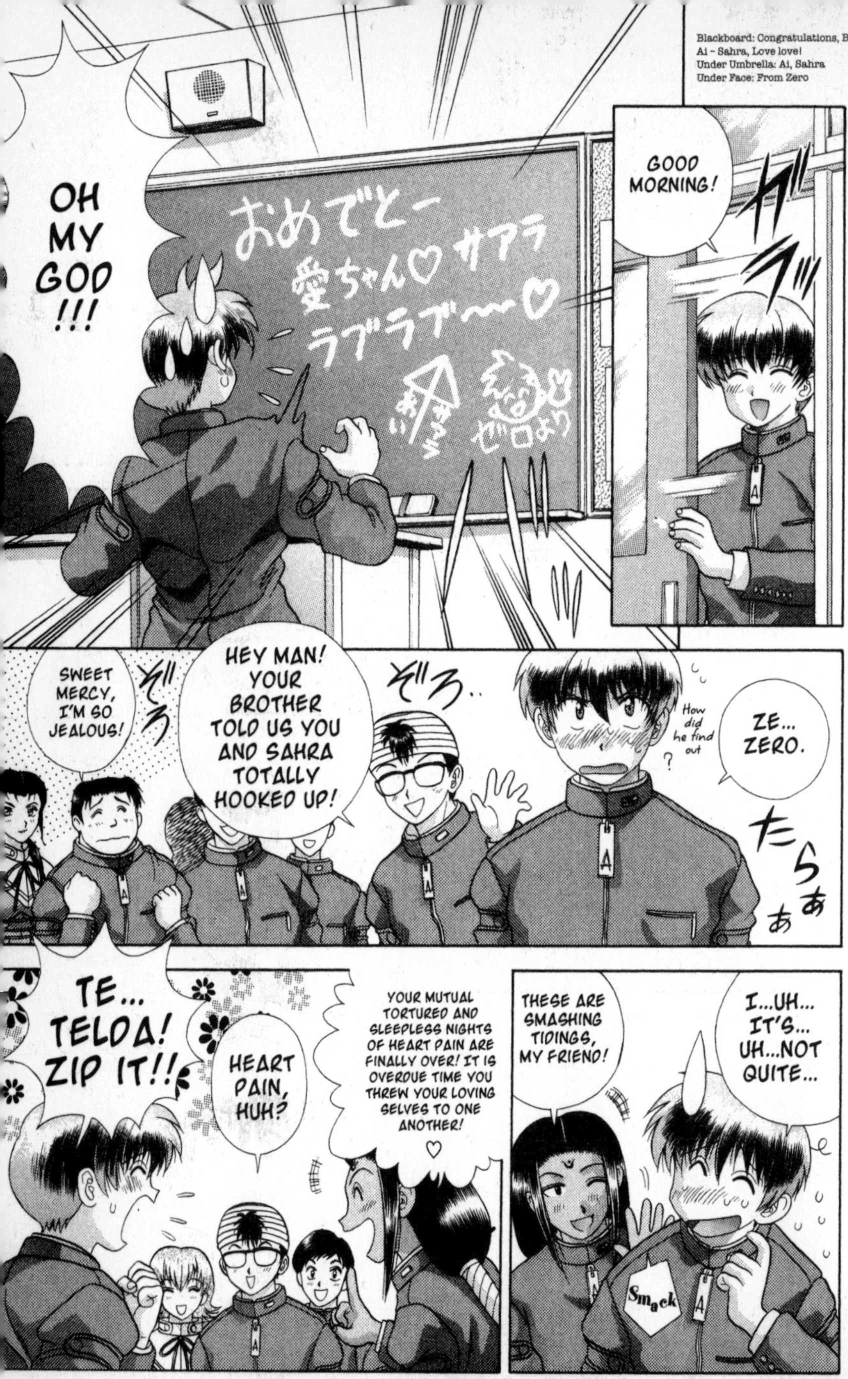
GOOD MORNING!
OH MY GOD!!!
おめでとー
愛ちゃん♡サアラ
ラブラブ~~♡
ZE... ZERO.
How did he find out
たらぁぁ
ぞろ..
HEY MAN! YOUR BROTHER TOLD US YOU AND SAHRA TOTALLY HOOKED UP!
ぞろ
SWEET MERCY, I'M SO JEALOUS!
I...UH... IT'S... UH...NOT QUITE...
THESE ARE SMASHING TIDINGS, MY FRIEND!
Smack
YOUR MUTUAL TORTURED AND SLEEPLESS NIGHTS OF HEART PAIN ARE FINALLY OVER! IT IS OVERDUE TIME YOU THREW YOUR LOVING SELVES TO ONE ANOTHER!
HEART PAIN, HUH?
TE... TELDA! ZIP IT!!

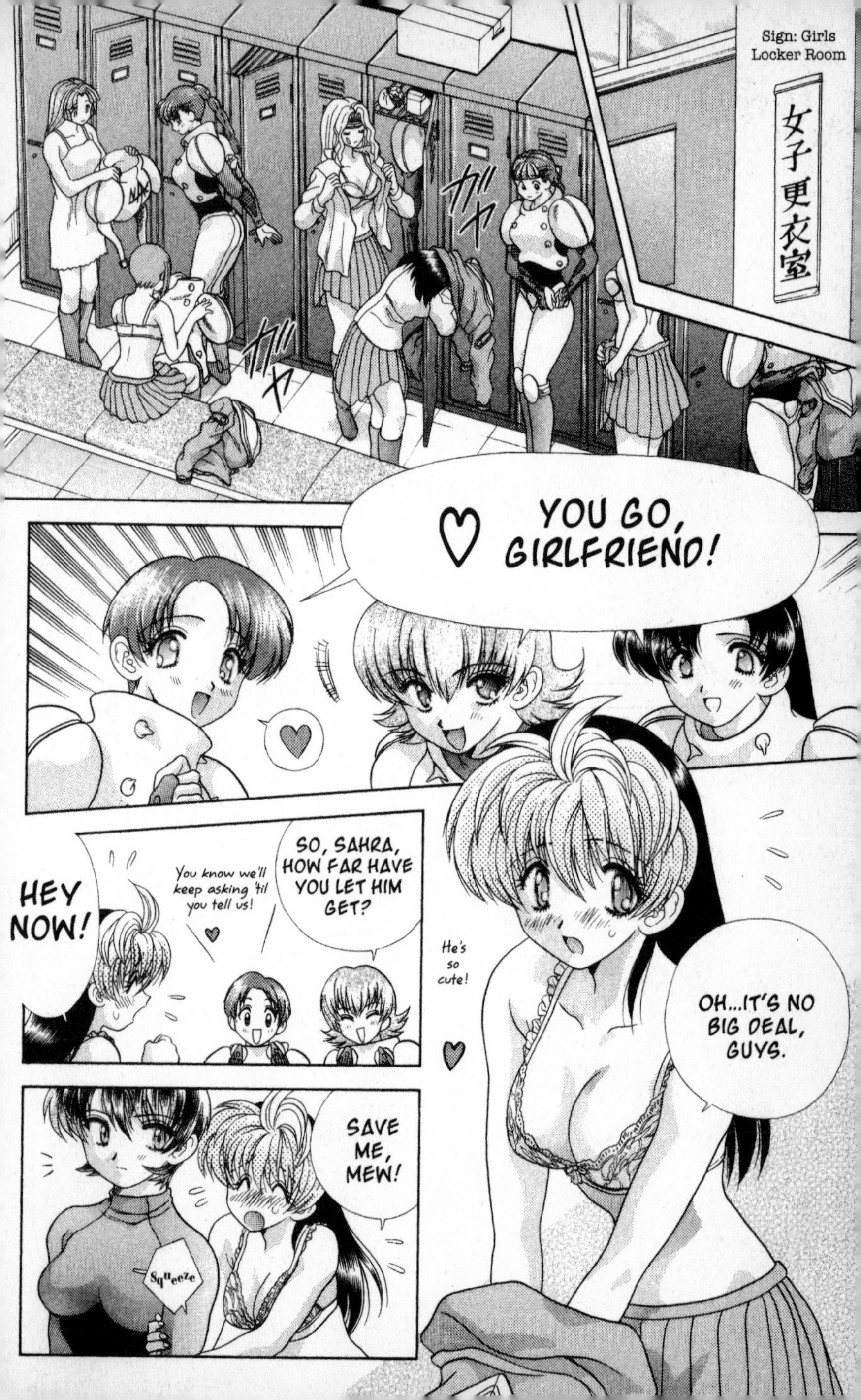
Sign: Girls Locker Room
女子更衣室
ガヤ
ガヤ
♡ YOU GO, GIRLFRIEND!
OH...IT'S NO BIG DEAL, GUYS.
SO, SAHRA, HOW FAR HAVE YOU LET HIM GET?
You know we'll keep asking 'til you tell us!
He's so cute!
HEY NOW!
SAVE ME, MEW!
Squeeze

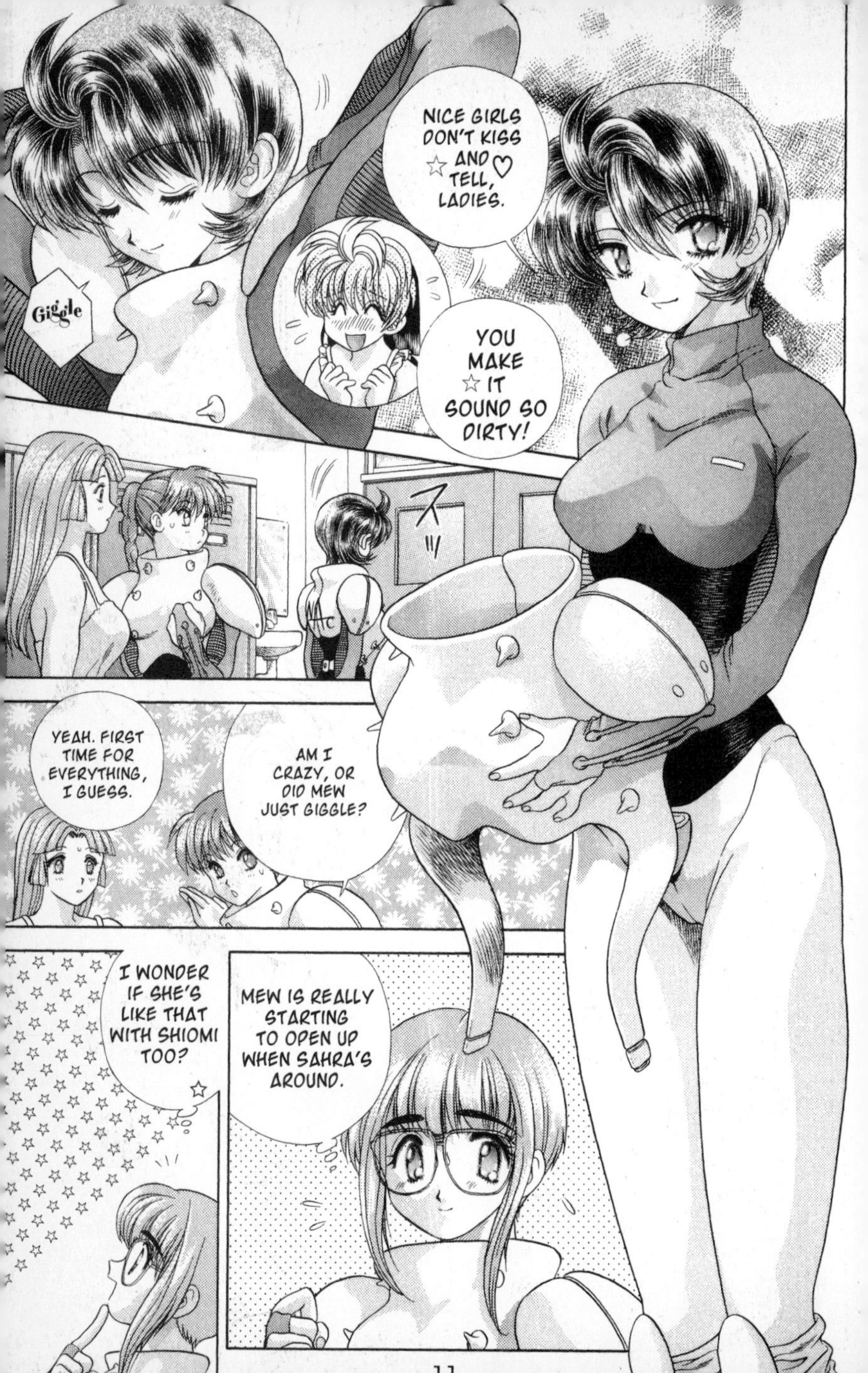
NICE GIRLS DON'T KISS ☆ AND ♡ TELL, LADIES.
YOU MAKE ☆ IT SOUND SO DIRTY!
Giggle
ス
AM I CRAZY, OR DID MEW JUST GIGGLE?
YEAH. FIRST TIME FOR EVERYTHING, I GUESS.
MEW IS REALLY STARTING TO OPEN UP WHEN SAHRA'S AROUND.
I WONDER IF SHE'S LIKE THAT WITH SHIOMI TOO?

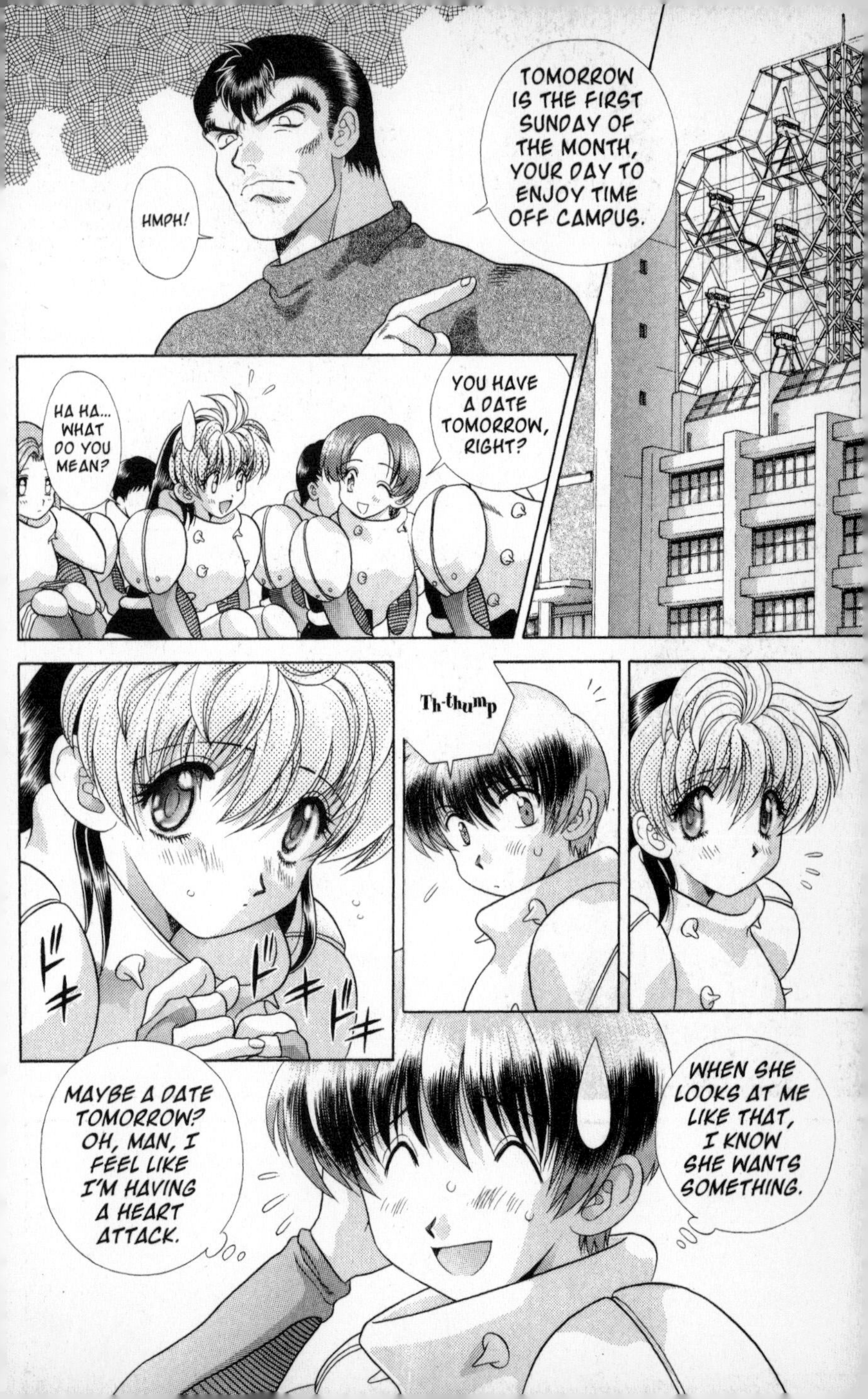
TOMORROW IS THE FIRST SUNDAY OF THE MONTH, YOUR DAY TO ENJOY TIME OFF CAMPUS.
HMPH!
YOU HAVE A DATE TOMORROW, RIGHT?
HA HA... WHAT DO YOU MEAN?
Th-thump
ドキ ドキ ドキ
WHEN SHE LOOKS AT ME LIKE THAT, I KNOW SHE WANTS SOMETHING.
MAYBE A DATE TOMORROW? OH, MAN, I FEEL LIKE I'M HAVING A HEART ATTACK.

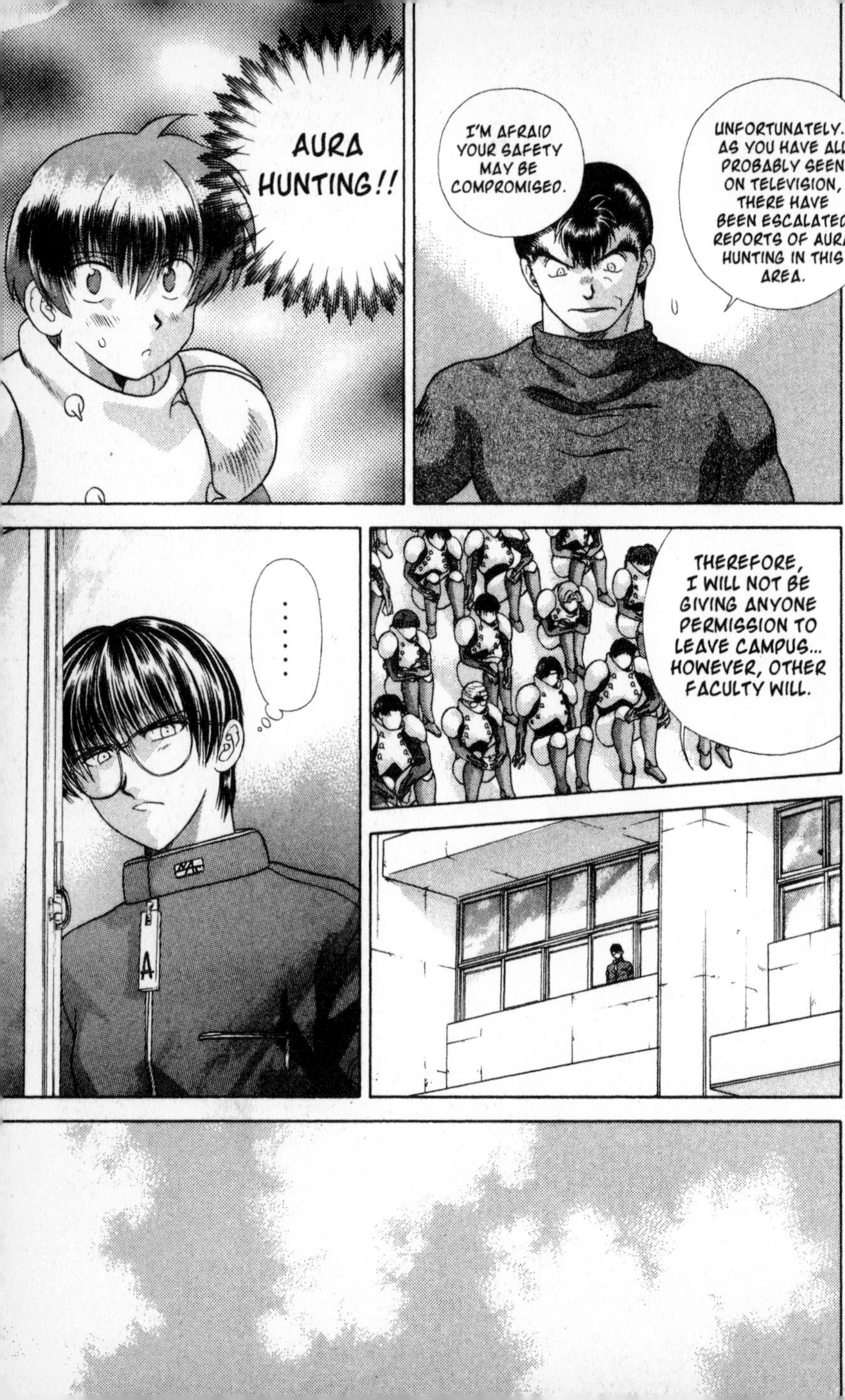
UNFORTUNATELY... AS YOU HAVE ALL PROBABLY SEEN ON TELEVISION, THERE HAVE BEEN ESCALATED REPORTS OF AURA HUNTING IN THIS AREA.
I'M AFRAID YOUR SAFETY MAY BE COMPROMISED.
AURA HUNTING!!
THEREFORE, I WILL NOT BE GIVING ANYONE PERMISSION TO LEAVE CAMPUS... HOWEVER, OTHER FACULTY WILL.
......

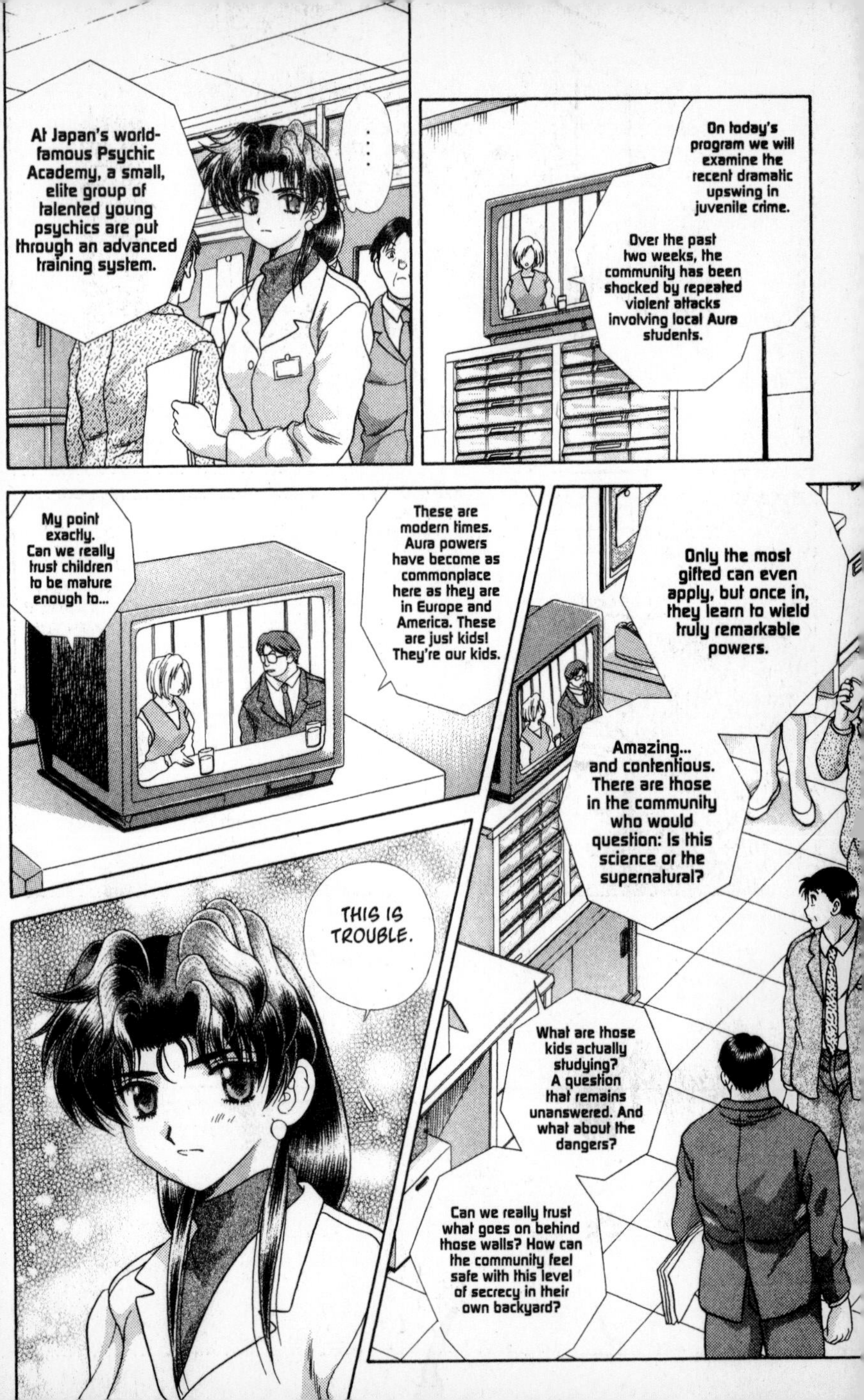
On today's program we will examine the recent dramatic upswing in juvenile crime.
Over the past two weeks, the community has been shocked by repeated violent attacks involving local Aura students.
....
At Japan's world-famous Psychic Academy, a small, elite group of talented young psychics are put through an advanced training system.
Only the most gifted can even apply, but once in, they learn to wield truly remarkable powers.
Amazing... and contentious. There are those in the community who would question: Is this science or the supernatural?
What are those kids actually studying? A question that remains unanswered. And what about the dangers?
Can we really trust what goes on behind those walls? How can the community feel safe with this level of secrecy in their own backyard?
These are modern times. Aura powers have become as commonplace here as they are in Europe and America. These are just kids! They're our kids.
My point exactly. Can we really trust children to be mature enough to...
THIS IS TROUBLE.

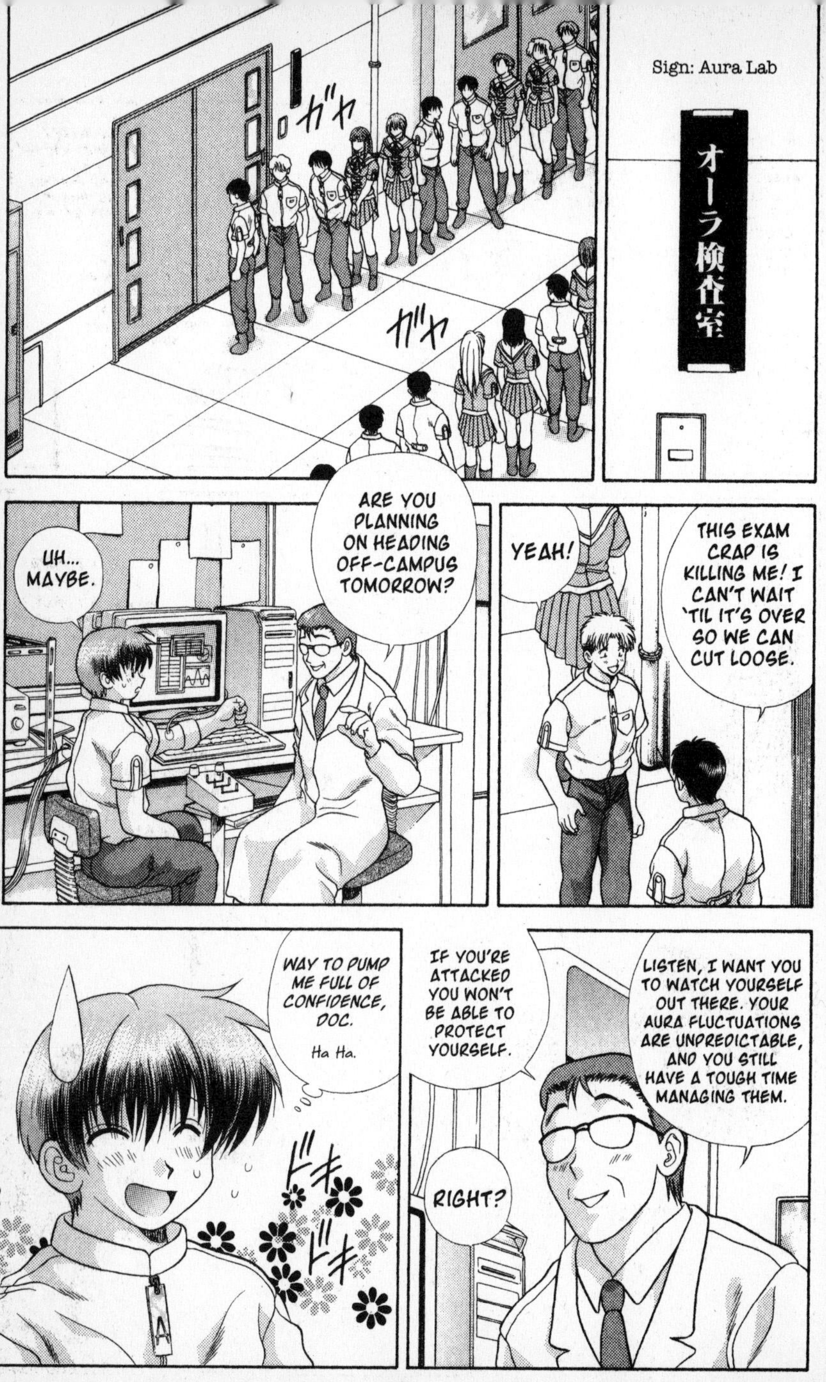
Sign: Aura Lab
オーラ検査室
ガヤ
ガヤ
THIS EXAM CRAP IS KILLING ME! I CAN'T WAIT 'TIL IT'S OVER SO WE CAN CUT LOOSE.
YEAH!
ARE YOU PLANNING ON HEADING OFF-CAMPUS TOMORROW?
UH... MAYBE.
LISTEN, I WANT YOU TO WATCH YOURSELF OUT THERE. YOUR AURA FLUCTUATIONS ARE UNPREDICTABLE, AND YOU STILL HAVE A TOUGH TIME MANAGING THEM.
IF YOU'RE ATTACKED YOU WON'T BE ABLE TO PROTECT YOURSELF.
RIGHT?
WAY TO PUMP ME FULL OF CONFIDENCE, DOC.
Ha Ha.
ドキ
ドキ

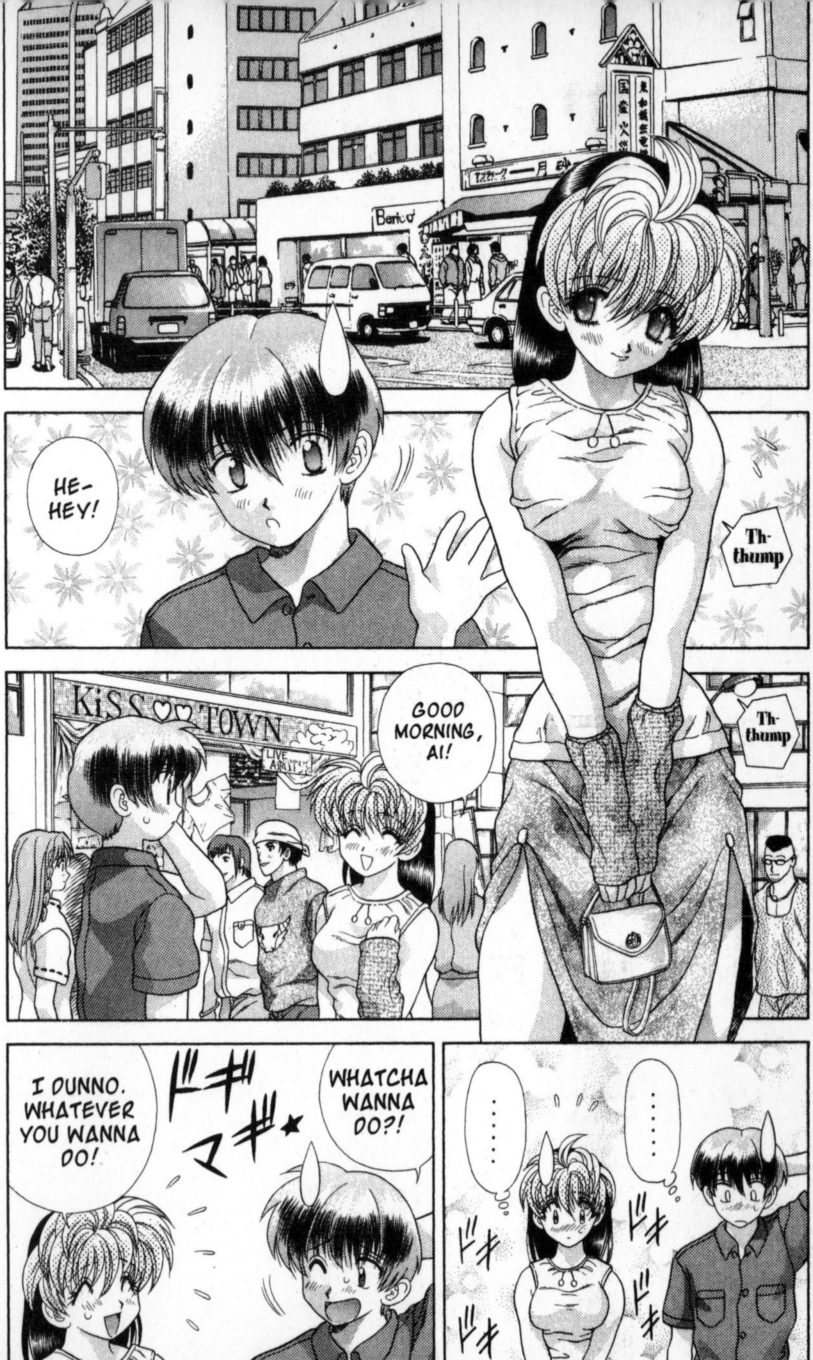
Th-thump
HE-HEY!
Th-thump
GOOD MORNING, AI!
KiSS TOWN
......
......
ドキ
ドキ
ドキ
ドキ
WHATCHA WANNA DO?!
ドギマギ★
I DUNNO. WHATEVER YOU WANNA DO!

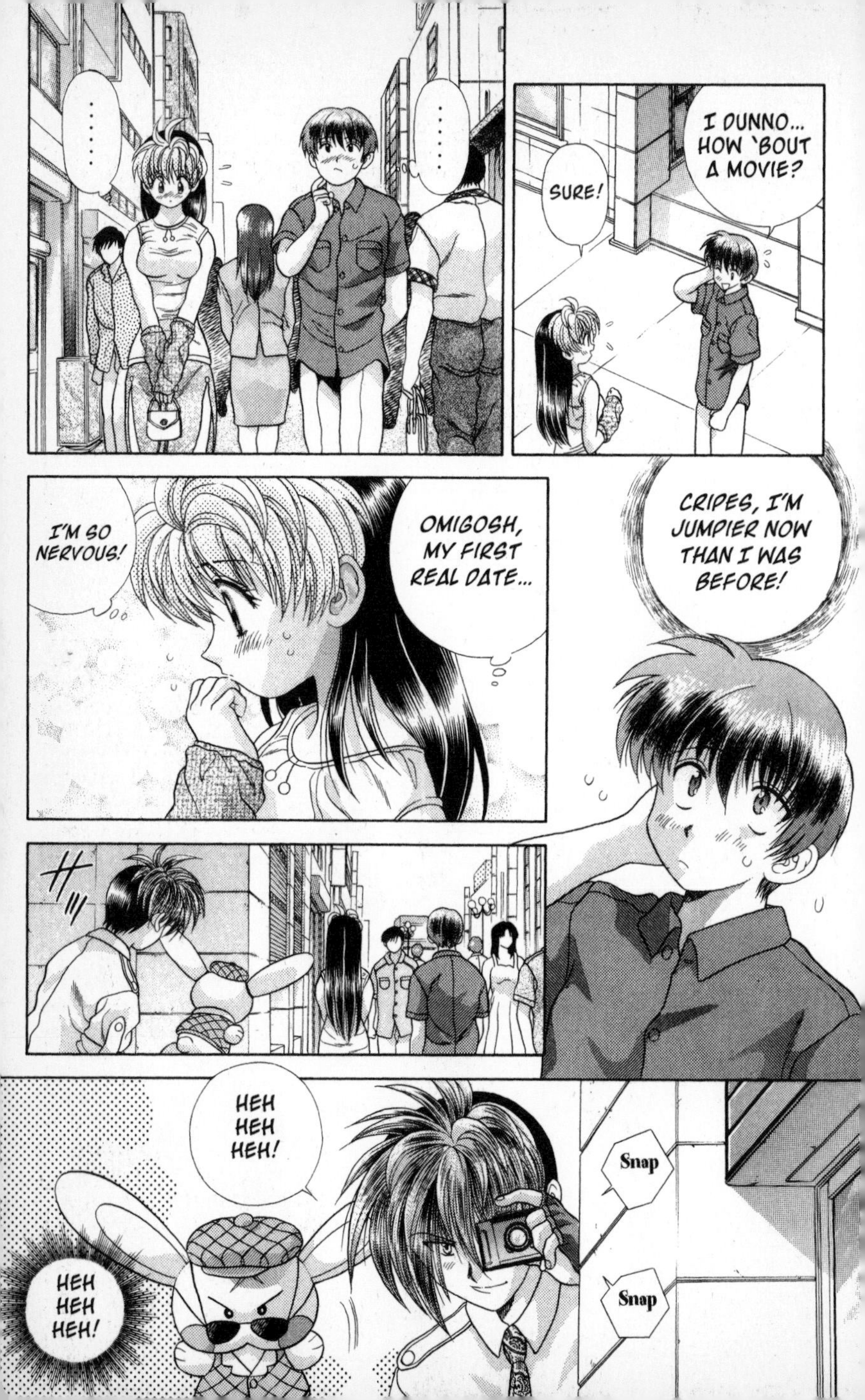
I DUNNO... HOW `BOUT A MOVIE?
SURE!
......
......
CRIPES, I'M JUMPIER NOW THAN I WAS BEFORE!
OMIGOSH, MY FIRST REAL DATE...
I'M SO NERVOUS!
Snap
Snap
HEH HEH HEH!
HEH HEH HEH!

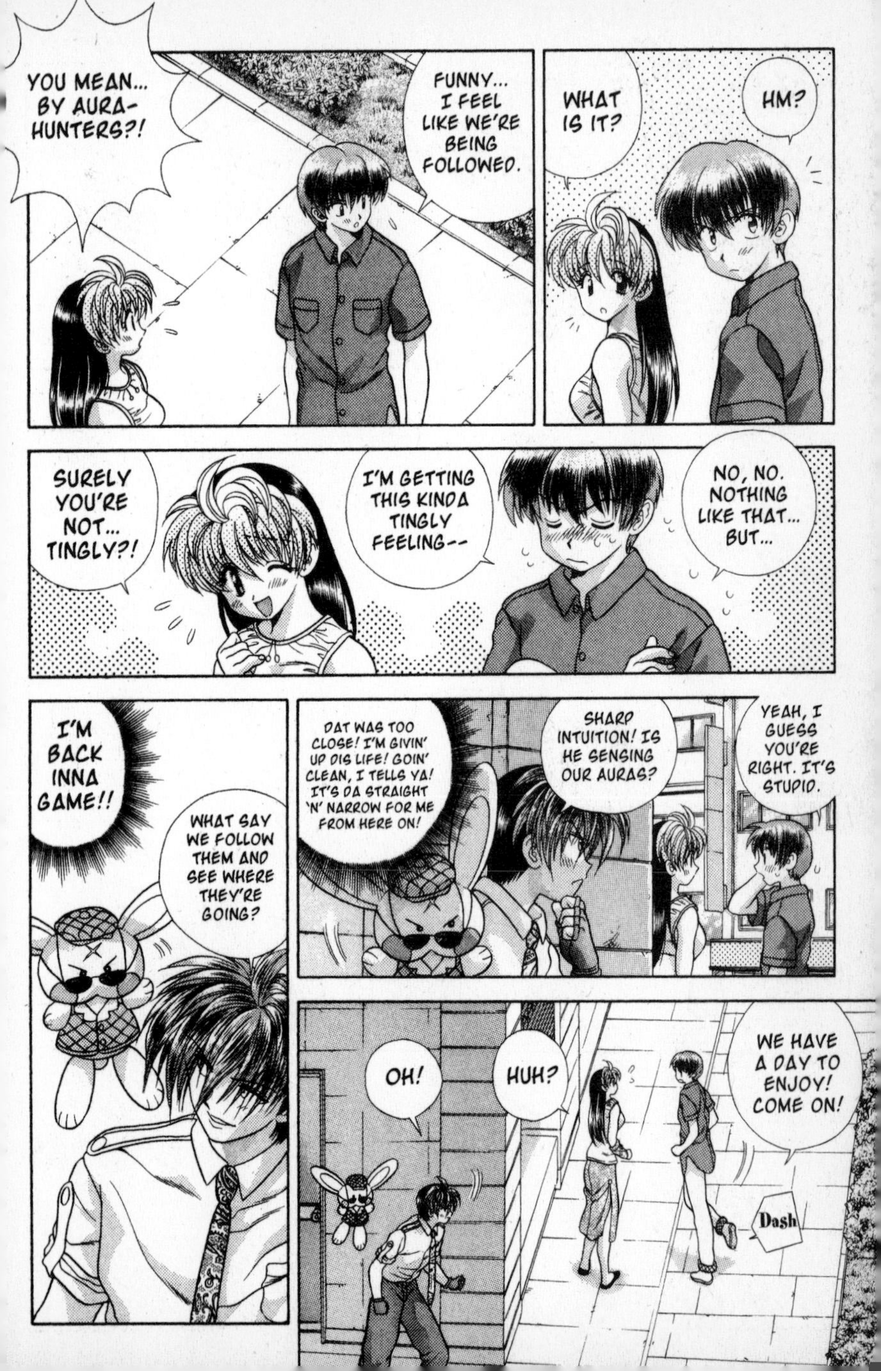

HM?
WHAT IS IT?
FUNNY... I FEEL LIKE WE'RE BEING FOLLOWED.
YOU MEAN... BY AURA-HUNTERS?!
NO, NO. NOTHING LIKE THAT... BUT...
I'M GETTING THIS KINDA TINGLY FEELING--
SURELY YOU'RE NOT... TINGLY?!
YEAH, I GUESS YOU'RE RIGHT. IT'S STUPID.
SHARP INTUITION! IS HE SENSING OUR AURAS?
DAT WAS TOO CLOSE! I'M GIVIN' UP DIS LIFE! GOIN' CLEAN, I TELLS YA! IT'S DA STRAIGHT 'N' NARROW FOR ME FROM HERE ON!
WE HAVE A DAY TO ENJOY! COME ON!
Dash
HUH?
OH!
WHAT SAY WE FOLLOW THEM AND SEE WHERE THEY'RE GOING?
I'M BACK INNA GAME!!

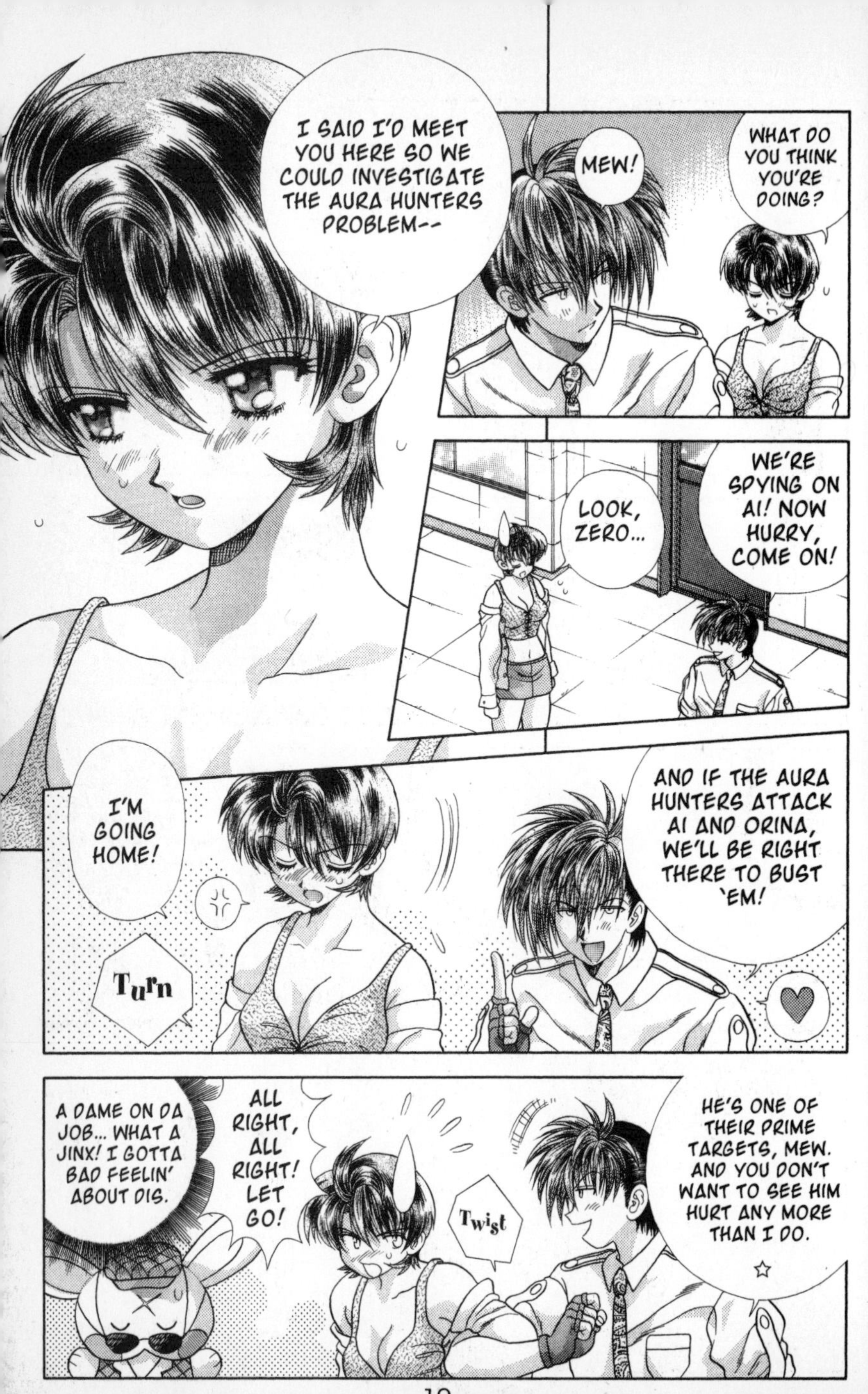
WHAT DO YOU THINK YOU'RE DOING?
MEW!
WE'RE SPYING ON AI! NOW HURRY, COME ON!
LOOK, ZERO...
I SAID I'D MEET YOU HERE SO WE COULD INVESTIGATE THE AURA HUNTERS PROBLEM--
AND IF THE AURA HUNTERS ATTACK AI AND ORINA, WE'LL BE RIGHT THERE TO BUST 'EM!
I'M GOING HOME!
Turn
HE'S ONE OF THEIR PRIME TARGETS, MEW. AND YOU DON'T WANT TO SEE HIM HURT ANY MORE THAN I DO.
Twist
ALL RIGHT, ALL RIGHT! LET GO!
A DAME ON DA JOB... WHAT A JINX! I GOTTA BAD FEELIN' ABOUT DIS.

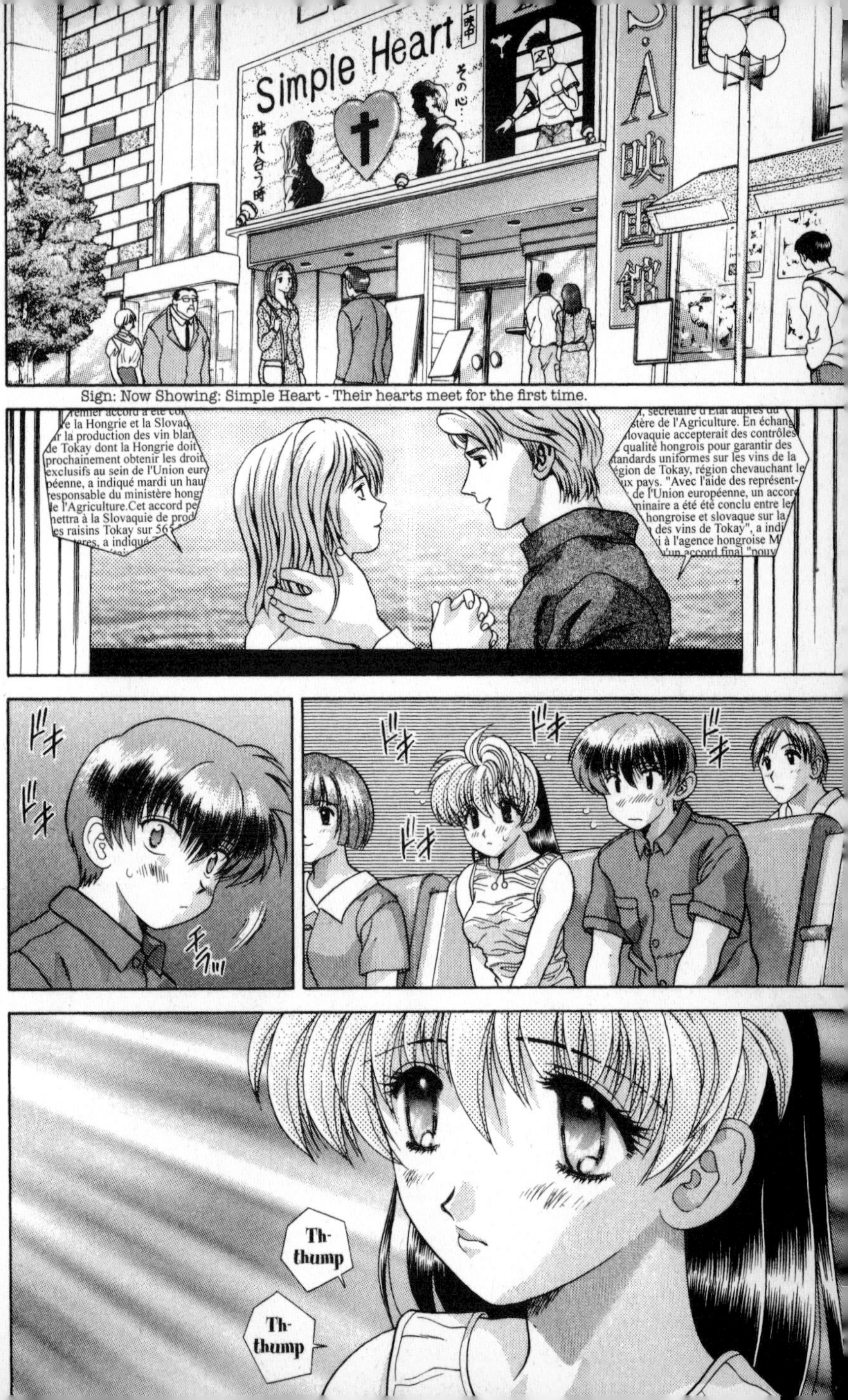

上映中
Simple Heart
その心…
触れ合う時
映画館
Sign: Now Showing: Simple Heart - Their hearts meet for the first time.
stère de l'Agriculture. En échang slovaquie accepterait des contrôles qualité hongrois pour garantir des standards uniformes sur les vins de la égion de Tokay, région chevauchant le ux pays. "Avec l'aide des représent- de l'Union européenne, un accor minaire a été été conclu entre le hongroise et slovaque sur la des vins de Tokay", a indi i à l'agence hongroise M
e la Hongrie et la Slovaq r la production des vin blan de Tokay dont la Hongrie doit prochainement obtenir les droit exclusifs au sein de l'Union euro péenne, a indiqué mardi un hau responsable du ministère hong de l'Agriculture.Cet accord pe nettra à la Slovaquie de prod es raisins Tokay sur 56
ドキ
ドキ
ドキ
ドキ
ドキ
ドキ
Th-thump
Th-thump

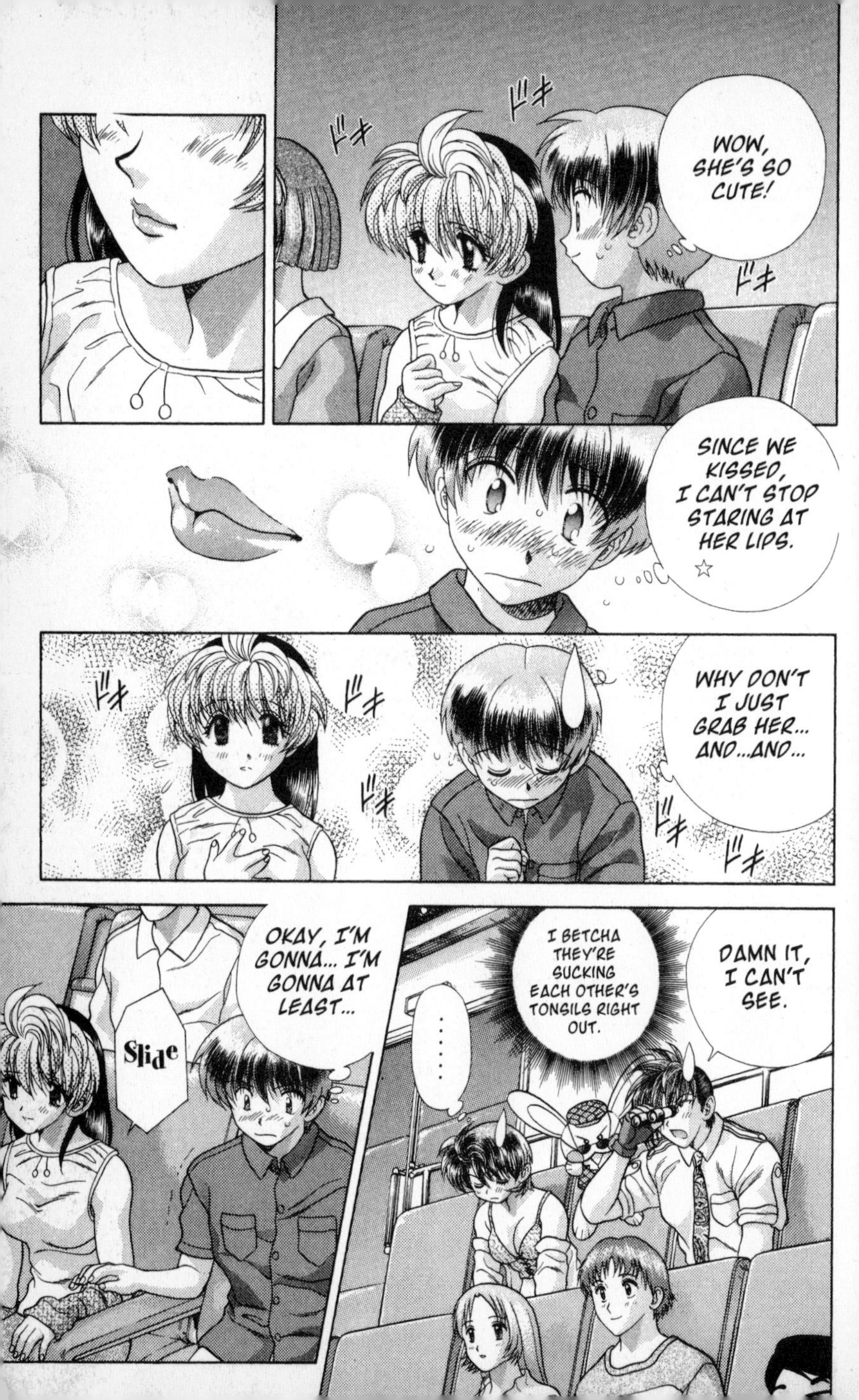
ドキ
ドキ
WOW, SHE'S SO CUTE!
ドキ
SINCE WE KISSED, I CAN'T STOP STARING AT HER LIPS. ☆
WHY DON'T I JUST GRAB HER... AND...AND...
ドキ
ドキ
ドキ
ドキ
ドキ
DAMN IT, I CAN'T SEE.
I BETCHA THEY'RE SUCKING EACH OTHER'S TONSILS RIGHT OUT.
......
OKAY, I'M GONNA... I'M GONNA AT LEAST...
Slide

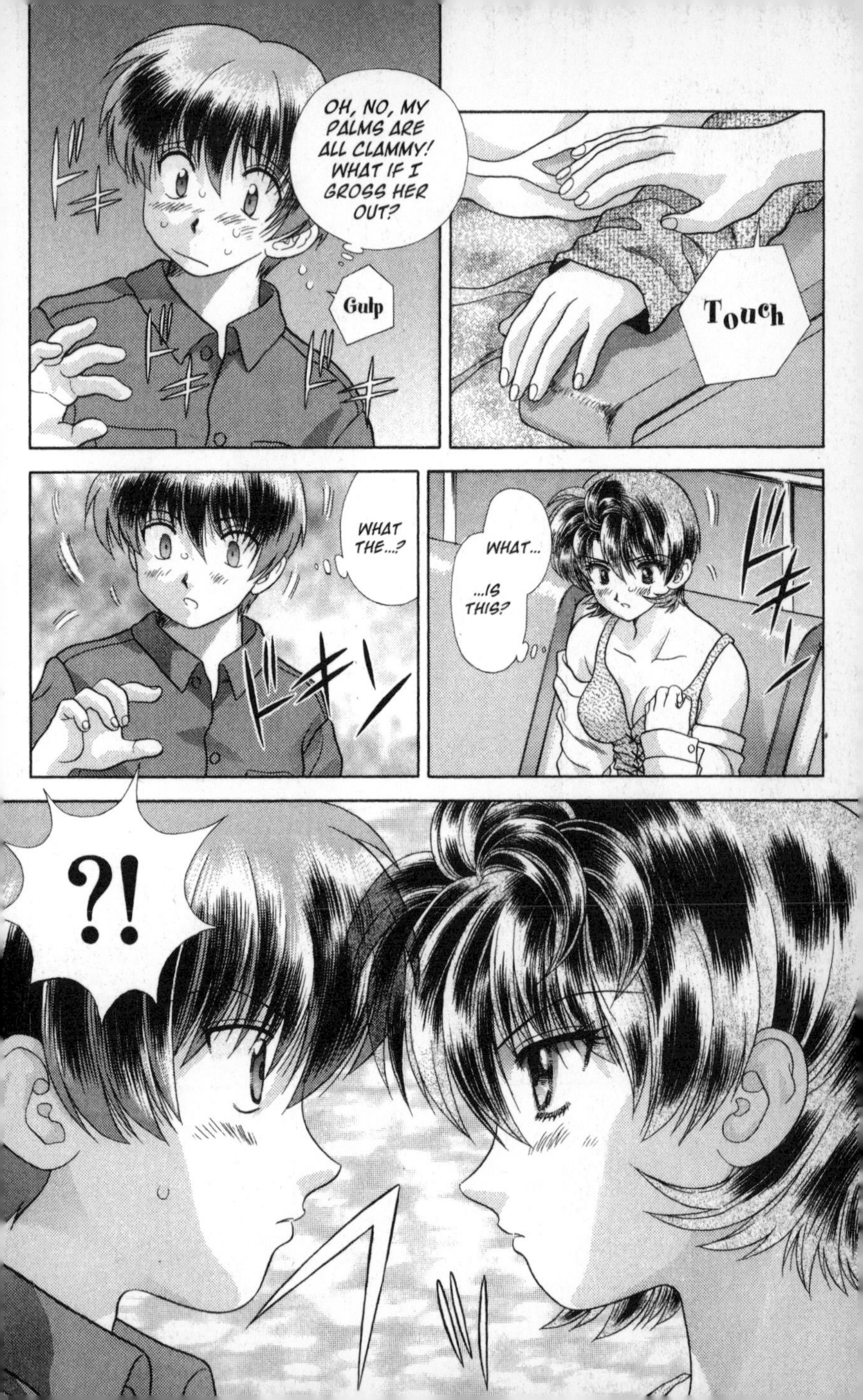
Touch
OH, NO, MY PALMS ARE ALL CLAMMY! WHAT IF I GROSS HER OUT?
Gulp
WHAT... ...IS THIS?
WHAT THE...?
?!

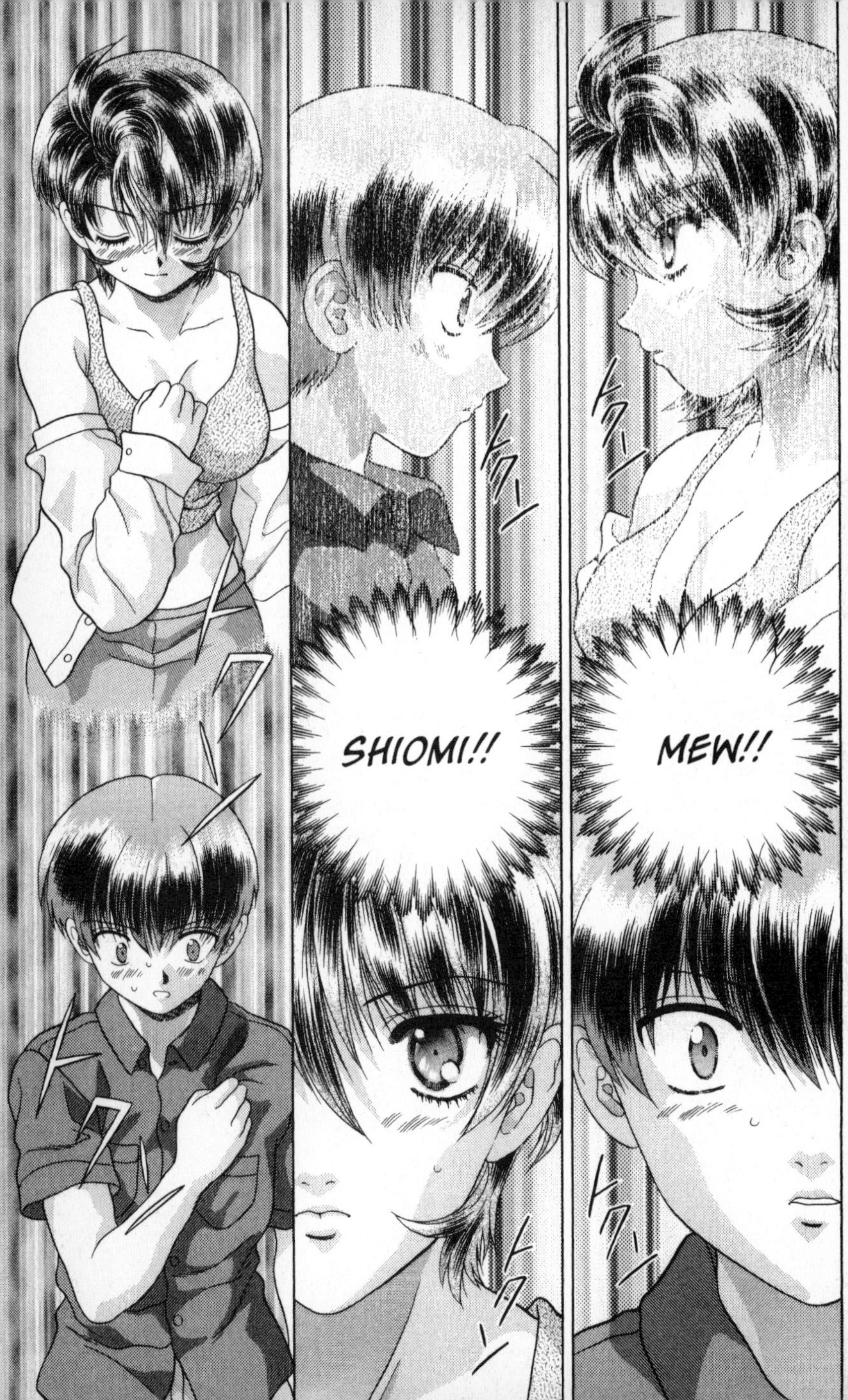
MEW!!
SHIOMI!!

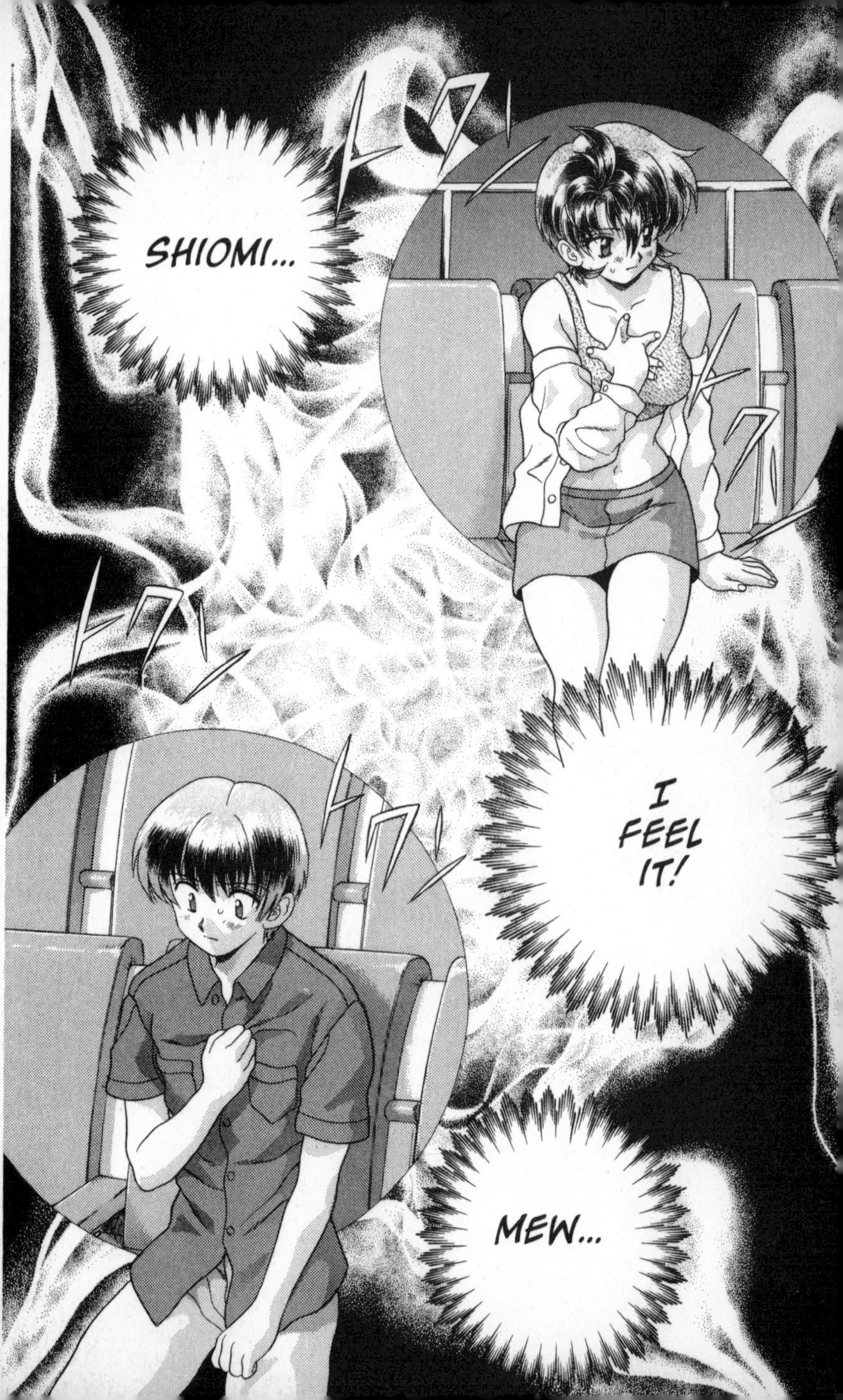
SHIOMI...
I FEEL IT!
MEW...

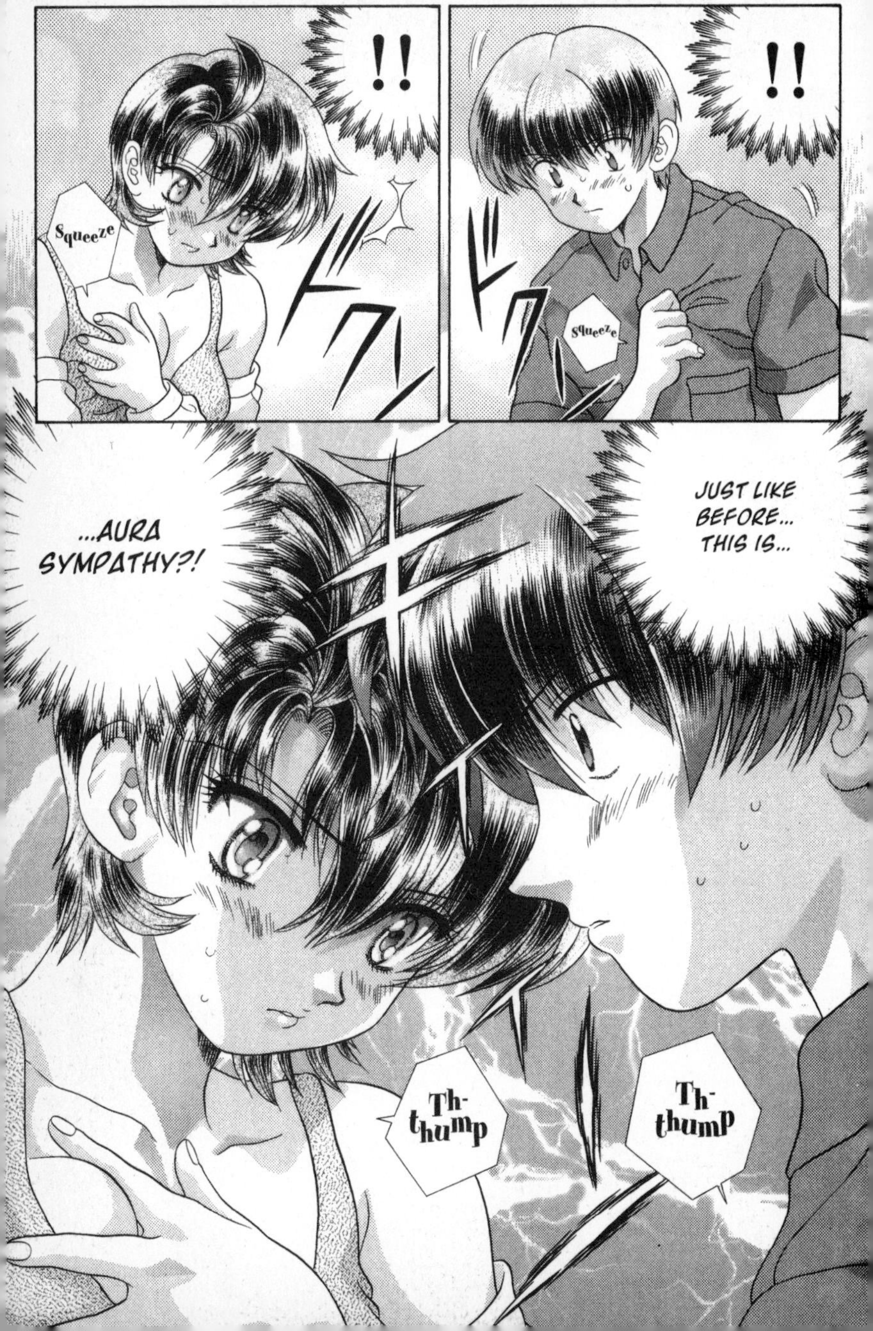
!!
Squeeze
!!
Squeeze
JUST LIKE BEFORE... THIS IS...
...AURA SYMPATHY?!
Th-thump
Th-thump

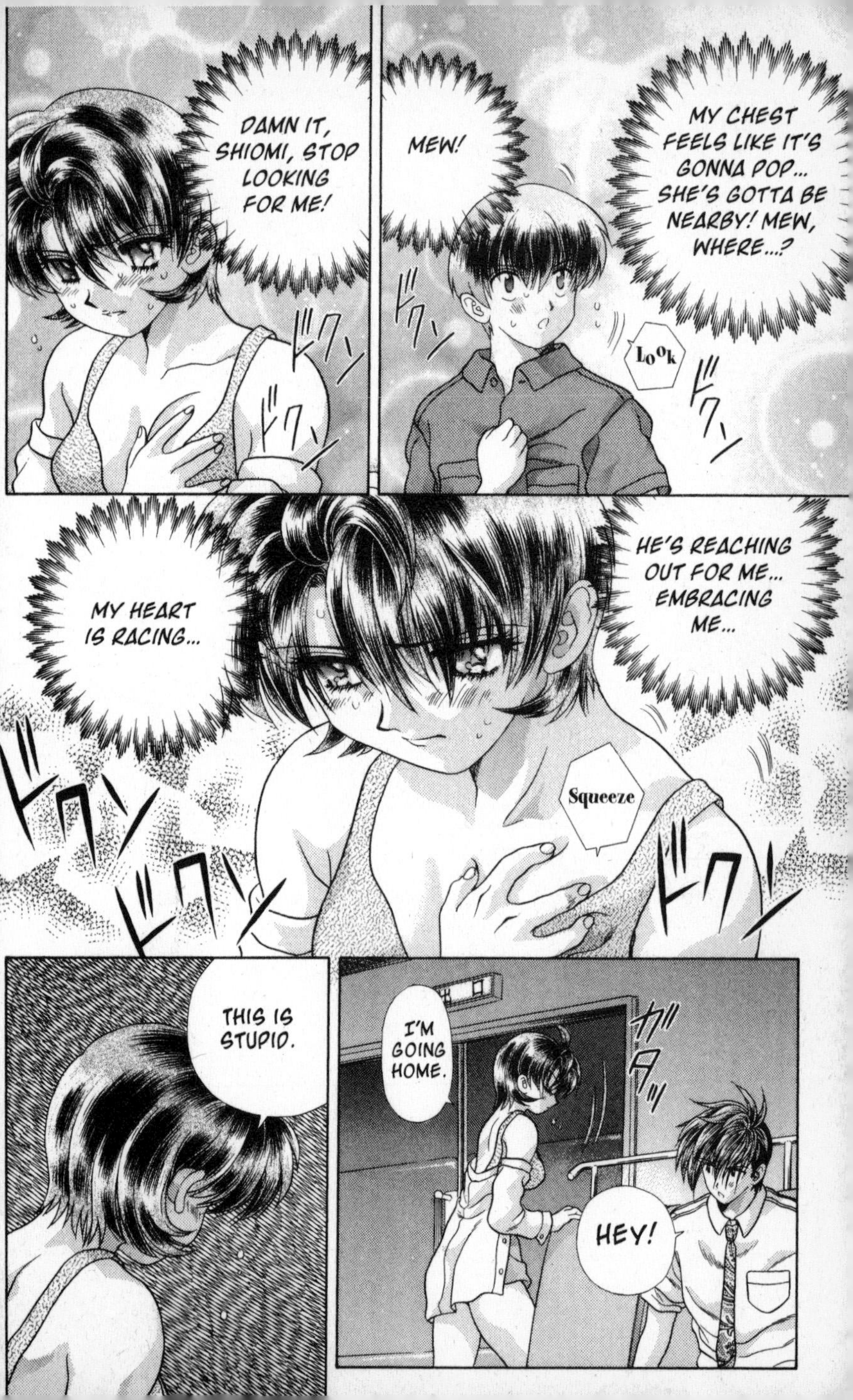
MY CHEST FEELS LIKE IT'S GONNA POP... SHE'S GOTTA BE NEARBY! MEW, WHERE...?
MEW!
ドクン
Look
ドクン
DAMN IT, SHIOMI, STOP LOOKING FOR ME!
ドクン
ドクン
HE'S REACHING OUT FOR ME... EMBRACING ME...
MY HEART IS RACING...
Squeeze
ドクン
ドクン
ドクン
ガタッ
I'M GOING HOME.
HEY!
THIS IS STUPID.

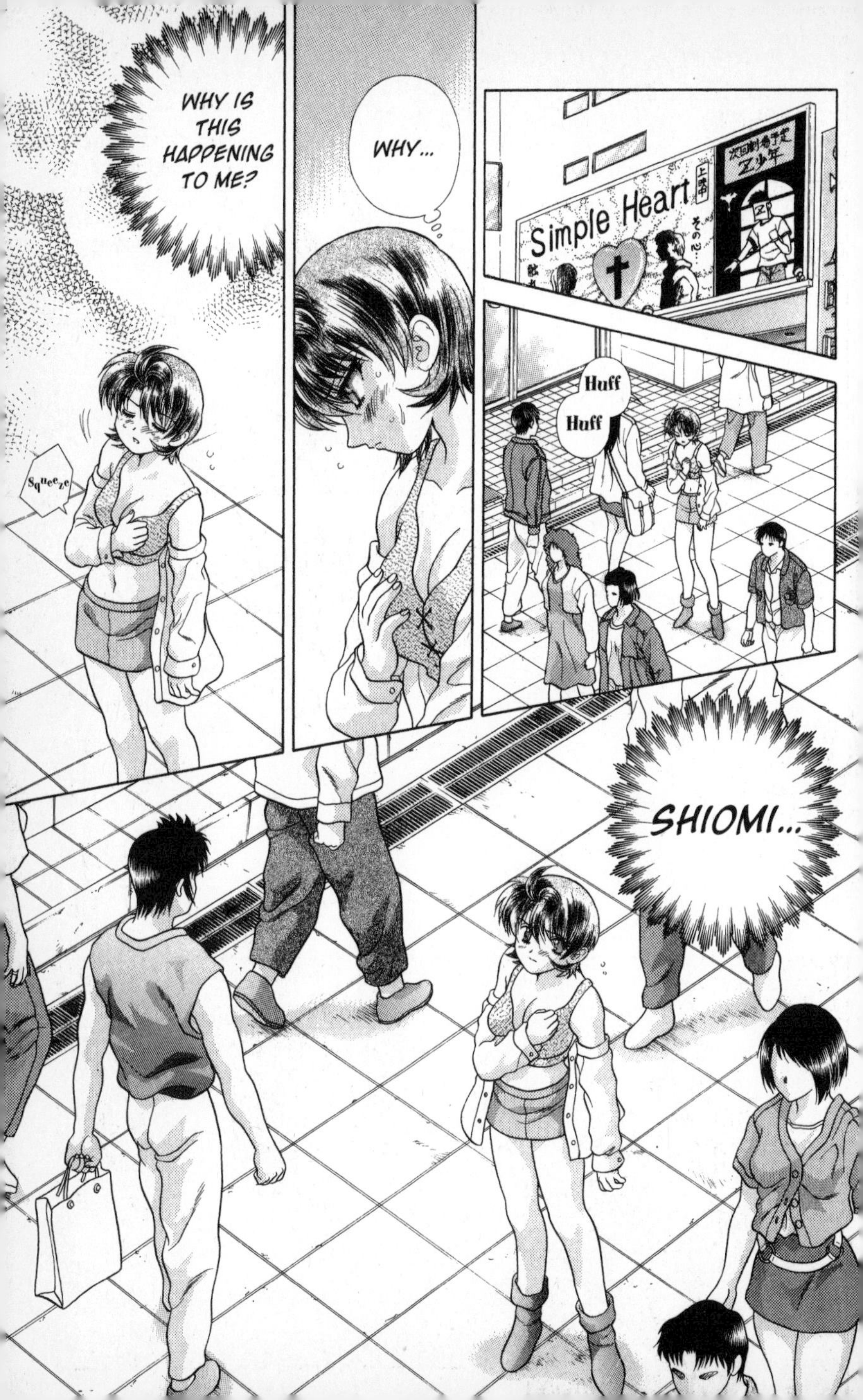
Simple Heart
Huff
Huff
WHY...
WHY IS THIS HAPPENING TO ME?
Squeeze
SHIOMI...

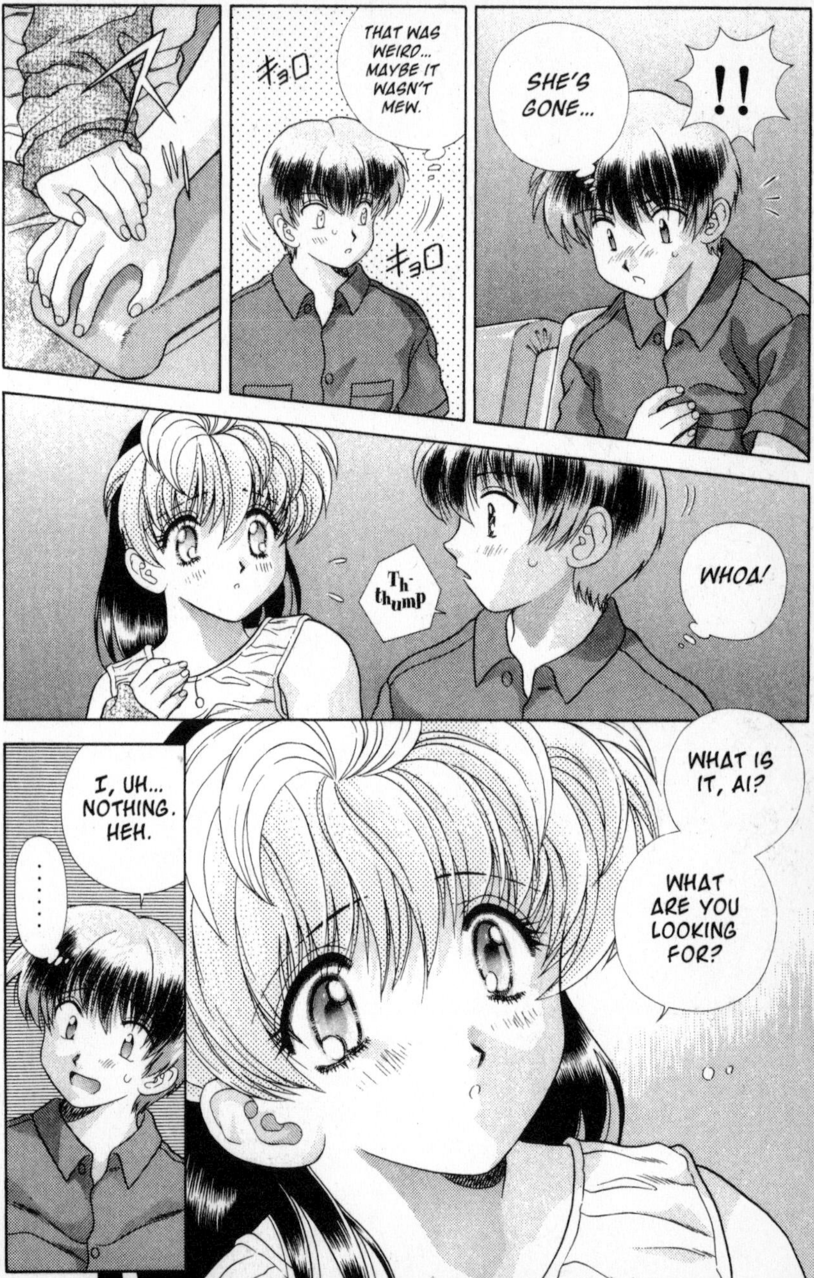

!!
SHE'S GONE...
THAT WAS WEIRD... MAYBE IT WASN'T MEW.
キョロ
キョロ
WHOA!
Th-thump
WHAT IS IT, AI?
WHAT ARE YOU LOOKING FOR?
I, UH... NOTHING. HEH.
......

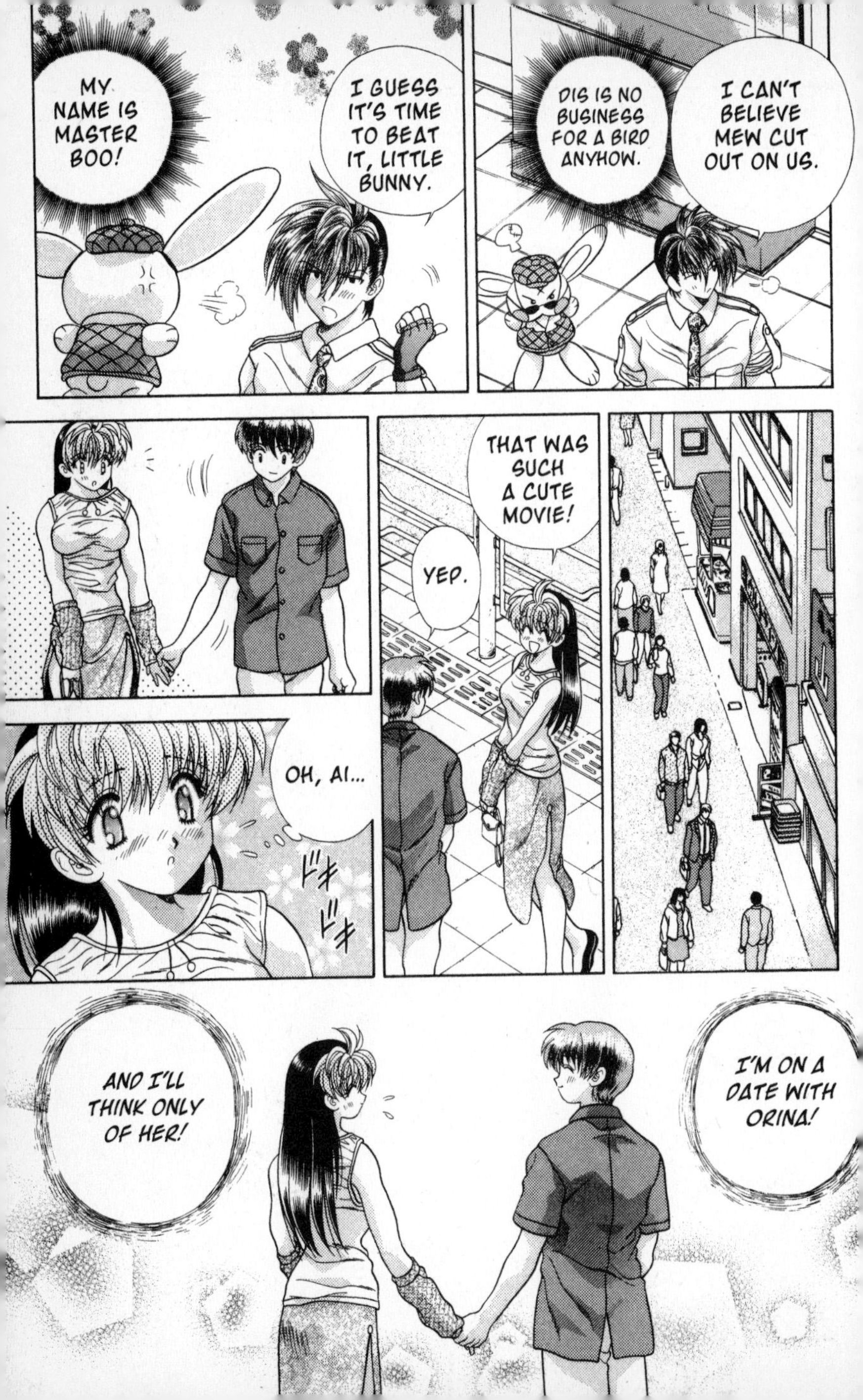
I CAN'T BELIEVE MEW CUT OUT ON US.
DIS IS NO BUSINESS FOR A BIRD ANYHOW.
I GUESS IT'S TIME TO BEAT IT, LITTLE BUNNY.
MY NAME IS MASTER BOO!
THAT WAS SUCH A CUTE MOVIE!
YEP.
OH, AI...
ドキ
ドキ
I'M ON A DATE WITH ORINA!
AND I'LL THINK ONLY OF HER!

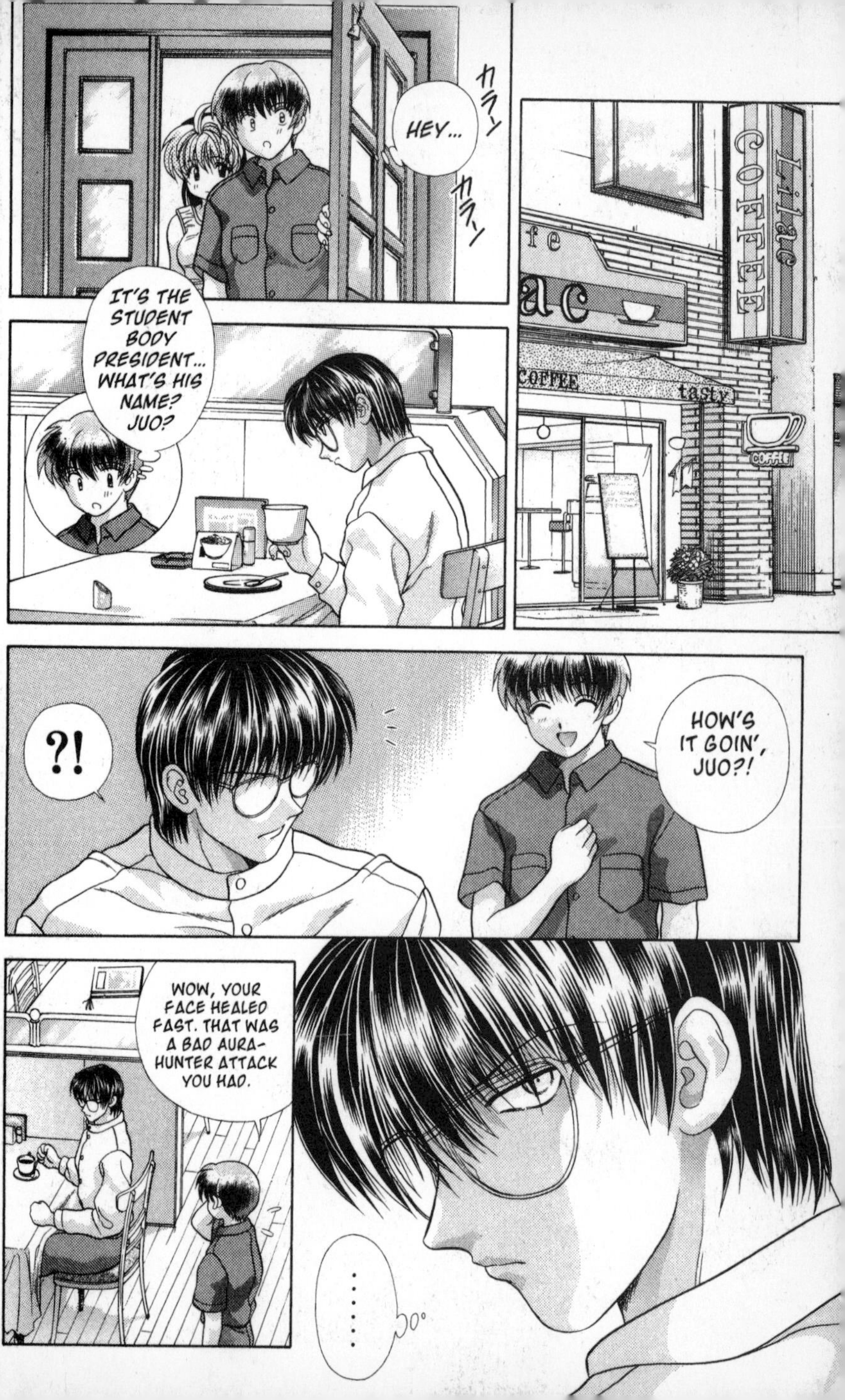
Lilac
COFFEE
COFFEE
tasty
COFFEE
HEY...
カラーン
カラーン
IT'S THE STUDENT BODY PRESIDENT... WHAT'S HIS NAME? JUO?
HOW'S IT GOIN', JUO?!
?!
......
WOW, YOUR FACE HEALED FAST. THAT WAS A BAD AURA-HUNTER ATTACK YOU HAD.

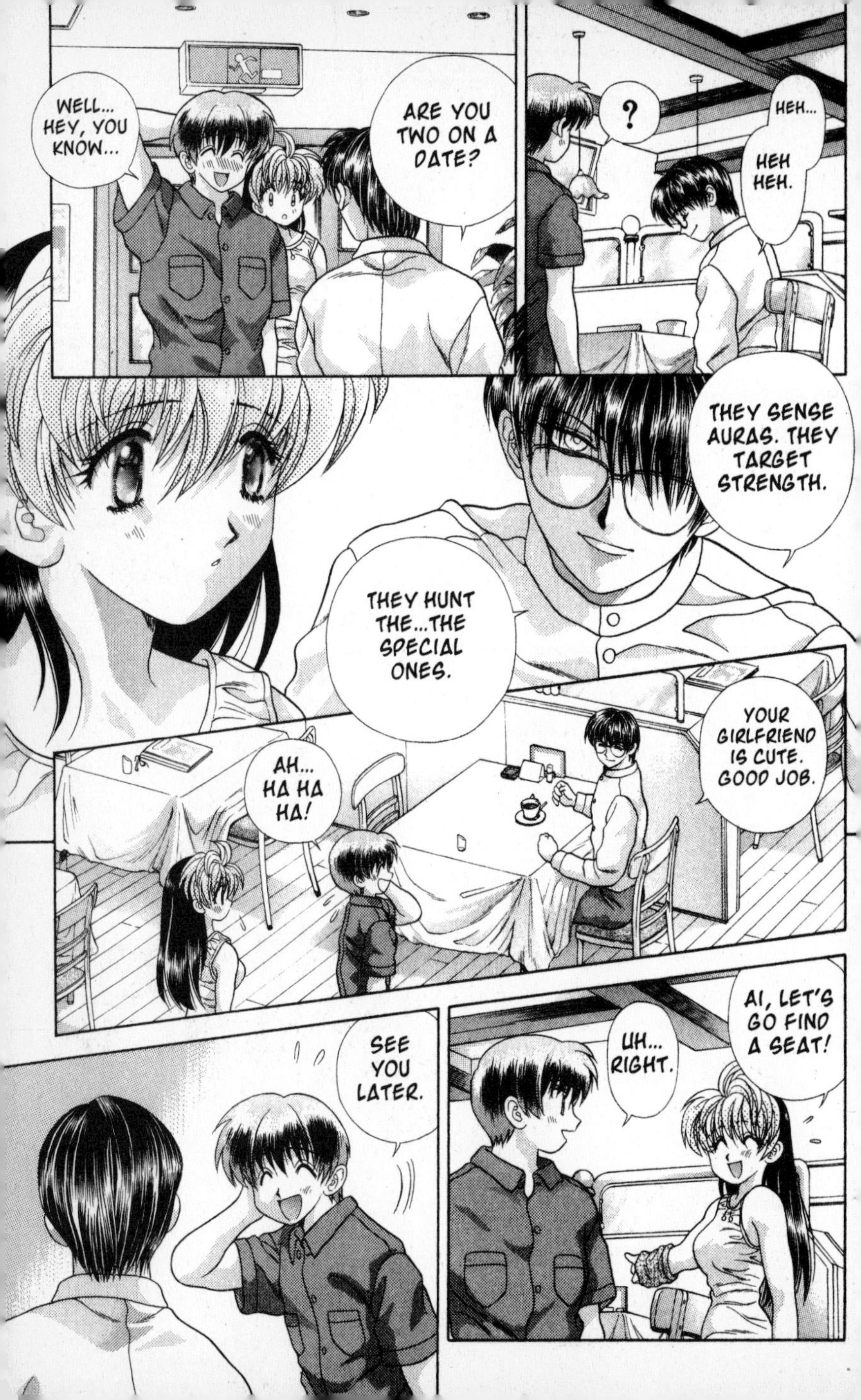
HEH...
HEH HEH.
?
ARE YOU TWO ON A DATE?
WELL... HEY, YOU KNOW...
THEY SENSE AURAS. THEY TARGET STRENGTH.
THEY HUNT THE...THE SPECIAL ONES.
YOUR GIRLFRIEND IS CUTE. GOOD JOB.
AH... HA HA HA!
AI, LET'S GO FIND A SEAT!
UH... RIGHT.
SEE YOU LATER.

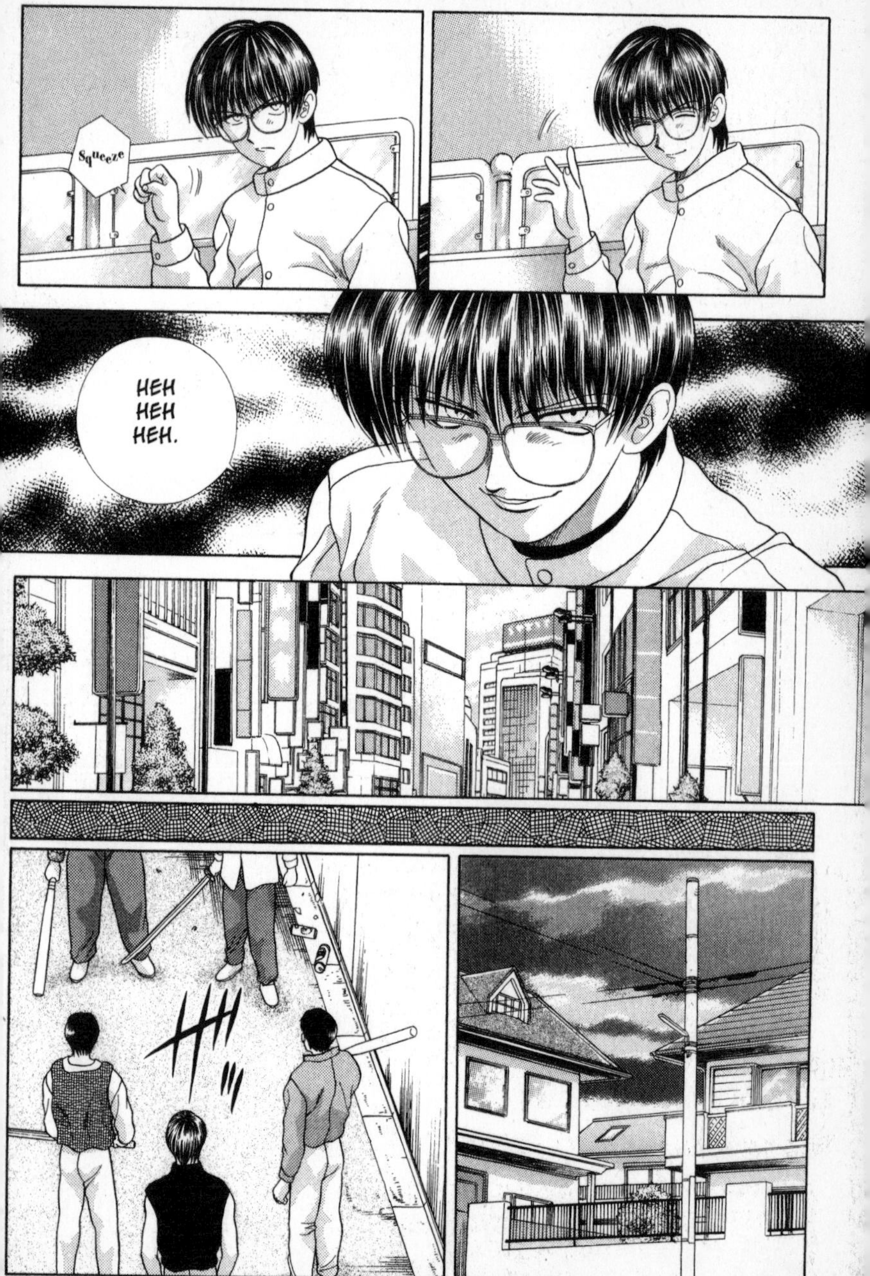
Squeeze
HEH HEH HEH.

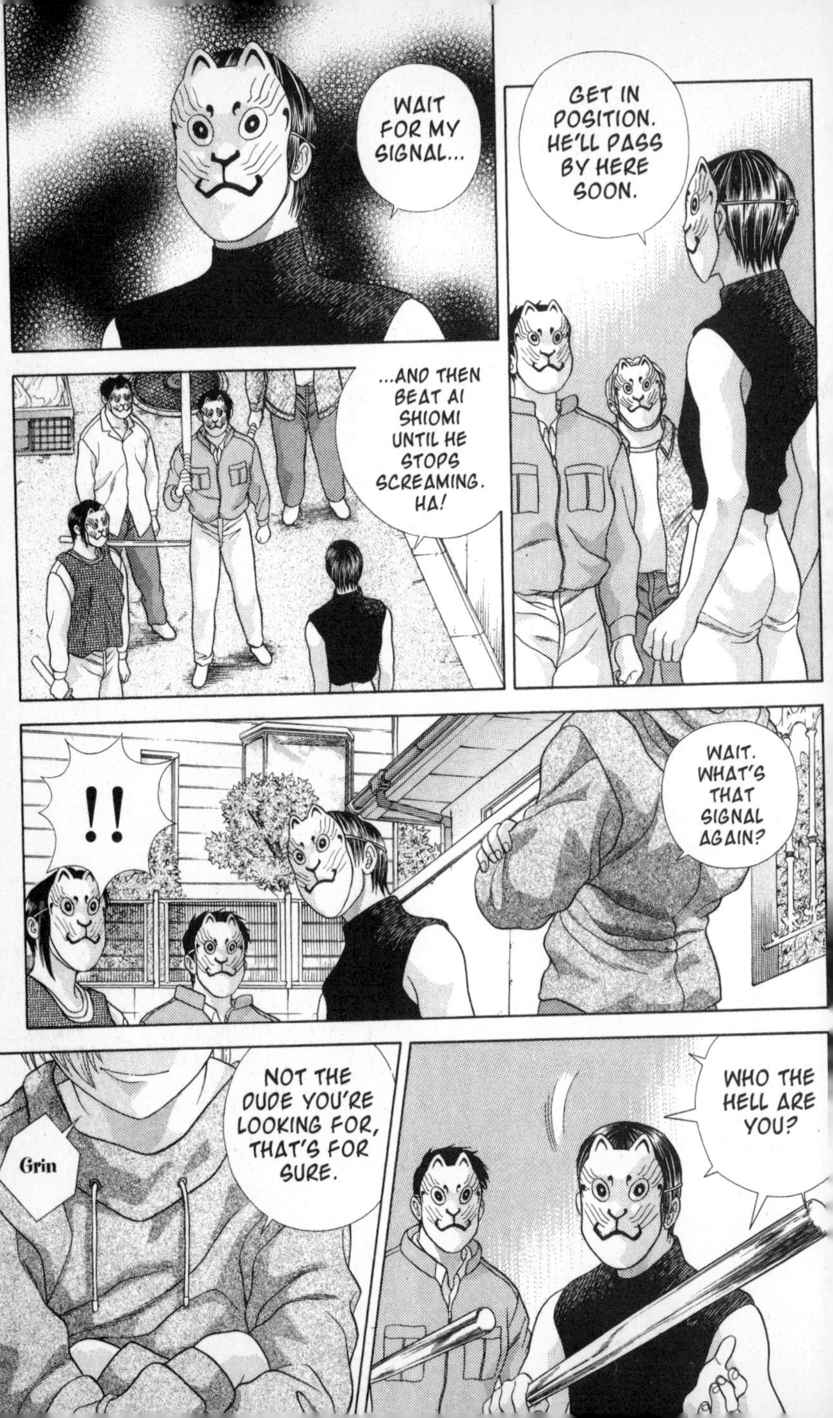
GET IN POSITION. HE'LL PASS BY HERE SOON.
WAIT FOR MY SIGNAL...
...AND THEN BEAT AI SHIOMI UNTIL HE STOPS SCREAMING. HA!
WAIT. WHAT'S THAT SIGNAL AGAIN?
!!
WHO THE HELL ARE YOU?
NOT THE DUDE YOU'RE LOOKING FOR, THAT'S FOR SURE.
Grin

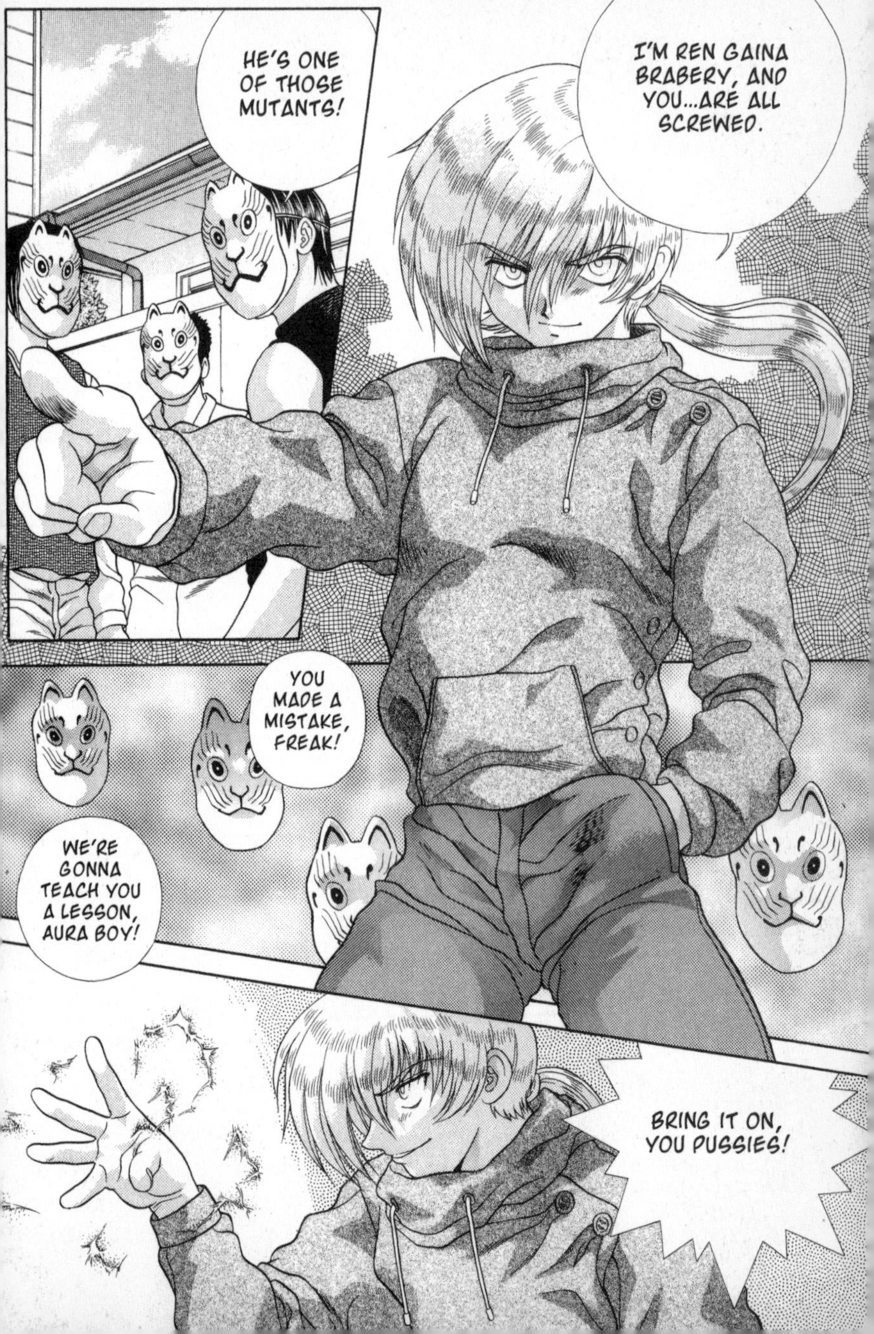
I'M REN GAINA BRABERY, AND YOU...ARE ALL SCREWED.
HE'S ONE OF THOSE MUTANTS!
YOU MADE A MISTAKE, FREAK!
WE'RE GONNA TEACH YOU A LESSON, AURA BOY!
BRING IT ON, YOU PUSSIES!

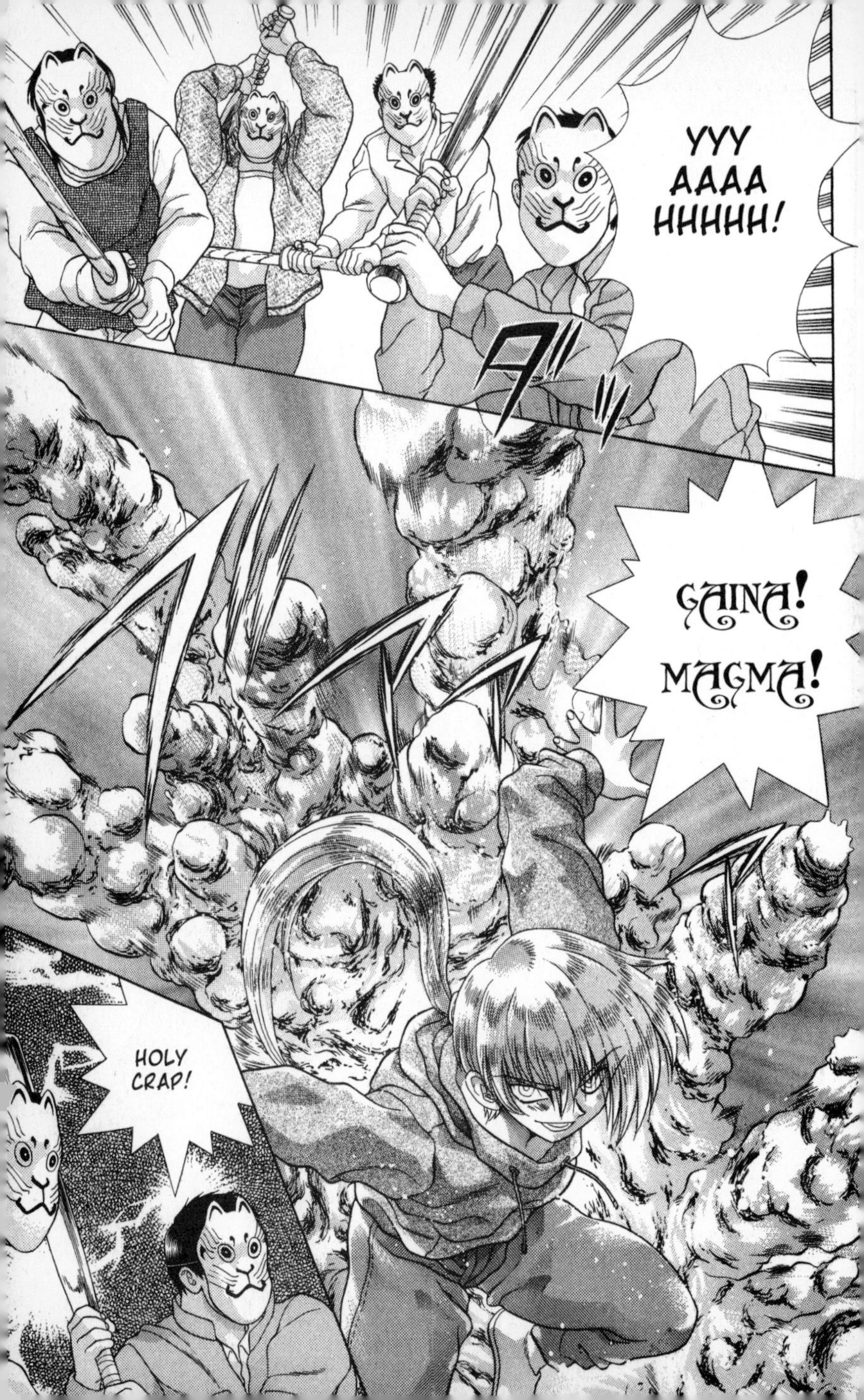

YYY AAAA HHHHH!
ダッ
GAINA! MAGMA!
HOLY CRAP!

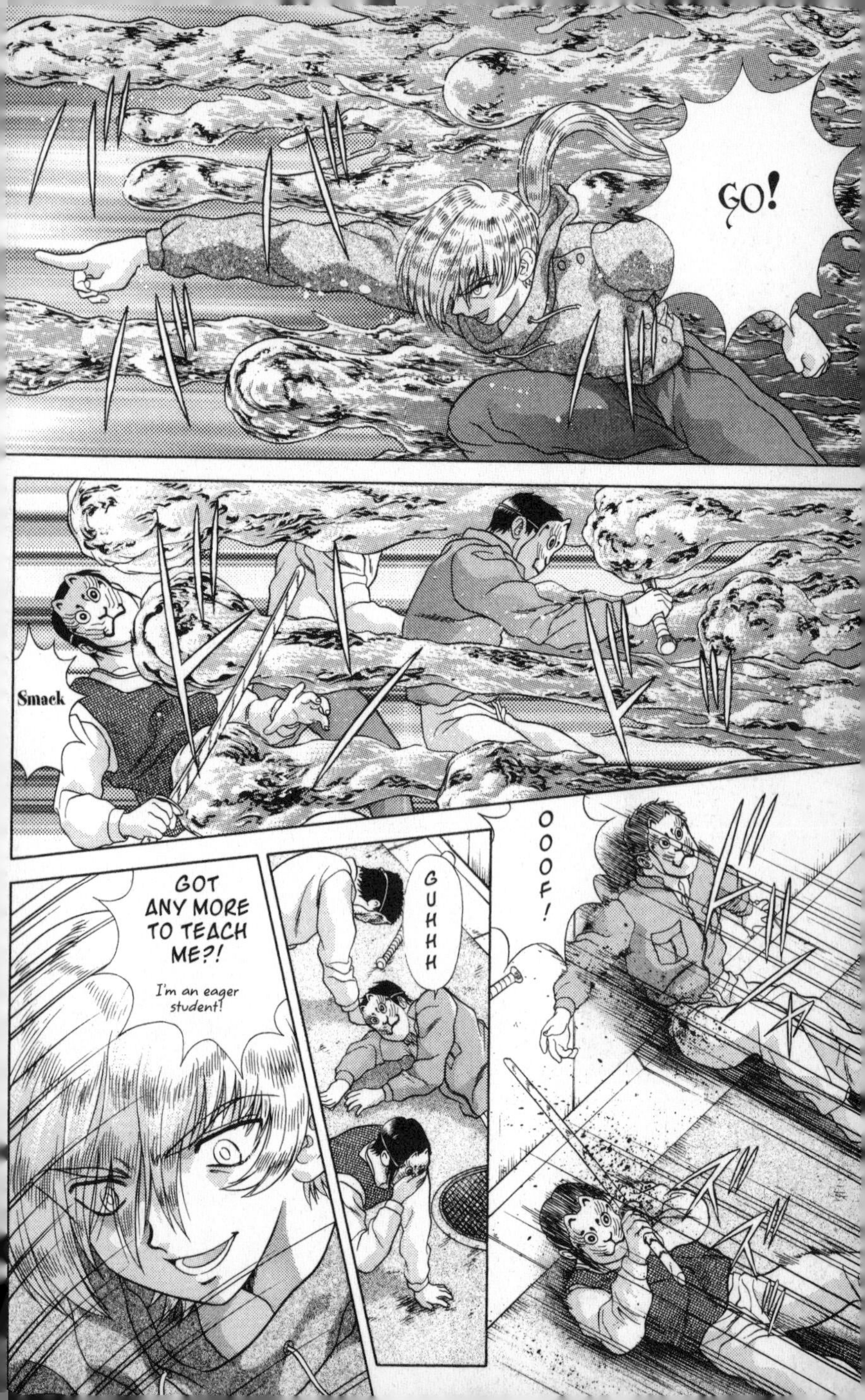
GO!
Smack
OOOF!
GUHHH
GOT ANY MORE TO TEACH ME?!
I'm an eager student!

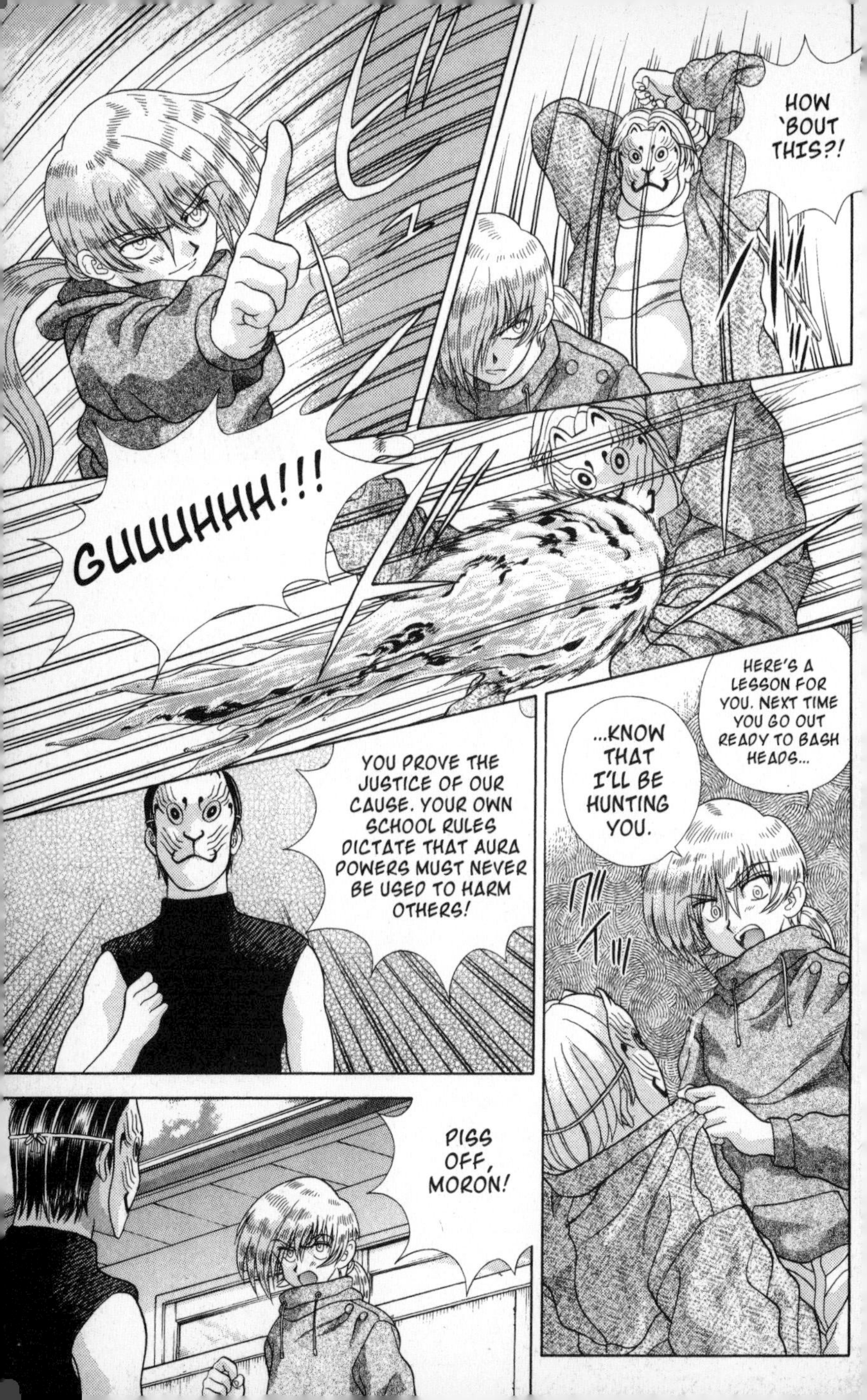
HOW `BOUT THIS?!
GUUUHHH!!!
HERE'S A LESSON FOR YOU. NEXT TIME YOU GO OUT READY TO BASH HEADS...
...KNOW THAT I'LL BE HUNTING YOU.
YOU PROVE THE JUSTICE OF OUR CAUSE. YOUR OWN SCHOOL RULES DICTATE THAT AURA POWERS MUST NEVER BE USED TO HARM OTHERS!
PISS OFF, MORON!

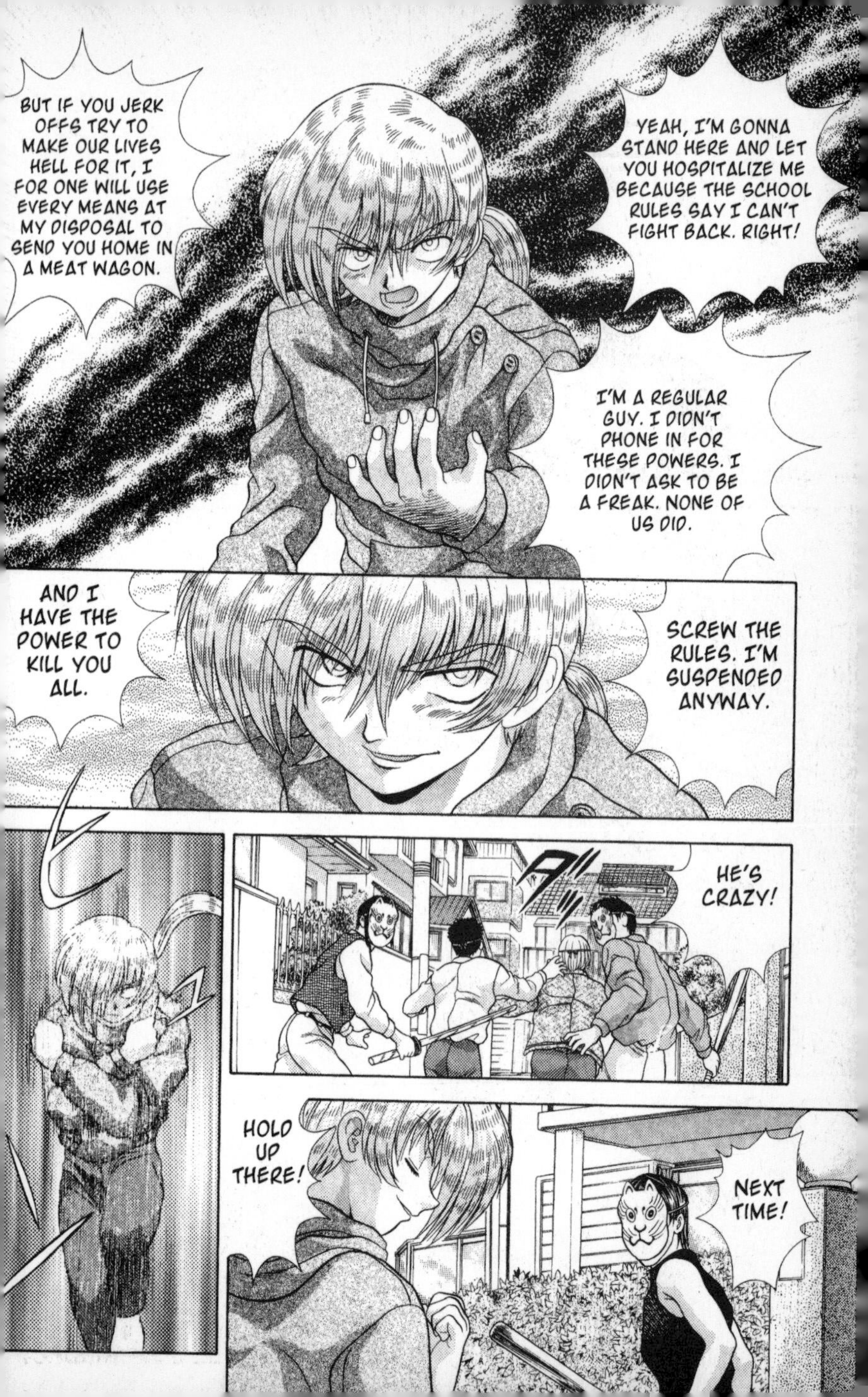
YEAH, I'M GONNA STAND HERE AND LET YOU HOSPITALIZE ME BECAUSE THE SCHOOL RULES SAY I CAN'T FIGHT BACK. RIGHT!
I'M A REGULAR GUY. I DIDN'T PHONE IN FOR THESE POWERS. I DIDN'T ASK TO BE A FREAK. NONE OF US DID.
BUT IF YOU JERK OFFS TRY TO MAKE OUR LIVES HELL FOR IT, I FOR ONE WILL USE EVERY MEANS AT MY DISPOSAL TO SEND YOU HOME IN A MEAT WAGON.
SCREW THE RULES. I'M SUSPENDED ANYWAY.
AND I HAVE THE POWER TO KILL YOU ALL.
HE'S CRAZY!
NEXT TIME!
HOLD UP THERE!

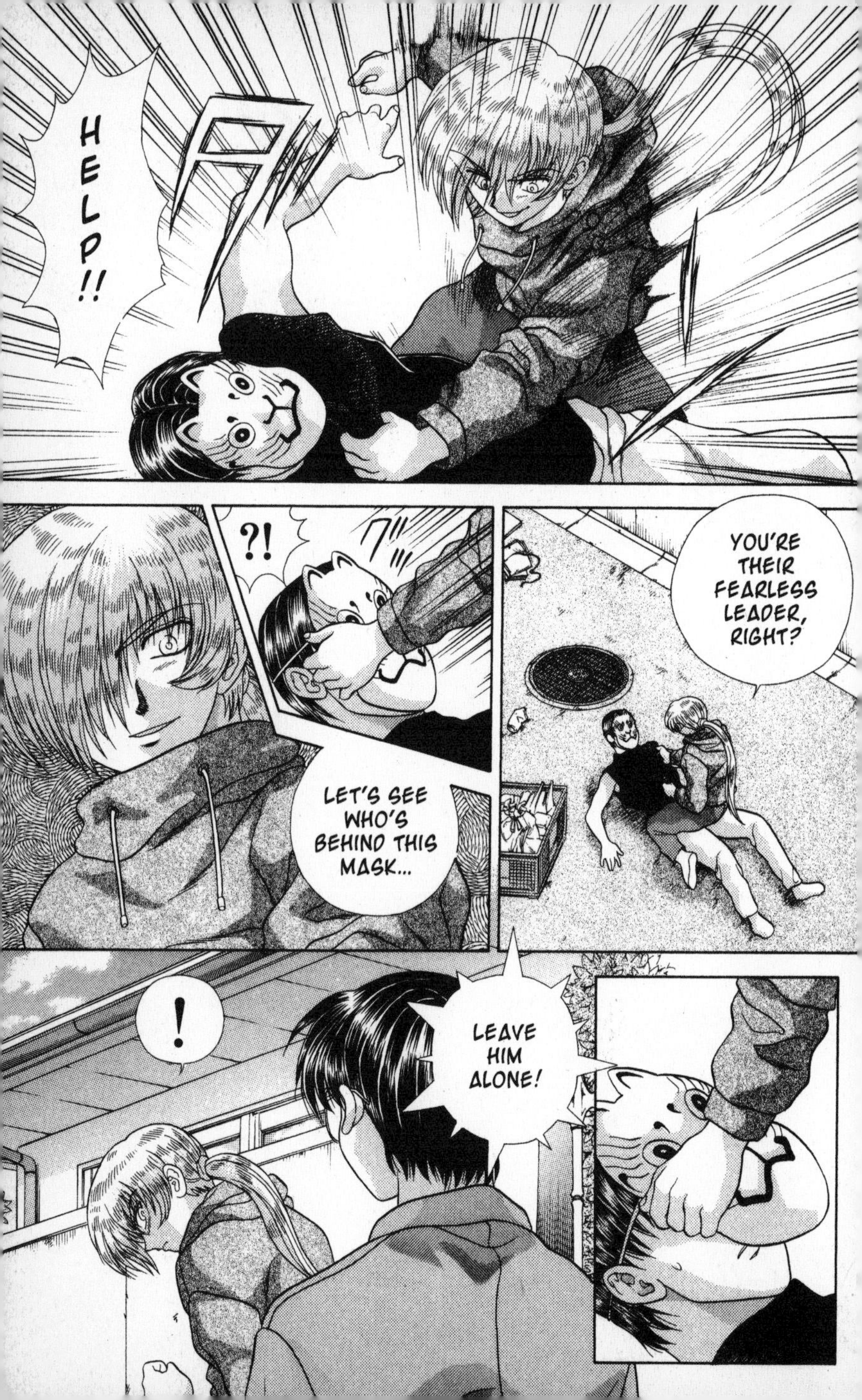
HELP!!
YOU'RE THEIR FEARLESS LEADER, RIGHT?
?!
LET'S SEE WHO'S BEHIND THIS MASK...
LEAVE HIM ALONE!
!

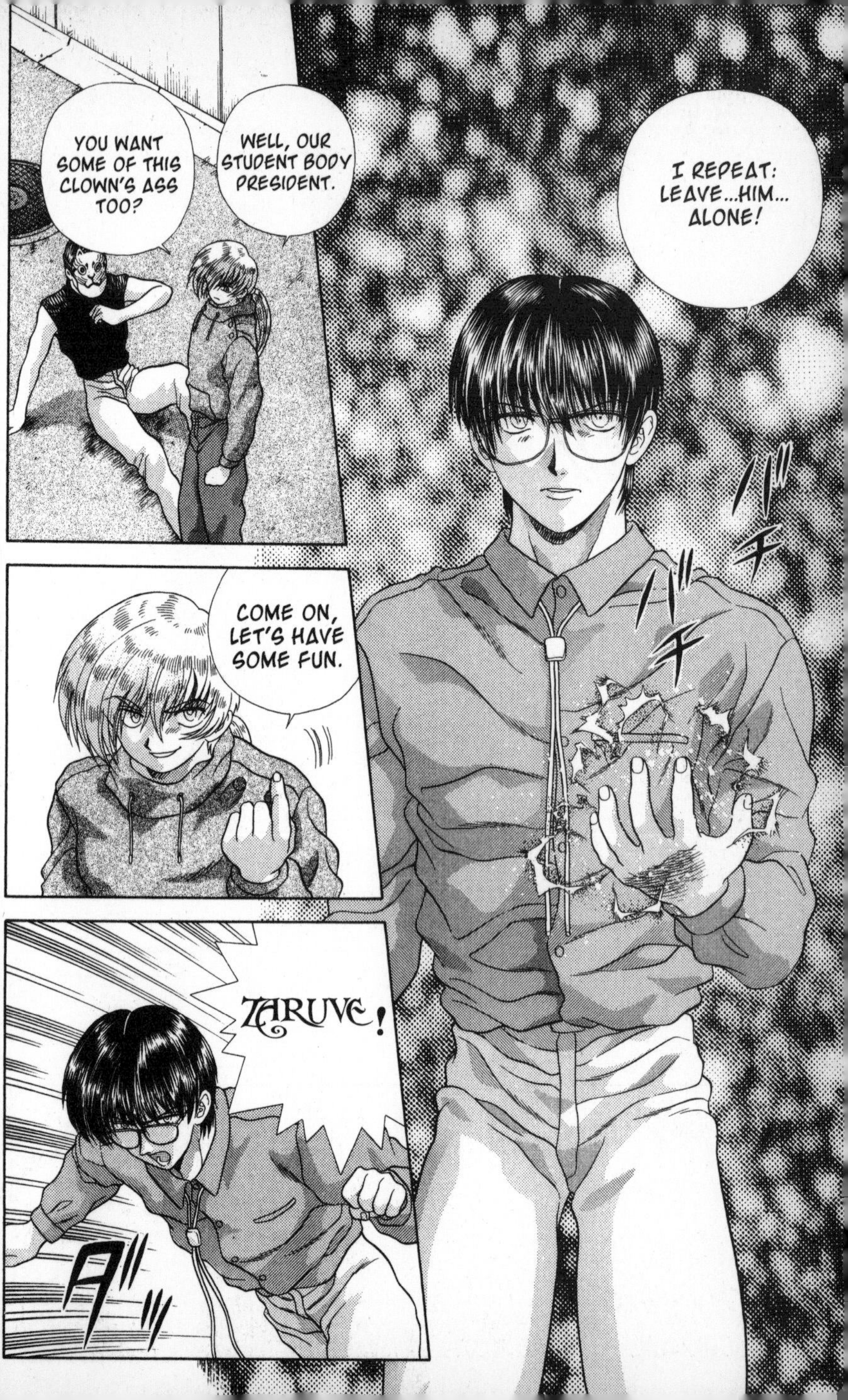
I REPEAT: LEAVE...HIM... ALONE!
バチ
バチ
WELL, OUR STUDENT BODY PRESIDENT.
YOU WANT SOME OF THIS CLOWN'S ASS TOO?
COME ON, LET'S HAVE SOME FUN.
ZARUVE!

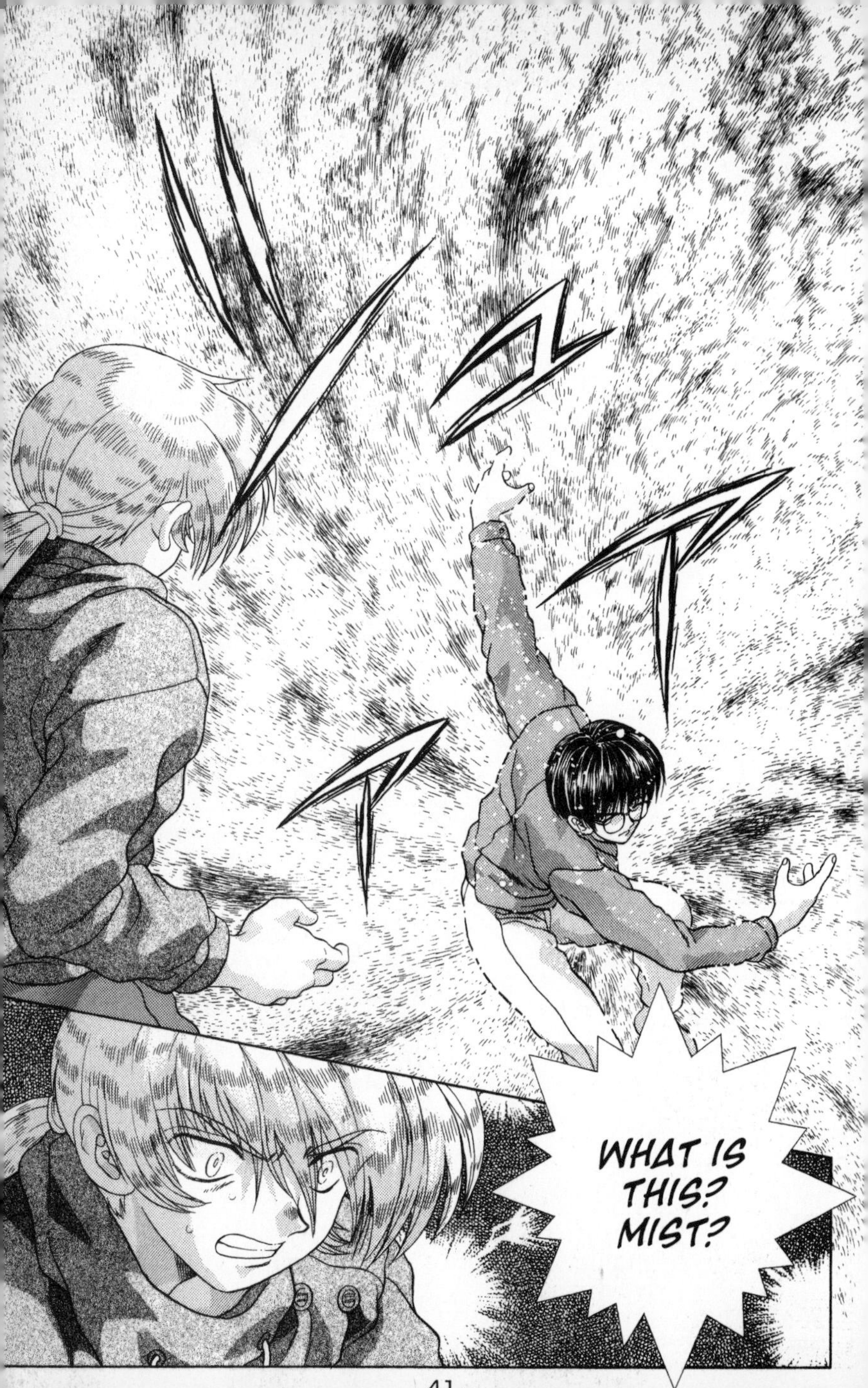
WHAT IS THIS? MIST?

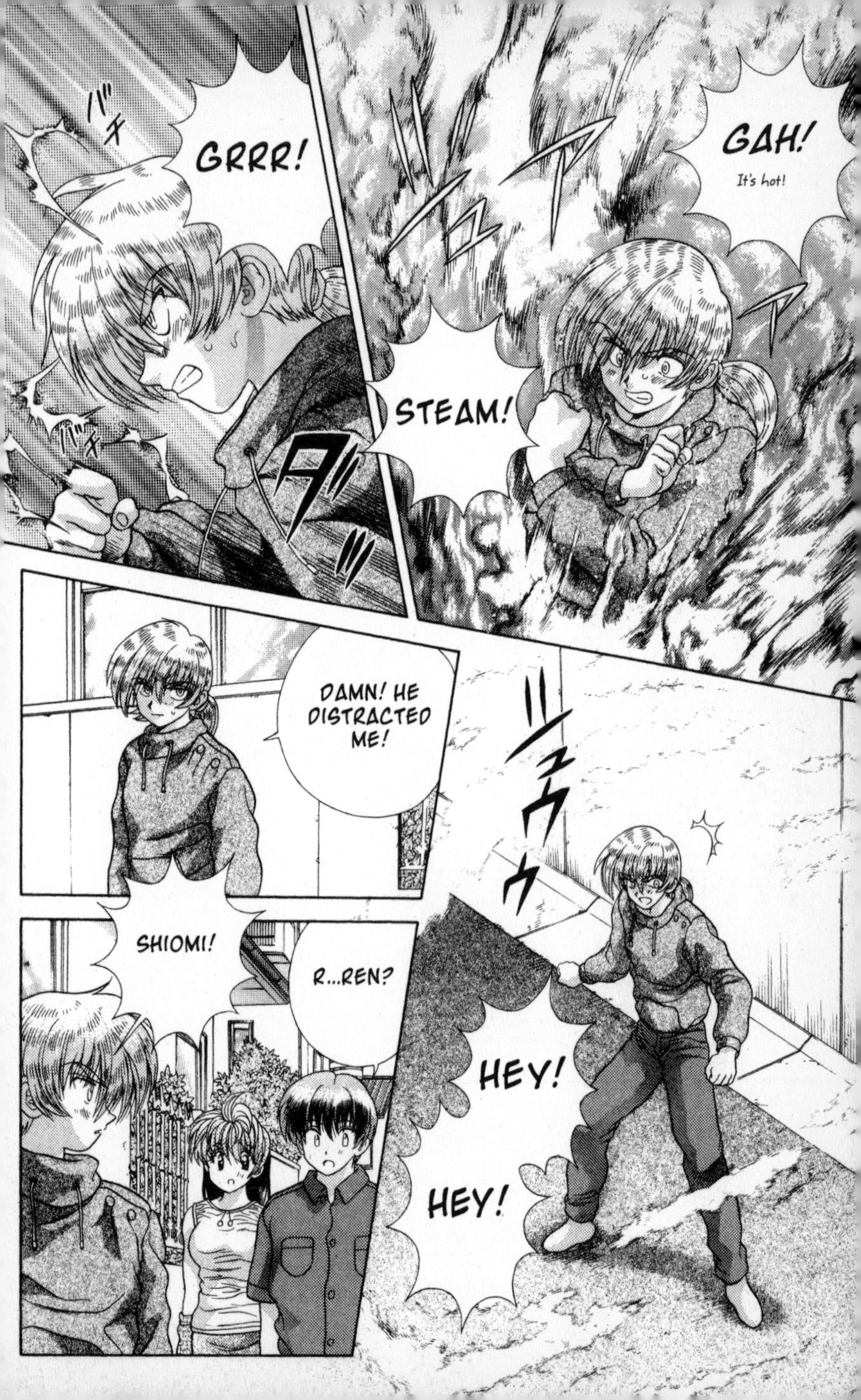

GAH!
It's hot!
STEAM!
GRRR!
HEY!
HEY!
DAMN! HE DISTRACTED ME!
SHIOMI!
R...REN?

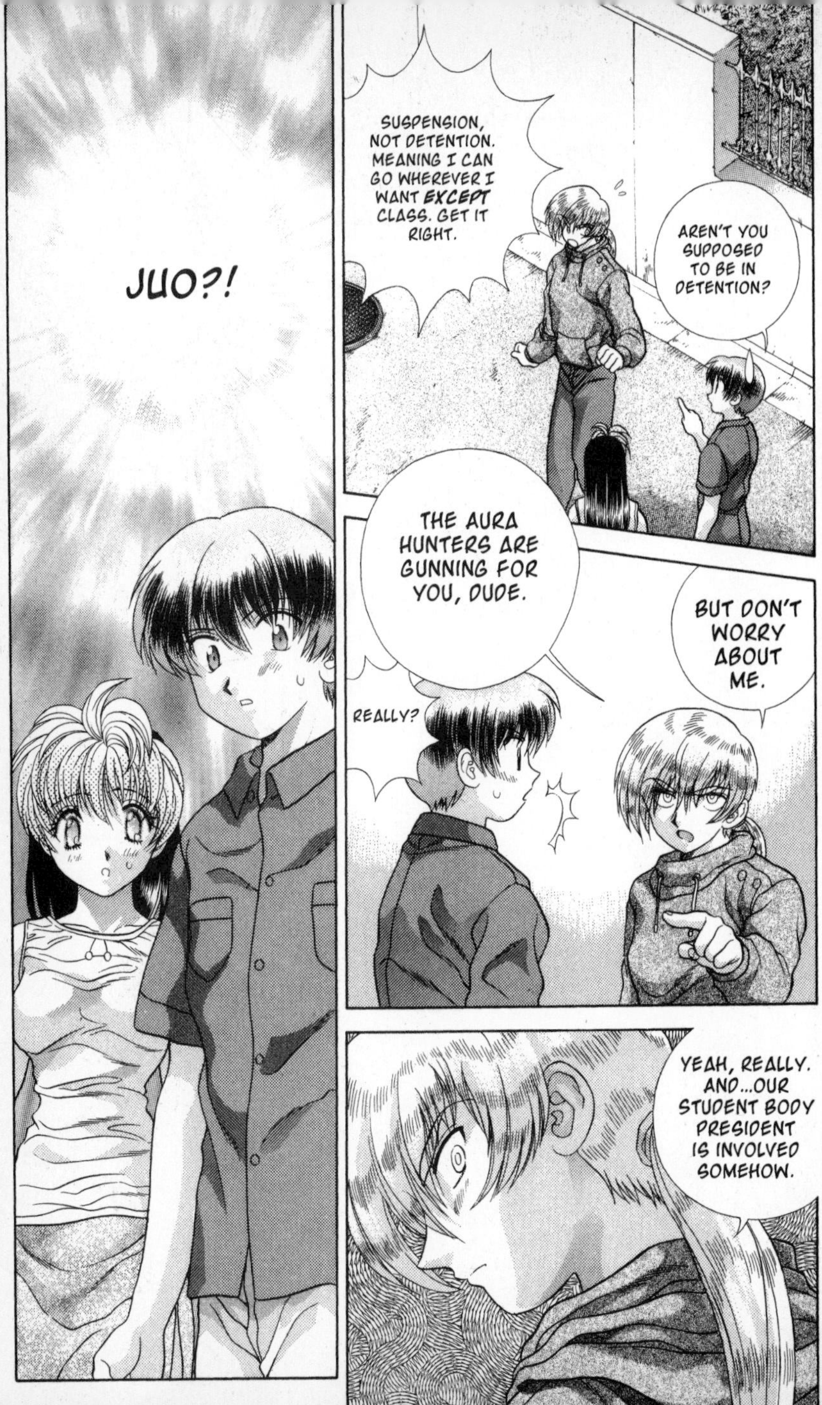
AREN'T YOU SUPPOSED TO BE IN DETENTION?
SUSPENSION, NOT DETENTION. MEANING I CAN GO WHEREVER I WANT *EXCEPT* CLASS. GET IT RIGHT.
THE AURA HUNTERS ARE GUNNING FOR YOU, DUDE.
BUT DON'T WORRY ABOUT ME.
REALLY?
YEAH, REALLY. AND...OUR STUDENT BODY PRESIDENT IS INVOLVED SOMEHOW.
JUO?!

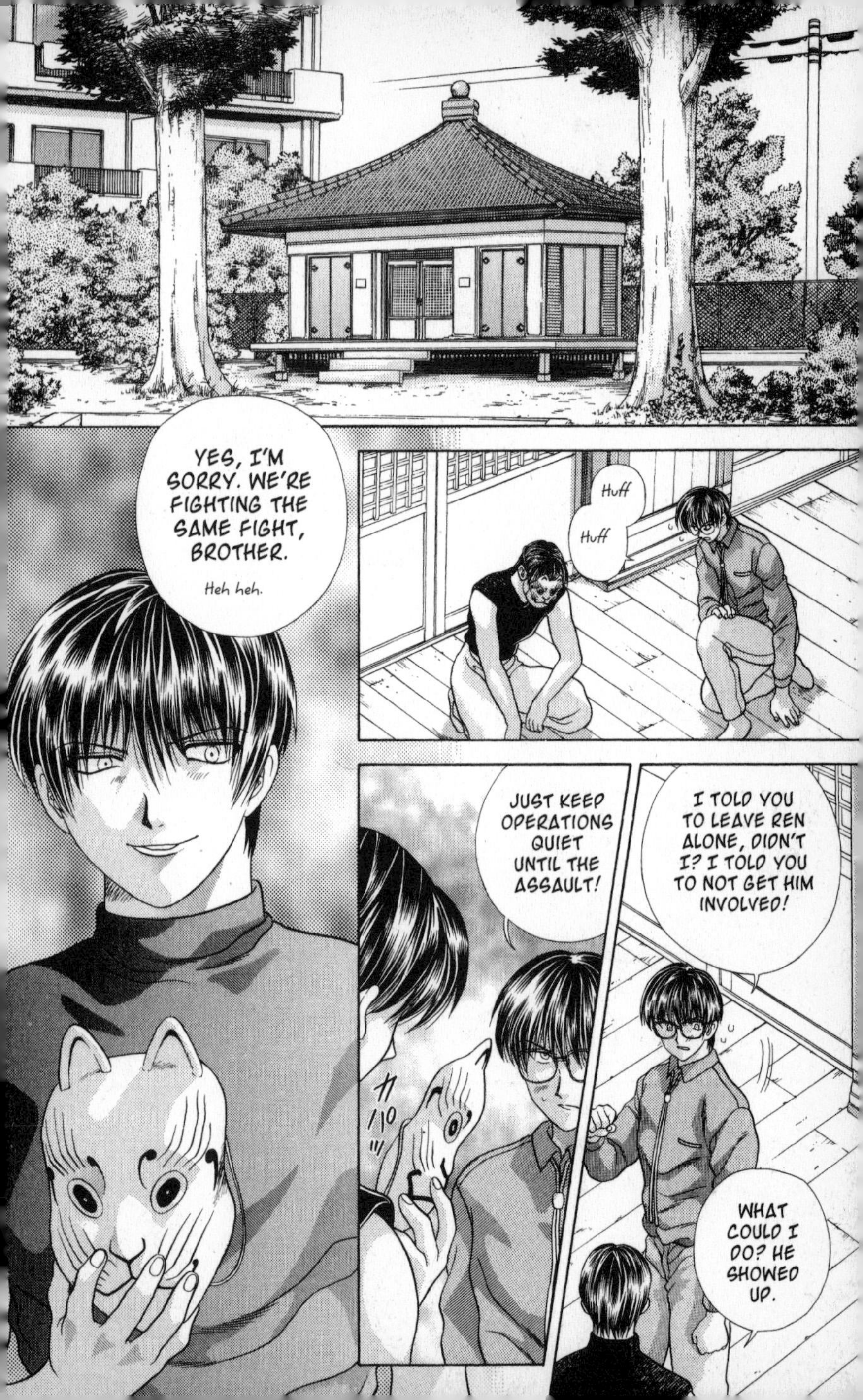
Huff
Huff
I TOLD YOU TO LEAVE REN ALONE, DIDN'T I? I TOLD YOU TO NOT GET HIM INVOLVED!
WHAT COULD I DO? HE SHOWED UP.
JUST KEEP OPERATIONS QUIET UNTIL THE ASSAULT!
YES, I'M SORRY. WE'RE FIGHTING THE SAME FIGHT, BROTHER.
Heh heh.

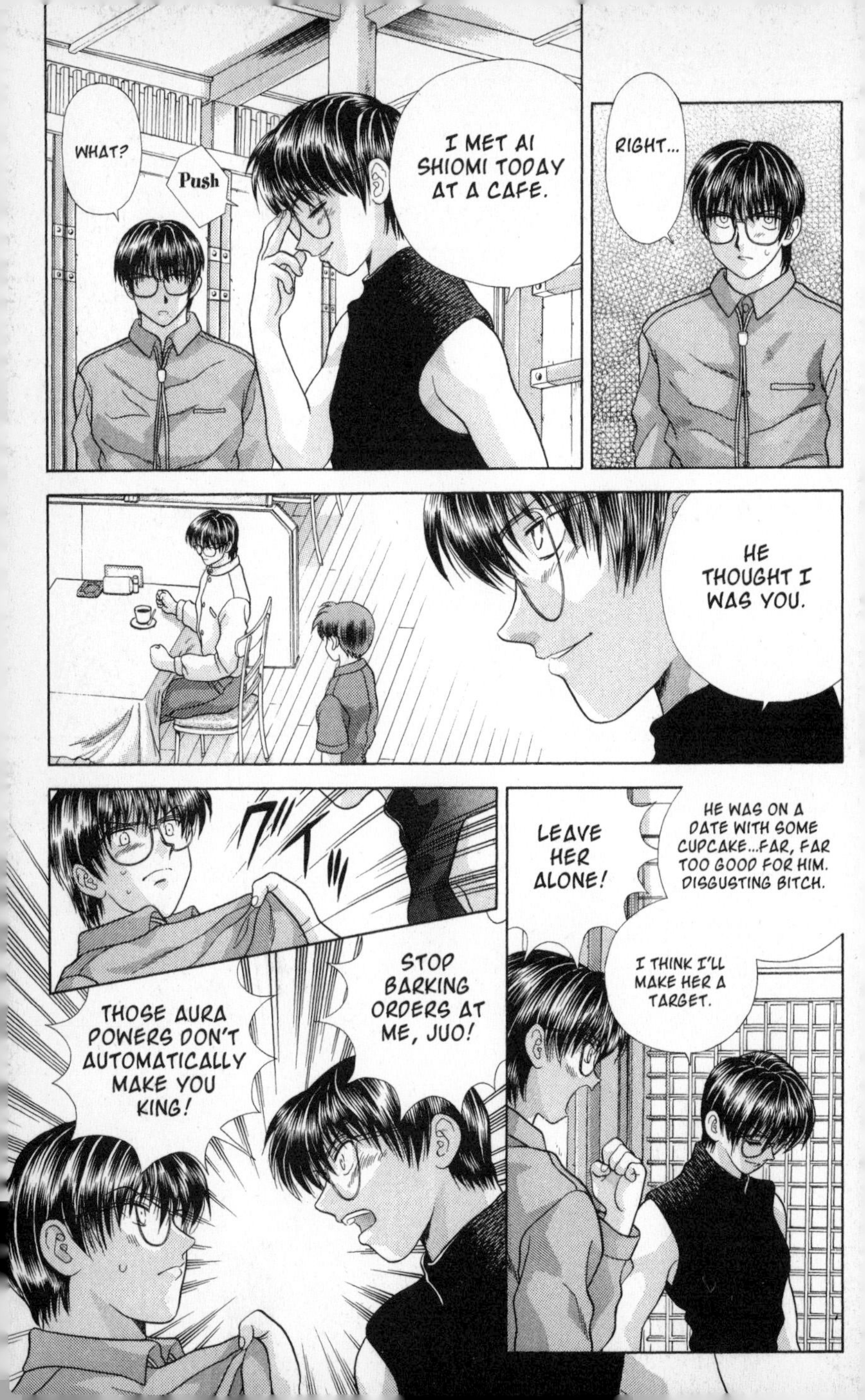
RIGHT...
I MET AI SHIOMI TODAY AT A CAFE.
Push
WHAT?
HE THOUGHT I WAS YOU.
HE WAS ON A DATE WITH SOME CUPCAKE...FAR, FAR TOO GOOD FOR HIM. DISGUSTING BITCH.
I THINK I'LL MAKE HER A TARGET.
LEAVE HER ALONE!
STOP BARKING ORDERS AT ME, JUO!
THOSE AURA POWERS DON'T AUTOMATICALLY MAKE YOU KING!

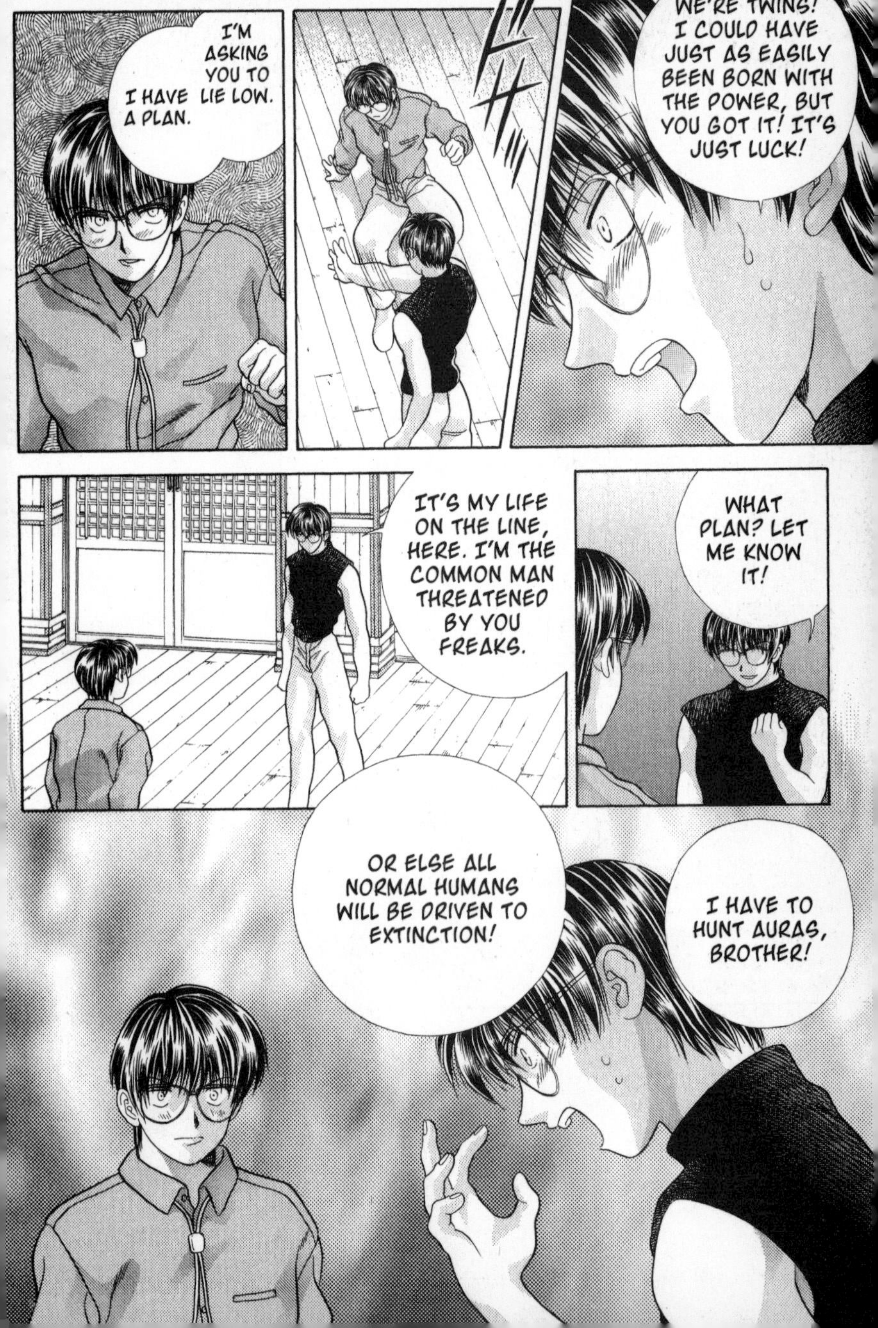
WE'RE TWINS! I COULD HAVE JUST AS EASILY BEEN BORN WITH THE POWER, BUT YOU GOT IT! IT'S JUST LUCK!
I'M ASKING YOU TO LIE LOW. I HAVE A PLAN.
WHAT PLAN? LET ME KNOW IT!
IT'S MY LIFE ON THE LINE, HERE. I'M THE COMMON MAN THREATENED BY YOU FREAKS.
I HAVE TO HUNT AURAS, BROTHER!
OR ELSE ALL NORMAL HUMANS WILL BE DRIVEN TO EXTINCTION!

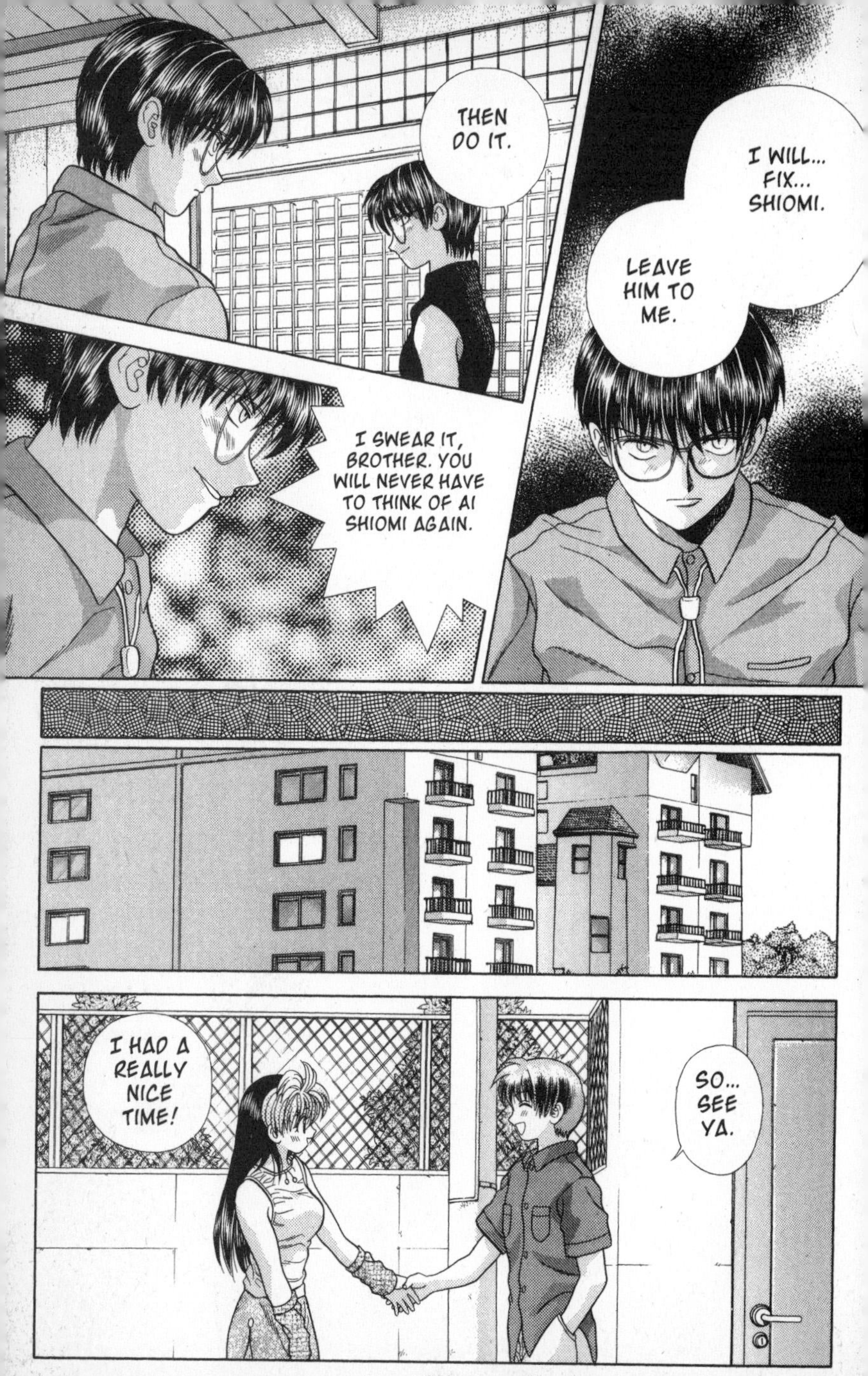
I WILL... FIX... SHIOMI.
LEAVE HIM TO ME.
THEN DO IT.
I SWEAR IT, BROTHER. YOU WILL NEVER HAVE TO THINK OF AI SHIOMI AGAIN.
SO... SEE YA.
I HAD A REALLY NICE TIME!

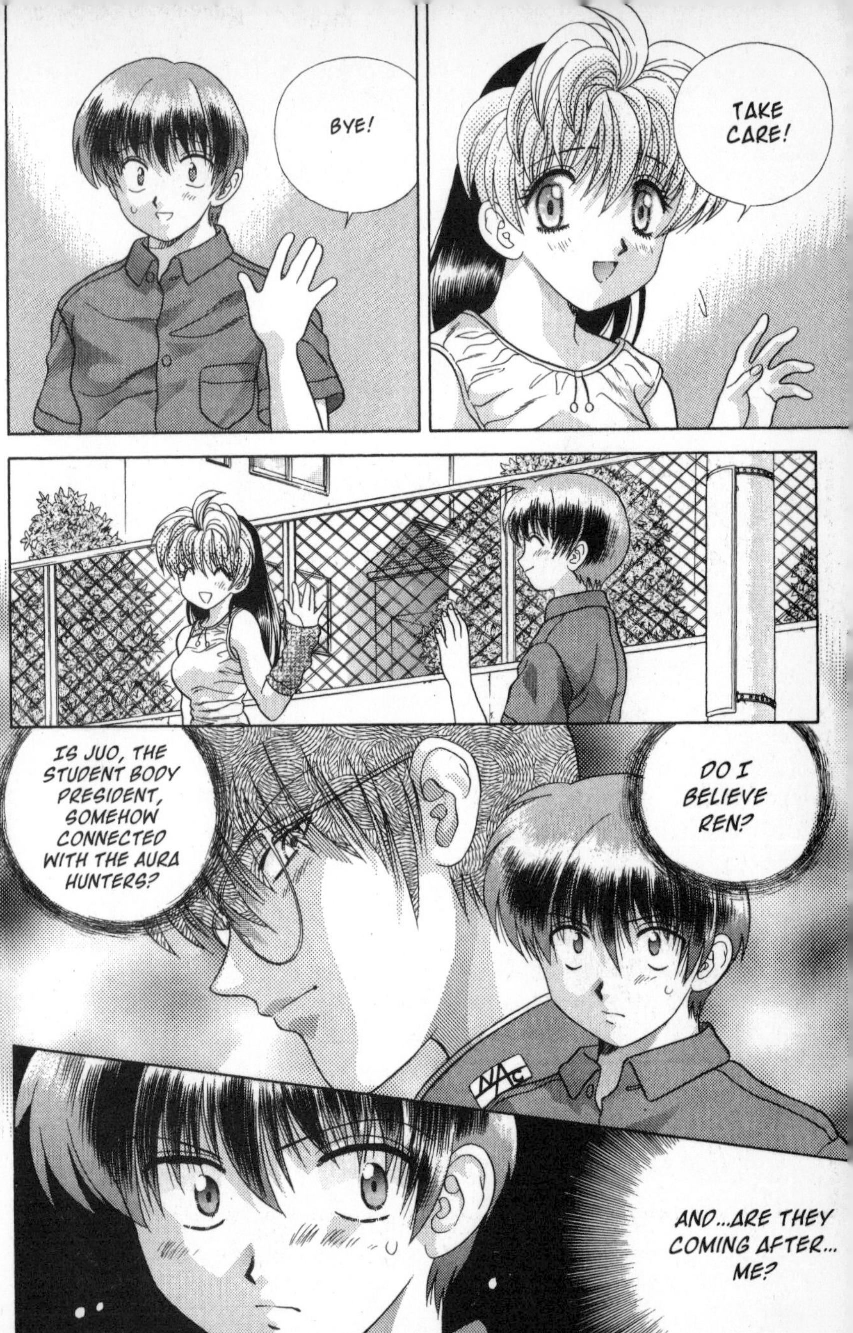
TAKE CARE!
BYE!
DO I BELIEVE REN?
IS JUO, THE STUDENT BODY PRESIDENT, SOMEHOW CONNECTED WITH THE AURA HUNTERS?
AND...ARE THEY COMING AFTER... ME?

Shadowed Friends and Masked Enemies - END

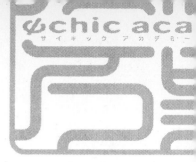

Chapter 12: The Aura Conspiracy

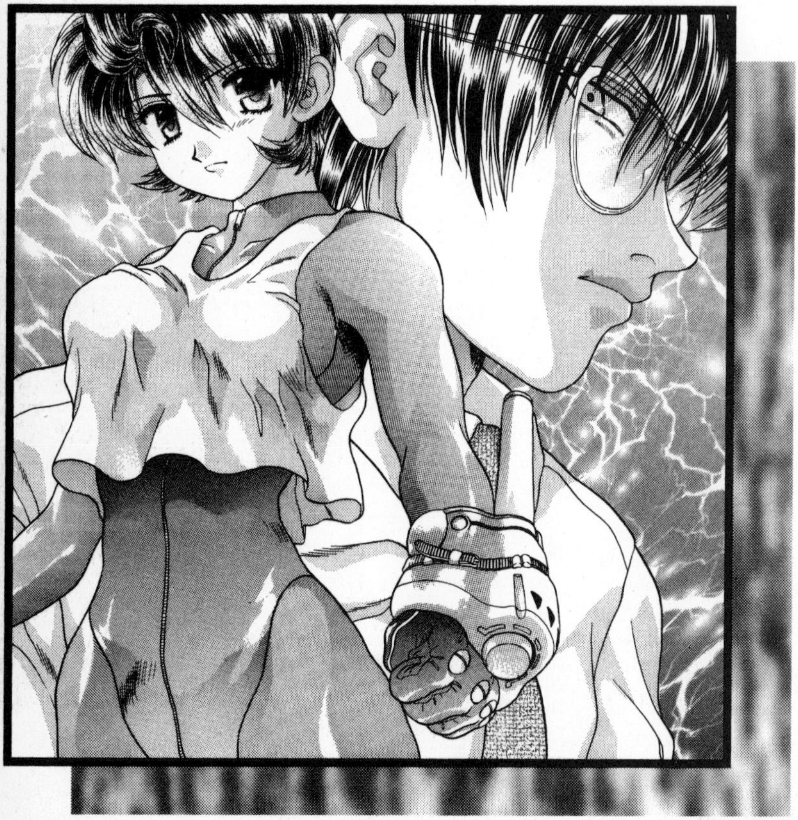

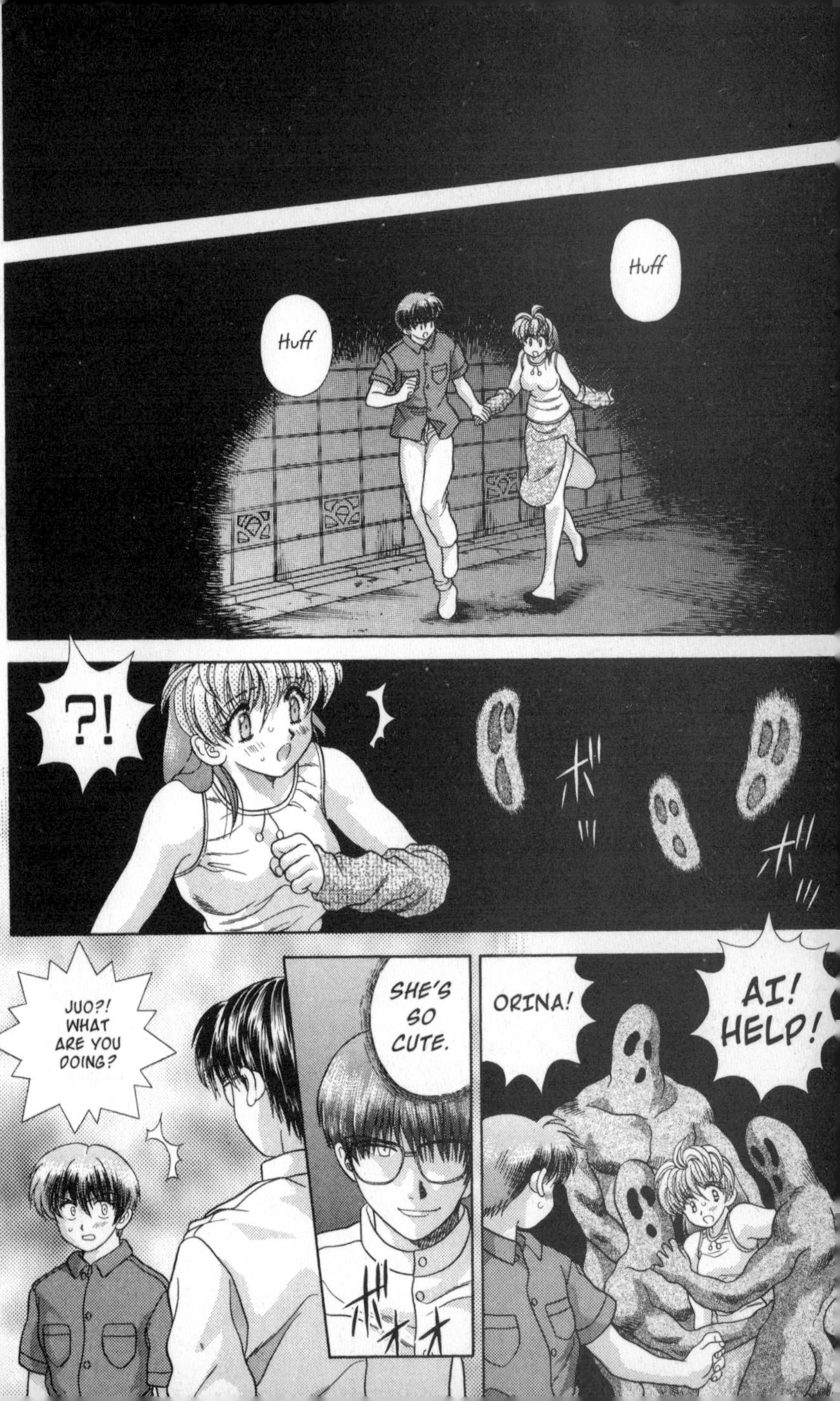
Huff
Huff
?!
AI! HELP!
ORINA!
SHE'S SO CUTE.
JUO?! WHAT ARE YOU DOING?

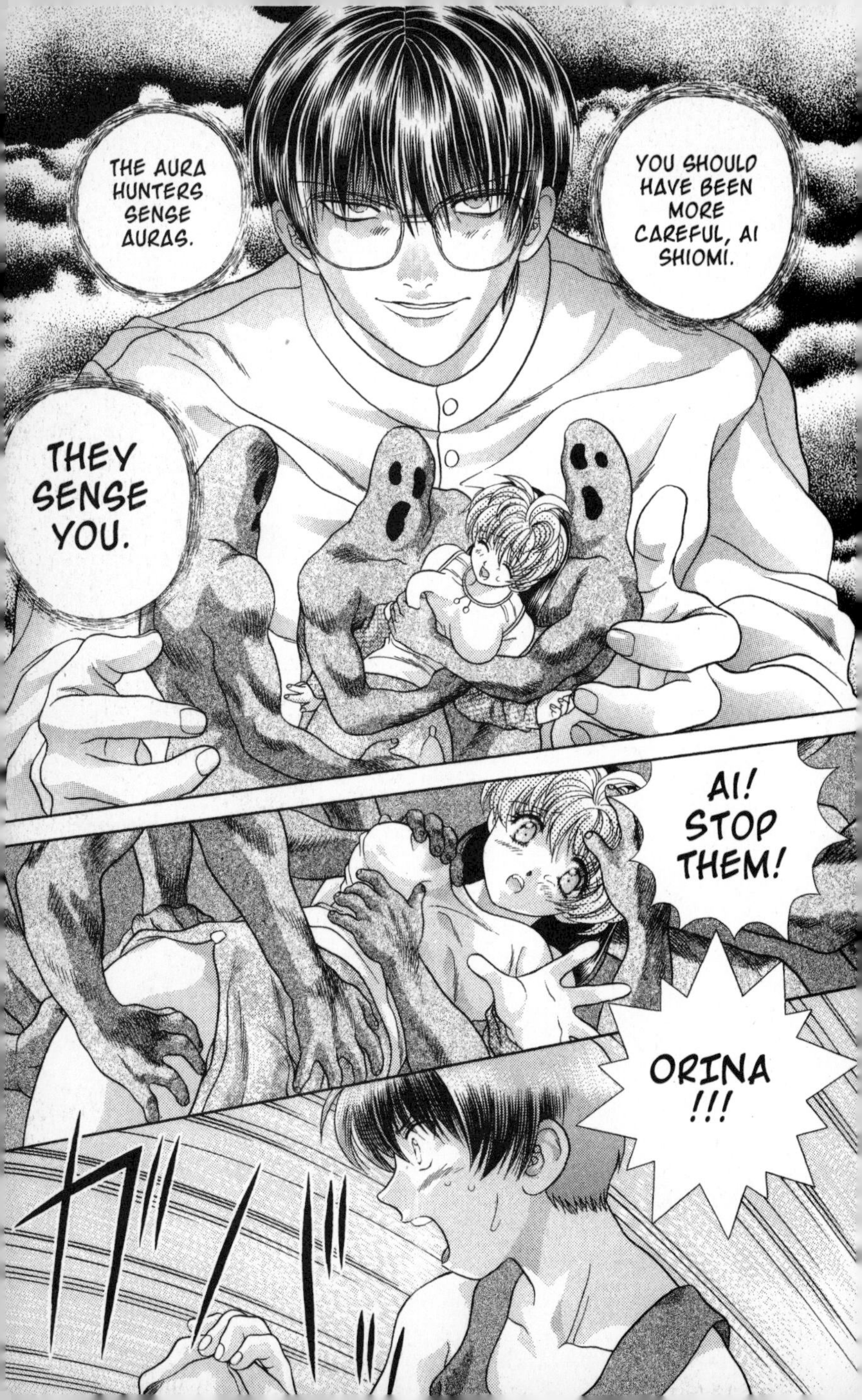
YOU SHOULD HAVE BEEN MORE CAREFUL, AI SHIOMI.
THE AURA HUNTERS SENSE AURAS.
THEY SENSE YOU.
AI! STOP THEM!
ORINA !!!

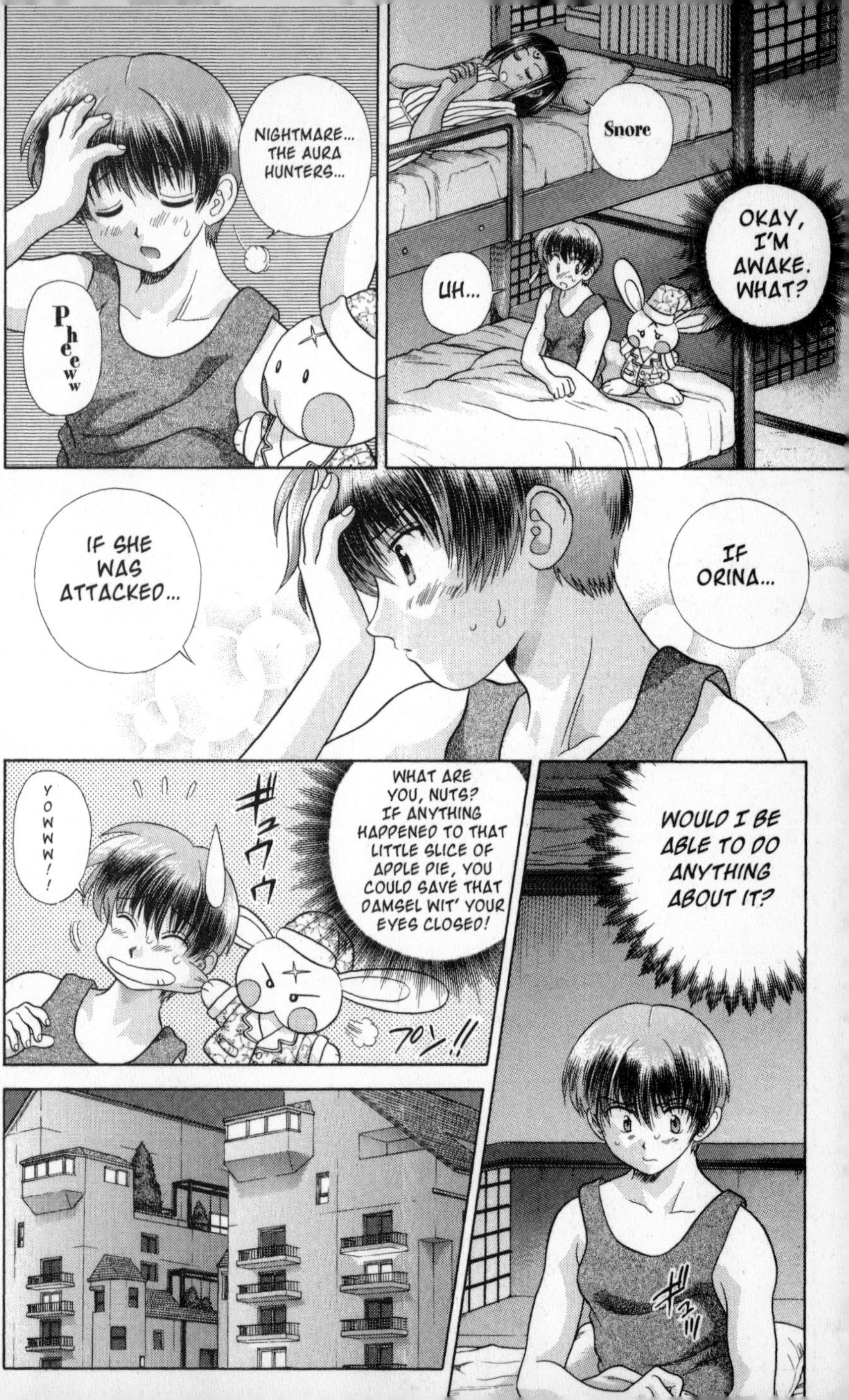
Snore
OKAY, I'M AWAKE. WHAT?
UH...
NIGHTMARE... THE AURA HUNTERS...
Pheeww
IF ORINA...
IF SHE WAS ATTACKED...
WOULD I BE ABLE TO DO ANYTHING ABOUT IT?
WHAT ARE YOU, NUTS? IF ANYTHING HAPPENED TO THAT LITTLE SLICE OF APPLE PIE, YOU COULD SAVE THAT DAMSEL WIT' YOUR EYES CLOSED!
YOWWW!!

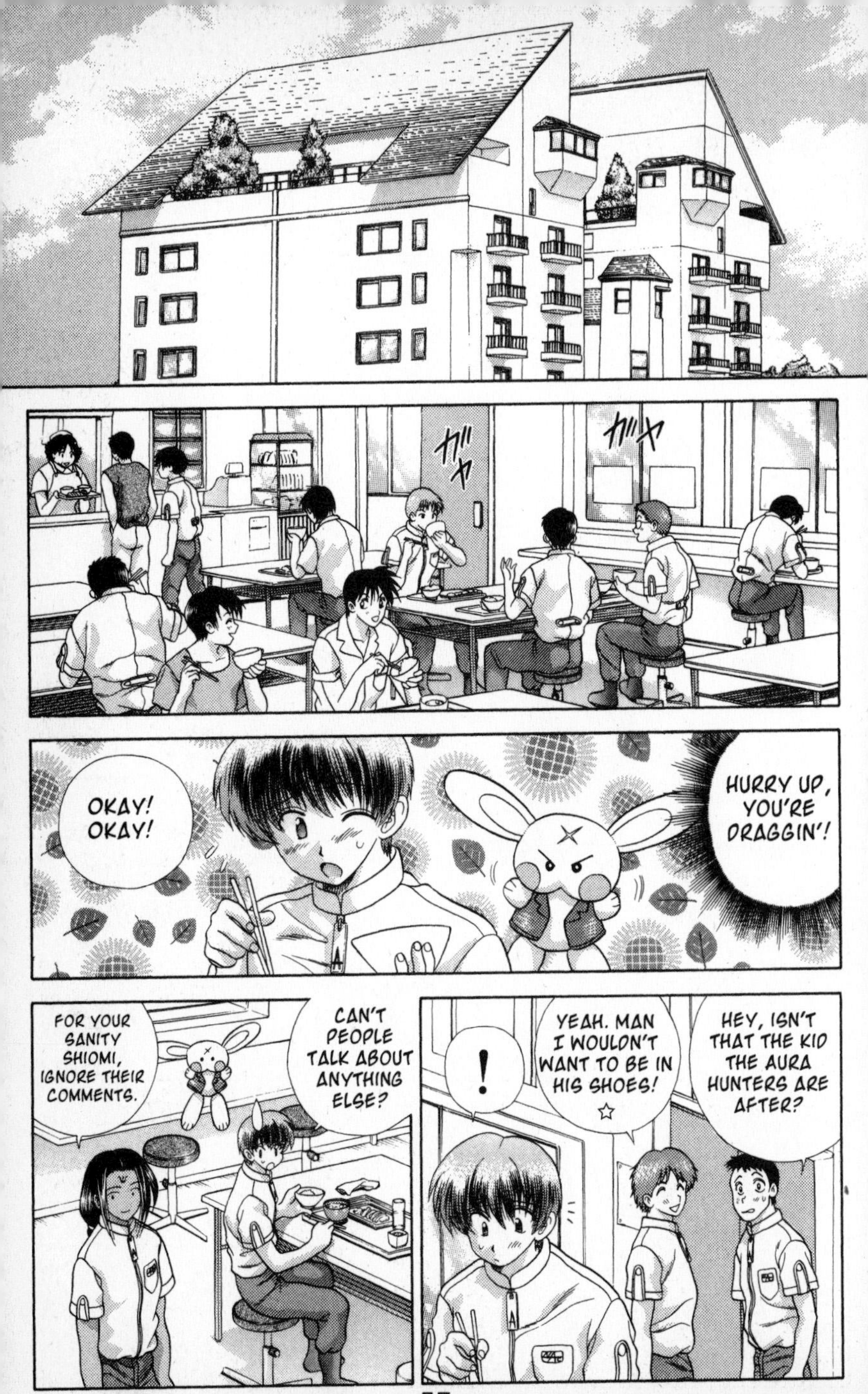
ガヤ
ガヤ
HURRY UP, YOU'RE DRAGGIN'!
OKAY! OKAY!
HEY, ISN'T THAT THE KID THE AURA HUNTERS ARE AFTER?
YEAH. MAN I WOULDN'T WANT TO BE IN HIS SHOES! ☆
!
CAN'T PEOPLE TALK ABOUT ANYTHING ELSE?
FOR YOUR SANITY SHIOMI, IGNORE THEIR COMMENTS.

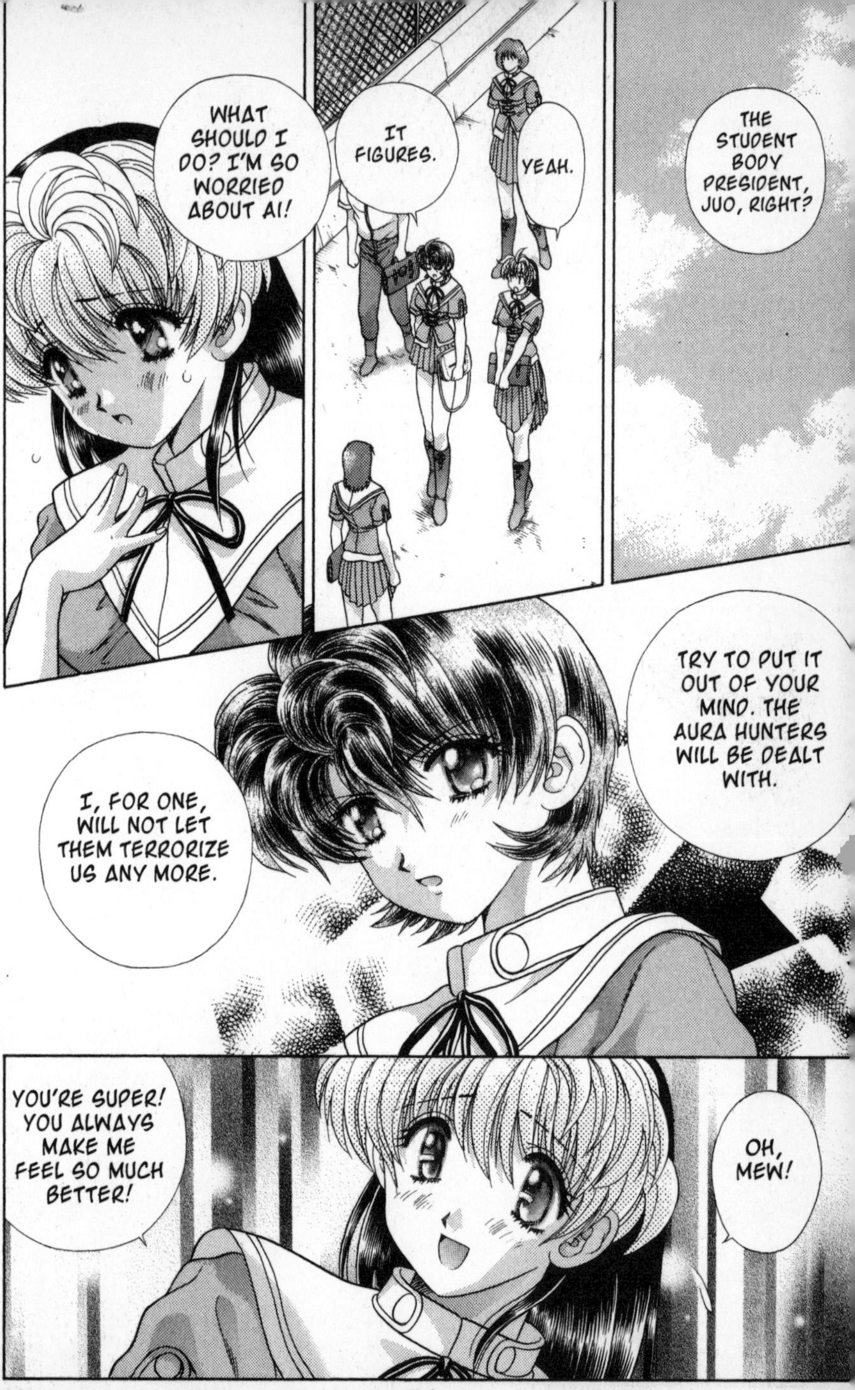
THE STUDENT BODY PRESIDENT, JUO, RIGHT?
YEAH.
IT FIGURES.
WHAT SHOULD I DO? I'M SO WORRIED ABOUT AI!
TRY TO PUT IT OUT OF YOUR MIND. THE AURA HUNTERS WILL BE DEALT WITH.
I, FOR ONE, WILL NOT LET THEM TERRORIZE US ANY MORE.
OH, MEW!
YOU'RE SUPER! YOU ALWAYS MAKE ME FEEL SO MUCH BETTER!

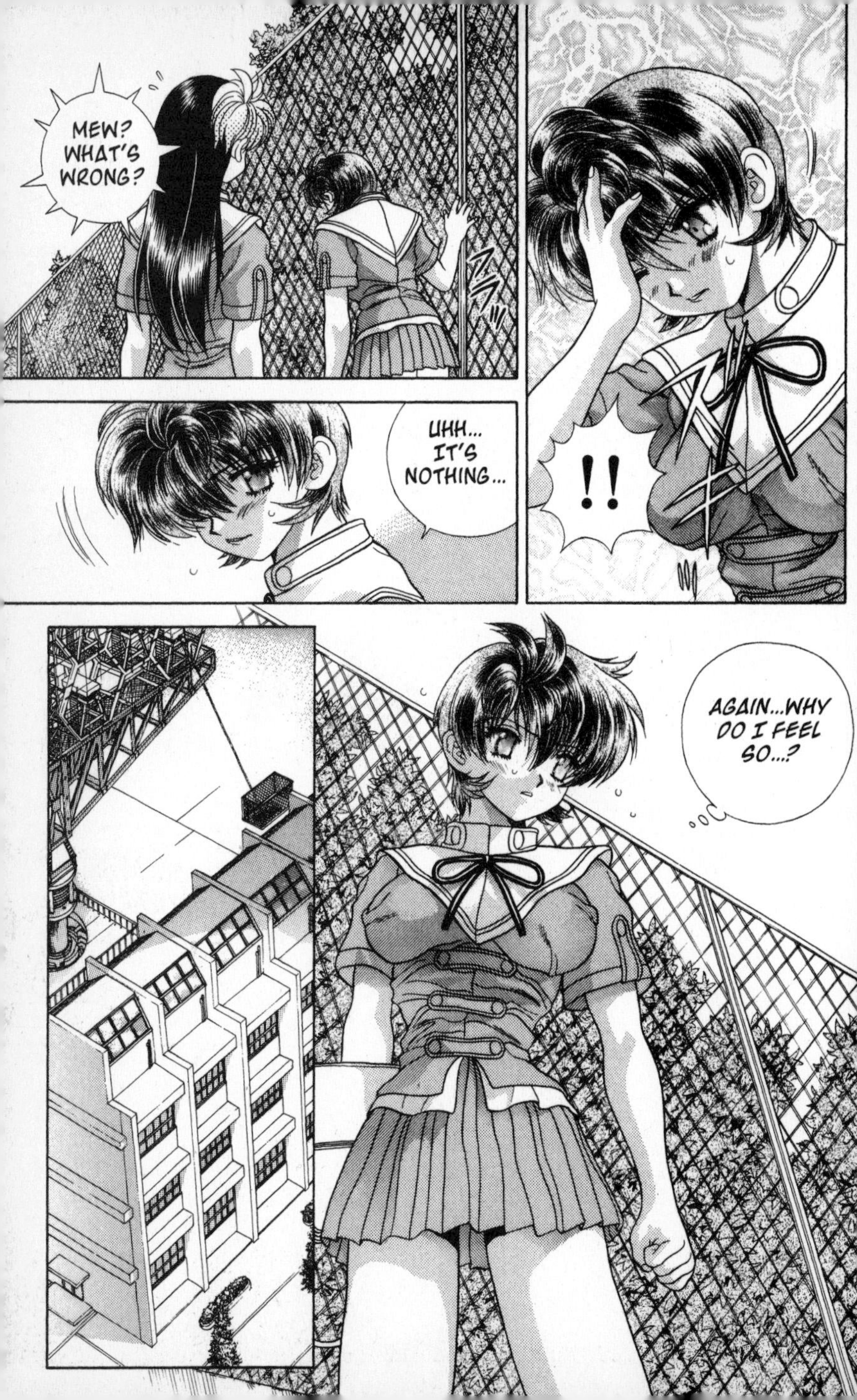
!!
MEW? WHAT'S WRONG?
UHH... IT'S NOTHING...
AGAIN...WHY DO I FEEL SO...?

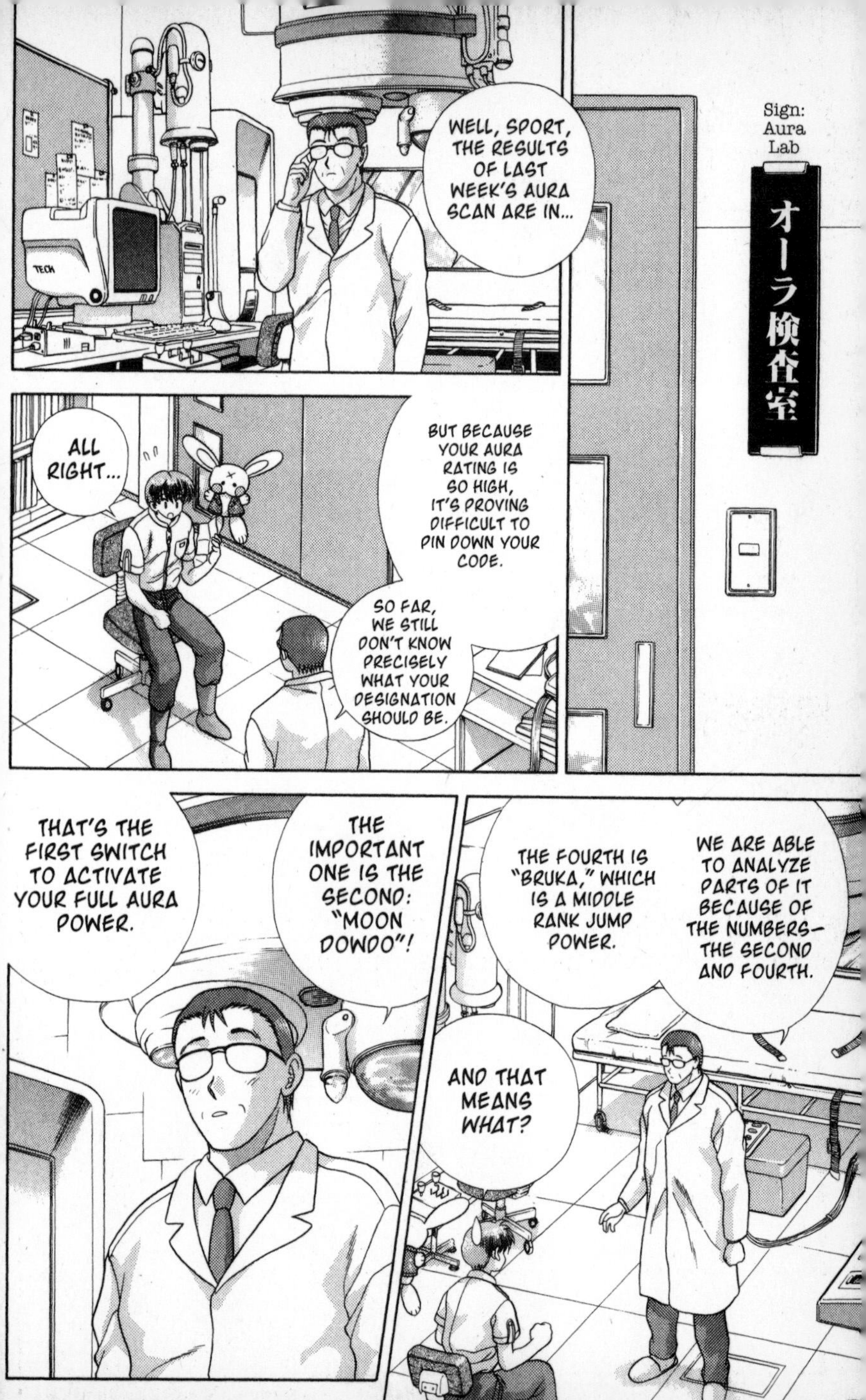
Sign: Aura Lab
オーラ検査室
WELL, SPORT, THE RESULTS OF LAST WEEK'S AURA SCAN ARE IN...
BUT BECAUSE YOUR AURA RATING IS SO HIGH, IT'S PROVING DIFFICULT TO PIN DOWN YOUR CODE.
SO FAR, WE STILL DON'T KNOW PRECISELY WHAT YOUR DESIGNATION SHOULD BE.
ALL RIGHT...
WE ARE ABLE TO ANALYZE PARTS OF IT BECAUSE OF THE NUMBERS— THE SECOND AND FOURTH.
THE FOURTH IS "BRUKA," WHICH IS A MIDDLE RANK JUMP POWER.
AND THAT MEANS WHAT?
THE IMPORTANT ONE IS THE SECOND: "MOON DOWDO"!
THAT'S THE FIRST SWITCH TO ACTIVATE YOUR FULL AURA POWER.

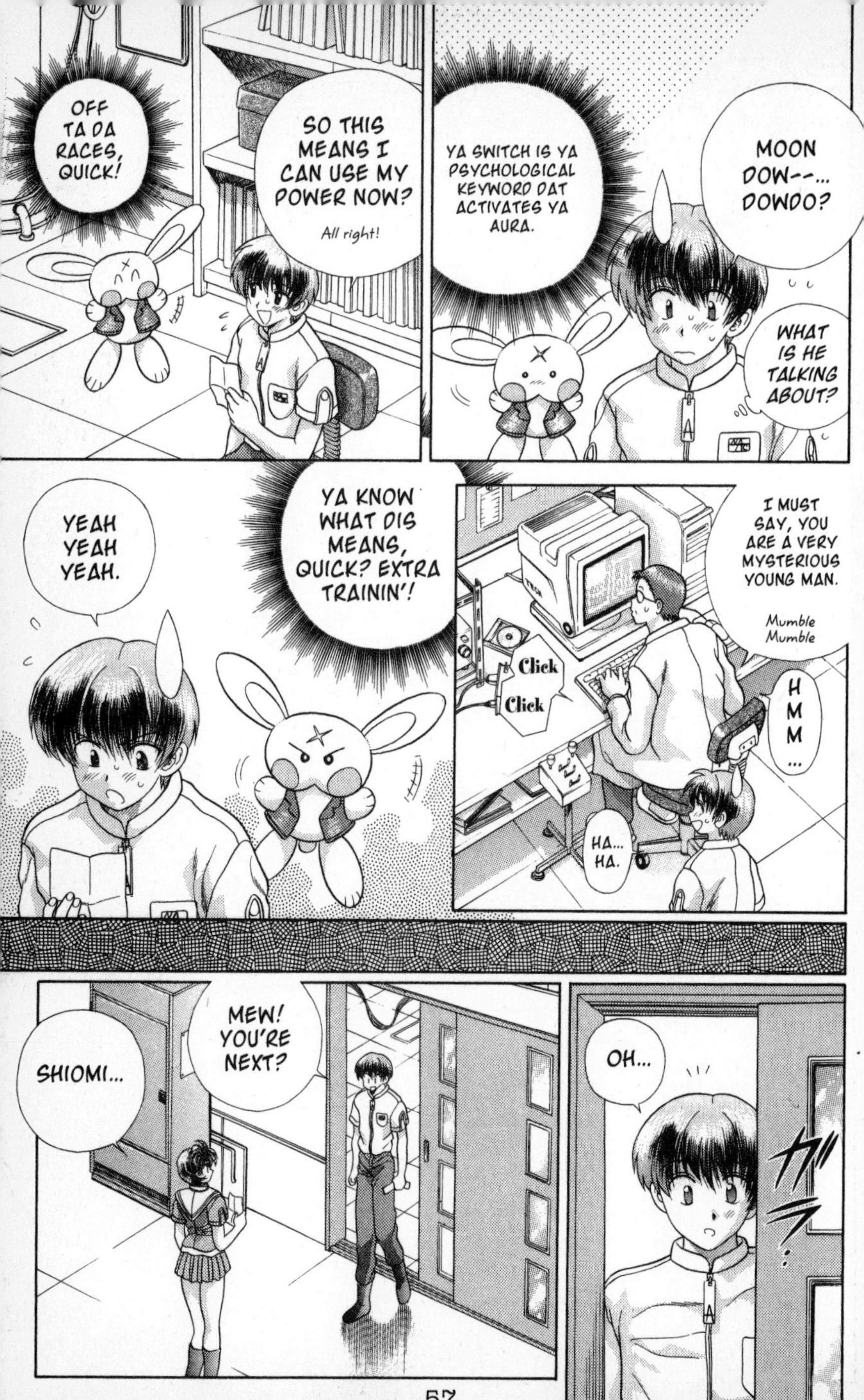
MOON DOW--... DOWDO?
YA SWITCH IS YA PSYCHOLOGICAL KEYWORD DAT ACTIVATES YA AURA.
WHAT IS HE TALKING ABOUT?
SO THIS MEANS I CAN USE MY POWER NOW?
All right!
OFF TA DA RACES, QUICK!
I MUST SAY, YOU ARE A VERY MYSTERIOUS YOUNG MAN.
Mumble Mumble
HMM...
Click
Click
HA... HA.
YA KNOW WHAT DIS MEANS, QUICK? EXTRA TRAININ'!
YEAH YEAH YEAH.
OH...
MEW! YOU'RE NEXT?
SHIOMI...

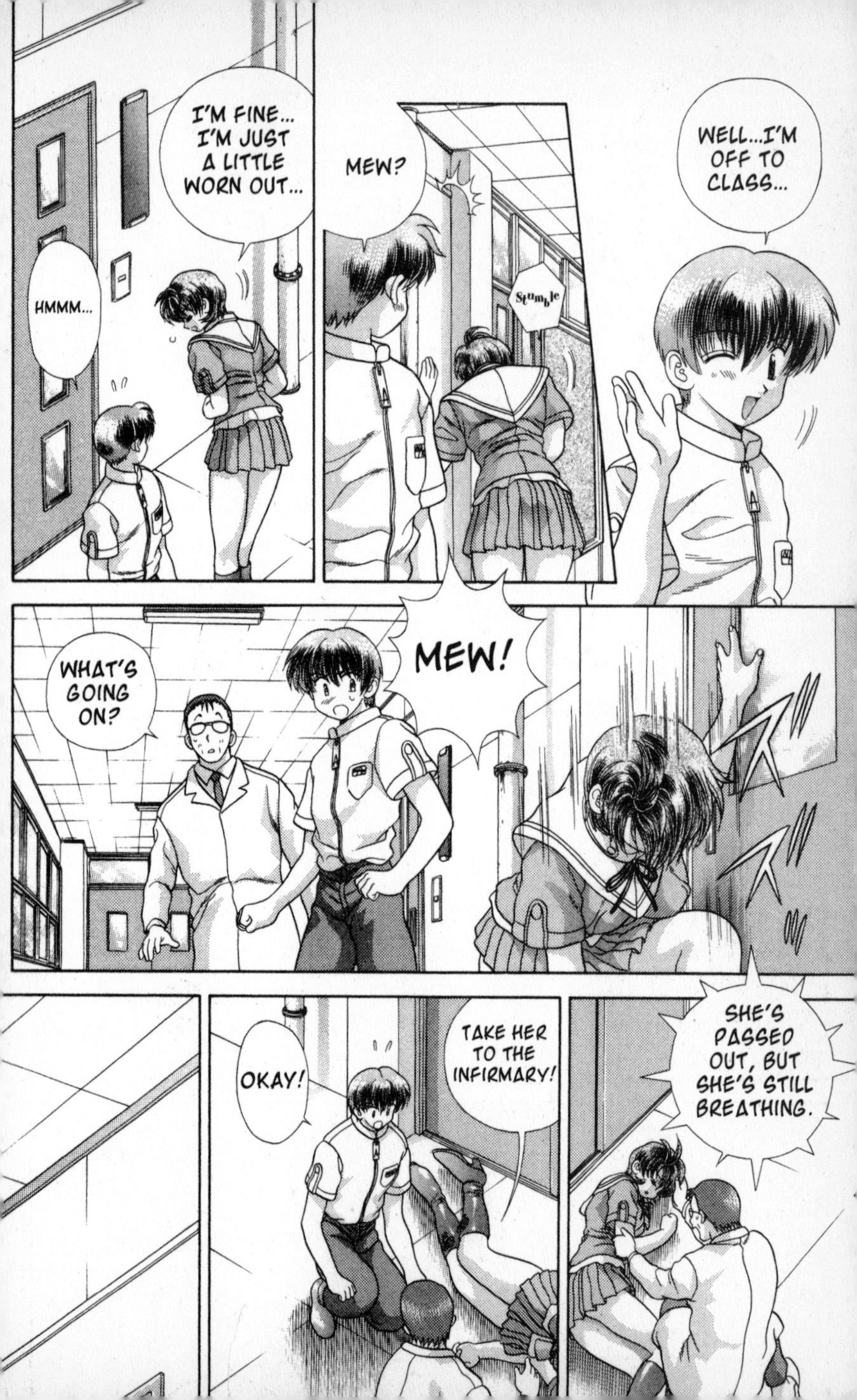
WELL...I'M OFF TO CLASS...
MEW?
Stumble
I'M FINE... I'M JUST A LITTLE WORN OUT...
HMMM...
MEW!
WHAT'S GOING ON?
SHE'S PASSED OUT, BUT SHE'S STILL BREATHING.
TAKE HER TO THE INFIRMARY!
OKAY!

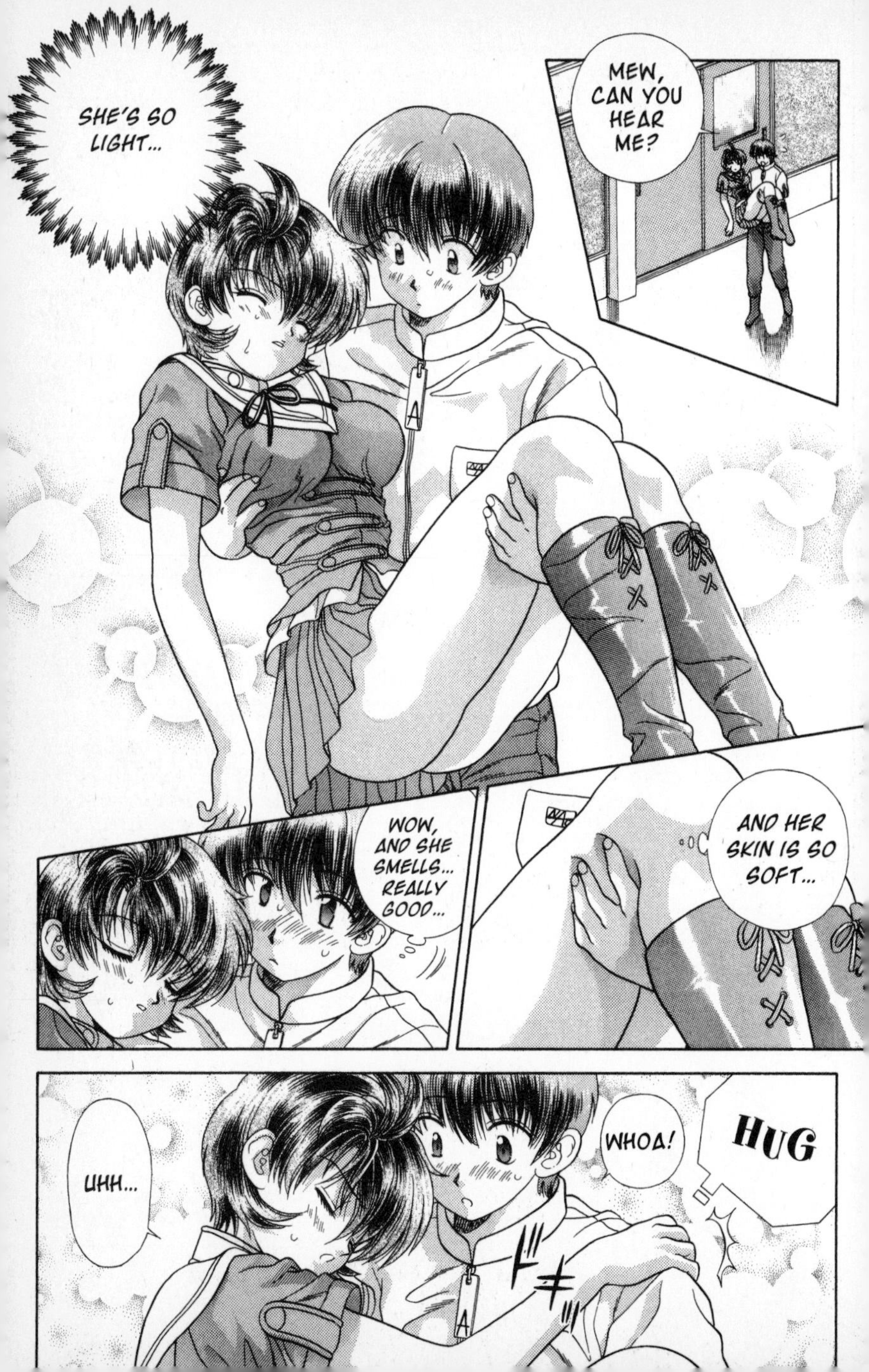
MEW, CAN YOU HEAR ME?
SHE'S SO LIGHT...
AND HER SKIN IS SO SOFT...
WOW, AND SHE SMELLS... REALLY GOOD...
HUG
WHOA!
UHH...

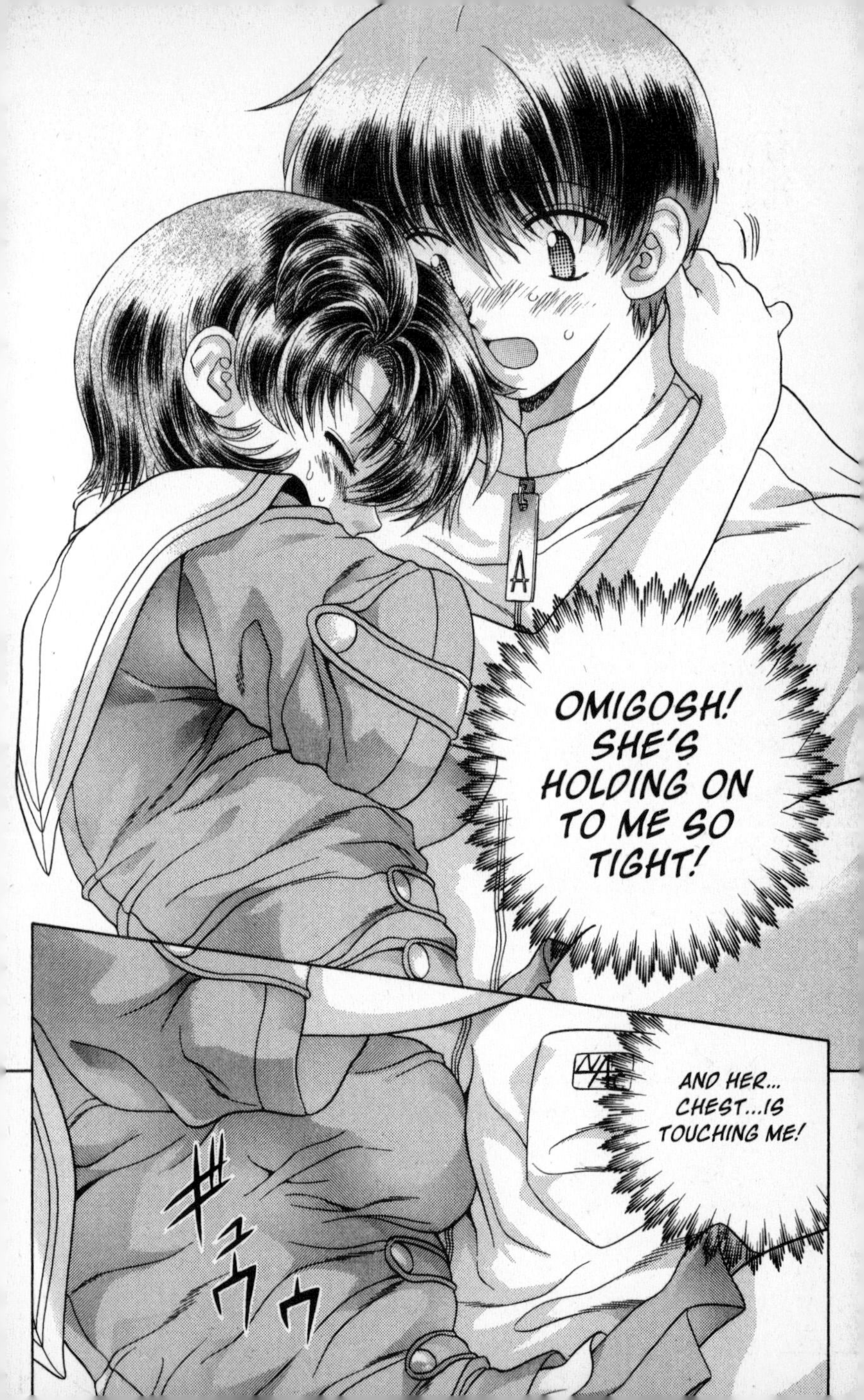
OMIGOSH! SHE'S HOLDING ON TO ME SO TIGHT!
AND HER... CHEST...IS TOUCHING ME!
ギュウウ

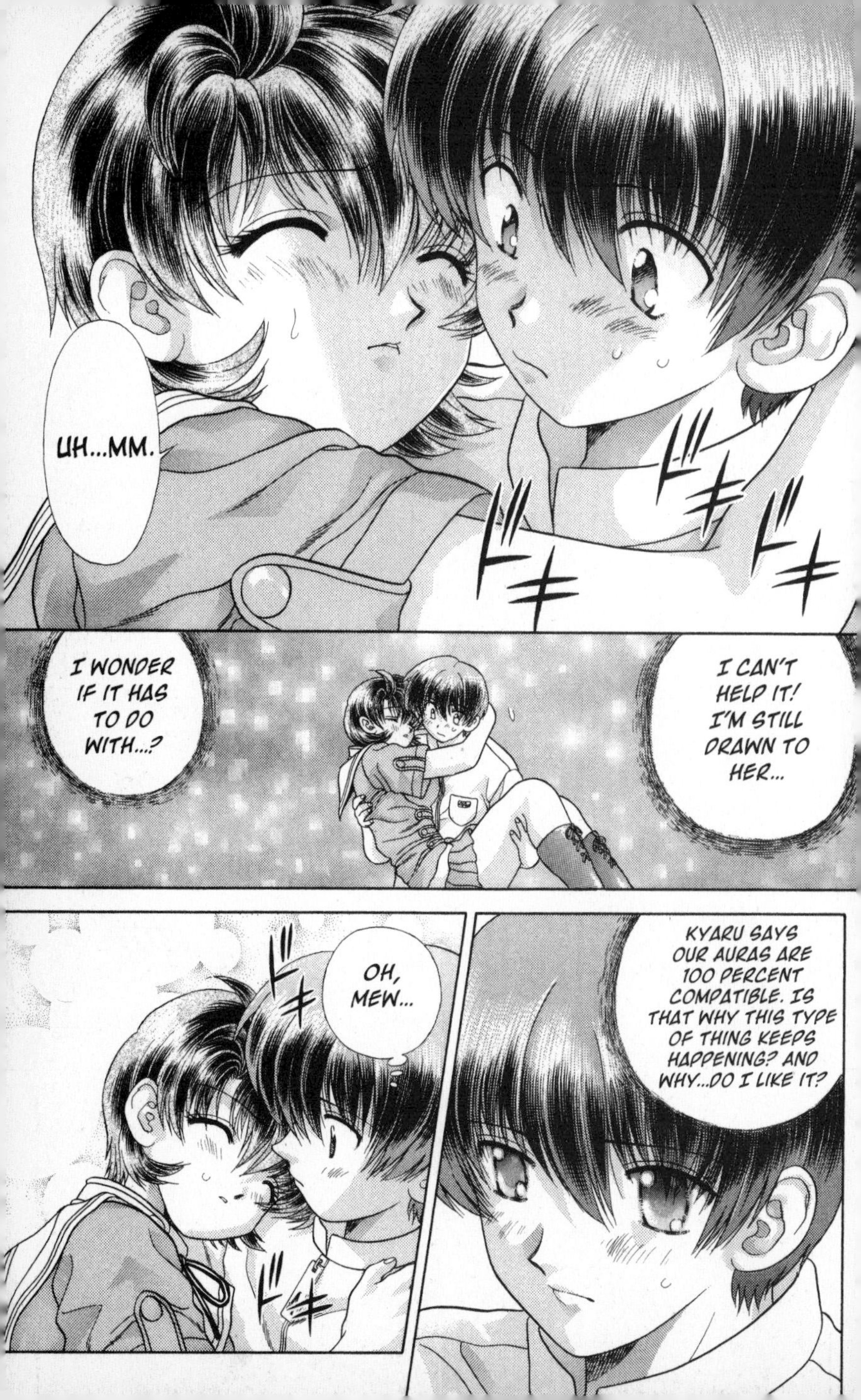
ドキ ドキ
ドキ
UH...MM.
I CAN'T HELP IT! I'M STILL DRAWN TO HER...
I WONDER IF IT HAS TO DO WITH...?
KYARU SAYS OUR AURAS ARE 100 PERCENT COMPATIBLE. IS THAT WHY THIS TYPE OF THING KEEPS HAPPENING? AND WHY...DO I LIKE IT?
ドキ
OH, MEW...
ドキ

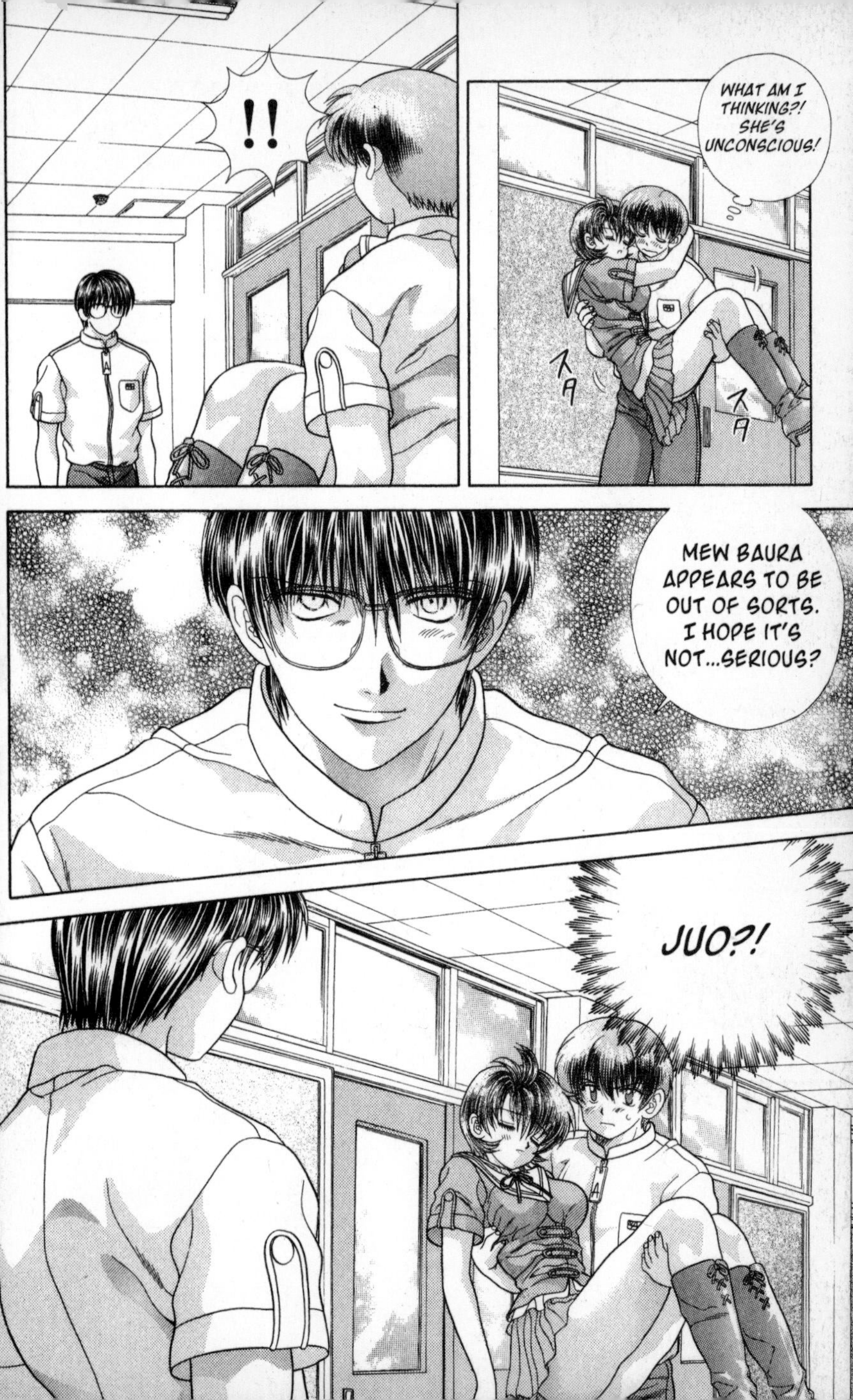
WHAT AM I THINKING?! SHE'S UNCONSCIOUS!
スタ
スタ
!!
MEW BAURA APPEARS TO BE OUT OF SORTS. I HOPE IT'S NOT...SERIOUS?
JUO?!

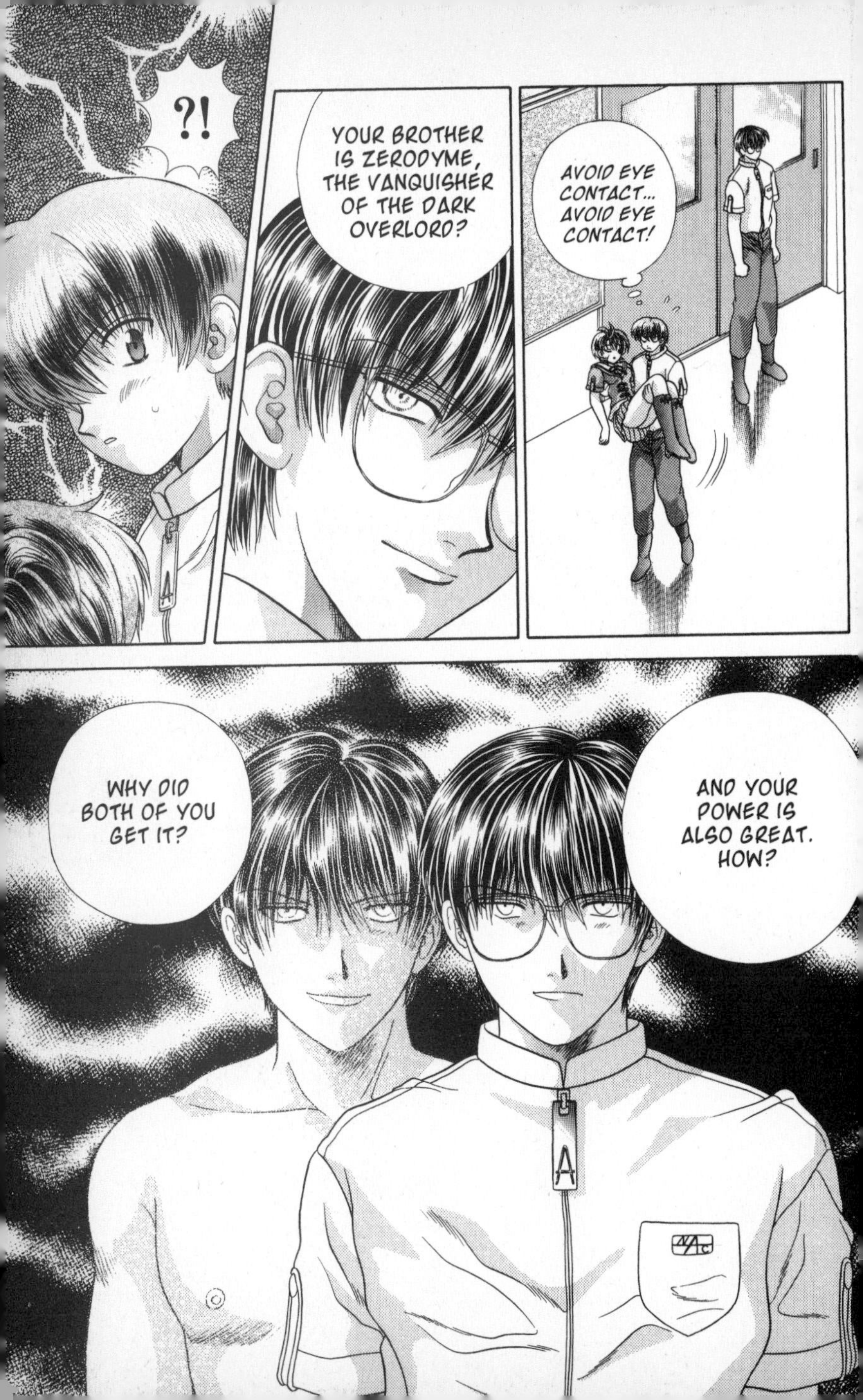
AVOID EYE CONTACT... AVOID EYE CONTACT!
YOUR BROTHER IS ZERODYME, THE VANQUISHER OF THE DARK OVERLORD?
?!
AND YOUR POWER IS ALSO GREAT. HOW?
WHY DID BOTH OF YOU GET IT?

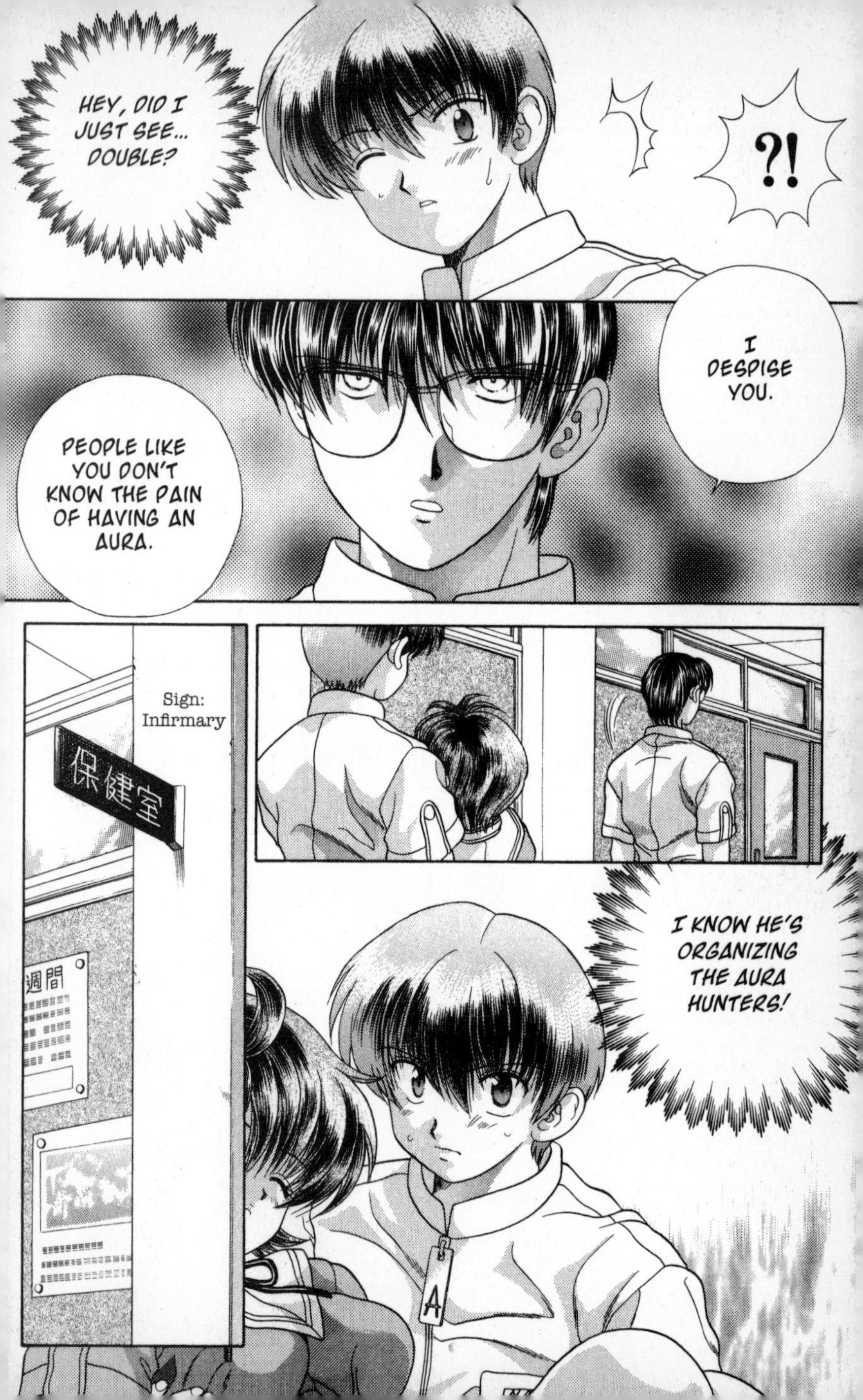
?!
HEY, DID I JUST SEE... DOUBLE?
I DESPISE YOU.
PEOPLE LIKE YOU DON'T KNOW THE PAIN OF HAVING AN AURA.
I KNOW HE'S ORGANIZING THE AURA HUNTERS!
保健室
Sign: Infirmary
週間

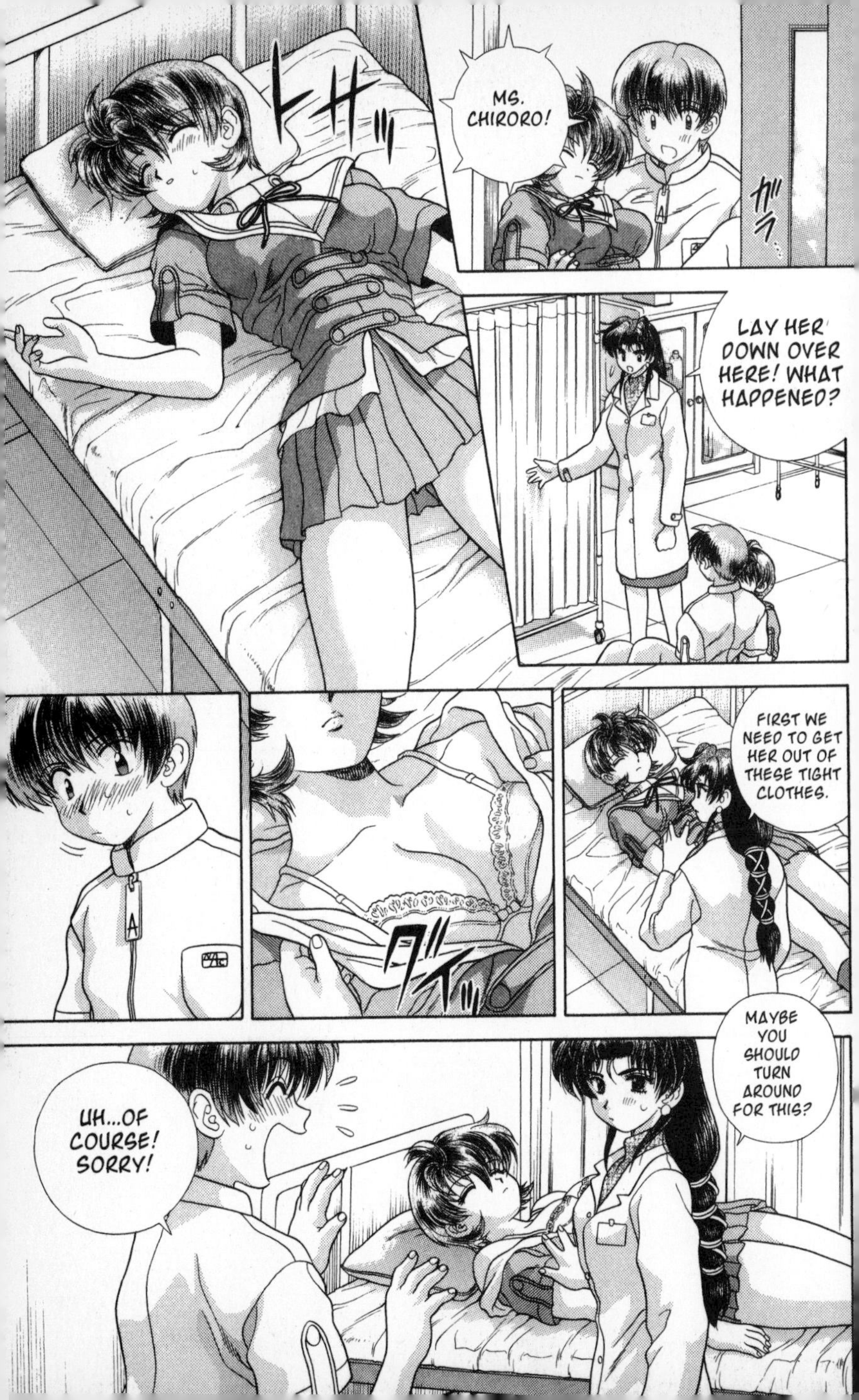
MS. CHIRORO!
ガラ…
LAY HER DOWN OVER HERE! WHAT HAPPENED?
トサッ
FIRST WE NEED TO GET HER OUT OF THESE TIGHT CLOTHES.
グイッ
MAYBE YOU SHOULD TURN AROUND FOR THIS?
UH...OF COURSE! SORRY!

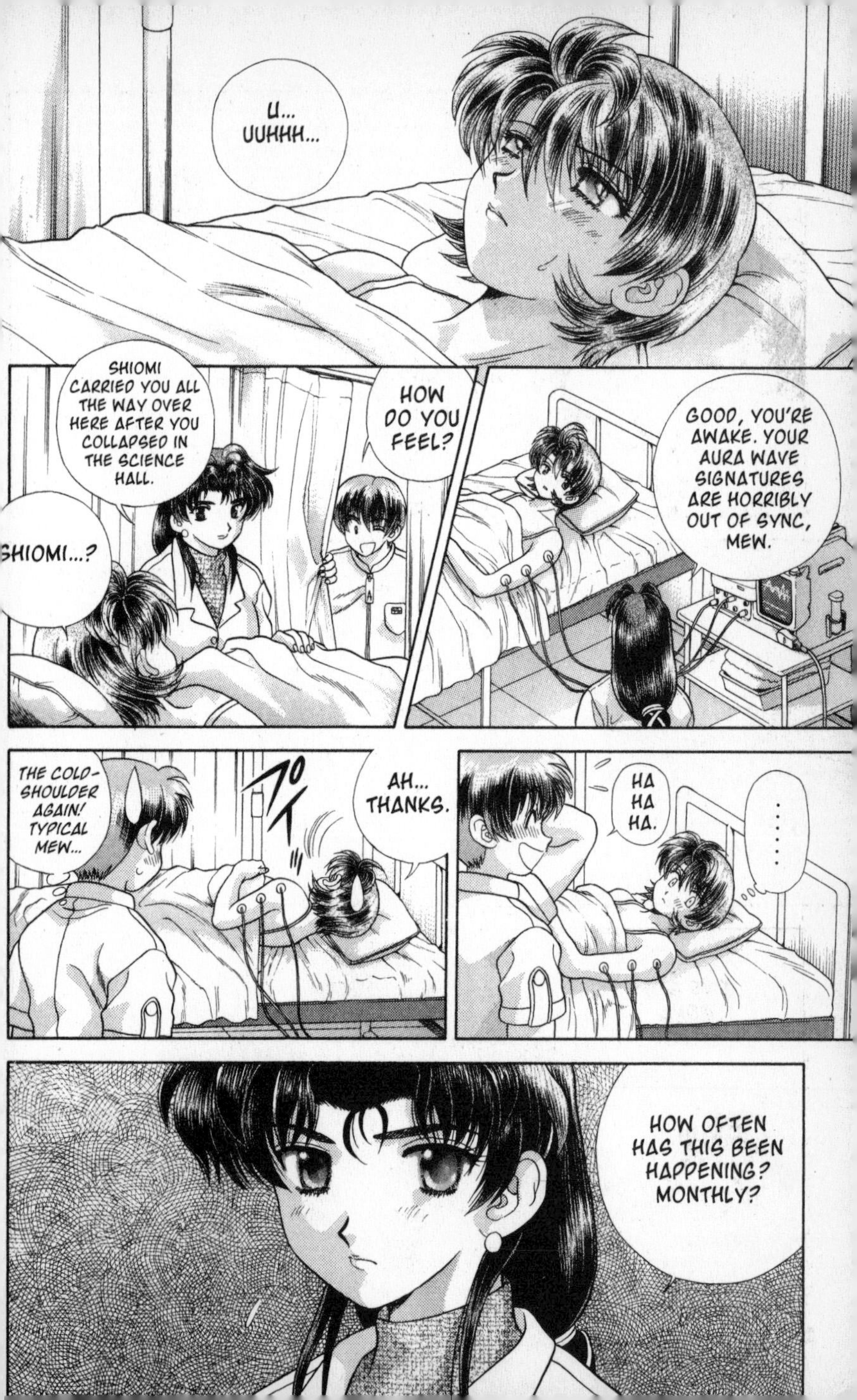
U... UUHHH...
GOOD, YOU'RE AWAKE. YOUR AURA WAVE SIGNATURES ARE HORRIBLY OUT OF SYNC, MEW.
HOW DO YOU FEEL?
SHIOMI CARRIED YOU ALL THE WAY OVER HERE AFTER YOU COLLAPSED IN THE SCIENCE HALL.
SHIOMI...?
......
HA HA HA.
AH... THANKS.
プイ
THE COLD-SHOULDER AGAIN! TYPICAL MEW...
HOW OFTEN HAS THIS BEEN HAPPENING? MONTHLY?

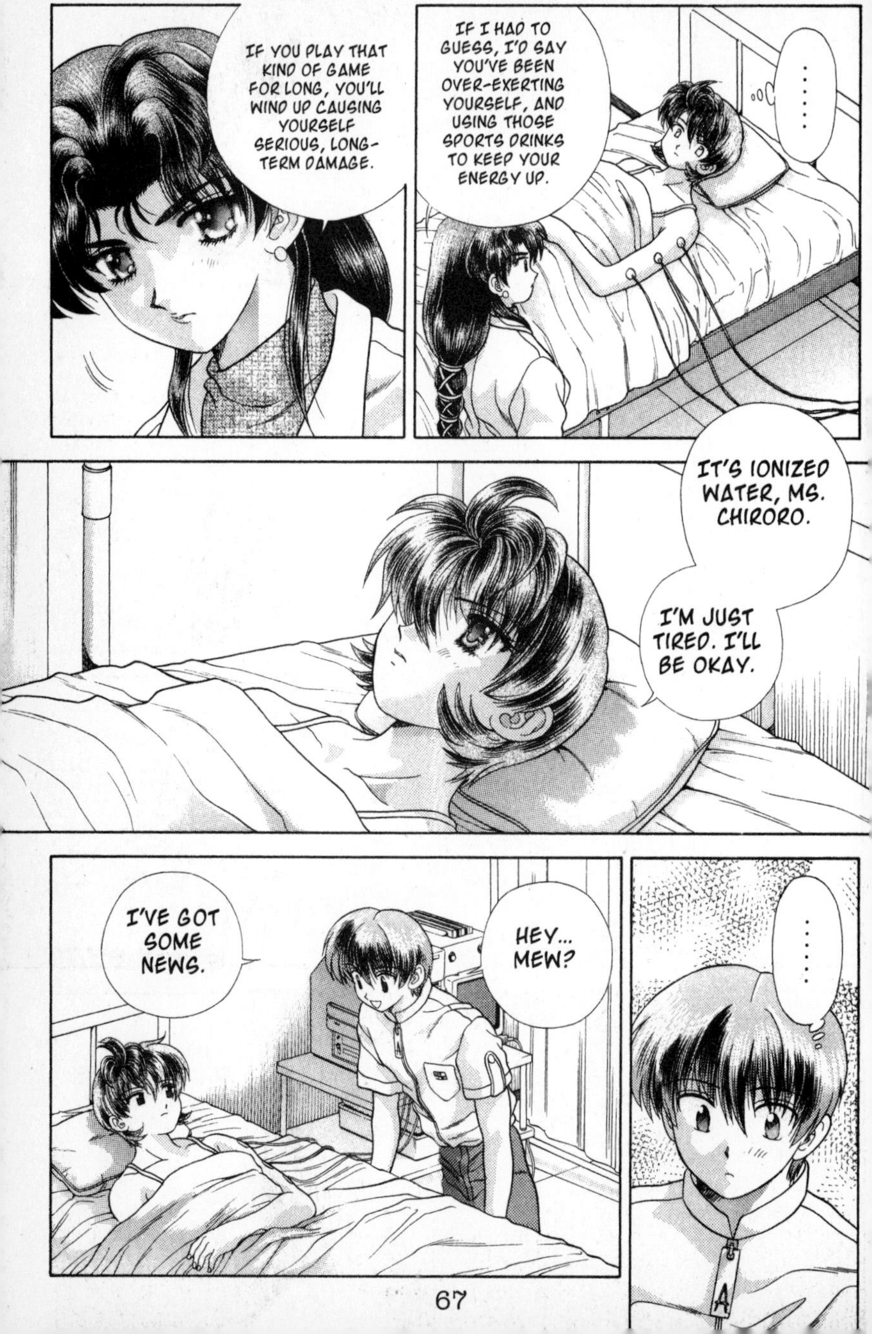

......
IF I HAD TO GUESS, I'D SAY YOU'VE BEEN OVER-EXERTING YOURSELF, AND USING THOSE SPORTS DRINKS TO KEEP YOUR ENERGY UP.
IF YOU PLAY THAT KIND OF GAME FOR LONG, YOU'LL WIND UP CAUSING YOURSELF SERIOUS, LONG-TERM DAMAGE.
IT'S IONIZED WATER, MS. CHIRORO.
I'M JUST TIRED. I'LL BE OKAY.
......
HEY... MEW?
I'VE GOT SOME NEWS.

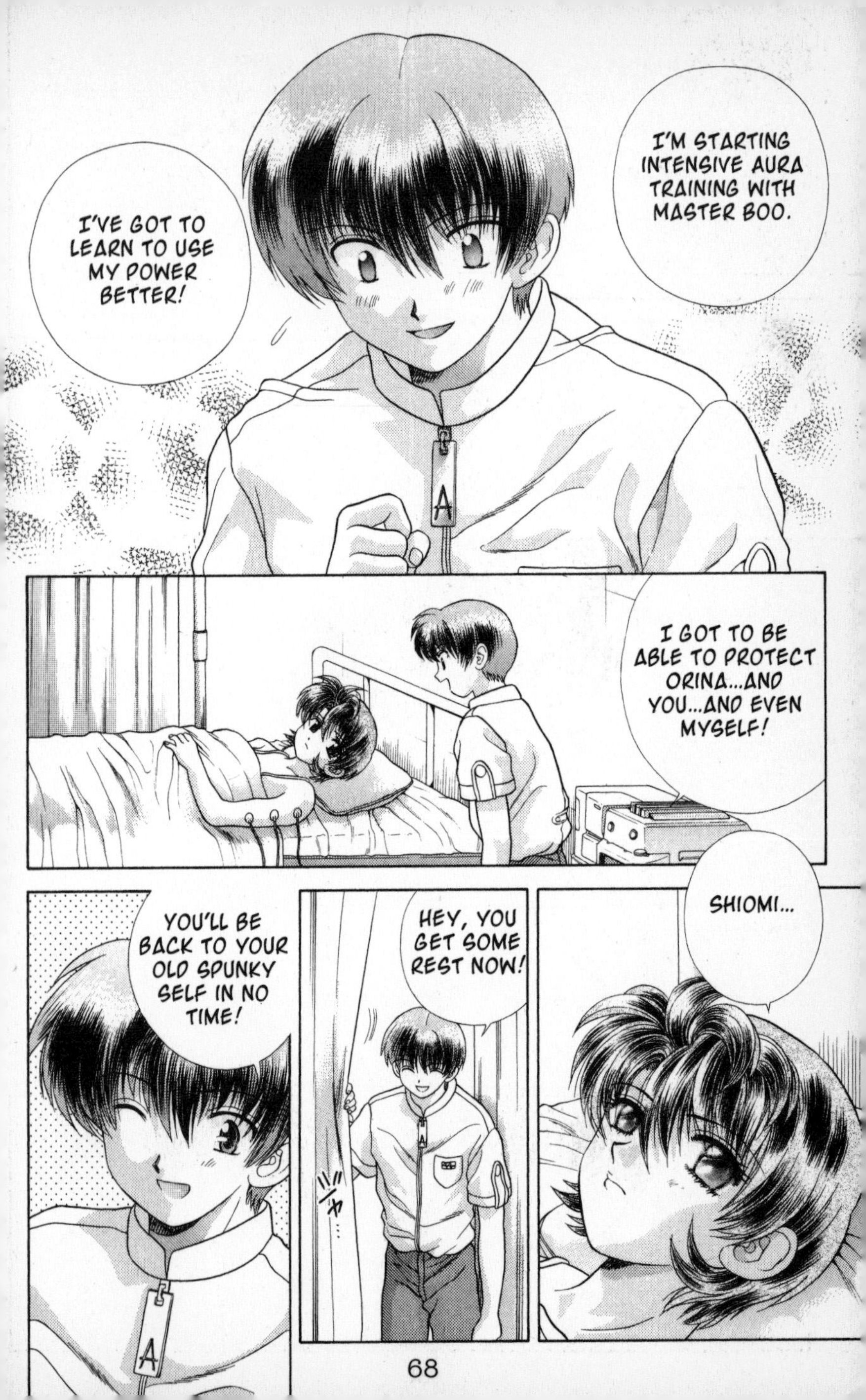
I'M STARTING INTENSIVE AURA TRAINING WITH MASTER BOO.
I'VE GOT TO LEARN TO USE MY POWER BETTER!
I GOT TO BE ABLE TO PROTECT ORINA...AND YOU...AND EVEN MYSELF!
SHIOMI...
HEY, YOU GET SOME REST NOW!
YOU'LL BE BACK TO YOUR OLD SPUNKY SELF IN NO TIME!

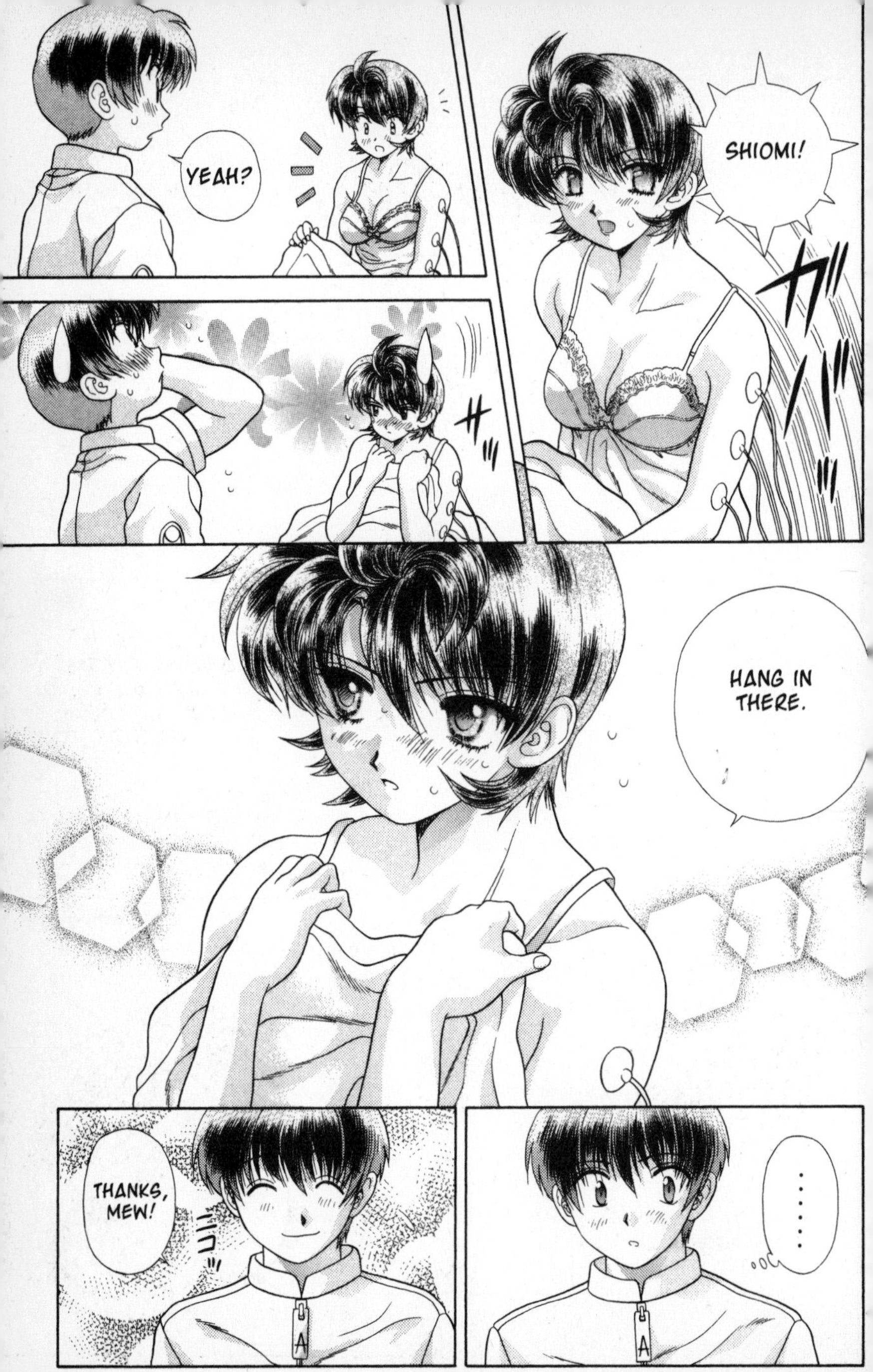
SHIOMI!
YEAH?
HANG IN THERE.
......
THANKS, MEW!

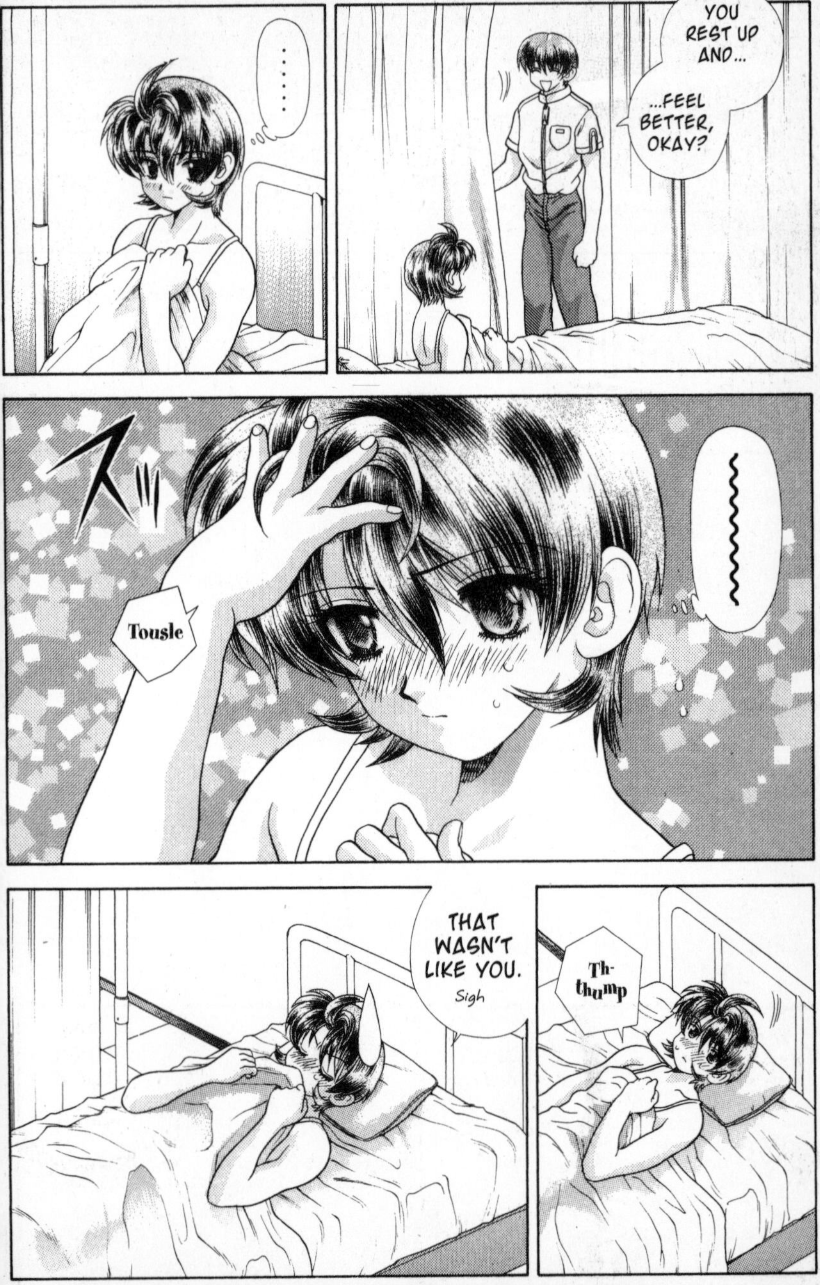
YOU REST UP AND...
...FEEL BETTER, OKAY?
......
ス
Tousle
Th-thump
THAT WASN'T LIKE YOU.
Sigh

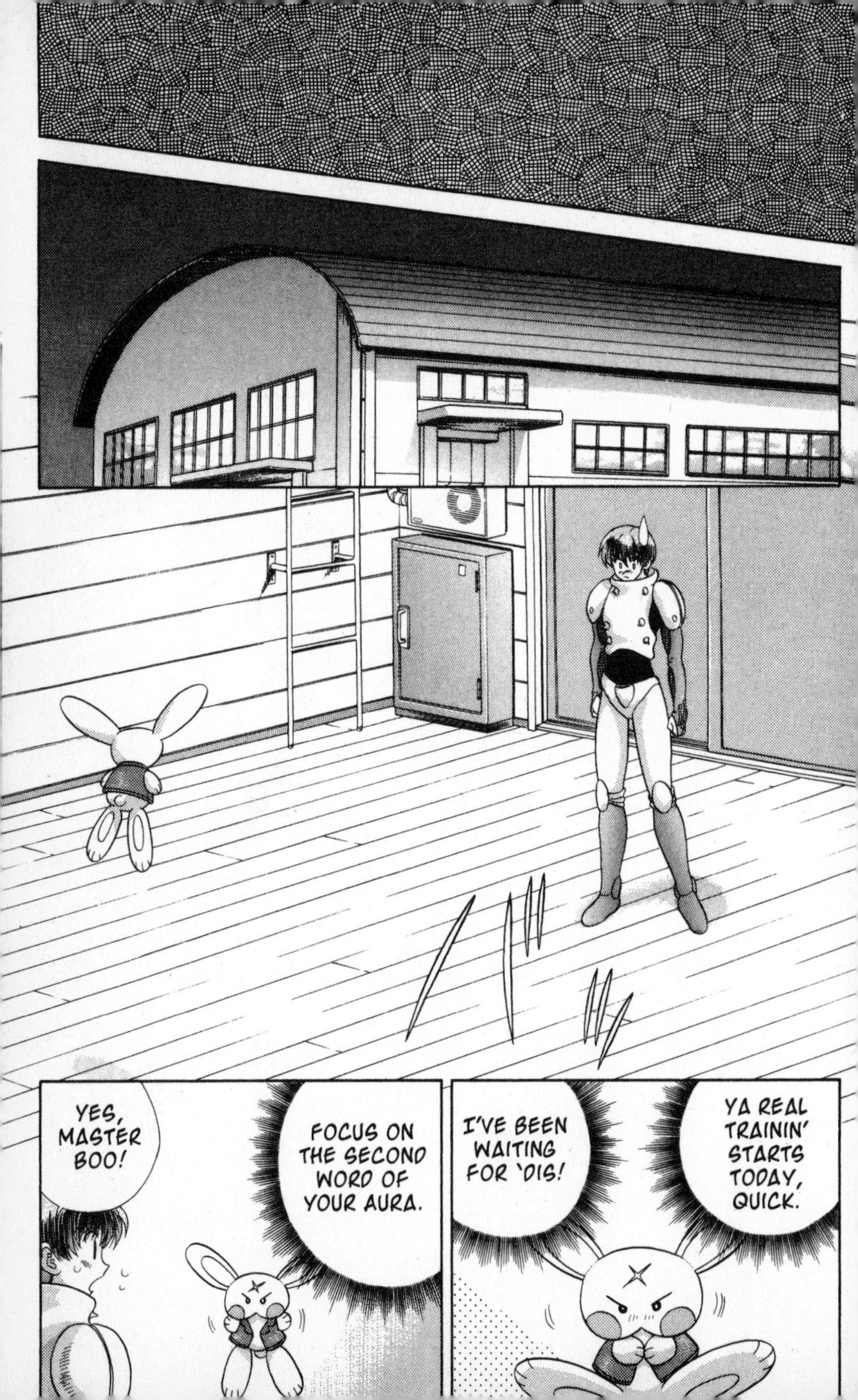
YA REAL TRAININ' STARTS TODAY, QUICK.
I'VE BEEN WAITING FOR 'DIS!
FOCUS ON THE SECOND WORD OF YOUR AURA.
YES, MASTER BOO!

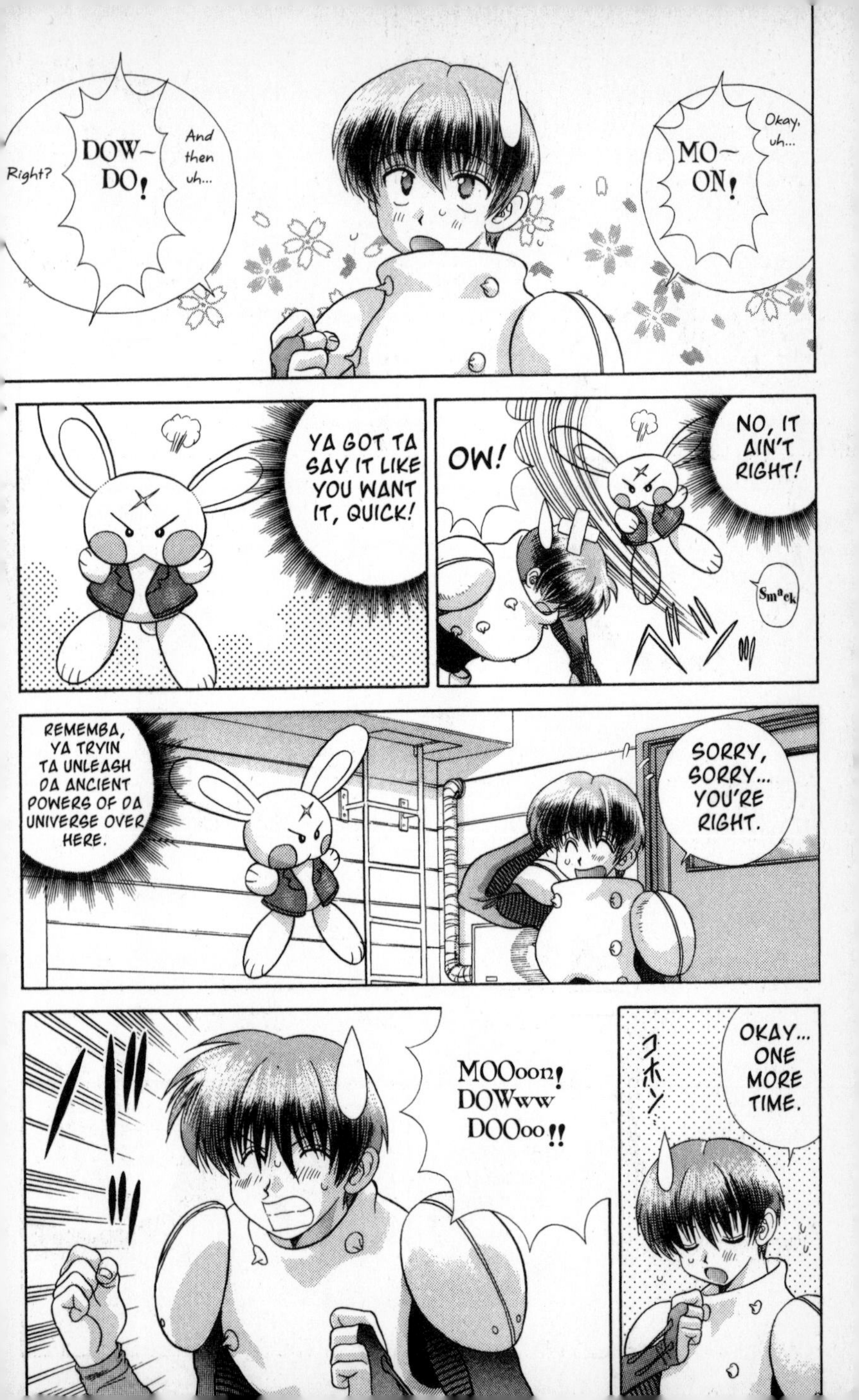
Okay, uh...
MO~ON!
And then uh...
DOW~DO!
Right?
NO, IT AIN'T RIGHT!
OW!
Smack
YA GOT TA SAY IT LIKE YOU WANT IT, QUICK!
SORRY, SORRY... YOU'RE RIGHT.
REMEMBA, YA TRYIN TA UNLEASH DA ANCIENT POWERS OF DA UNIVERSE OVER HERE.
OKAY... ONE MORE TIME.
コホン
MOOoon! DOWww DOOoo!!

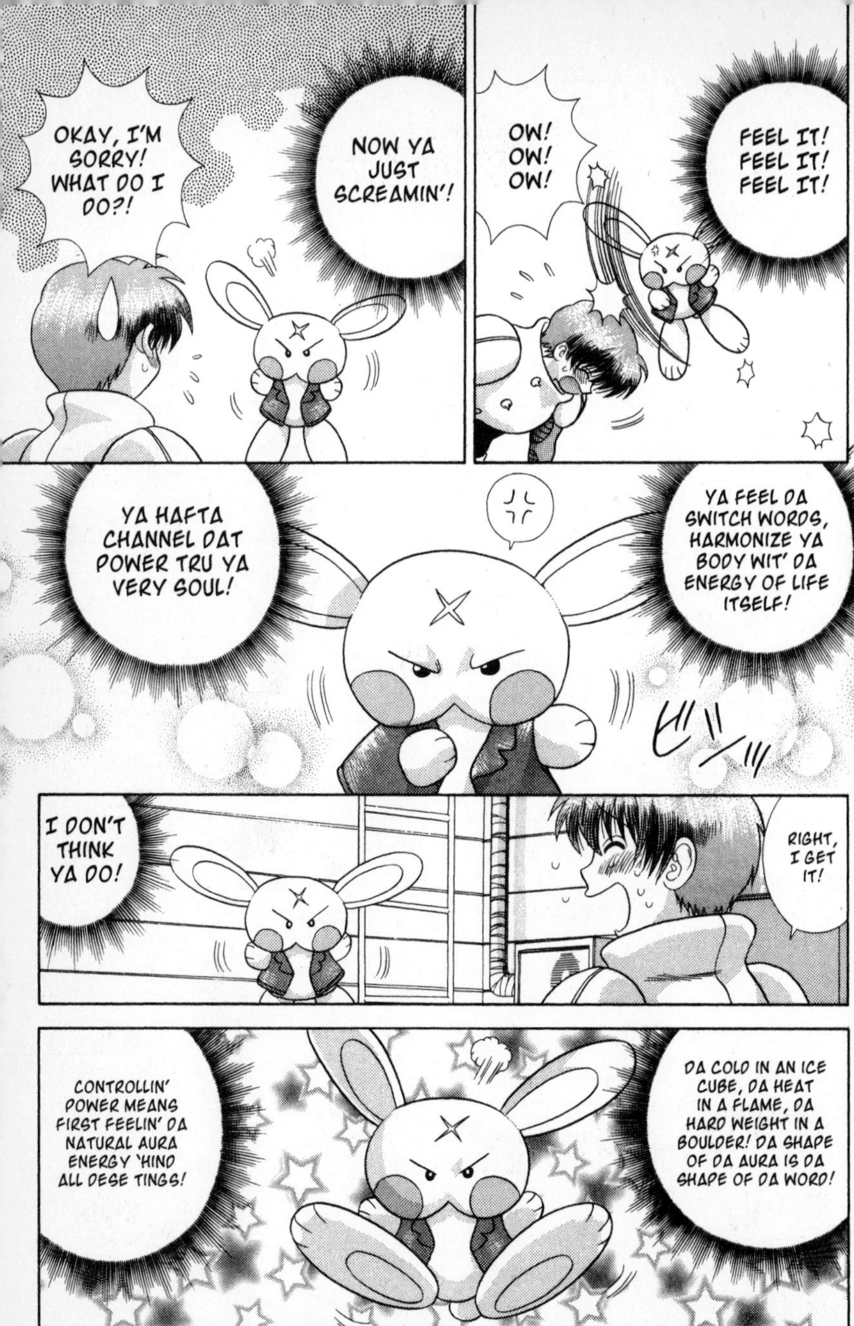
FEEL IT! FEEL IT! FEEL IT!
OW! OW! OW!
NOW YA JUST SCREAMIN'!
OKAY, I'M SORRY! WHAT DO I DO?!
YA FEEL DA SWITCH WORDS, HARMONIZE YA BODY WIT' DA ENERGY OF LIFE ITSELF!
YA HAFTA CHANNEL DAT POWER TRU YA VERY SOUL!
RIGHT, I GET IT!
I DON'T THINK YA DO!
DA COLD IN AN ICE CUBE, DA HEAT IN A FLAME, DA HARD WEIGHT IN A BOULDER! DA SHAPE OF DA AURA IS DA SHAPE OF DA WORD!
CONTROLLIN' POWER MEANS FIRST FEELIN' DA NATURAL AURA ENERGY 'HIND ALL DESE TINGS!

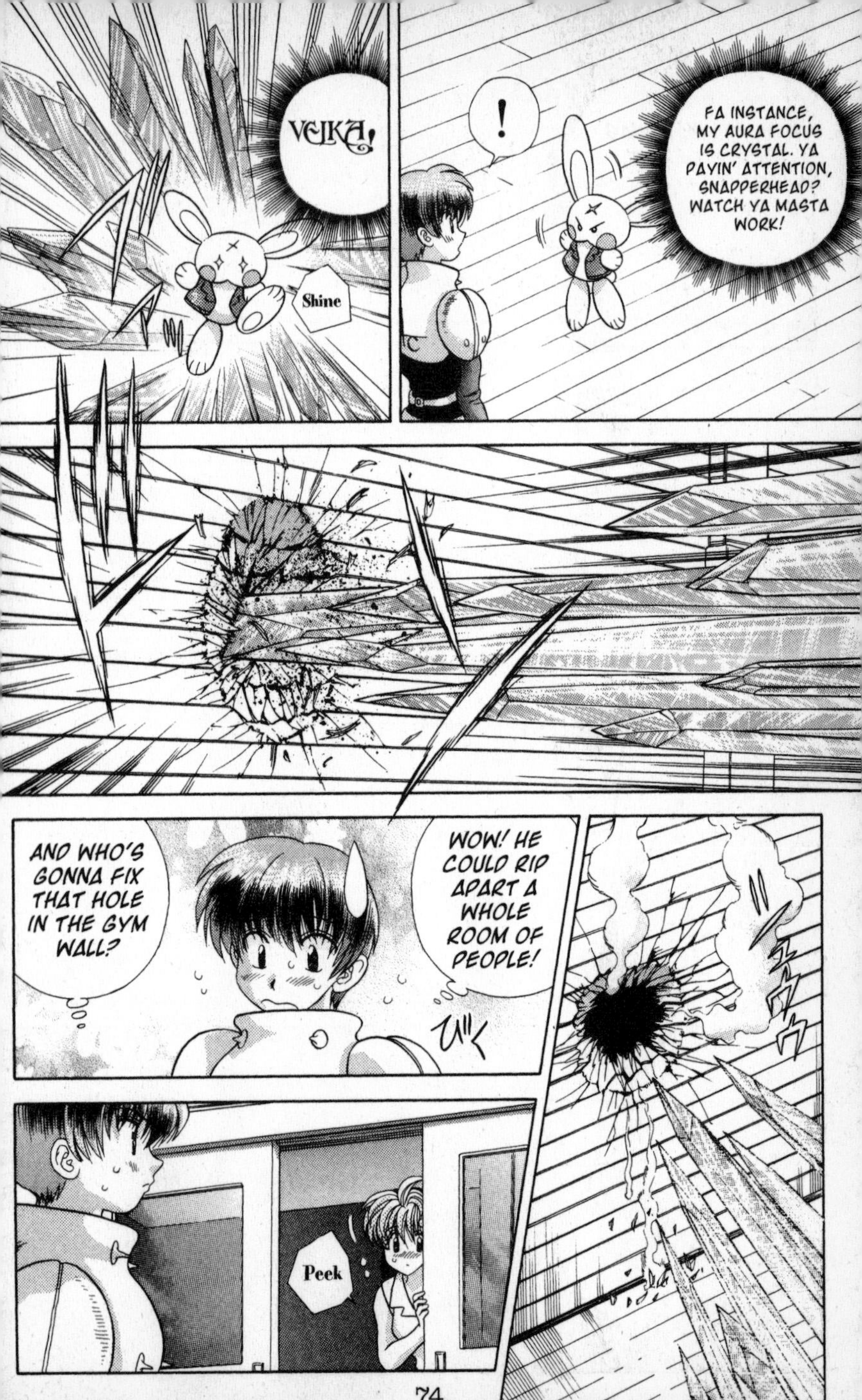
FA INSTANCE, MY AURA FOCUS IS CRYSTAL. YA PAYIN' ATTENTION, SNAPPERHEAD? WATCH YA MASTA WORK!
!
VELKA!
Shine
WOW! HE COULD RIP APART A WHOLE ROOM OF PEOPLE!
AND WHO'S GONNA FIX THAT HOLE IN THE GYM WALL?
Peek

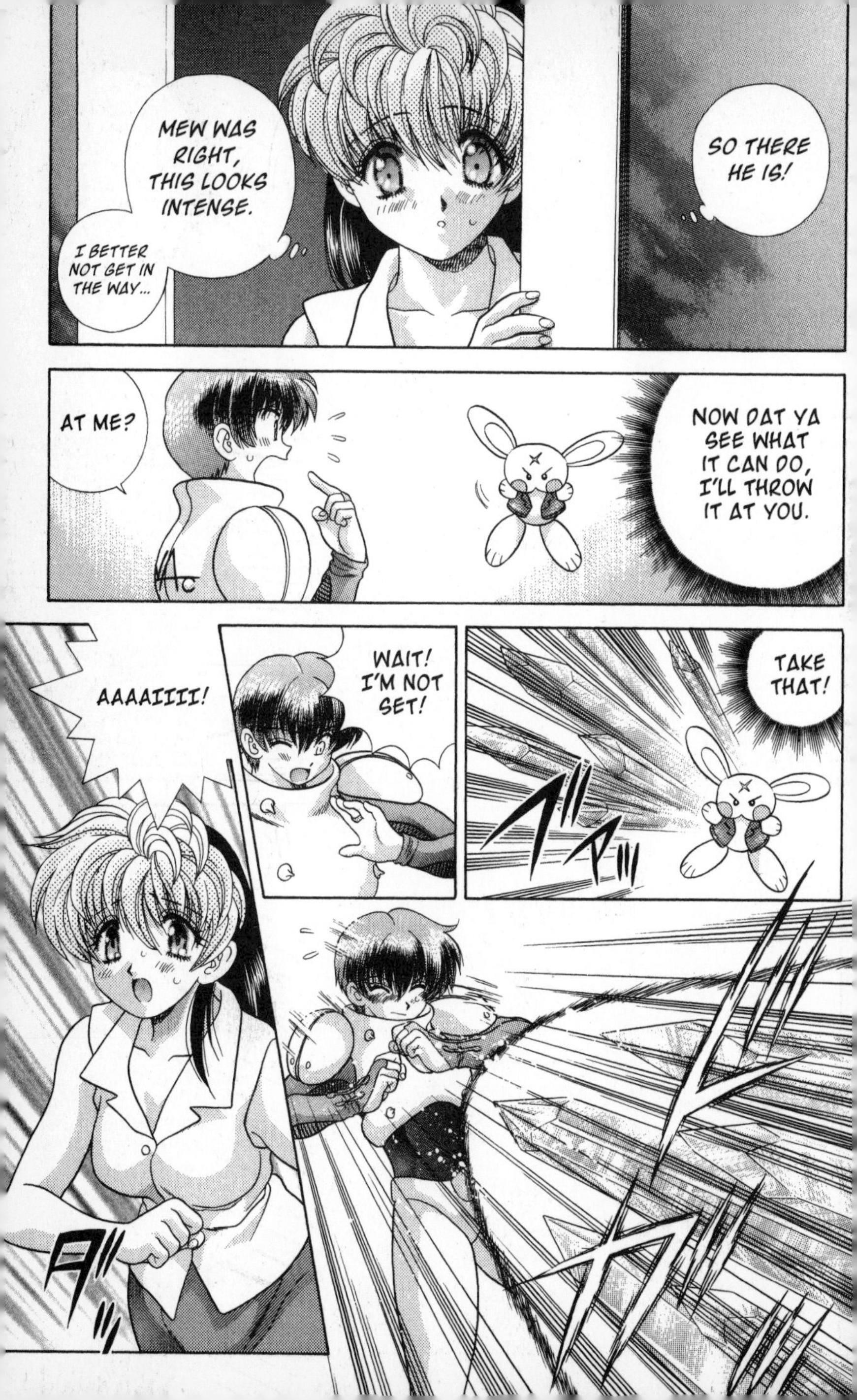
SO THERE HE IS!
MEW WAS RIGHT, THIS LOOKS INTENSE.
I BETTER NOT GET IN THE WAY...
NOW DAT YA SEE WHAT IT CAN DO, I'LL THROW IT AT YOU.
AT ME?
TAKE THAT!
WAIT! I'M NOT SET!
AAAAIIII!

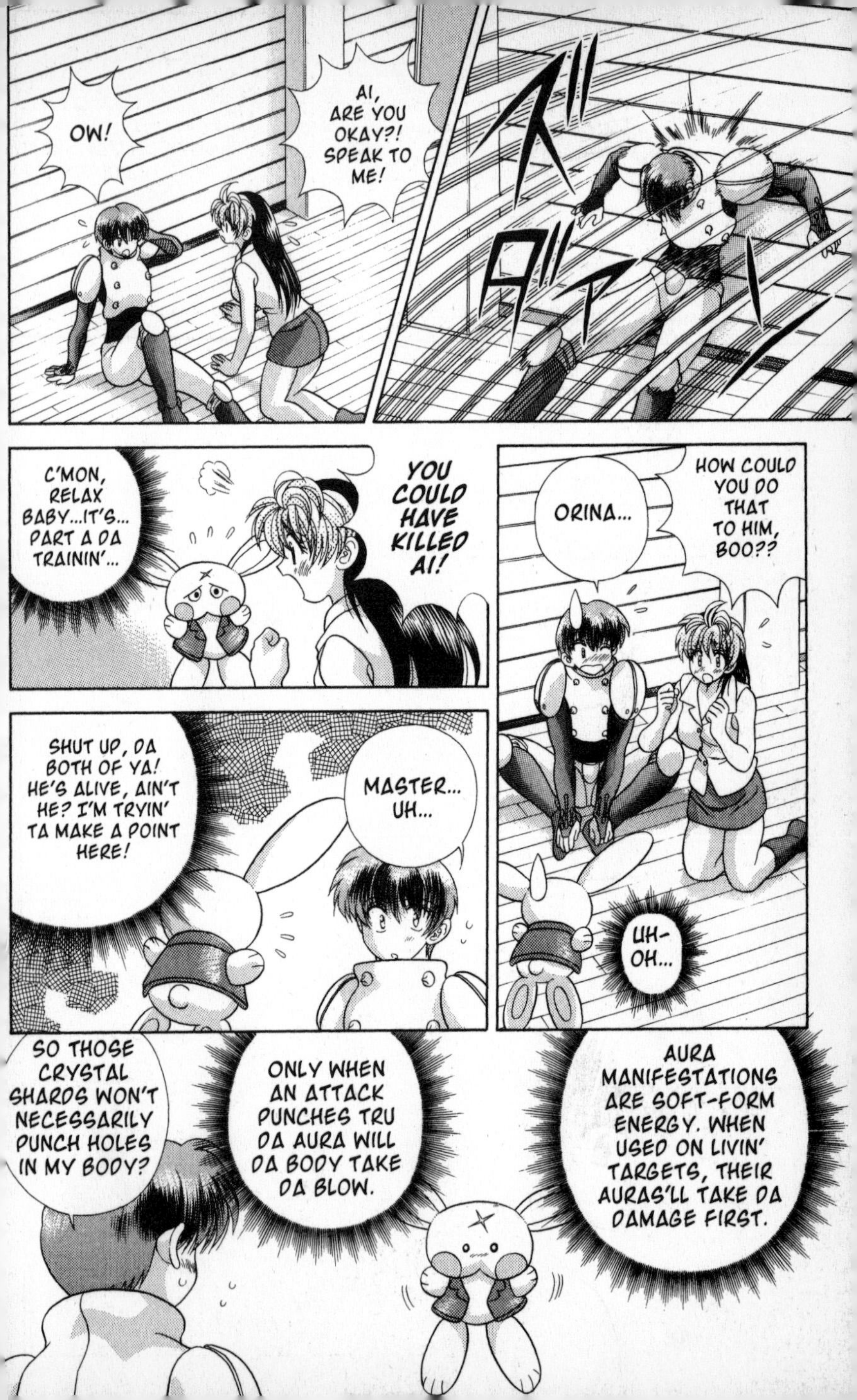
AI, ARE YOU OKAY?! SPEAK TO ME!
OW!
HOW COULD YOU DO THAT TO HIM, BOO??
ORINA...
YOU COULD HAVE KILLED AI!
C'MON, RELAX BABY...IT'S... PART A DA TRAININ'...
UH-OH...
MASTER... UH...
SHUT UP, DA BOTH OF YA! HE'S ALIVE, AIN'T HE? I'M TRYIN' TA MAKE A POINT HERE!
AURA MANIFESTATIONS ARE SOFT-FORM ENERGY. WHEN USED ON LIVIN' TARGETS, THEIR AURAS'LL TAKE DA DAMAGE FIRST.
ONLY WHEN AN ATTACK PUNCHES TRU DA AURA WILL DA BODY TAKE DA BLOW.
SO THOSE CRYSTAL SHARDS WON'T NECESSARILY PUNCH HOLES IN MY BODY?

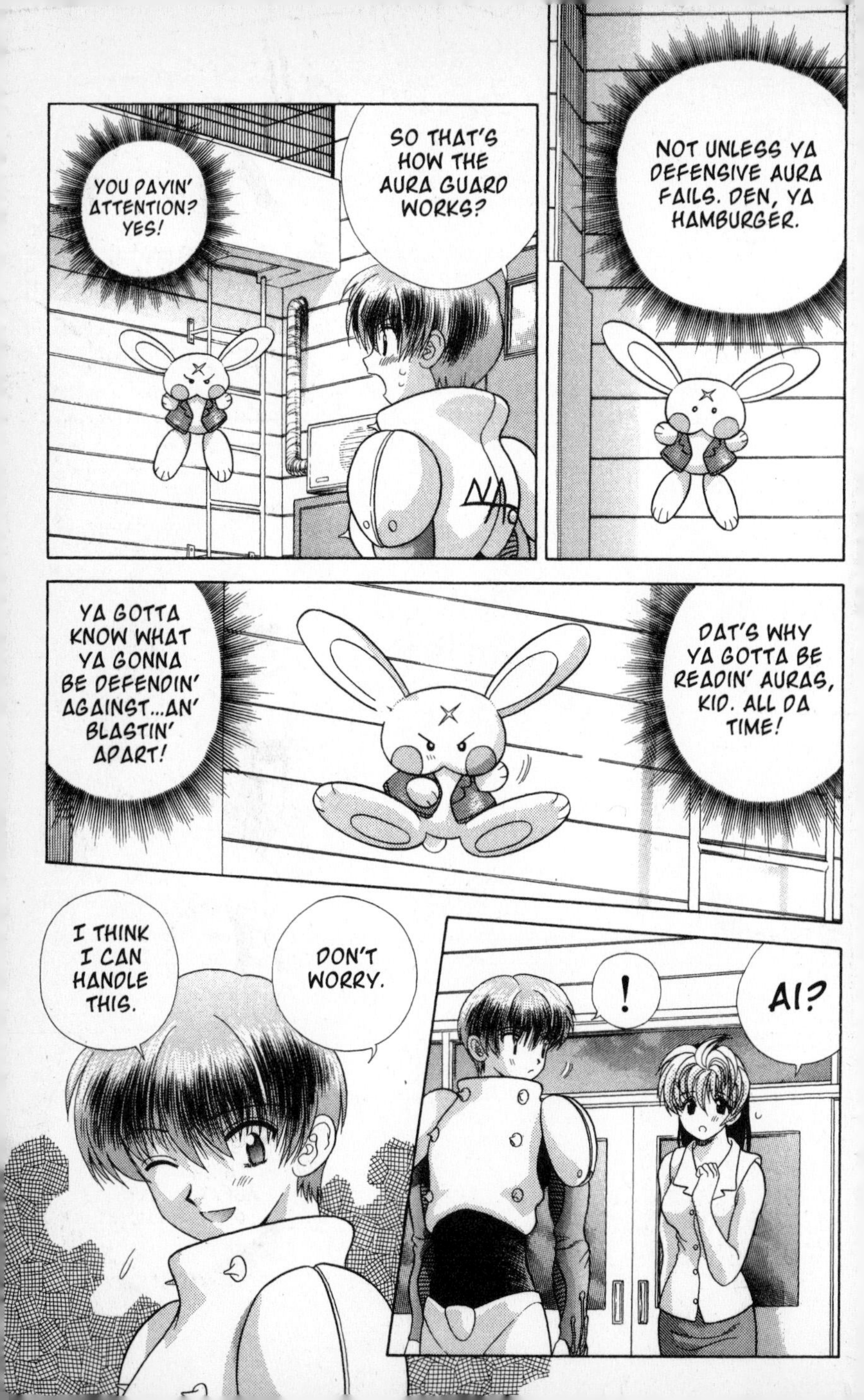
YOU PAYIN' ATTENTION? YES!
SO THAT'S HOW THE AURA GUARD WORKS?
NOT UNLESS YA DEFENSIVE AURA FAILS. DEN, YA HAMBURGER.
YA GOTTA KNOW WHAT YA GONNA BE DEFENDIN' AGAINST...AN' BLASTIN' APART!
DAT'S WHY YA GOTTA BE READIN' AURAS, KID. ALL DA TIME!
I THINK I CAN HANDLE THIS.
DON'T WORRY.
!
AI?

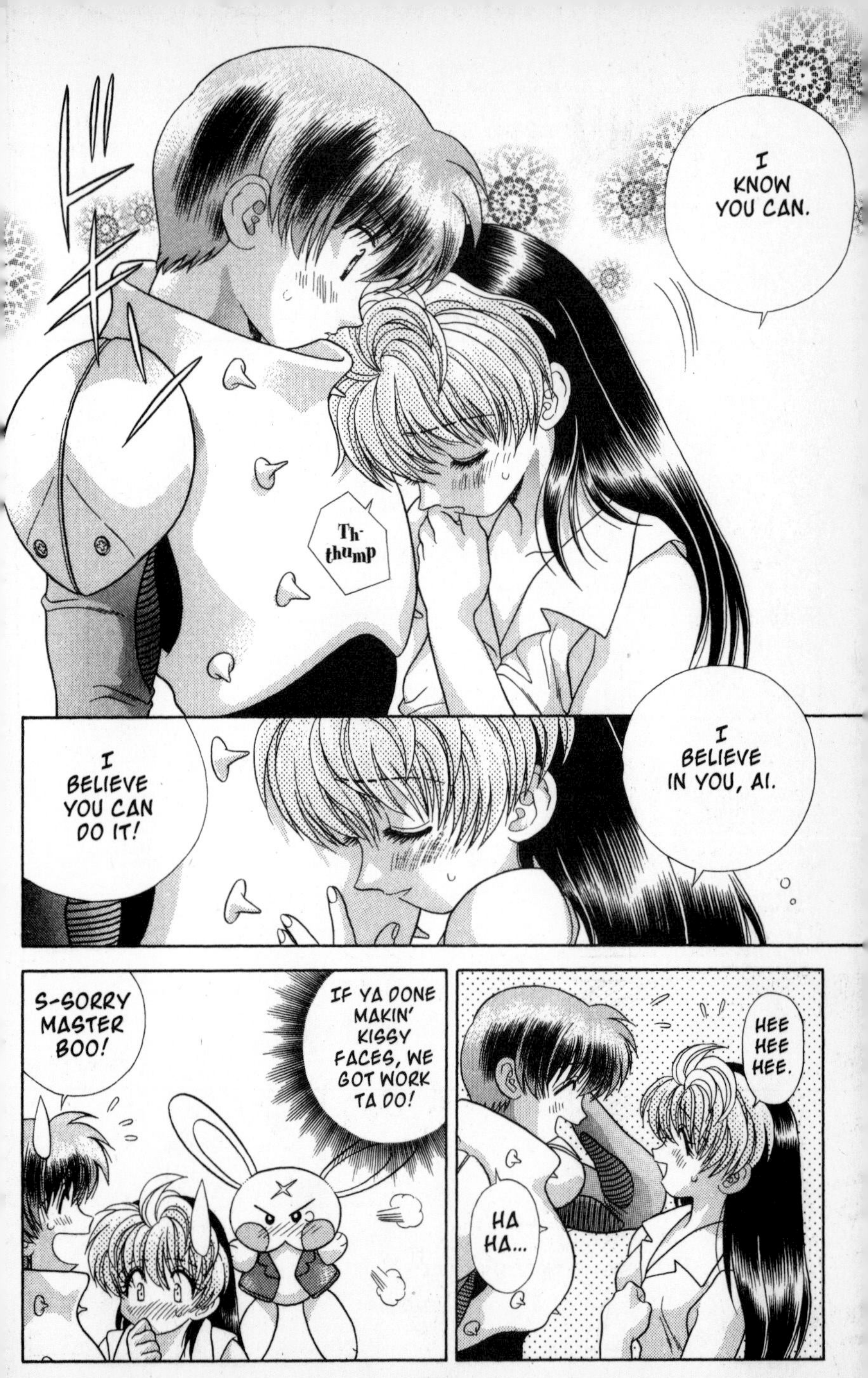
I KNOW YOU CAN.
ドキ
Th-thump
I BELIEVE IN YOU, AI.
I BELIEVE YOU CAN DO IT!
HEE HEE HEE.
HA HA...
IF YA DONE MAKIN' KISSY FACES, WE GOT WORK TA DO!
S-SORRY MASTER BOO!

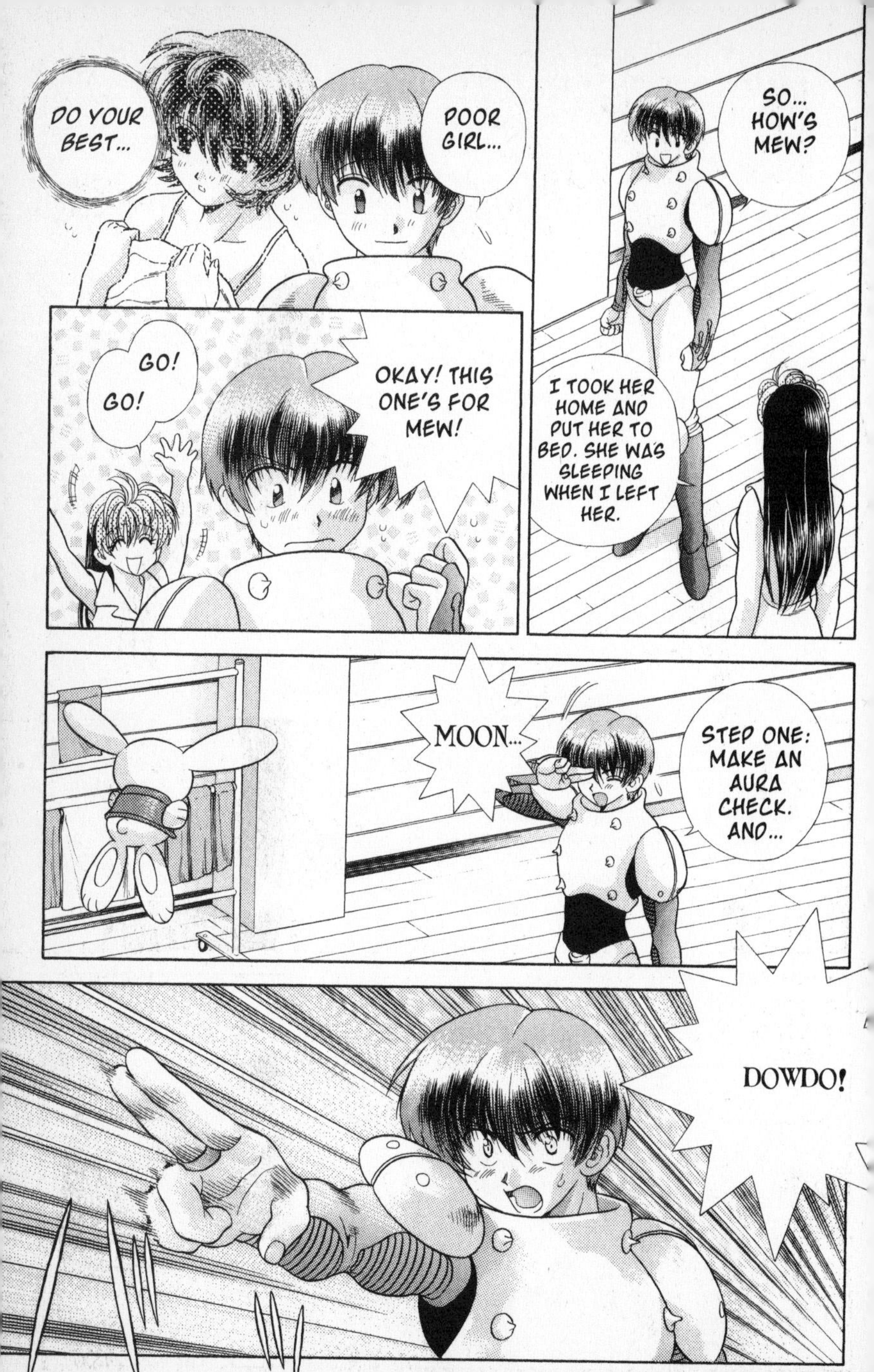
SO... HOW'S MEW?
I TOOK HER HOME AND PUT HER TO BED. SHE WAS SLEEPING WHEN I LEFT HER.
POOR GIRL...
DO YOUR BEST...
OKAY! THIS ONE'S FOR MEW!
GO! GO!
STEP ONE: MAKE AN AURA CHECK. AND...
MOON...
DOWDO!

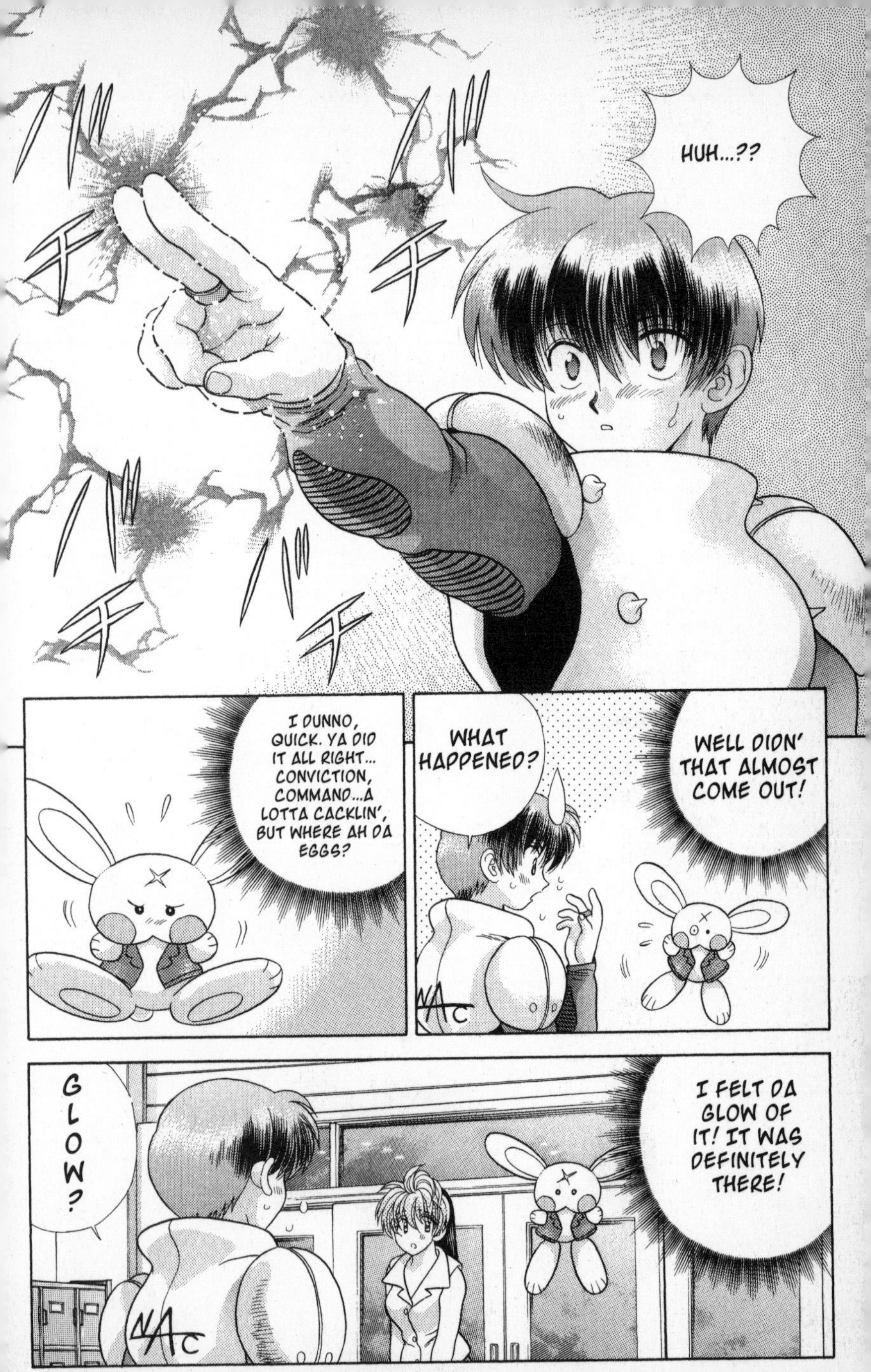
HUH...??
WELL DIDN' THAT ALMOST COME OUT!
WHAT HAPPENED?
I DUNNO, QUICK. YA DID IT ALL RIGHT... CONVICTION, COMMAND...A LOTTA CACKLIN', BUT WHERE AH DA EGGS?
I FELT DA GLOW OF IT! IT WAS DEFINITELY THERE!
GLOW?

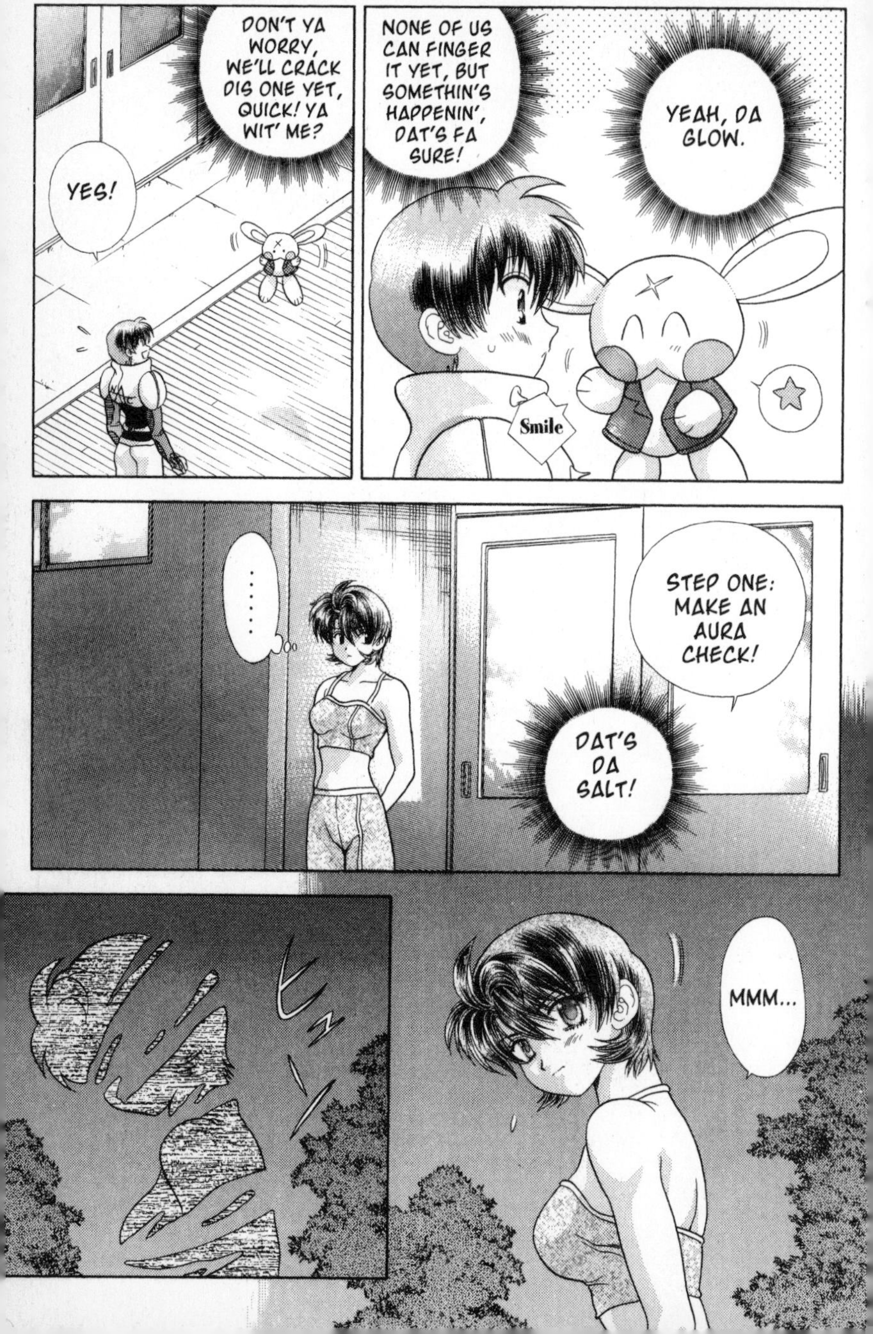
NONE OF US CAN FINGER IT YET, BUT SOMETHIN'S HAPPENIN', DAT'S FA SURE!
YEAH, DA GLOW.
Smile
DON'T YA WORRY, WE'LL CRACK DIS ONE YET, QUICK! YA WIT' ME?
YES!
STEP ONE: MAKE AN AURA CHECK!
DAT'S DA SALT!
......
MMM...

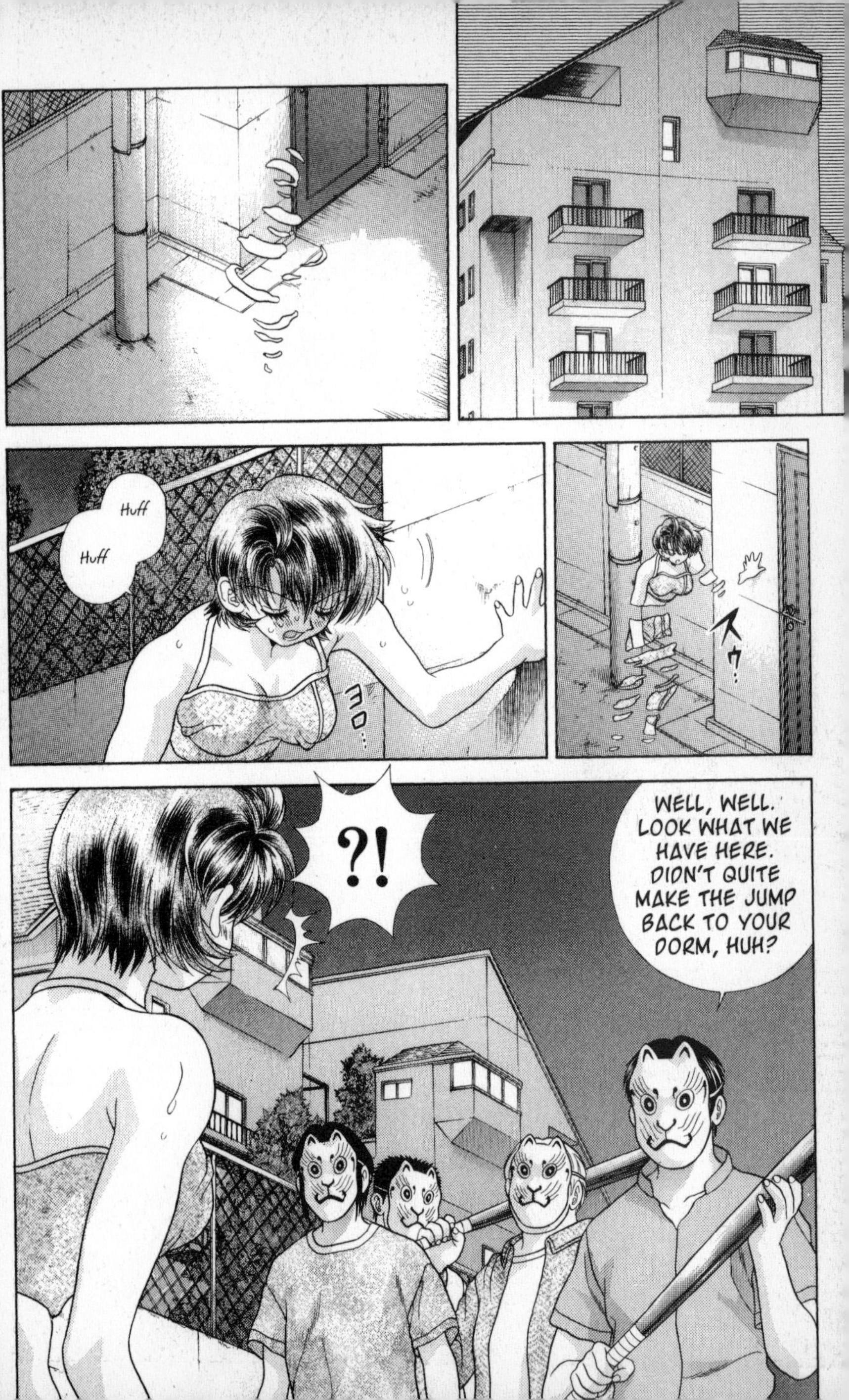
スゥ…
Huff
Huff
ヨロ…
WELL, WELL. LOOK WHAT WE HAVE HERE. DIDN'T QUITE MAKE THE JUMP BACK TO YOUR DORM, HUH?
?!

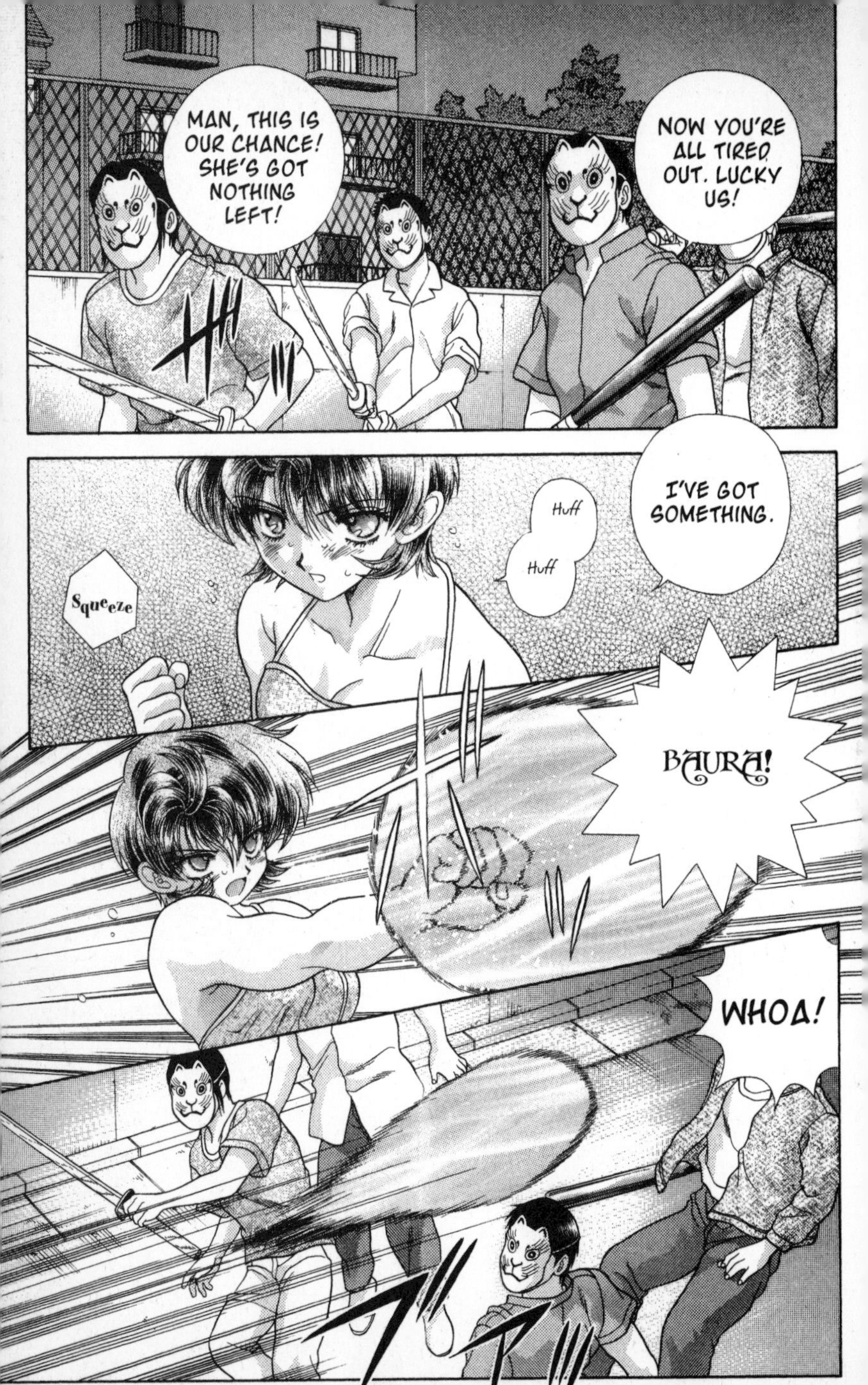
NOW YOU'RE ALL TIRED OUT. LUCKY US!
MAN, THIS IS OUR CHANCE! SHE'S GOT NOTHING LEFT!
I'VE GOT SOMETHING.
Huff
Huff
Squeeze
BAURA!
WHOA!

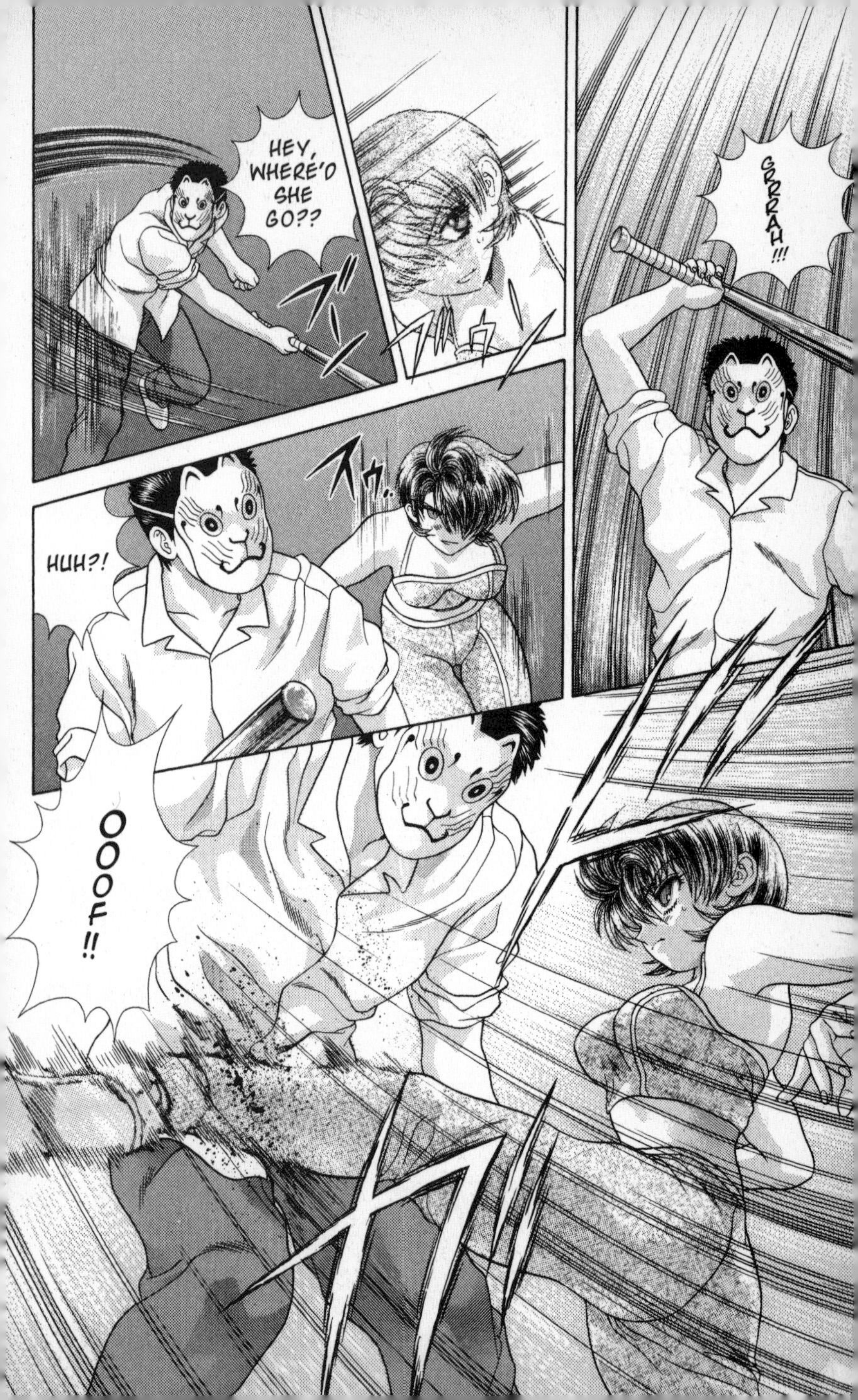
GRRRAH!!!
HEY, WHERE'D SHE GO??
HUH?!
OOOF!!

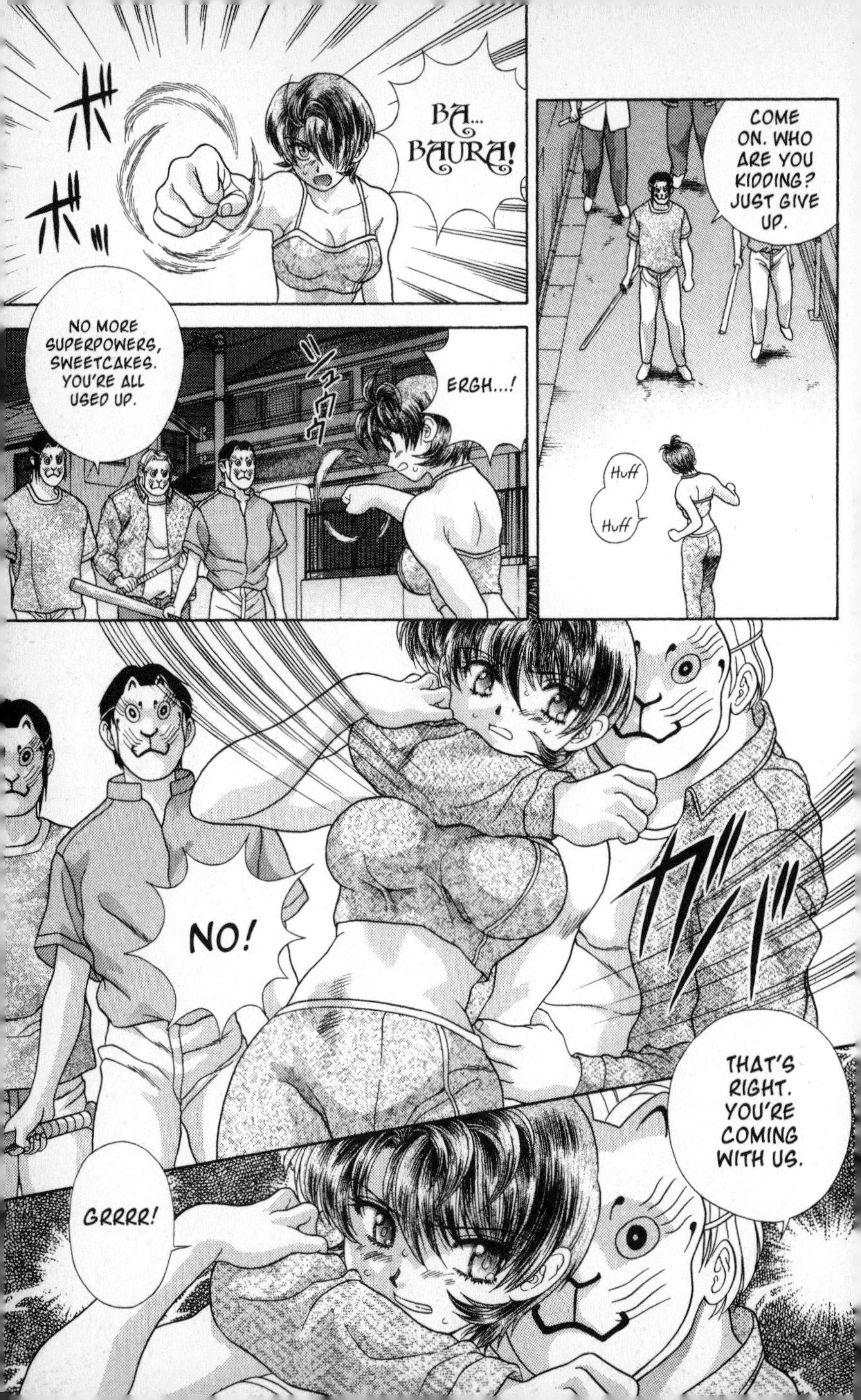
COME ON. WHO ARE YOU KIDDING? JUST GIVE UP.
Huff
Huff
BA... BAURA!
NO MORE SUPERPOWERS, SWEETCAKES. YOU'RE ALL USED UP.
ERGH...!
NO!
THAT'S RIGHT. YOU'RE COMING WITH US.
GRRRR!

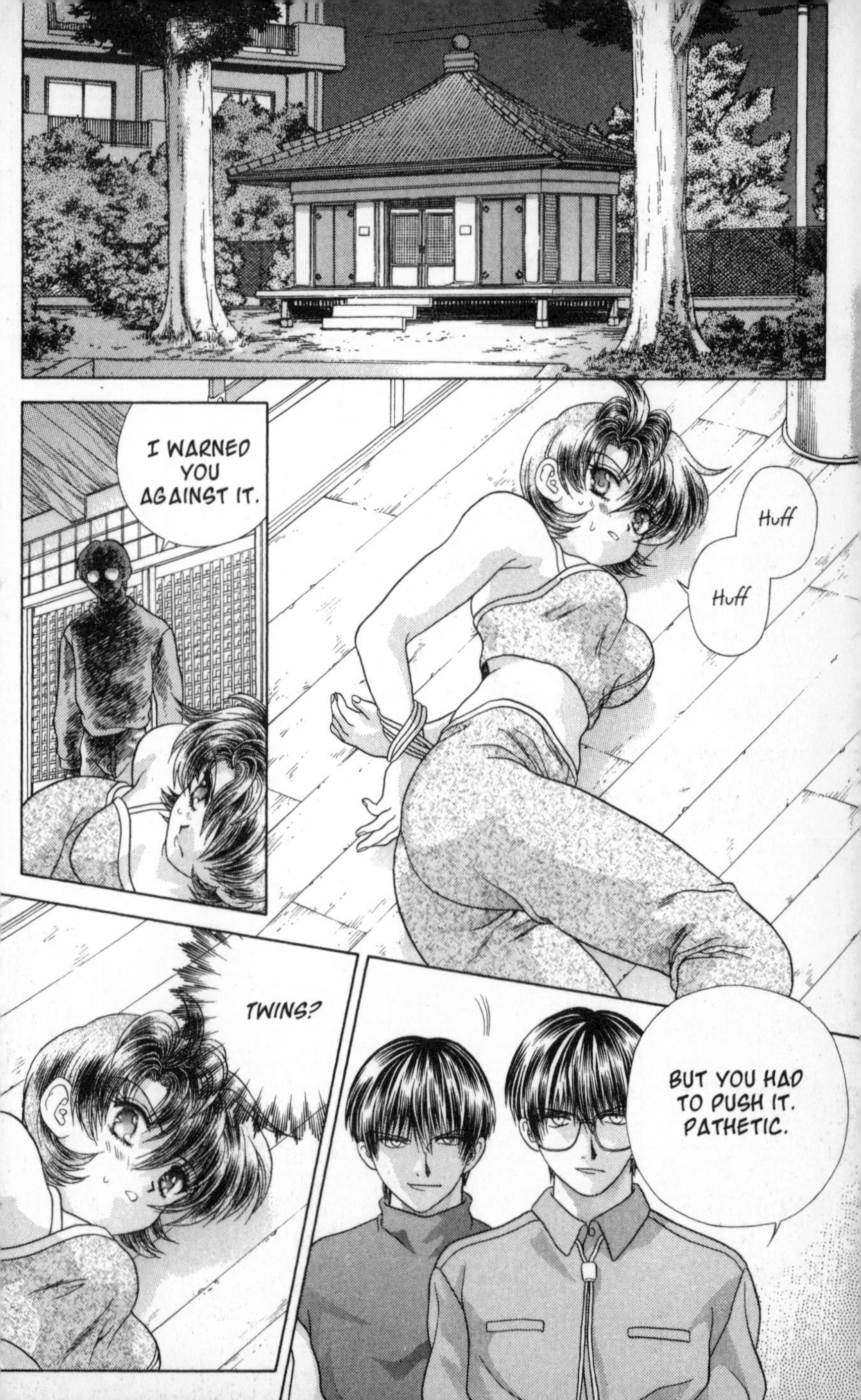
Huff
Huff
I WARNED YOU AGAINST IT.
BUT YOU HAD TO PUSH IT. PATHETIC.
TWINS?

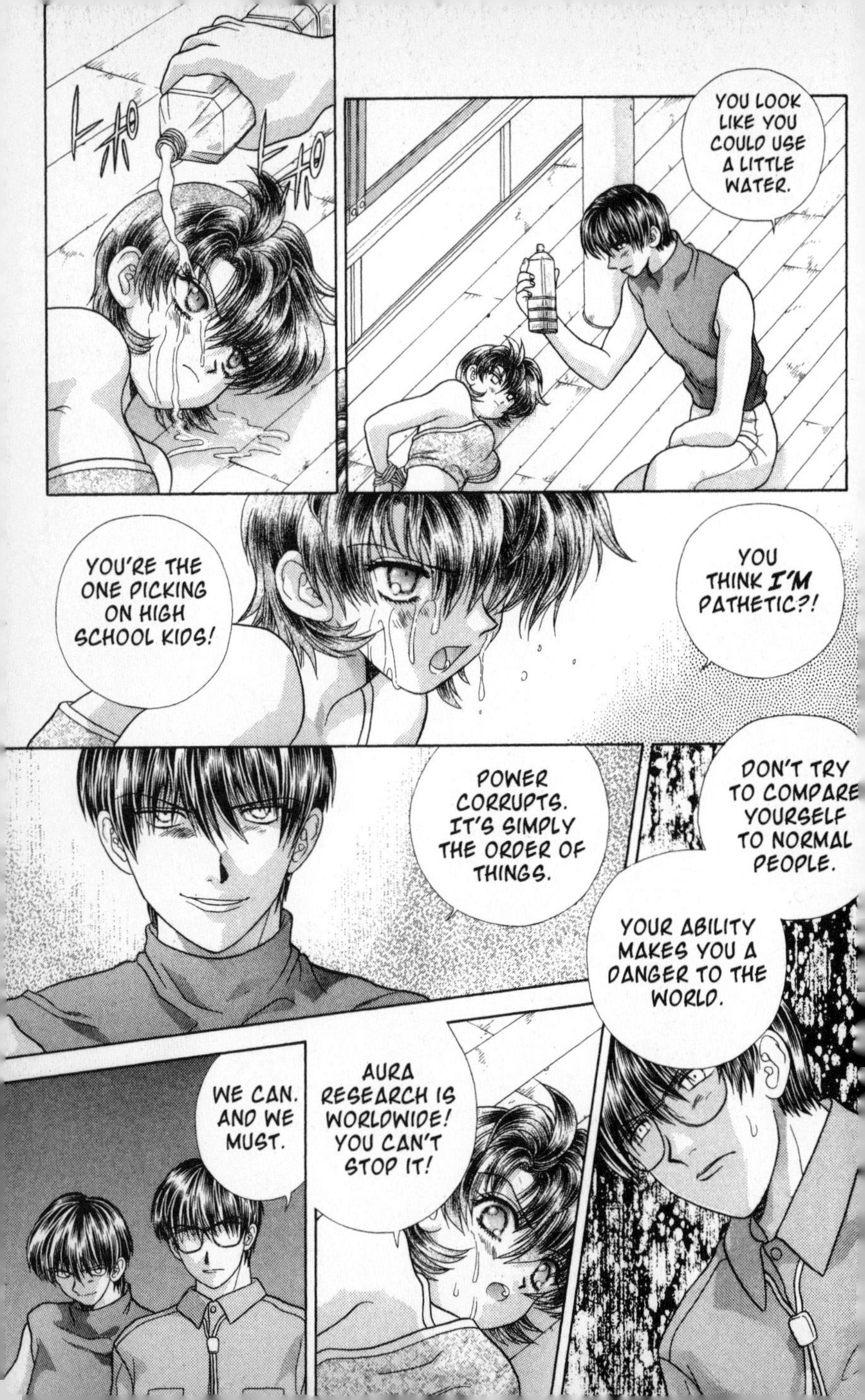
YOU LOOK LIKE YOU COULD USE A LITTLE WATER.
YOU THINK *I'M* PATHETIC?!
YOU'RE THE ONE PICKING ON HIGH SCHOOL KIDS!
DON'T TRY TO COMPARE YOURSELF TO NORMAL PEOPLE.
POWER CORRUPTS. IT'S SIMPLY THE ORDER OF THINGS.
YOUR ABILITY MAKES YOU A DANGER TO THE WORLD.
AURA RESEARCH IS WORLDWIDE! YOU CAN'T STOP IT!
WE CAN. AND WE MUST.

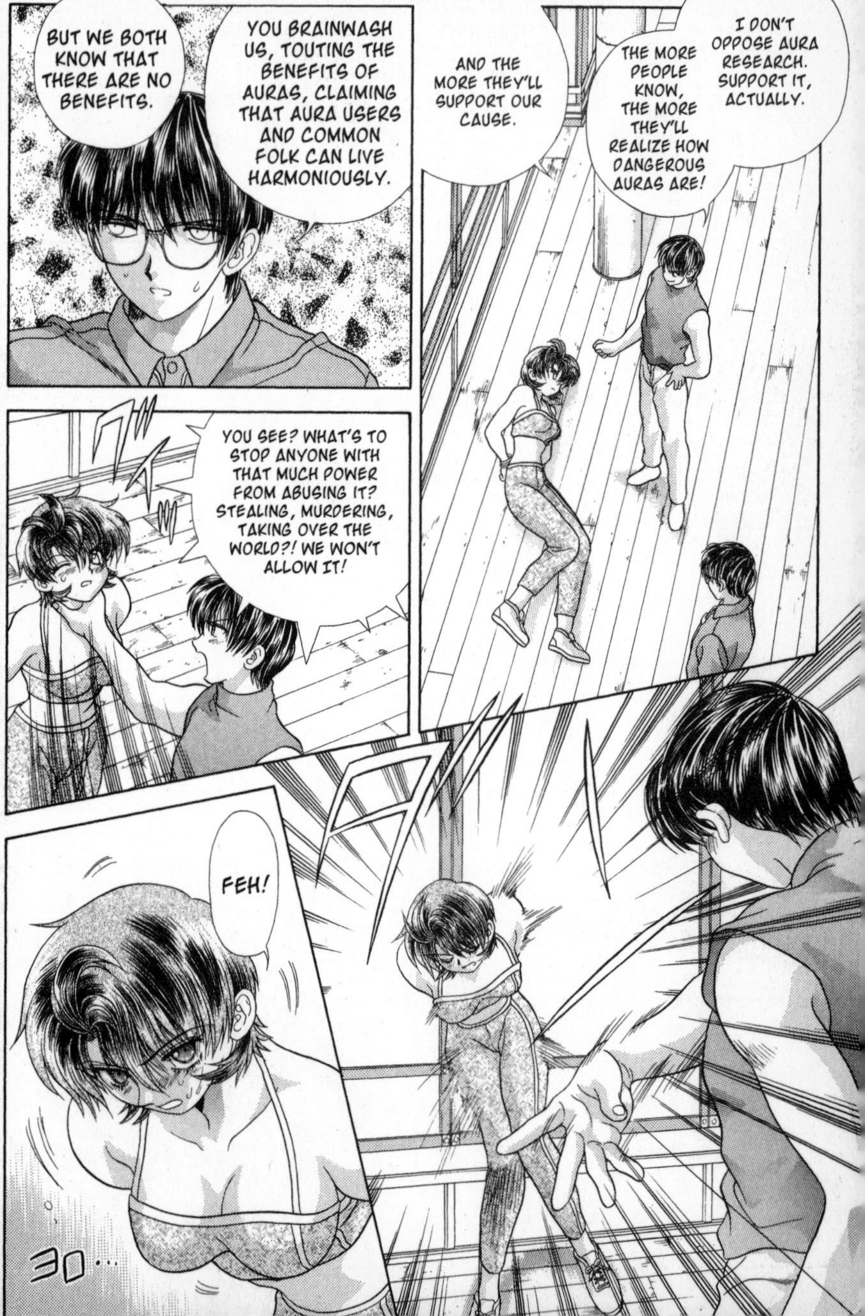
I DON'T OPPOSE AURA RESEARCH. SUPPORT IT, ACTUALLY.
THE MORE PEOPLE KNOW, THE MORE THEY'LL REALIZE HOW DANGEROUS AURAS ARE!
AND THE MORE THEY'LL SUPPORT OUR CAUSE.
YOU BRAINWASH US, TOUTING THE BENEFITS OF AURAS, CLAIMING THAT AURA USERS AND COMMON FOLK CAN LIVE HARMONIOUSLY.
BUT WE BOTH KNOW THAT THERE ARE NO BENEFITS.
YOU SEE? WHAT'S TO STOP ANYONE WITH THAT MUCH POWER FROM ABUSING IT? STEALING, MURDERING, TAKING OVER THE WORLD?! WE WON'T ALLOW IT!
FEH!
30...

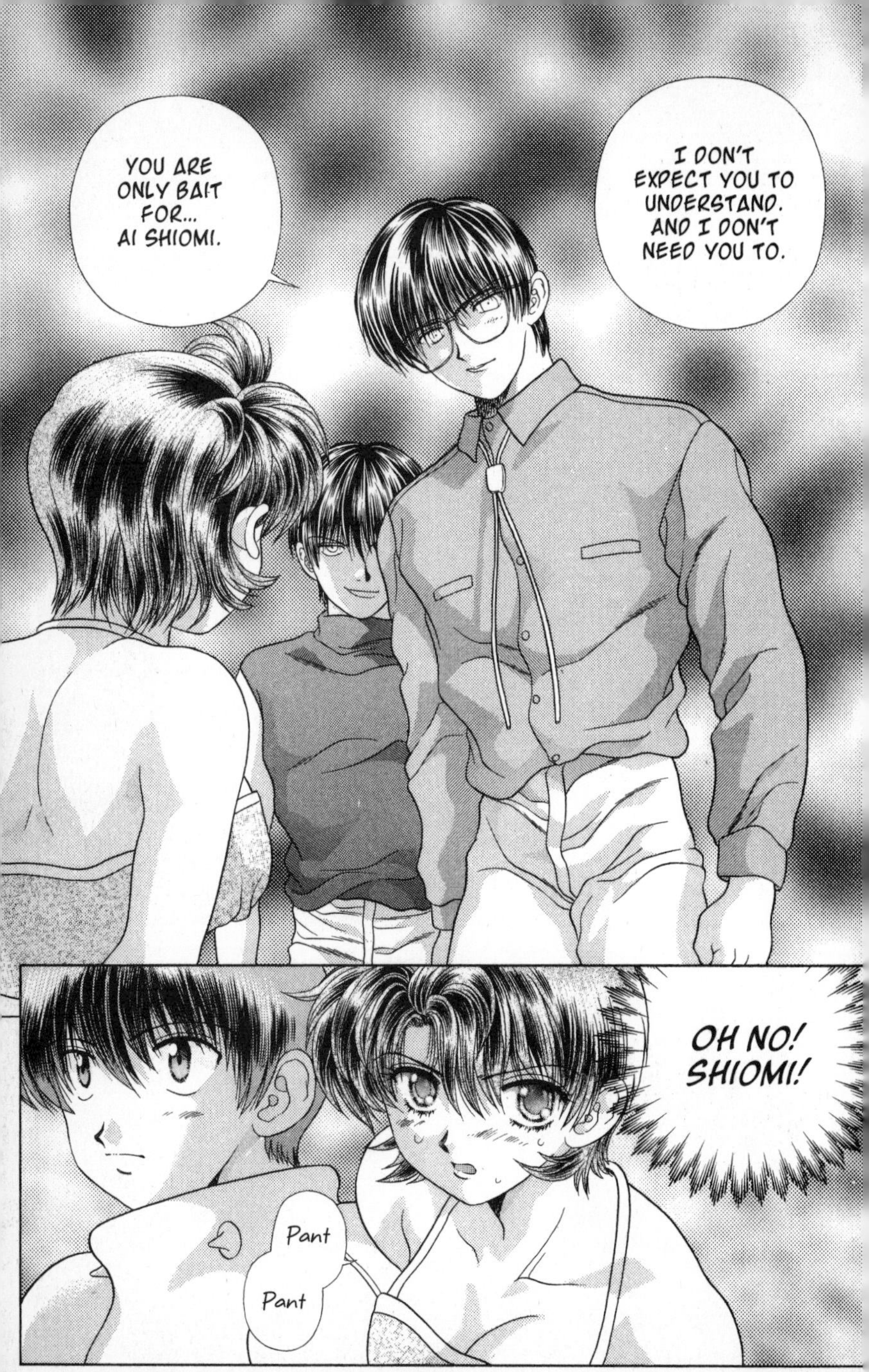
I DON'T EXPECT YOU TO UNDERSTAND. AND I DON'T NEED YOU TO.
YOU ARE ONLY BAIT FOR... AI SHIOMI.
OH NO! SHIOMI!
Pant
Pant

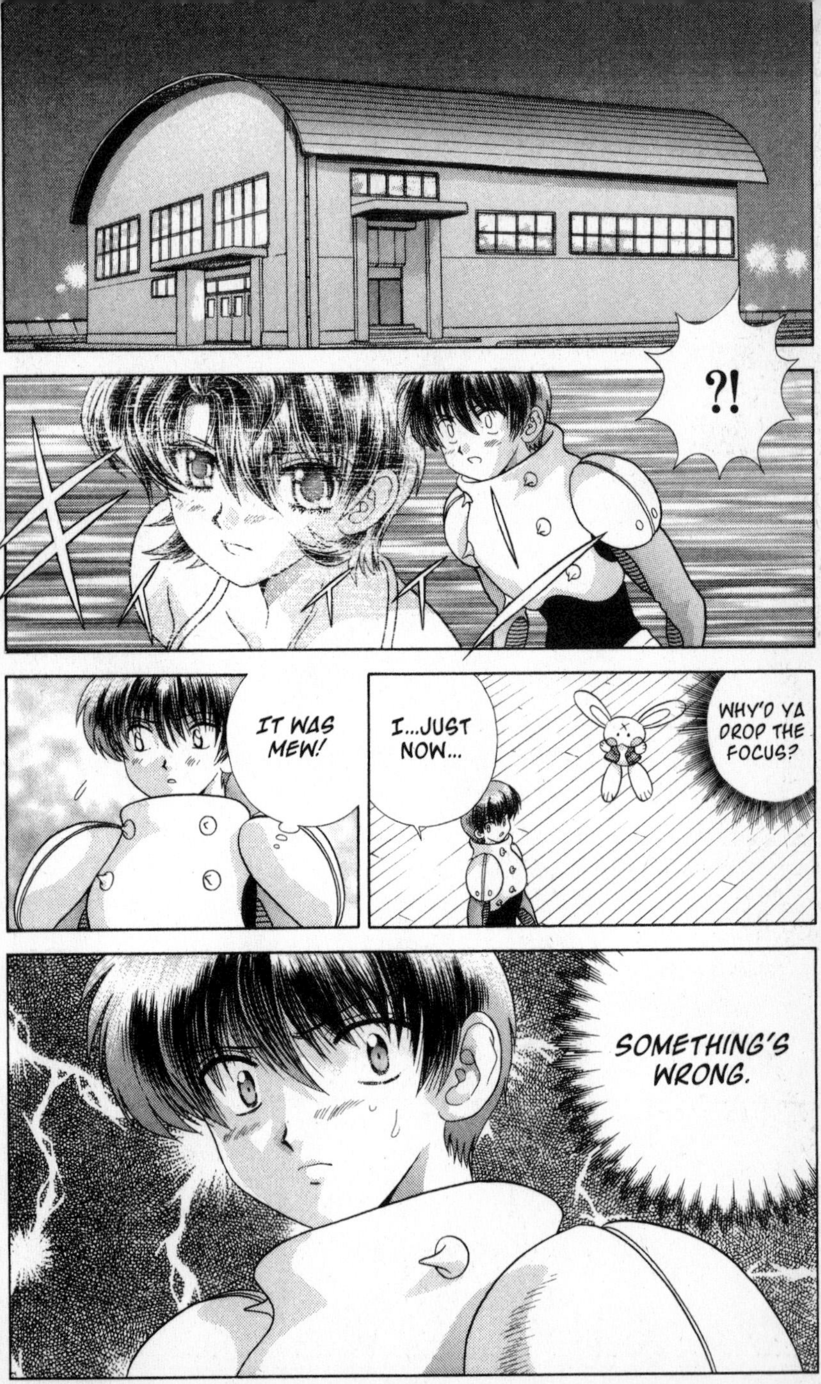
?!
WHY'D YA DROP THE FOCUS?
I...JUST NOW...
IT WAS MEW!
SOMETHING'S WRONG.

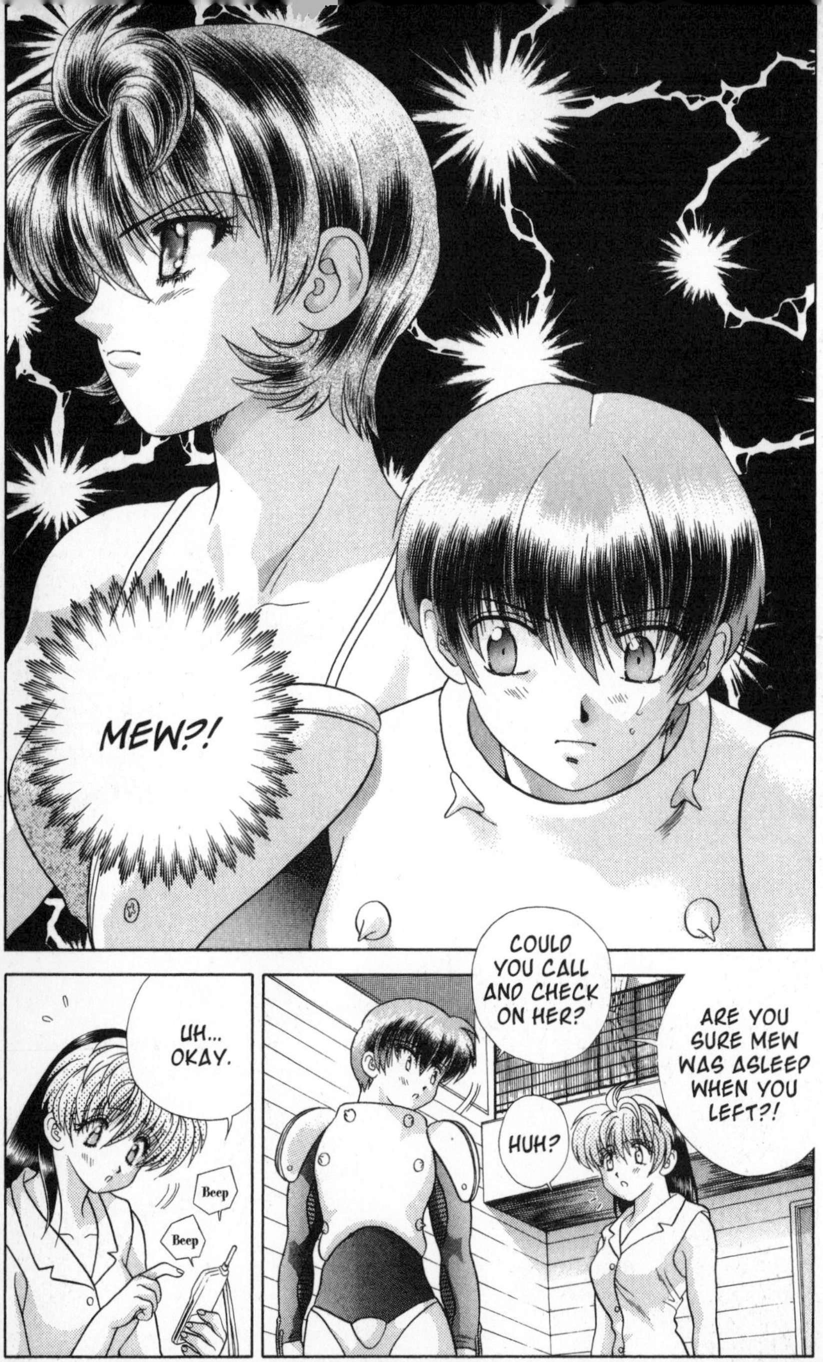
MEW?!
ARE YOU SURE MEW WAS ASLEEP WHEN YOU LEFT?!
HUH?
COULD YOU CALL AND CHECK ON HER?
UH... OKAY.
Beep
Beep

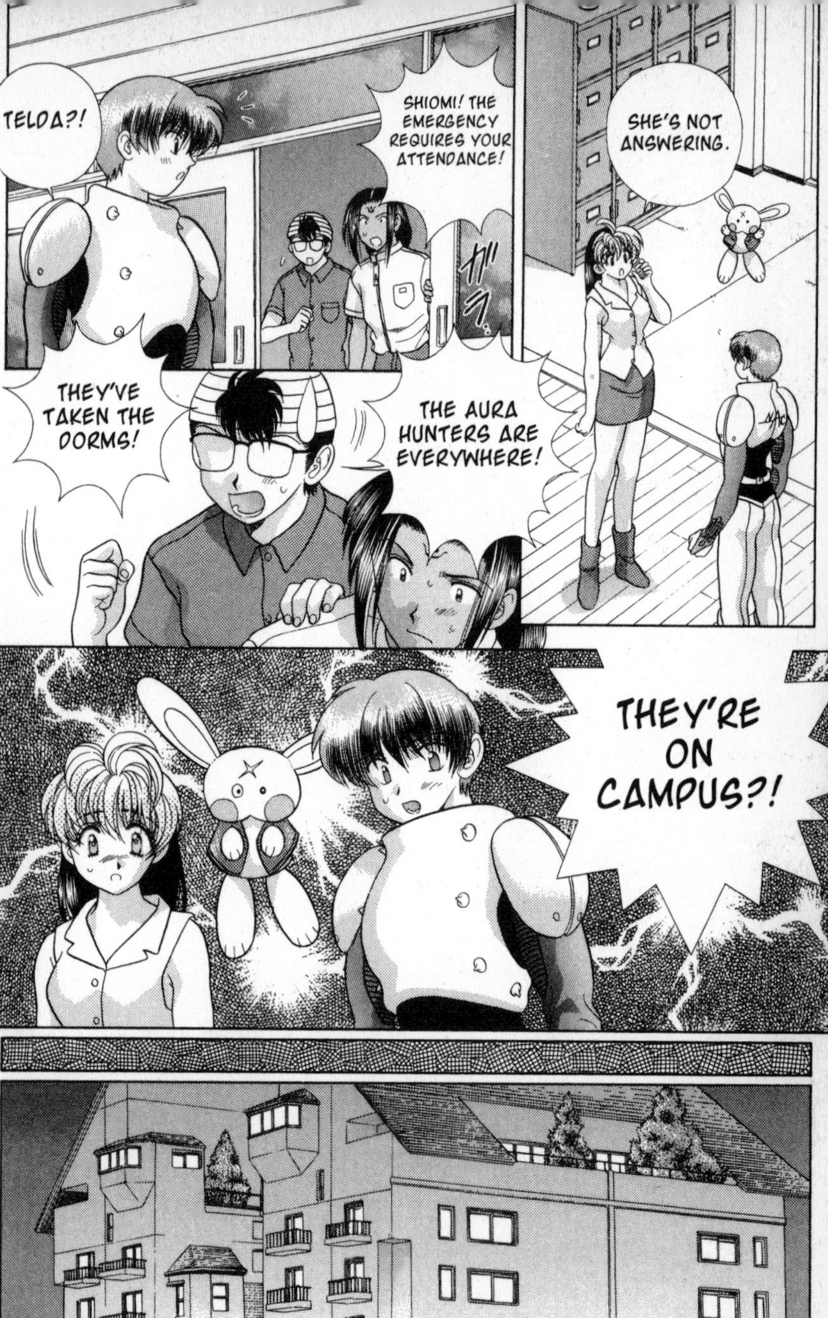

SHE'S NOT ANSWERING.
SHIOMI! THE EMERGENCY REQUIRES YOUR ATTENDANCE!
ガラ
TELDA?!
THE AURA HUNTERS ARE EVERYWHERE!
THEY'VE TAKEN THE DORMS!
THEY'RE ON CAMPUS?!

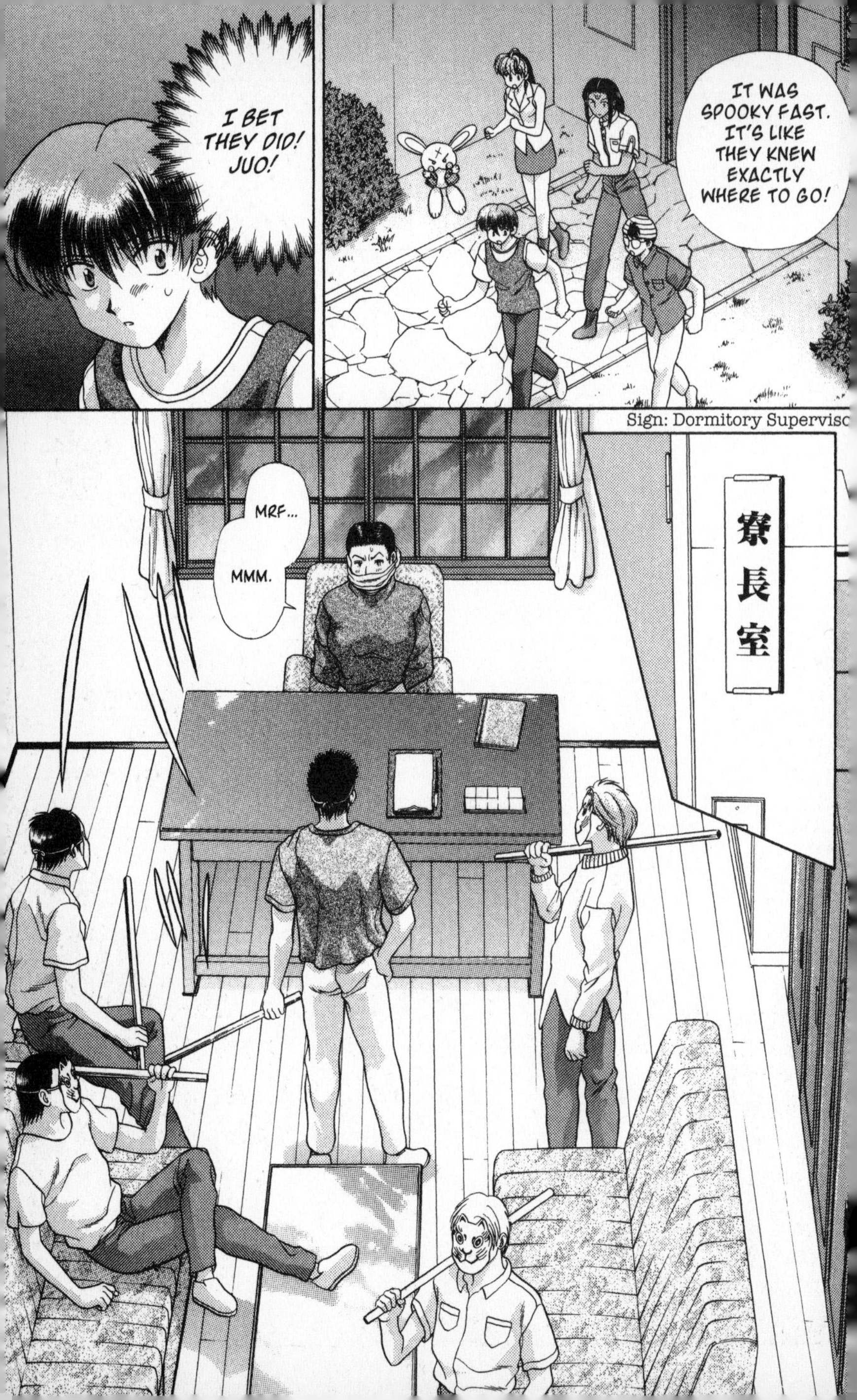
IT WAS SPOOKY FAST. IT'S LIKE THEY KNEW EXACTLY WHERE TO GO!
I BET THEY DID! JUO!
Sign: Dormitory Superviso
寮長室
MRF...
MMM.

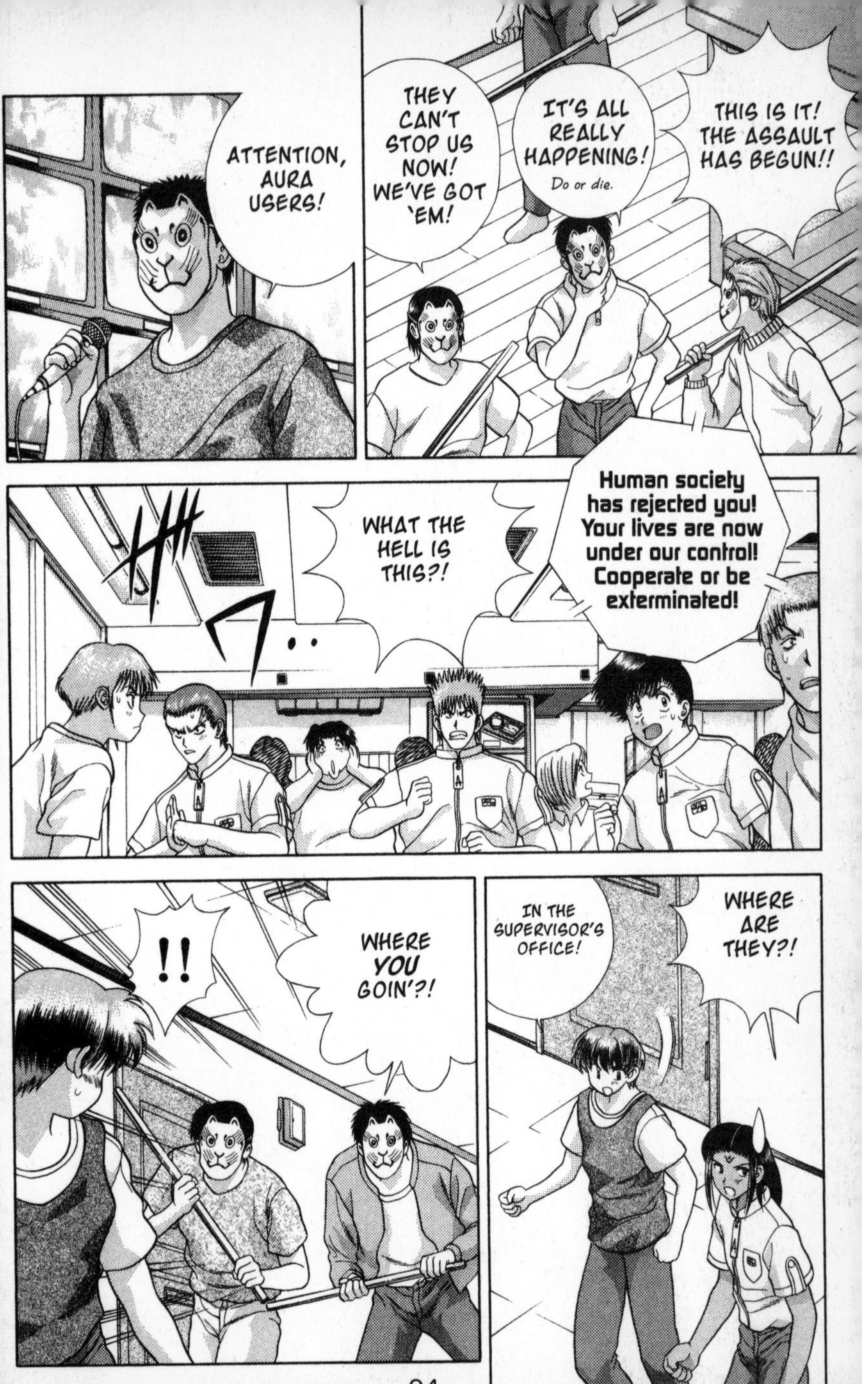
THIS IS IT! THE ASSAULT HAS BEGUN!!
IT'S ALL REALLY HAPPENING!
Do or die.
THEY CAN'T STOP US NOW! WE'VE GOT 'EM!
ATTENTION, AURA USERS!
Human society has rejected you! Your lives are now under our control! Cooperate or be exterminated!
WHAT THE HELL IS THIS?!
WHERE ARE THEY?!
IN THE SUPERVISOR'S OFFICE!
!!
WHERE *YOU* GOIN'?!

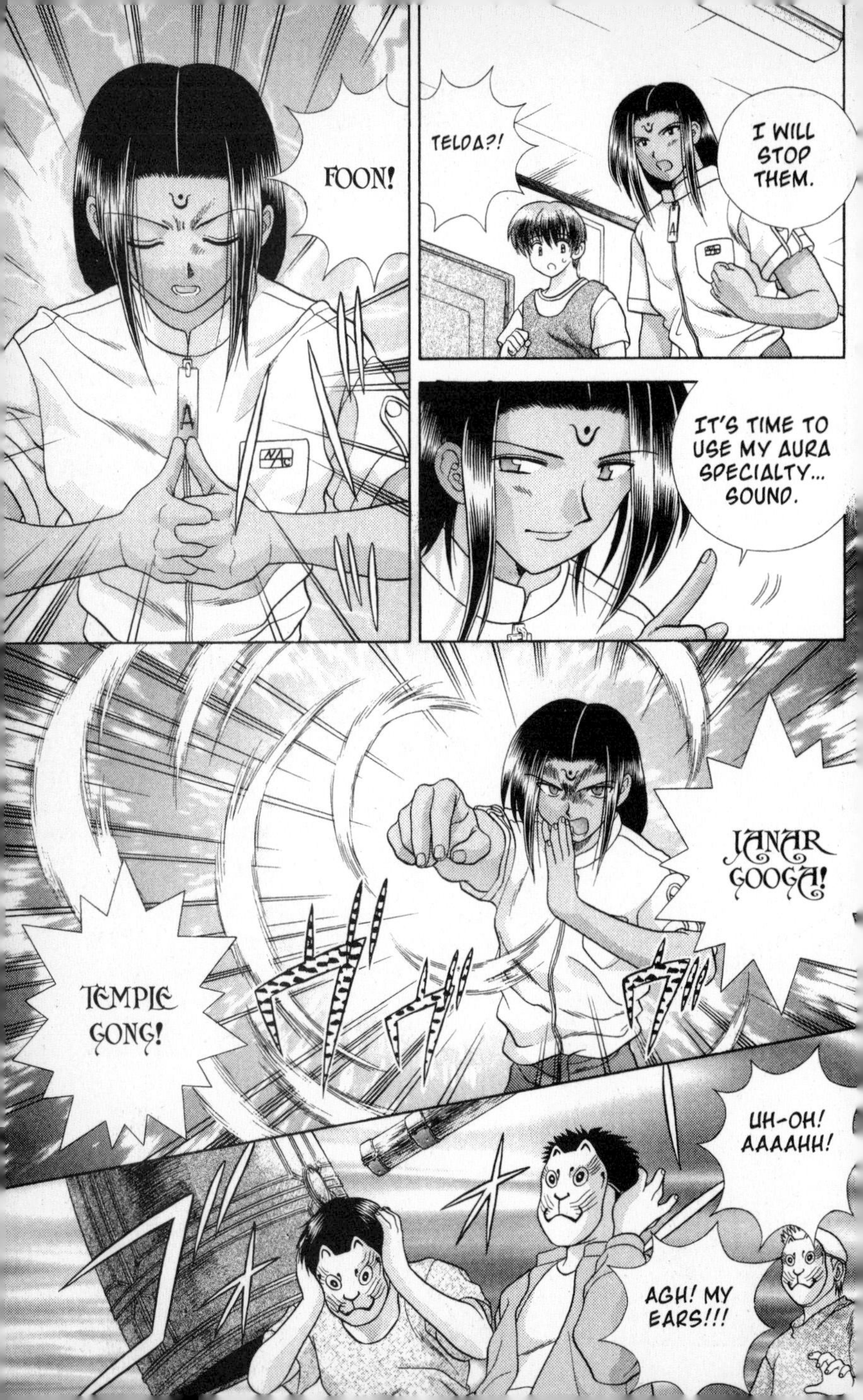

I WILL STOP THEM.
TELDA?!
IT'S TIME TO USE MY AURA SPECIALTY... SOUND.
FOON!
IANAR GOOGA!
TEMPLE GONG!
UH-OH! AAAAHH!
AGH! MY EARS!!!

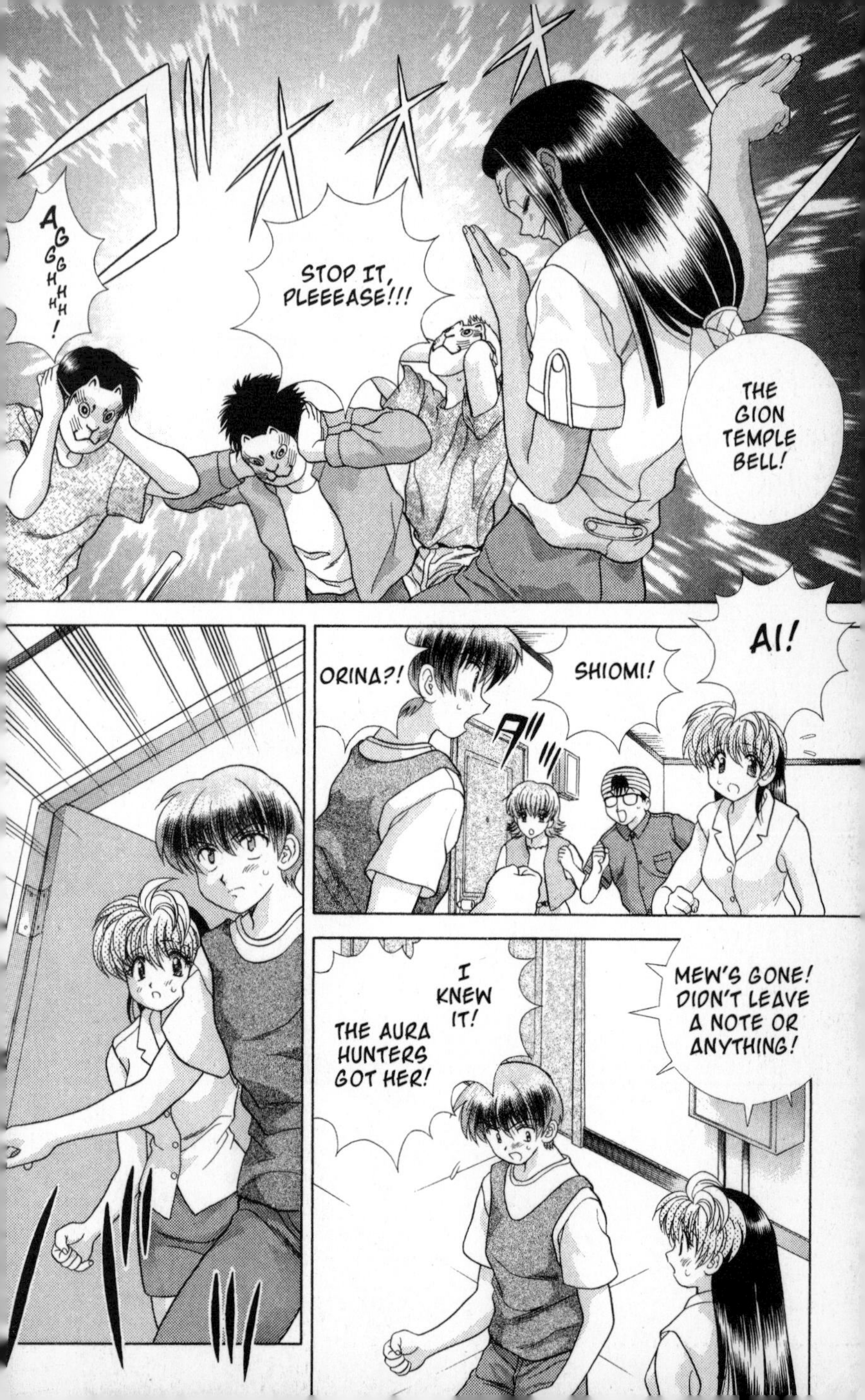
THE GION TEMPLE BELL!
STOP IT, PLEEEASE!!!
AGGGHHHH!
AI!
SHIOMI!
ORINA?!
MEW'S GONE! DIDN'T LEAVE A NOTE OR ANYTHING!
I KNEW IT!
THE AURA HUNTERS GOT HER!

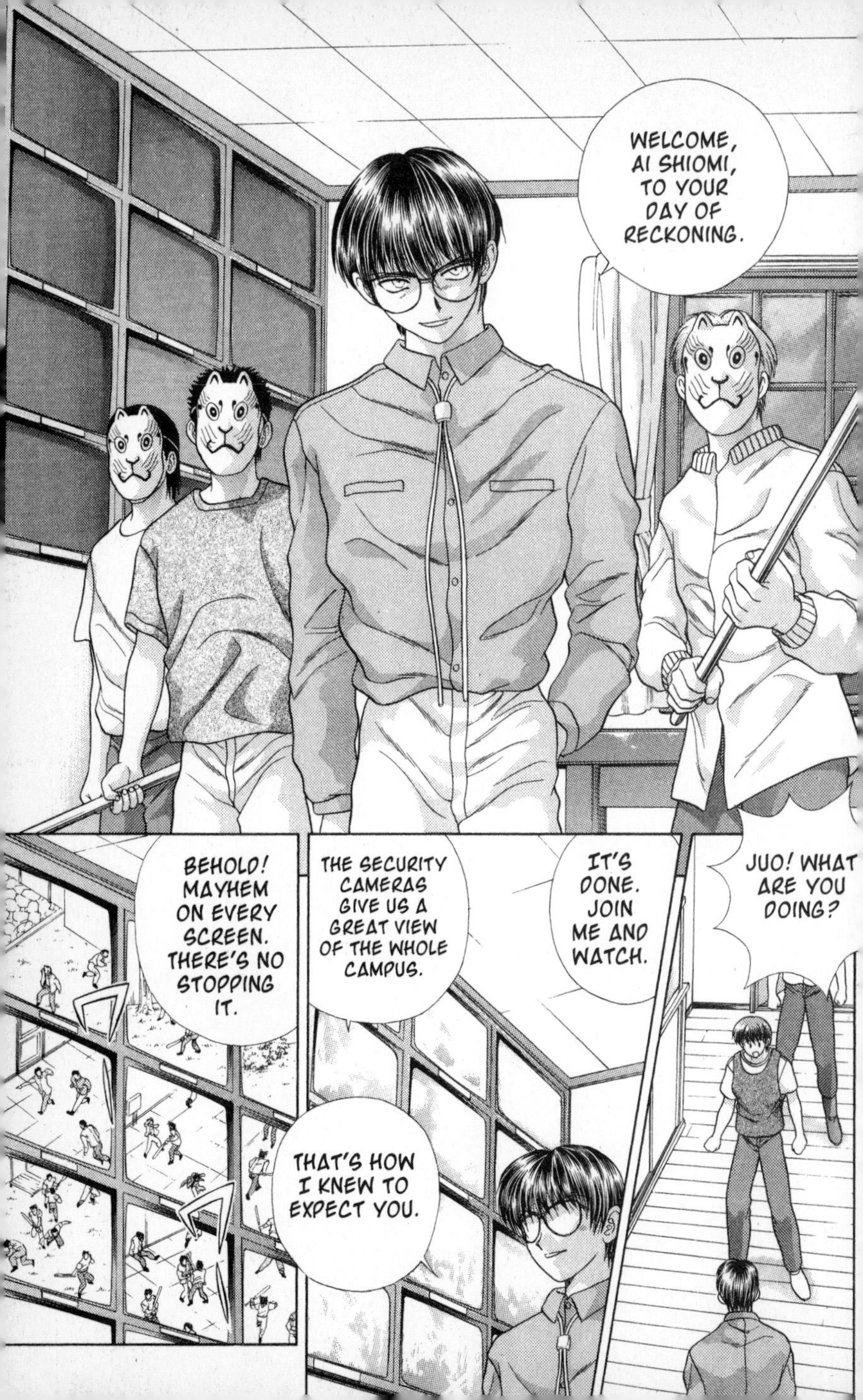
WELCOME, AI SHIOMI, TO YOUR DAY OF RECKONING.
JUO! WHAT ARE YOU DOING?
IT'S DONE. JOIN ME AND WATCH.
THE SECURITY CAMERAS GIVE US A GREAT VIEW OF THE WHOLE CAMPUS.
BEHOLD! MAYHEM ON EVERY SCREEN. THERE'S NO STOPPING IT.
THAT'S HOW I KNEW TO EXPECT YOU.

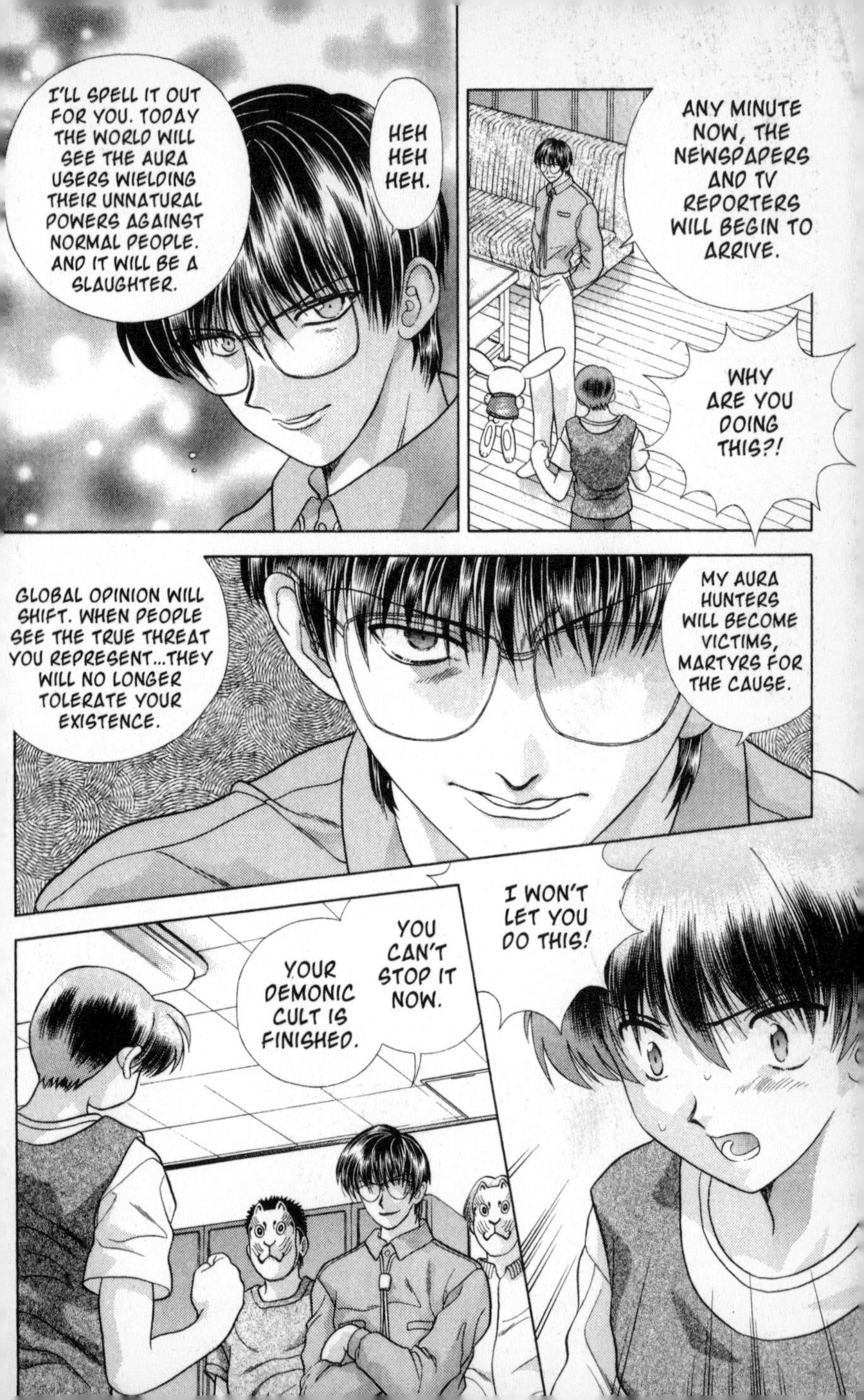
ANY MINUTE NOW, THE NEWSPAPERS AND TV REPORTERS WILL BEGIN TO ARRIVE.
WHY ARE YOU DOING THIS?!
HEH HEH HEH.
I'LL SPELL IT OUT FOR YOU. TODAY THE WORLD WILL SEE THE AURA USERS WIELDING THEIR UNNATURAL POWERS AGAINST NORMAL PEOPLE. AND IT WILL BE A SLAUGHTER.
MY AURA HUNTERS WILL BECOME VICTIMS, MARTYRS FOR THE CAUSE.
GLOBAL OPINION WILL SHIFT. WHEN PEOPLE SEE THE TRUE THREAT YOU REPRESENT...THEY WILL NO LONGER TOLERATE YOUR EXISTENCE.
I WON'T LET YOU DO THIS!
YOU CAN'T STOP IT NOW.
YOUR DEMONIC CULT IS FINISHED.

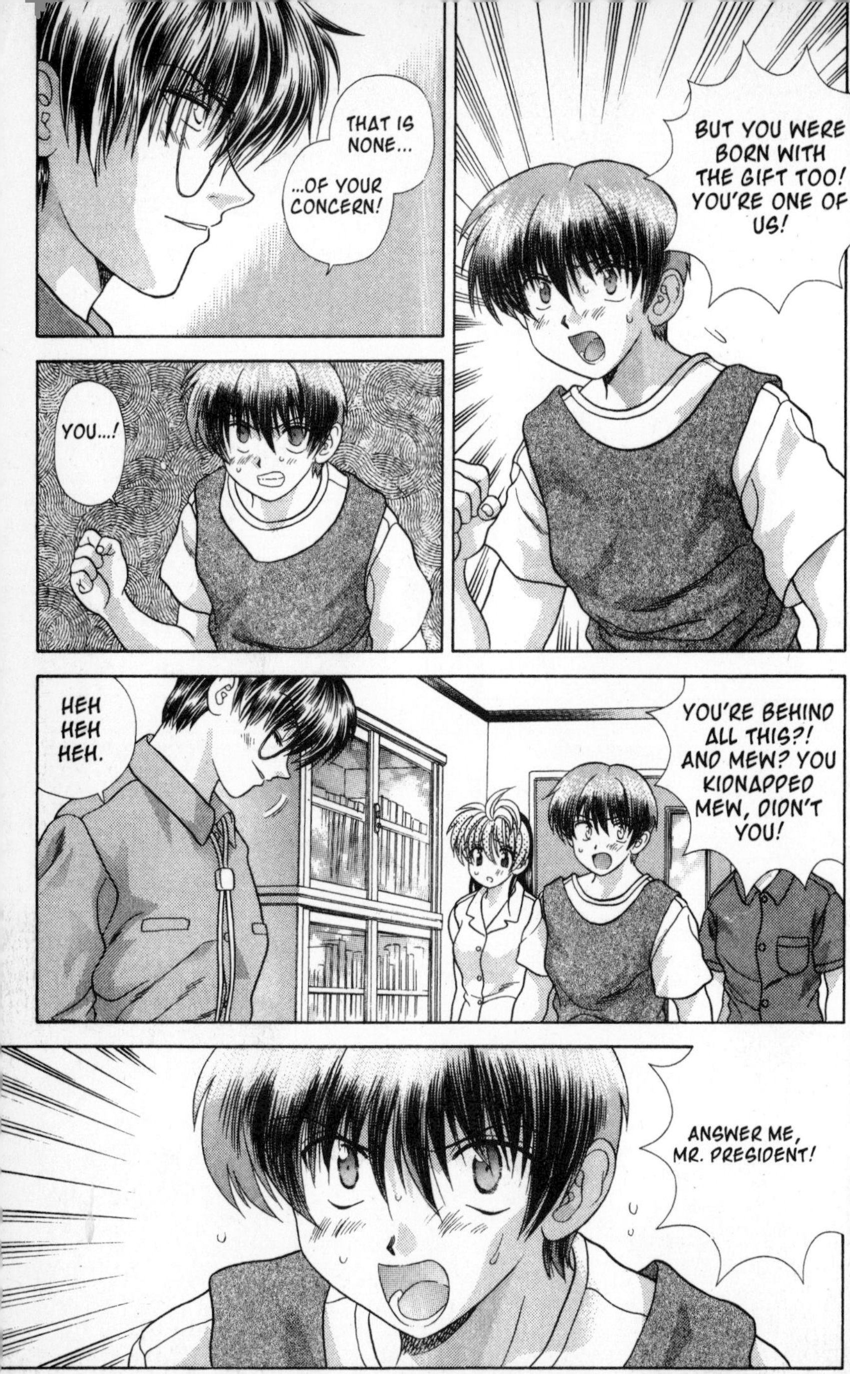
BUT YOU WERE BORN WITH THE GIFT TOO! YOU'RE ONE OF US!
THAT IS NONE...
...OF YOUR CONCERN!
YOU...!
YOU'RE BEHIND ALL THIS?! AND MEW? YOU KIDNAPPED MEW, DIDN'T YOU!
HEH HEH HEH.
ANSWER ME, MR. PRESIDENT!

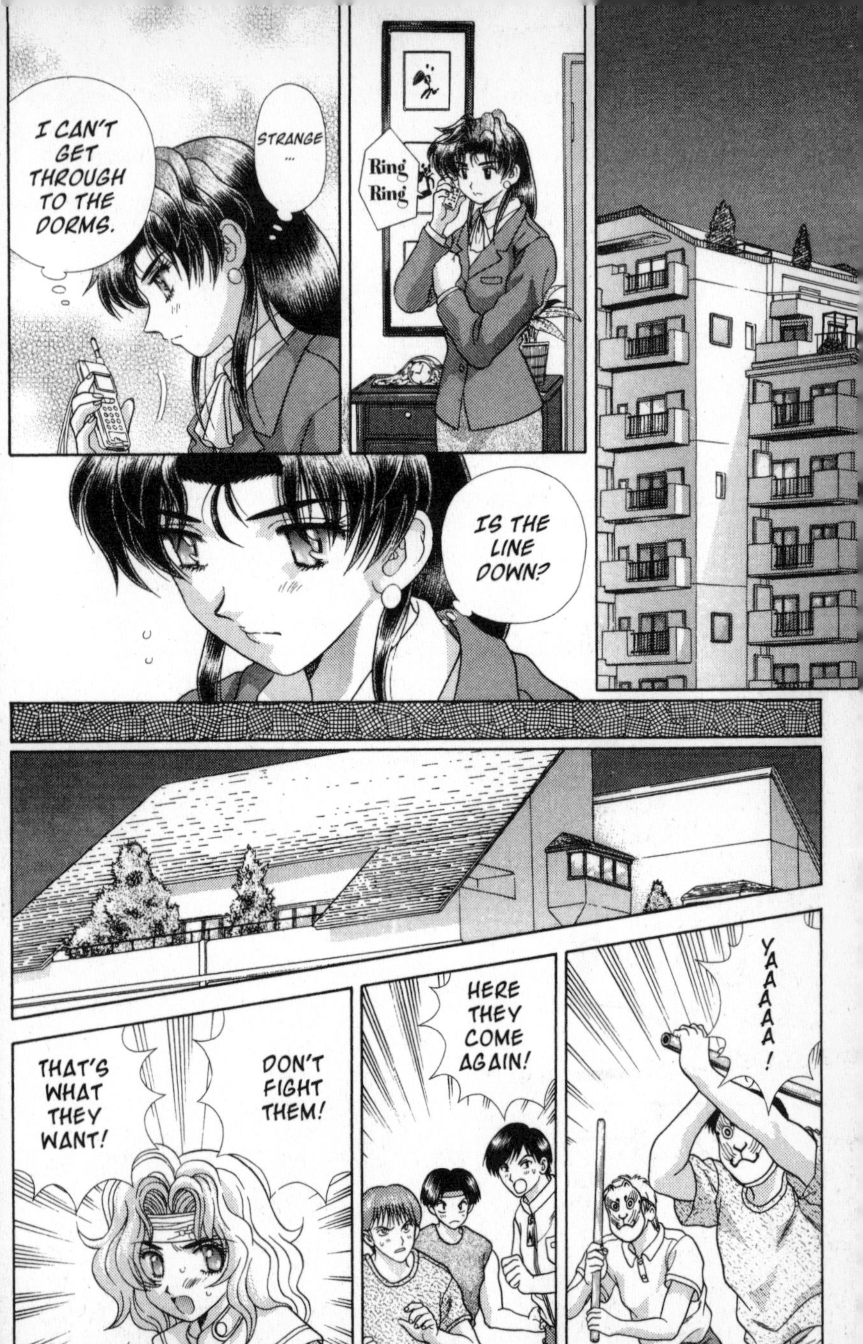
Ring Ring
STRANGE ...
I CAN'T GET THROUGH TO THE DORMS.
IS THE LINE DOWN?
YAAAAA!
HERE THEY COME AGAIN!
DON'T FIGHT THEM!
THAT'S WHAT THEY WANT!

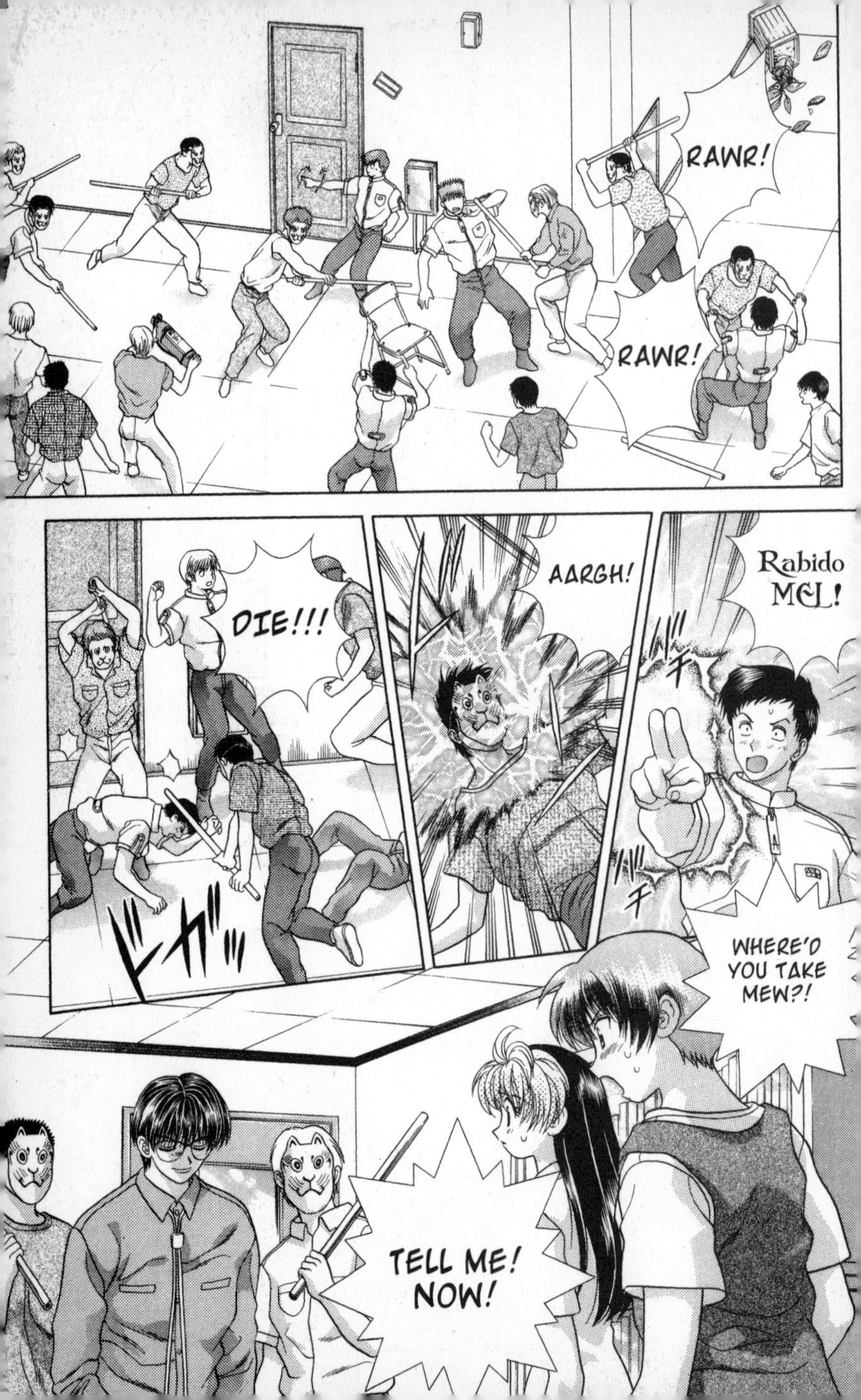
RAWR!
RAWR!
Rabido MEL!
AARGH!
DIE!!!
WHERE'D YOU TAKE MEW?!
TELL ME! NOW!

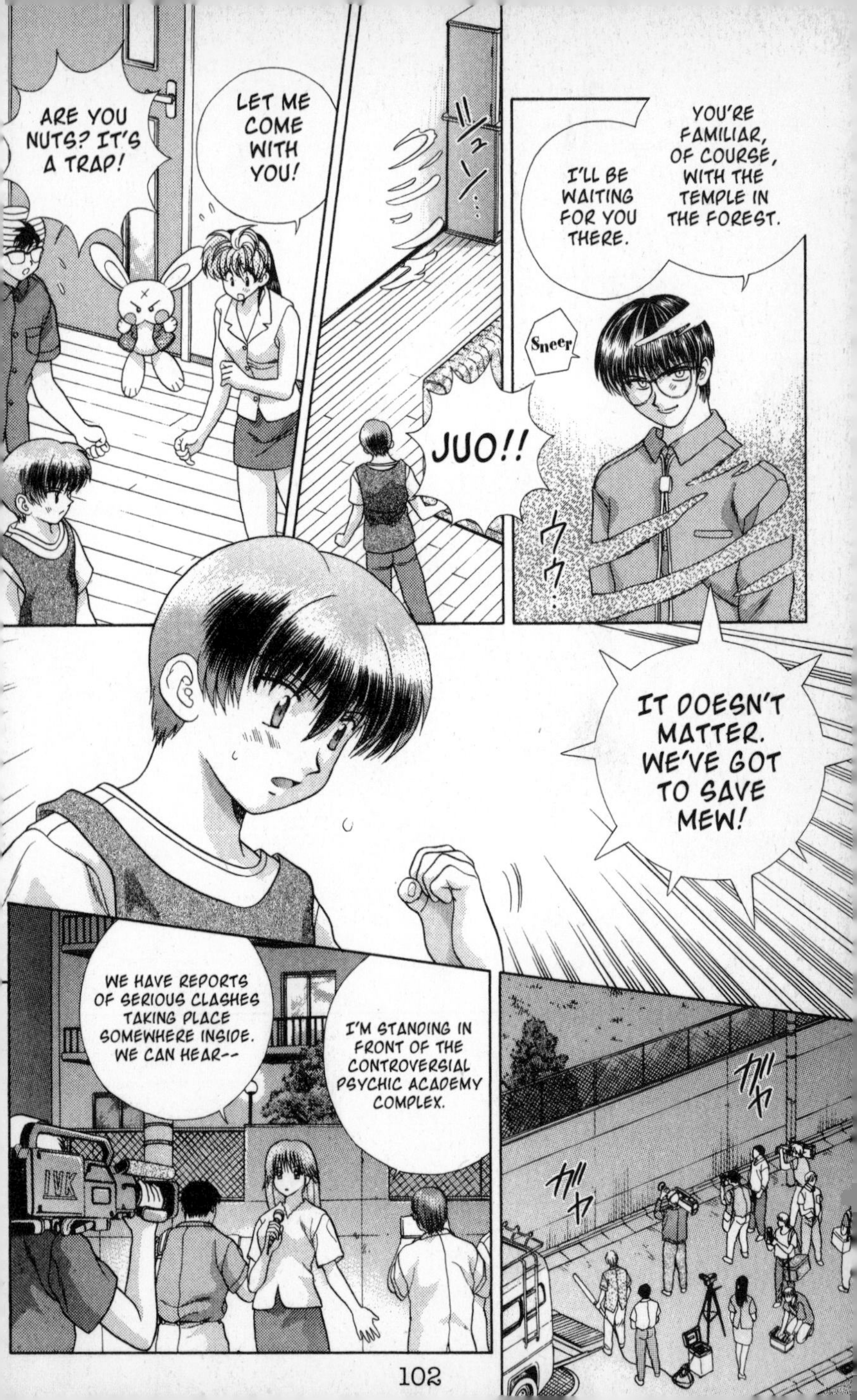
YOU'RE FAMILIAR, OF COURSE, WITH THE TEMPLE IN THE FOREST.
I'LL BE WAITING FOR YOU THERE.
Sneer
JUO!!
LET ME COME WITH YOU!
ARE YOU NUTS? IT'S A TRAP!
IT DOESN'T MATTER. WE'VE GOT TO SAVE MEW!
I'M STANDING IN FRONT OF THE CONTROVERSIAL PSYCHIC ACADEMY COMPLEX.
WE HAVE REPORTS OF SERIOUS CLASHES TAKING PLACE SOMEWHERE INSIDE. WE CAN HEAR--

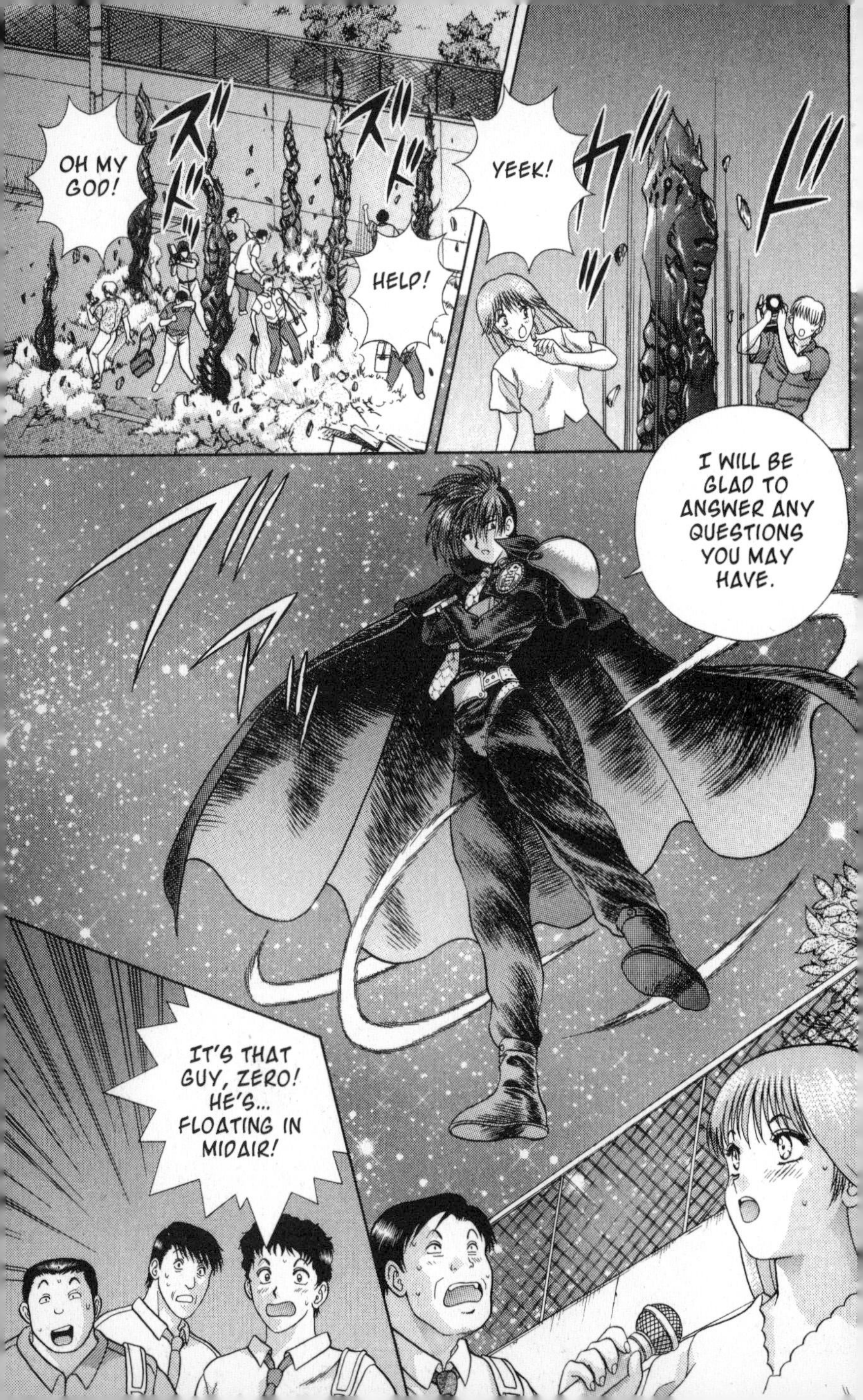
YEEK!
HELP!
OH MY GOD!
I WILL BE GLAD TO ANSWER ANY QUESTIONS YOU MAY HAVE.
IT'S THAT GUY, ZERO! HE'S... FLOATING IN MIDAIR!

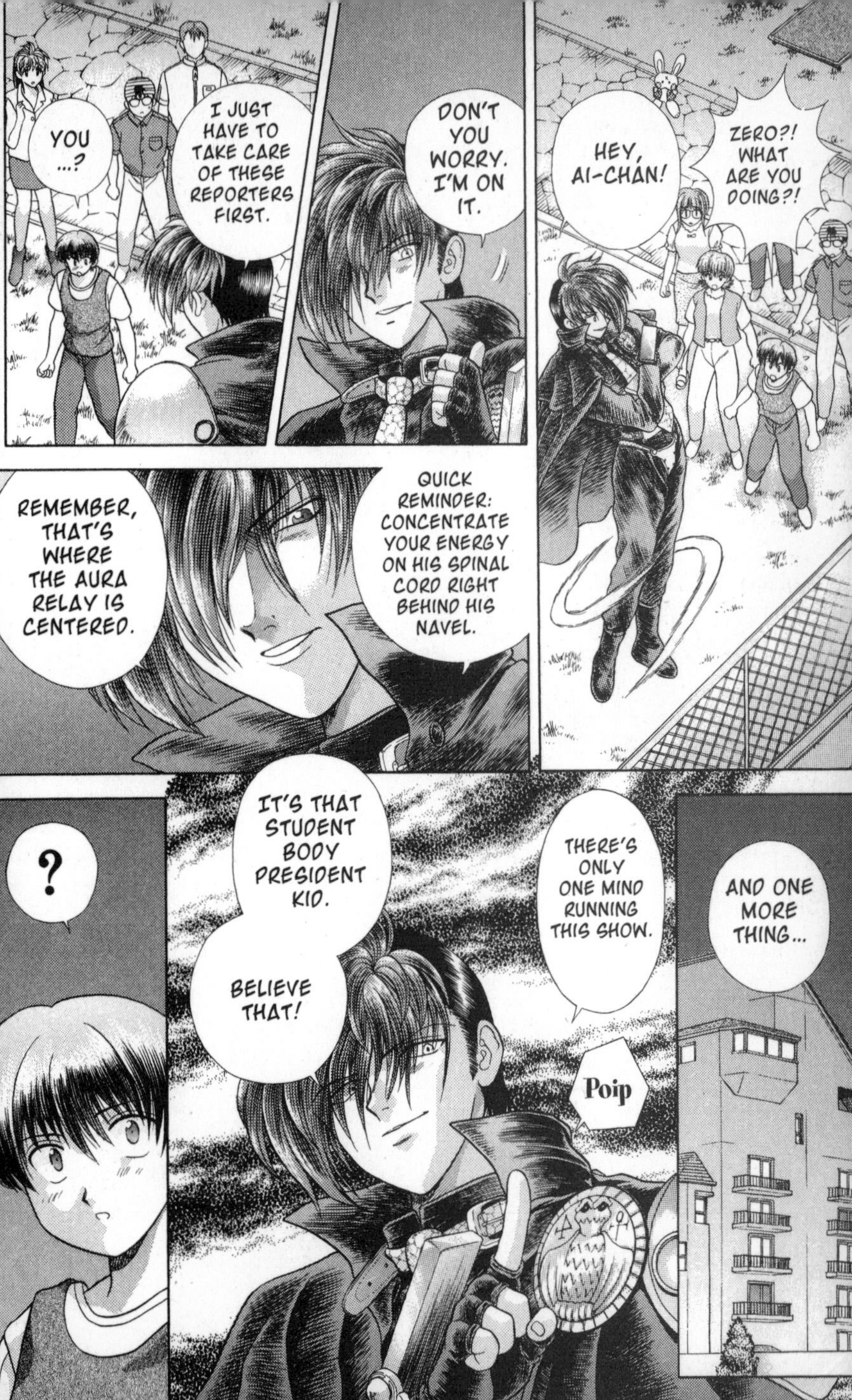
ZERO?! WHAT ARE YOU DOING?!
HEY, AI-CHAN!
DON'T YOU WORRY. I'M ON IT.
I JUST HAVE TO TAKE CARE OF THESE REPORTERS FIRST.
YOU ...?
QUICK REMINDER: CONCENTRATE YOUR ENERGY ON HIS SPINAL CORD RIGHT BEHIND HIS NAVEL.
REMEMBER, THAT'S WHERE THE AURA RELAY IS CENTERED.
AND ONE MORE THING...
THERE'S ONLY ONE MIND RUNNING THIS SHOW.
Poip
IT'S THAT STUDENT BODY PRESIDENT KID.
BELIEVE THAT!
?

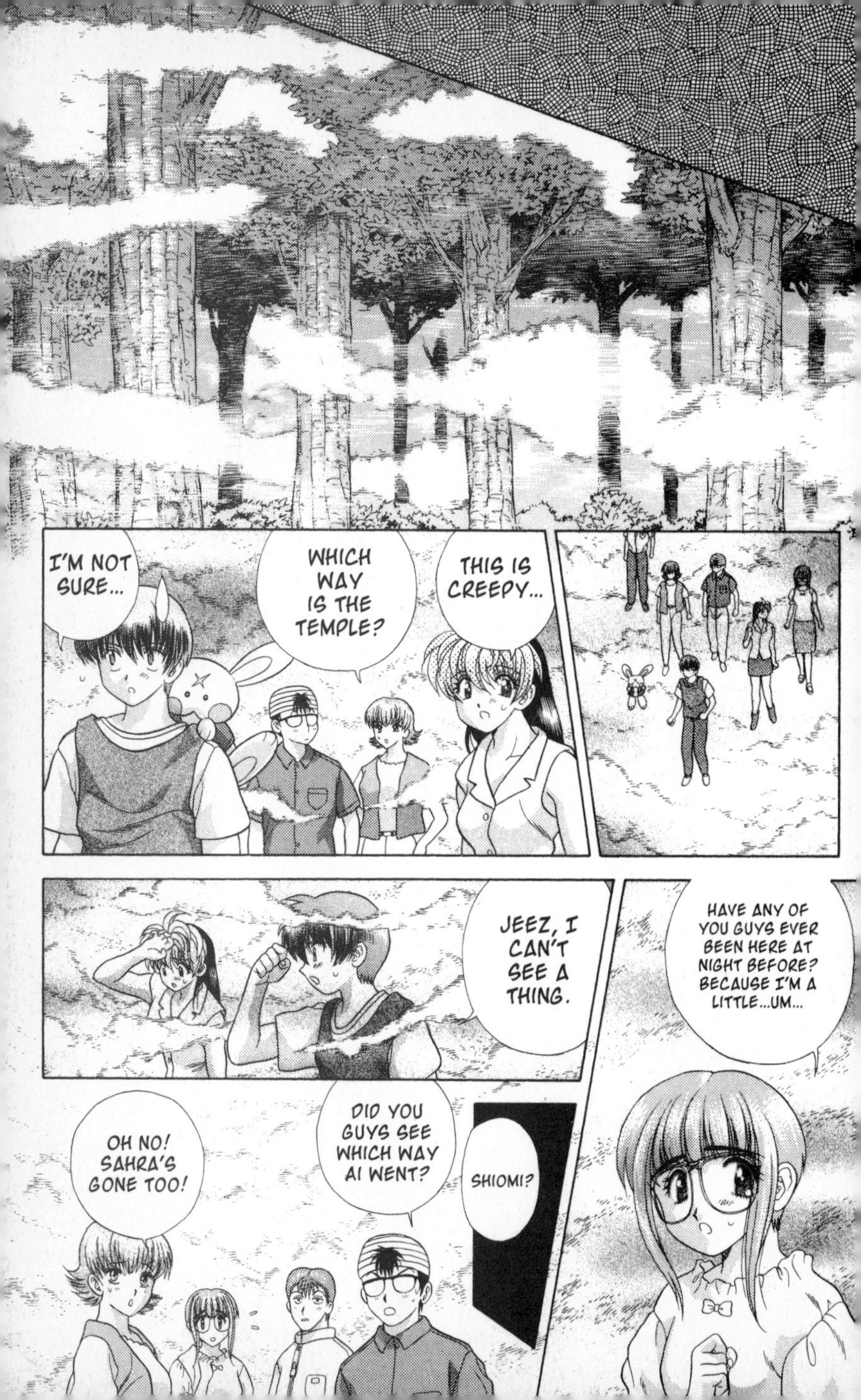
THIS IS CREEPY...
WHICH WAY IS THE TEMPLE?
I'M NOT SURE...
HAVE ANY OF YOU GUYS EVER BEEN HERE AT NIGHT BEFORE? BECAUSE I'M A LITTLE...UM...
JEEZ, I CAN'T SEE A THING.
SHIOMI?
DID YOU GUYS SEE WHICH WAY AI WENT?
OH NO! SAHRA'S GONE TOO!

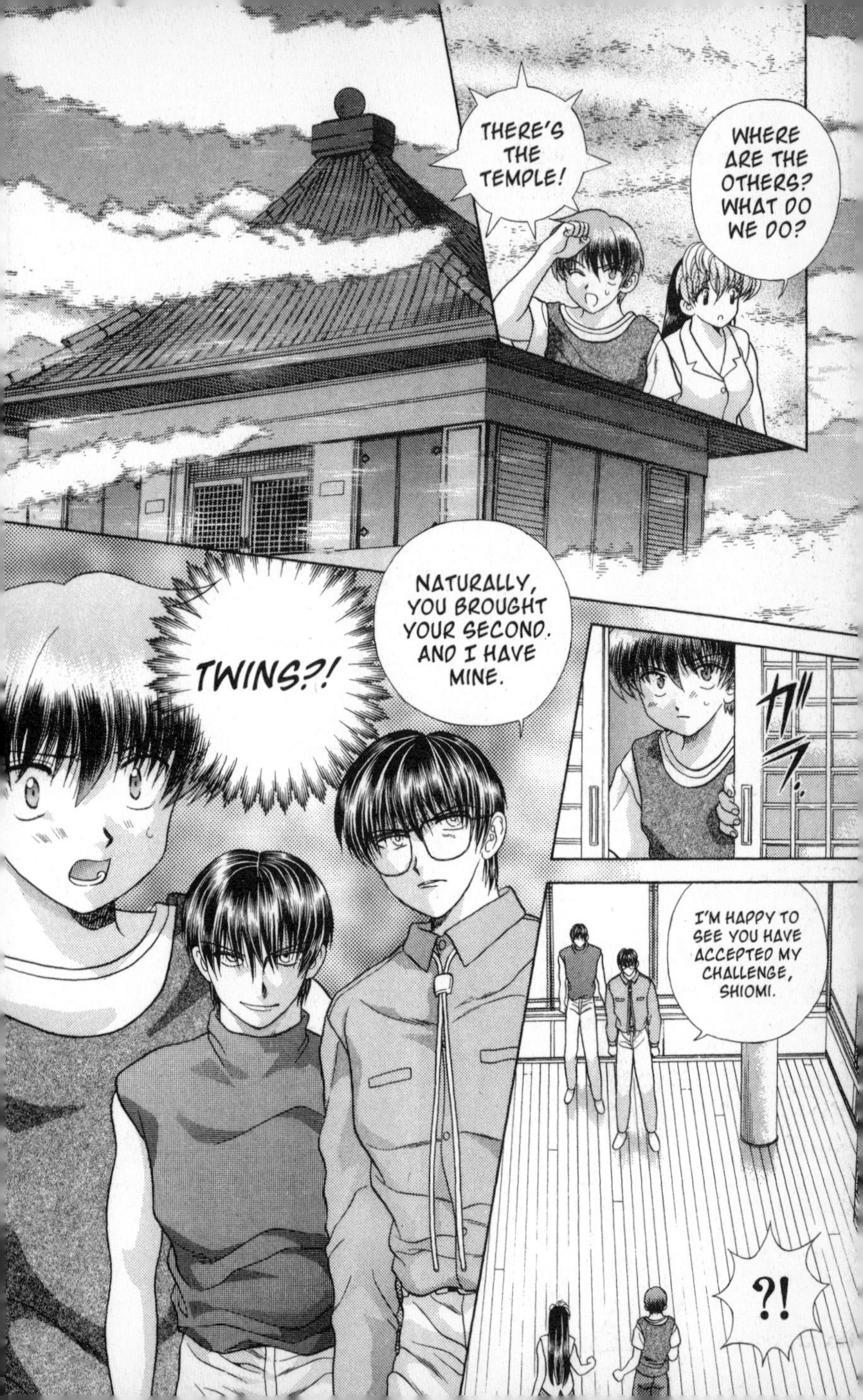
WHERE ARE THE OTHERS? WHAT DO WE DO?
THERE'S THE TEMPLE!
I'M HAPPY TO SEE YOU HAVE ACCEPTED MY CHALLENGE, SHIOMI.
?!
NATURALLY, YOU BROUGHT YOUR SECOND. AND I HAVE MINE.
TWINS?!

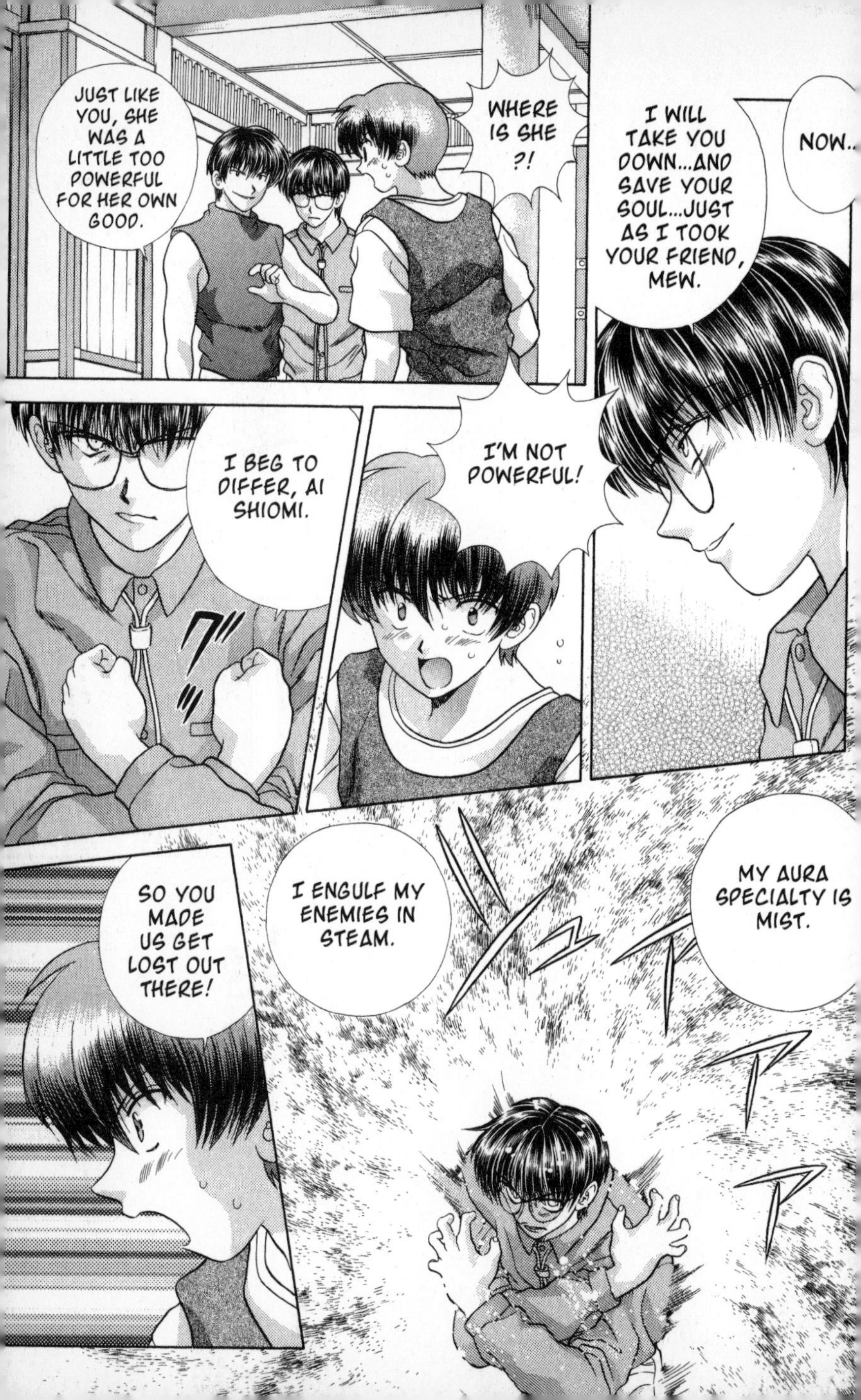
NOW..
I WILL TAKE YOU DOWN...AND SAVE YOUR SOUL...JUST AS I TOOK YOUR FRIEND, MEW.
WHERE IS SHE ?!
JUST LIKE YOU, SHE WAS A LITTLE TOO POWERFUL FOR HER OWN GOOD.
I'M NOT POWERFUL!
I BEG TO DIFFER, AI SHIOMI.
MY AURA SPECIALTY IS MIST.
I ENGULF MY ENEMIES IN STEAM.
SO YOU MADE US GET LOST OUT THERE!

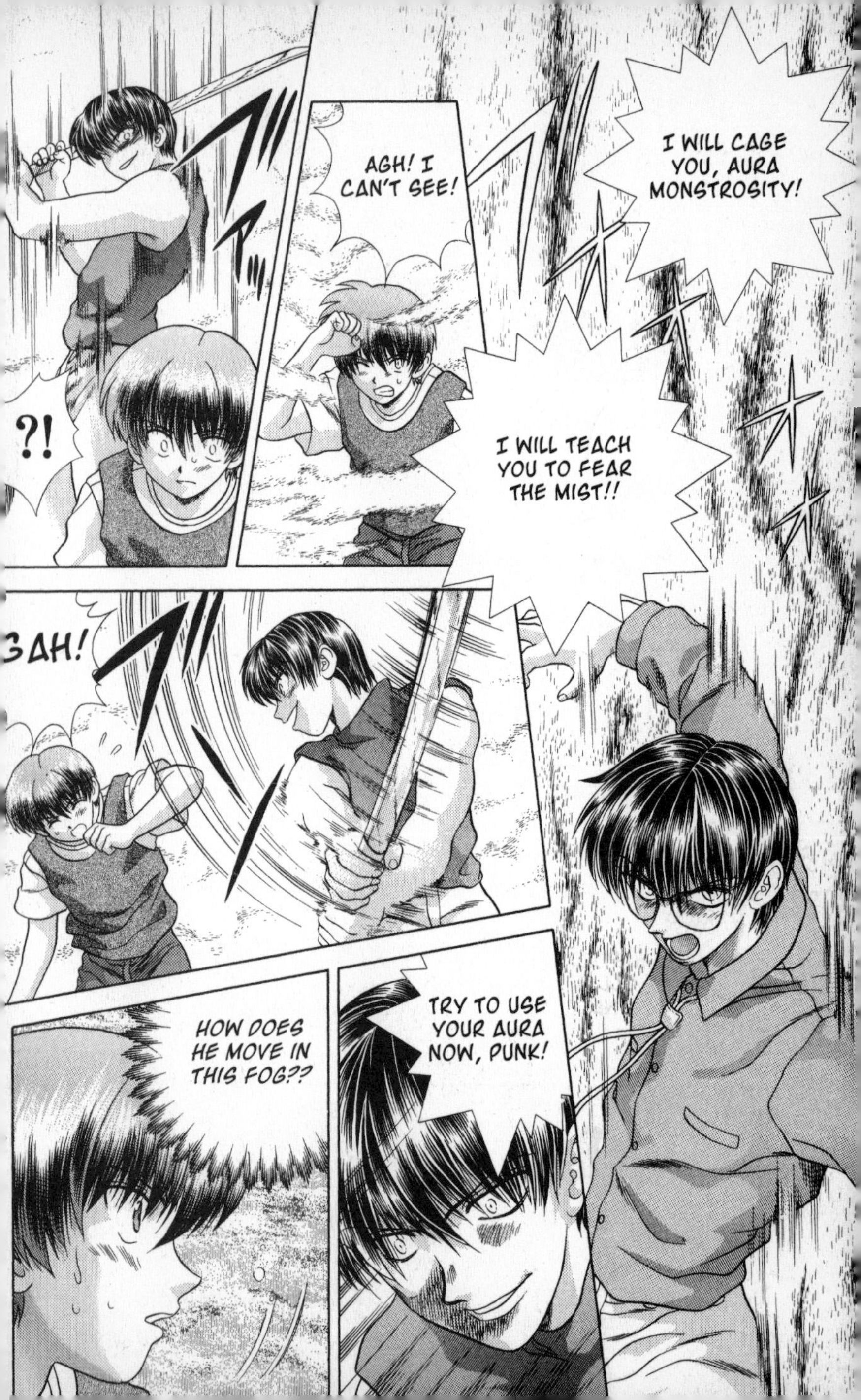
I WILL CAGE YOU, AURA MONSTROSITY!
I WILL TEACH YOU TO FEAR THE MIST!!
AGH! I CAN'T SEE!
?!
GAH!
TRY TO USE YOUR AURA NOW, PUNK!
HOW DOES HE MOVE IN THIS FOG??

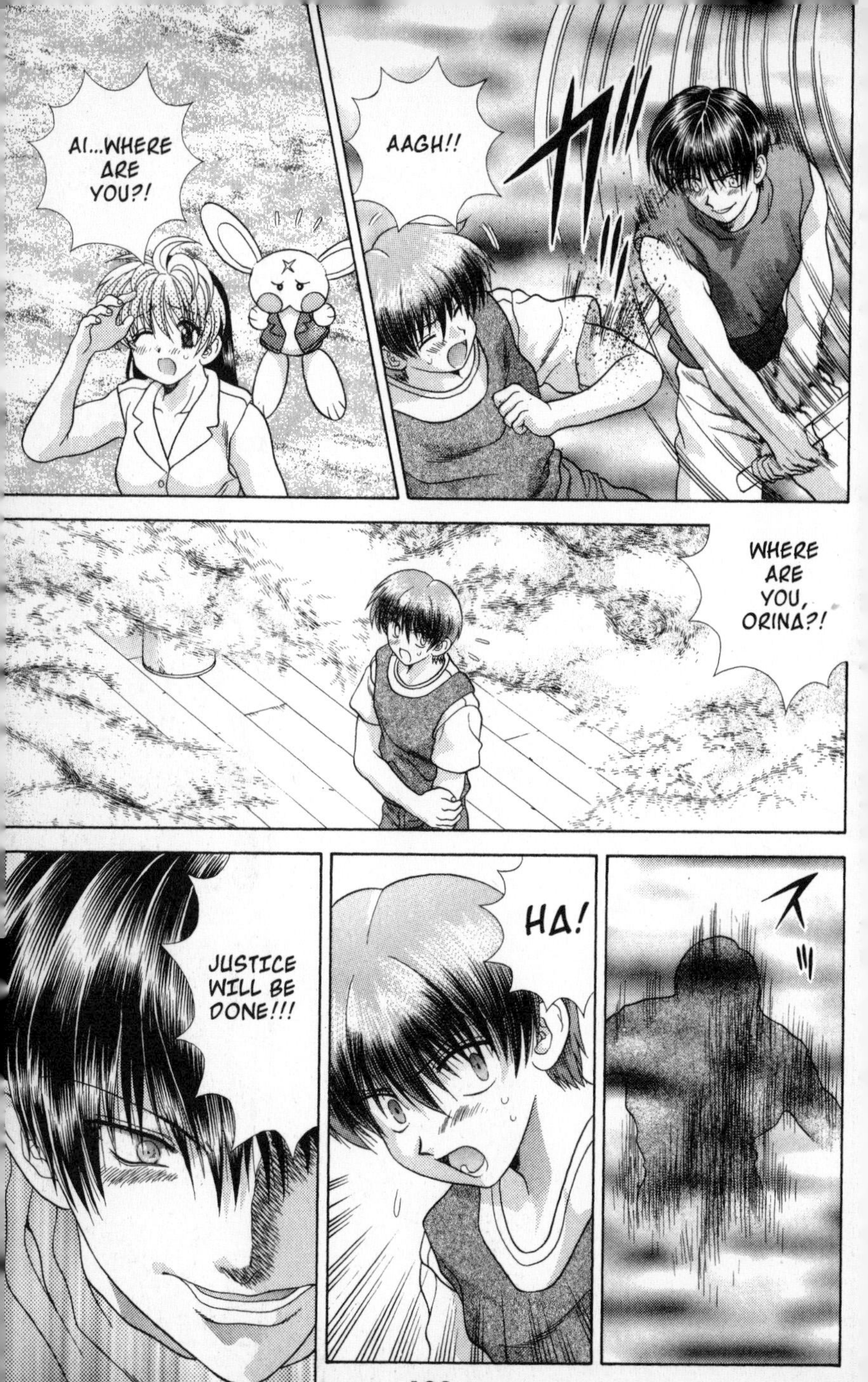

ガッ
AAGH!!
AI...WHERE ARE YOU?!
WHERE ARE YOU, ORINA?!
スッ
HA!
JUSTICE WILL BE DONE!!!

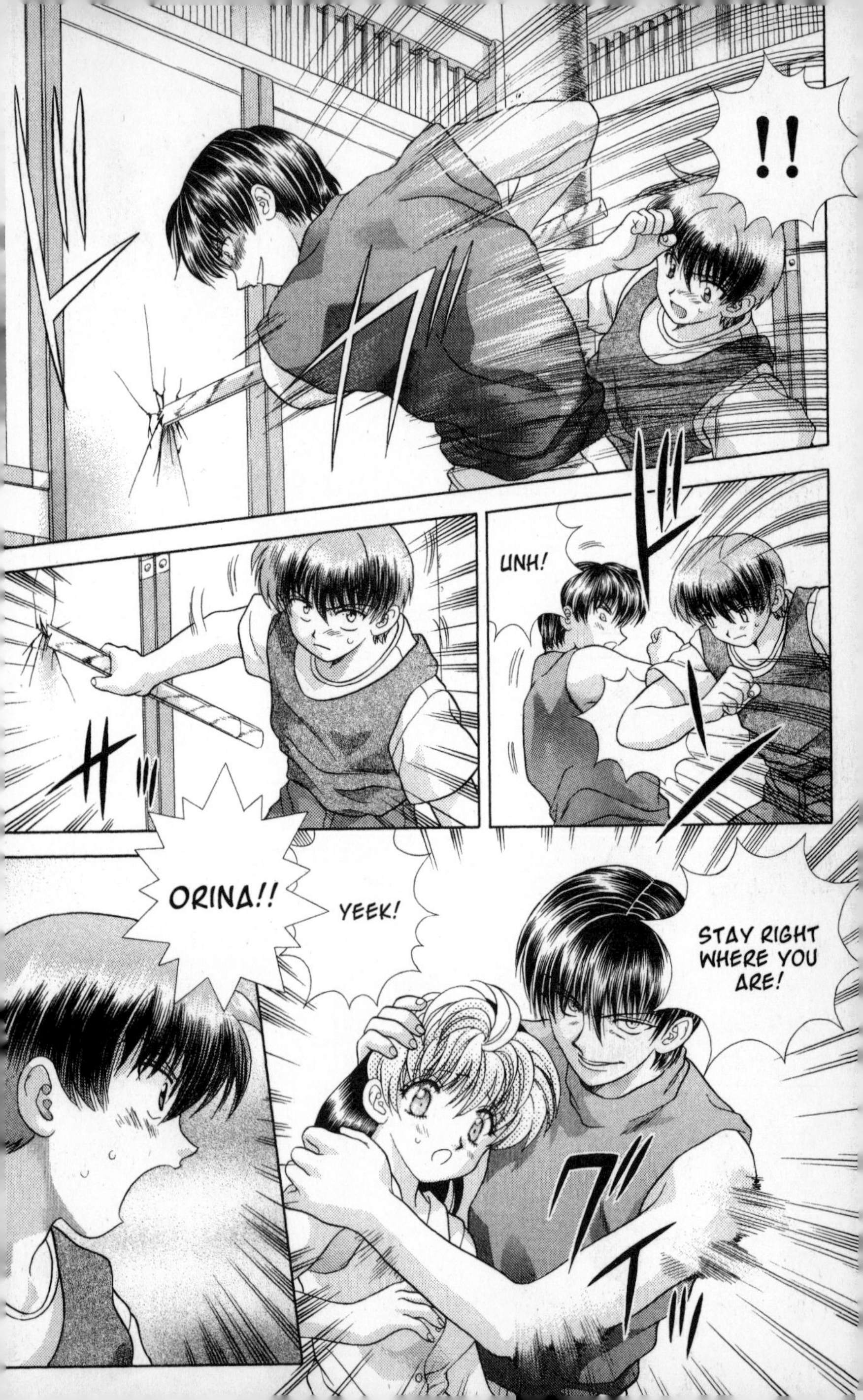
!!
UNH!
STAY RIGHT WHERE YOU ARE!
YEEK!
ORINA!!

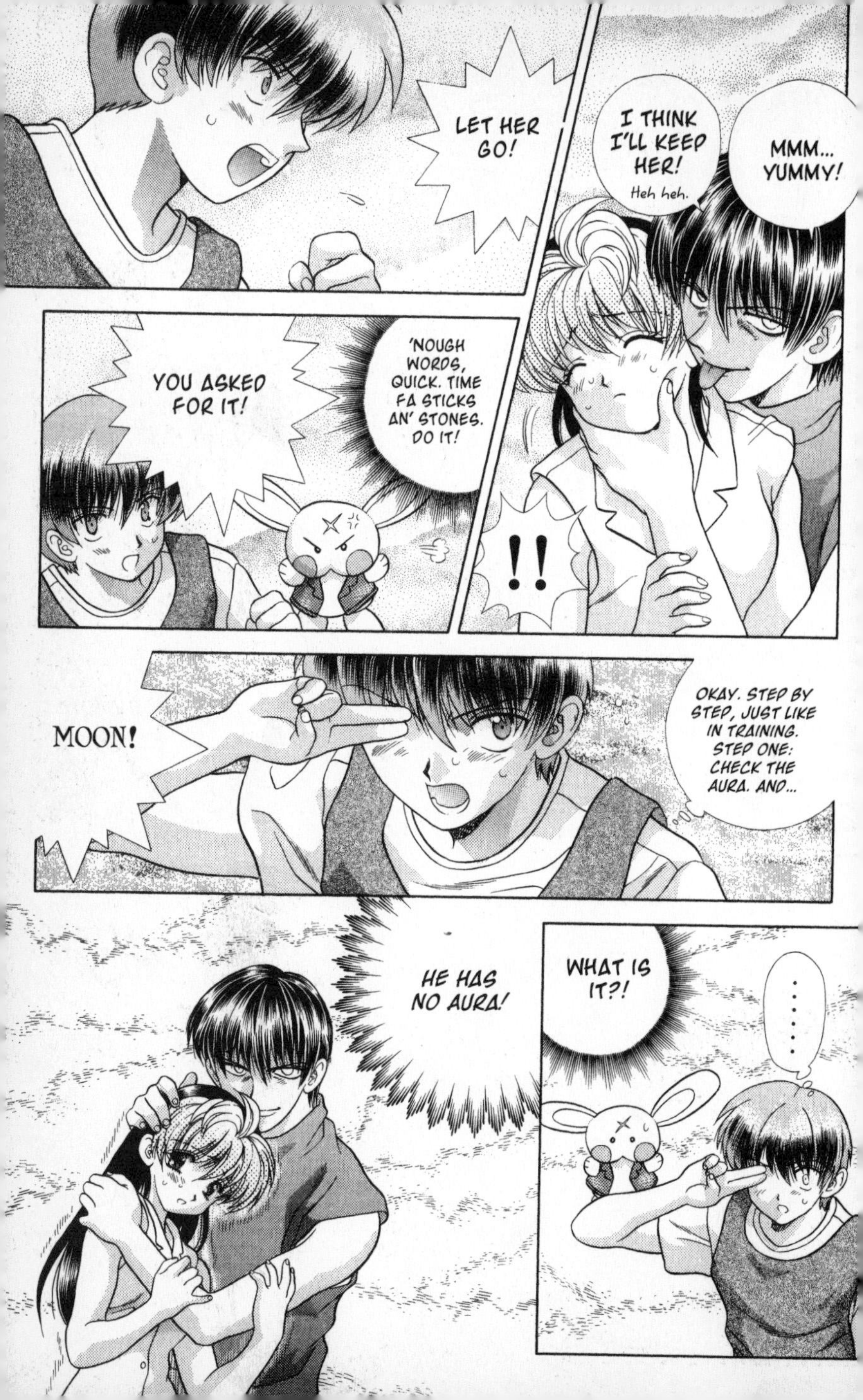
MMM... YUMMY!
I THINK I'LL KEEP HER!
Heh heh.
LET HER GO!
!!
'NOUGH WORDS, QUICK. TIME FA STICKS AN' STONES. DO IT!
YOU ASKED FOR IT!
OKAY. STEP BY STEP, JUST LIKE IN TRAINING. STEP ONE: CHECK THE AURA. AND...
MOON!
....
WHAT IS IT?!
HE HAS NO AURA!

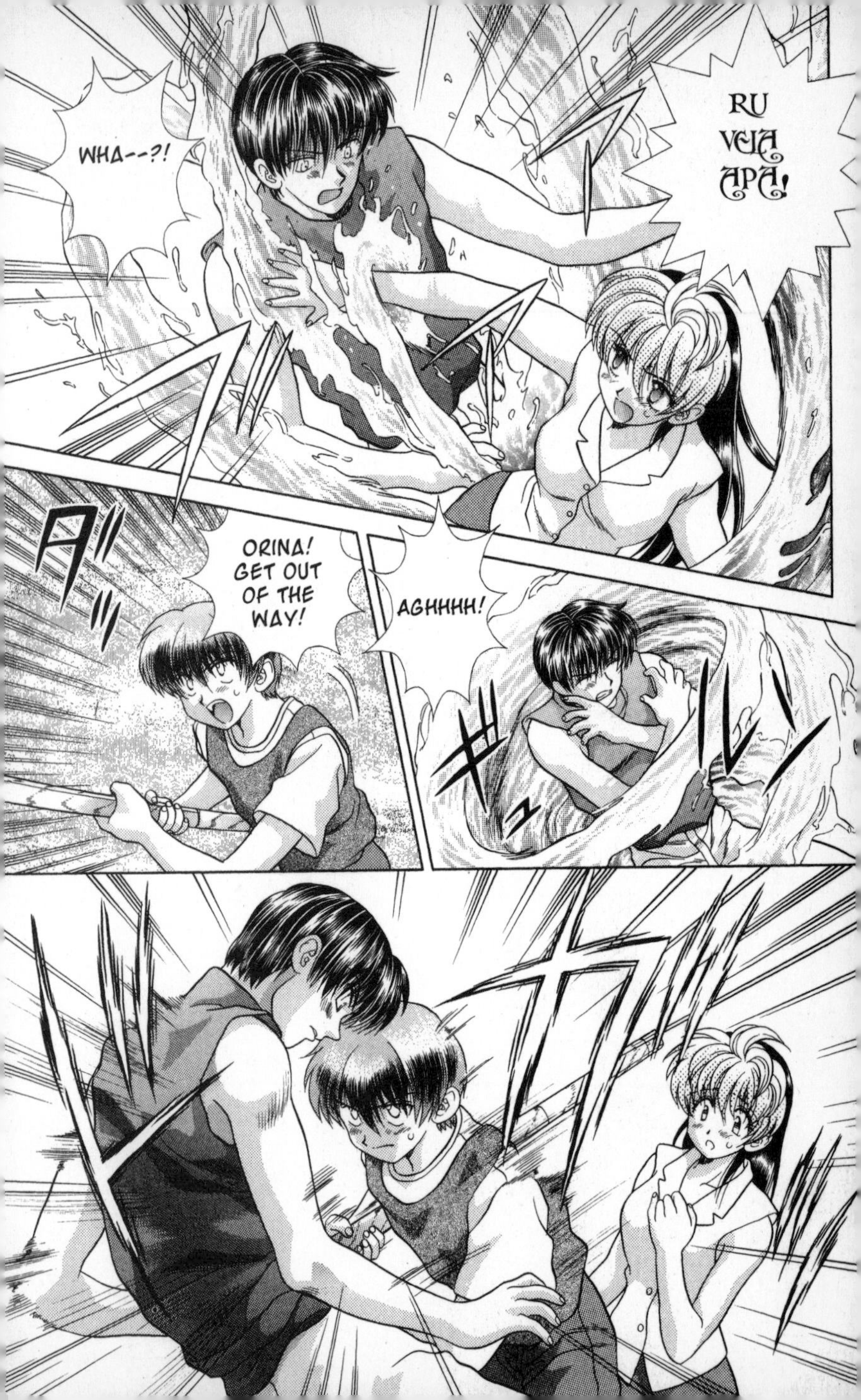
RU VEIA APA!
WHA--?!
AGHHHH!
ORINA! GET OUT OF THE WAY!

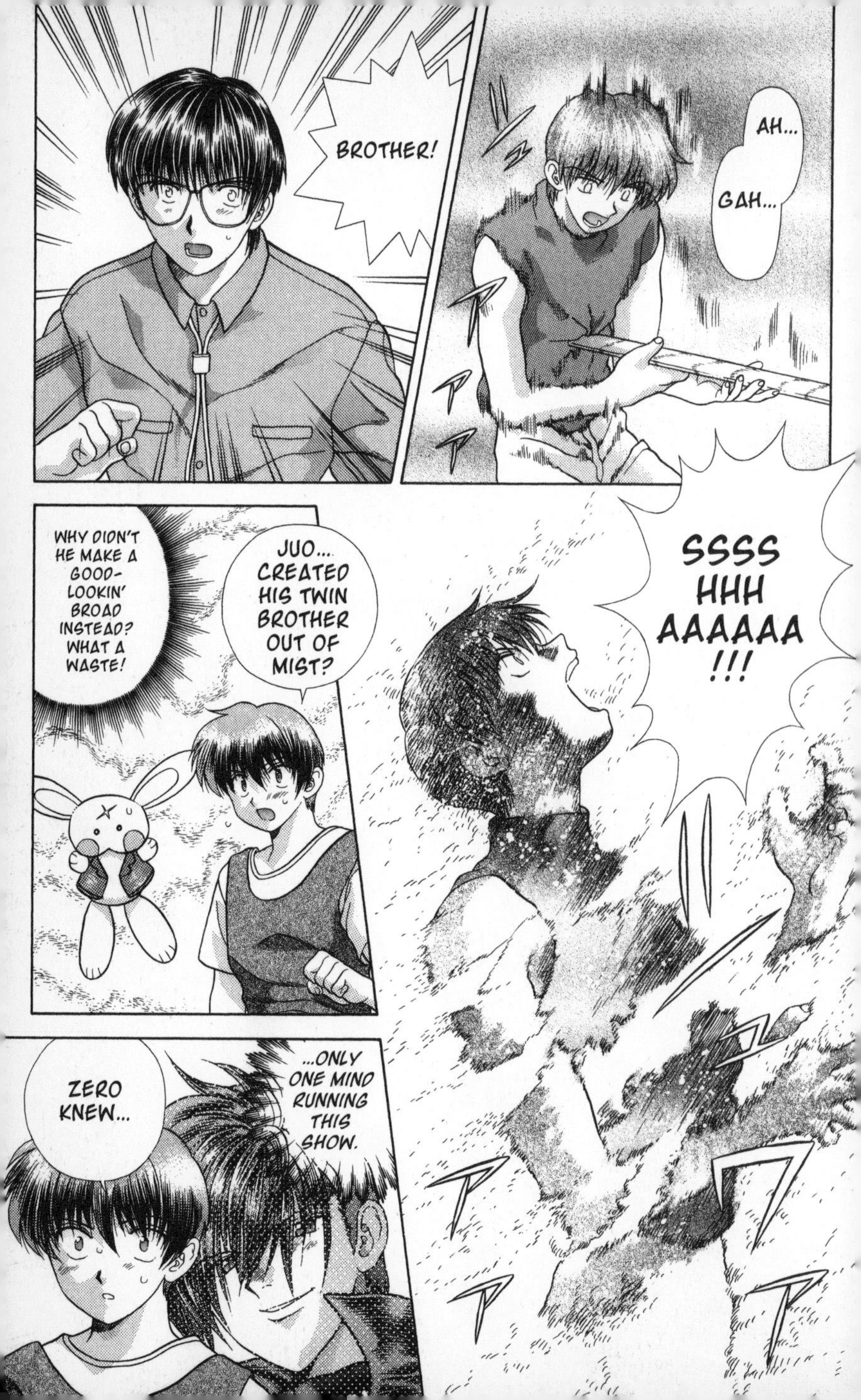
AH...
GAH...
BROTHER!
SSSS HHH AAAAAA !!!
JUO... CREATED HIS TWIN BROTHER OUT OF MIST?
WHY DIDN'T HE MAKE A GOOD-LOOKIN' BROAD INSTEAD? WHAT A WASTE!
ZERO KNEW...
...ONLY ONE MIND RUNNING THIS SHOW.

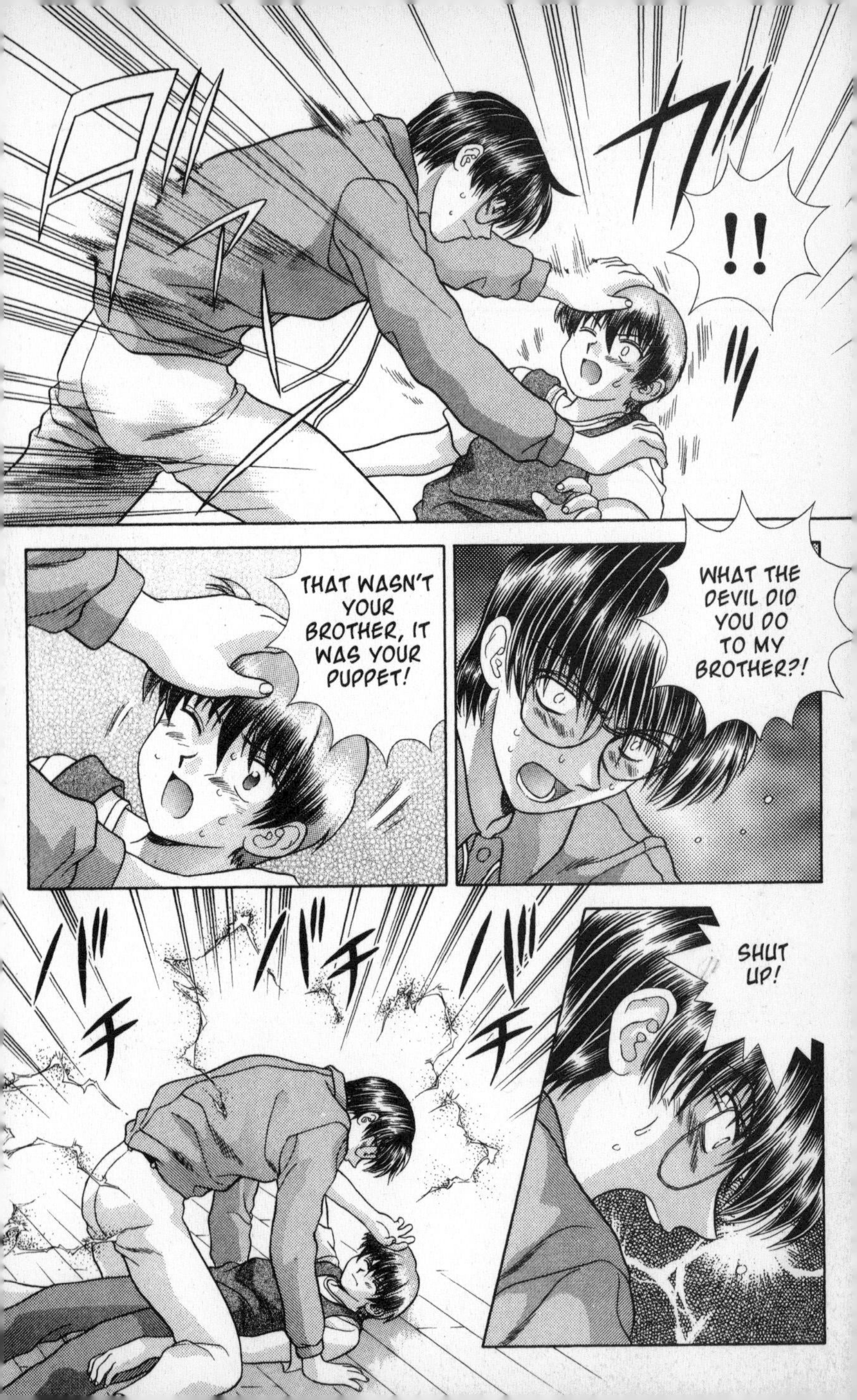
ガッ
!!
ダッ
WHAT THE DEVIL DID YOU DO TO MY BROTHER?!
THAT WASN'T YOUR BROTHER, IT WAS YOUR PUPPET!
SHUT UP!
バチ
バチ
バチ

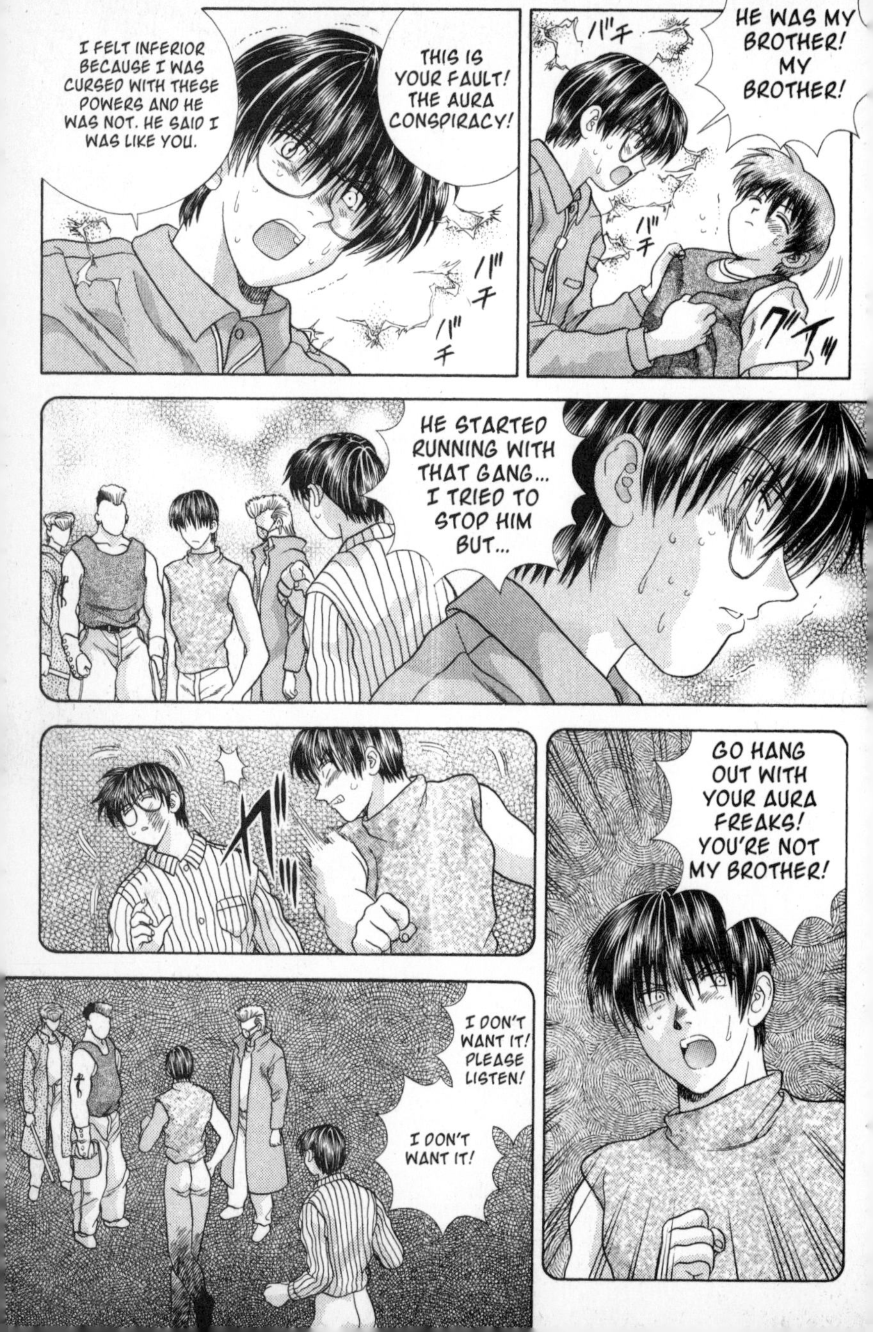
HE WAS MY BROTHER! MY BROTHER!
バチ
バチ
グイッ
THIS IS YOUR FAULT! THE AURA CONSPIRACY!
I FELT INFERIOR BECAUSE I WAS CURSED WITH THESE POWERS AND HE WAS NOT. HE SAID I WAS LIKE YOU.
バチ
バチ
HE STARTED RUNNING WITH THAT GANG... I TRIED TO STOP HIM BUT...
GO HANG OUT WITH YOUR AURA FREAKS! YOU'RE NOT MY BROTHER!
I DON'T WANT IT! PLEASE LISTEN!
I DON'T WANT IT!

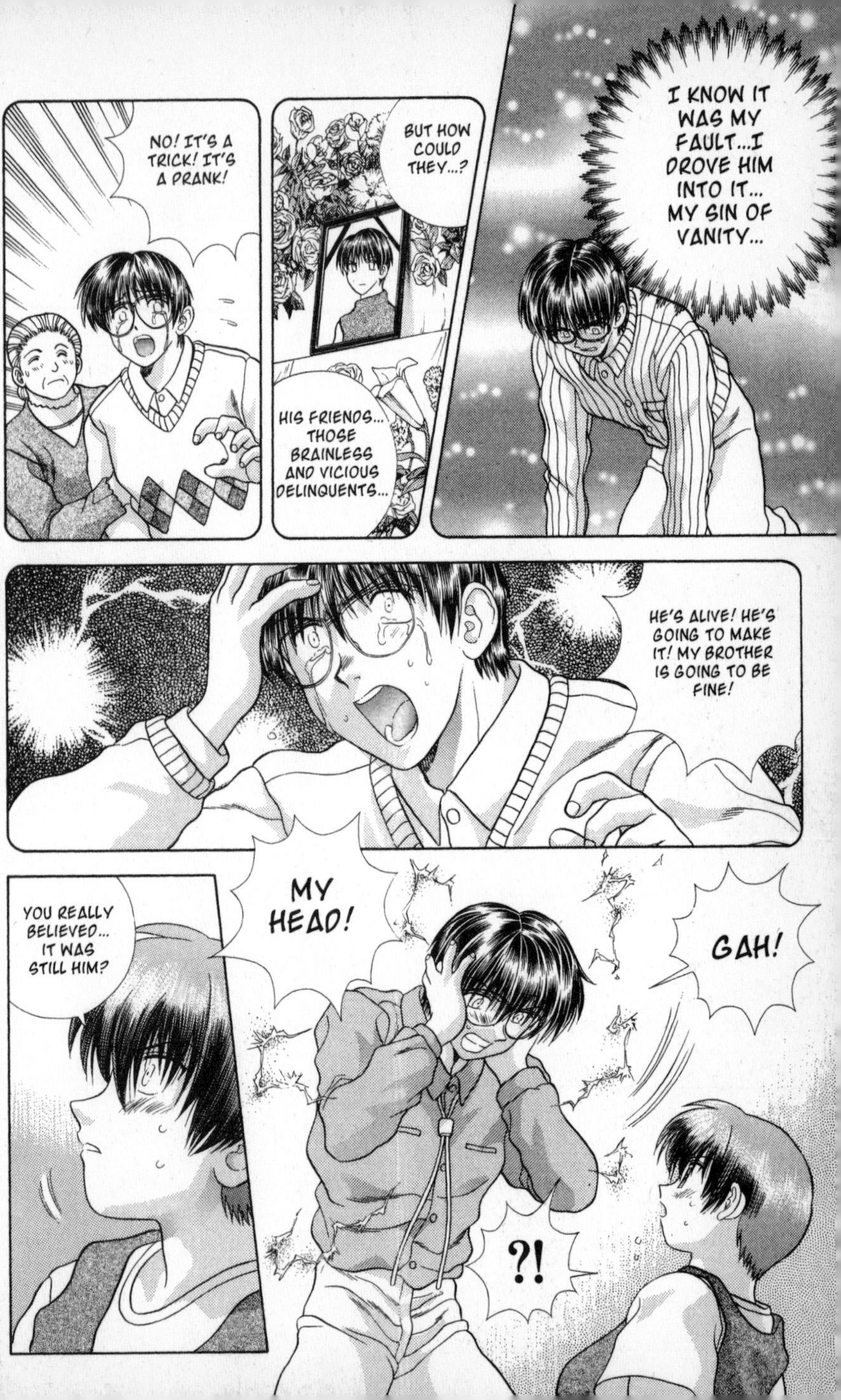
I KNOW IT WAS MY FAULT...I DROVE HIM INTO IT... MY SIN OF VANITY...
BUT HOW COULD THEY...?
HIS FRIENDS... THOSE BRAINLESS AND VICIOUS DELINQUENTS...
NO! IT'S A TRICK! IT'S A PRANK!
HE'S ALIVE! HE'S GOING TO MAKE IT! MY BROTHER IS GOING TO BE FINE!
GAH!
MY HEAD!
?!
YOU REALLY BELIEVED... IT WAS STILL HIM?

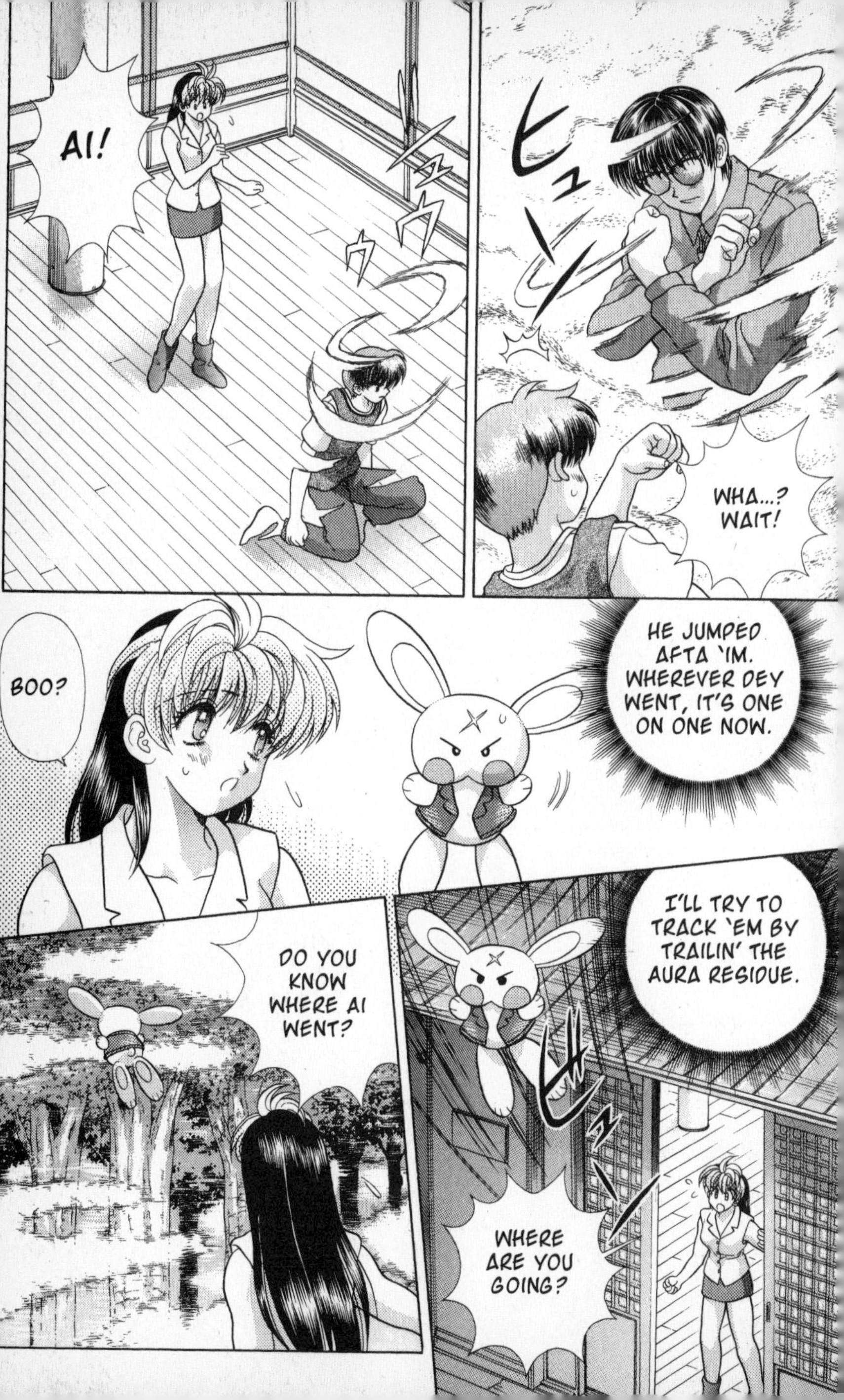
WHA...? WAIT!
AI!
HE JUMPED AFTA 'IM. WHEREVER DEY WENT, IT'S ONE ON ONE NOW.
BOO?
I'LL TRY TO TRACK 'EM BY TRAILIN' THE AURA RESIDUE.
WHERE ARE YOU GOING?
DO YOU KNOW WHERE AI WENT?

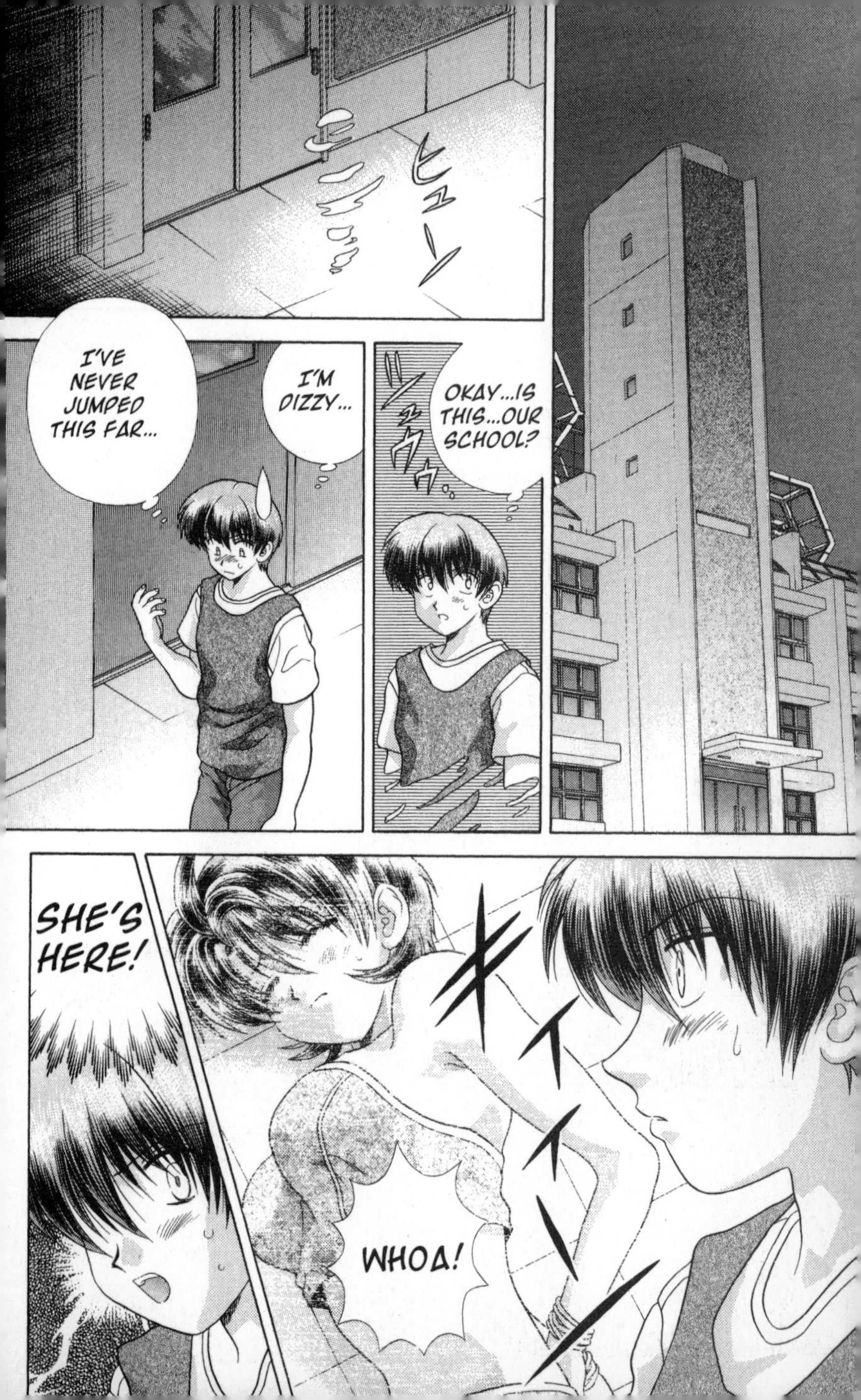

ヒューン
OKAY...IS THIS...OUR SCHOOL?
I'M DIZZY...
I'VE NEVER JUMPED THIS FAR...
SHE'S HERE!
WHOA!

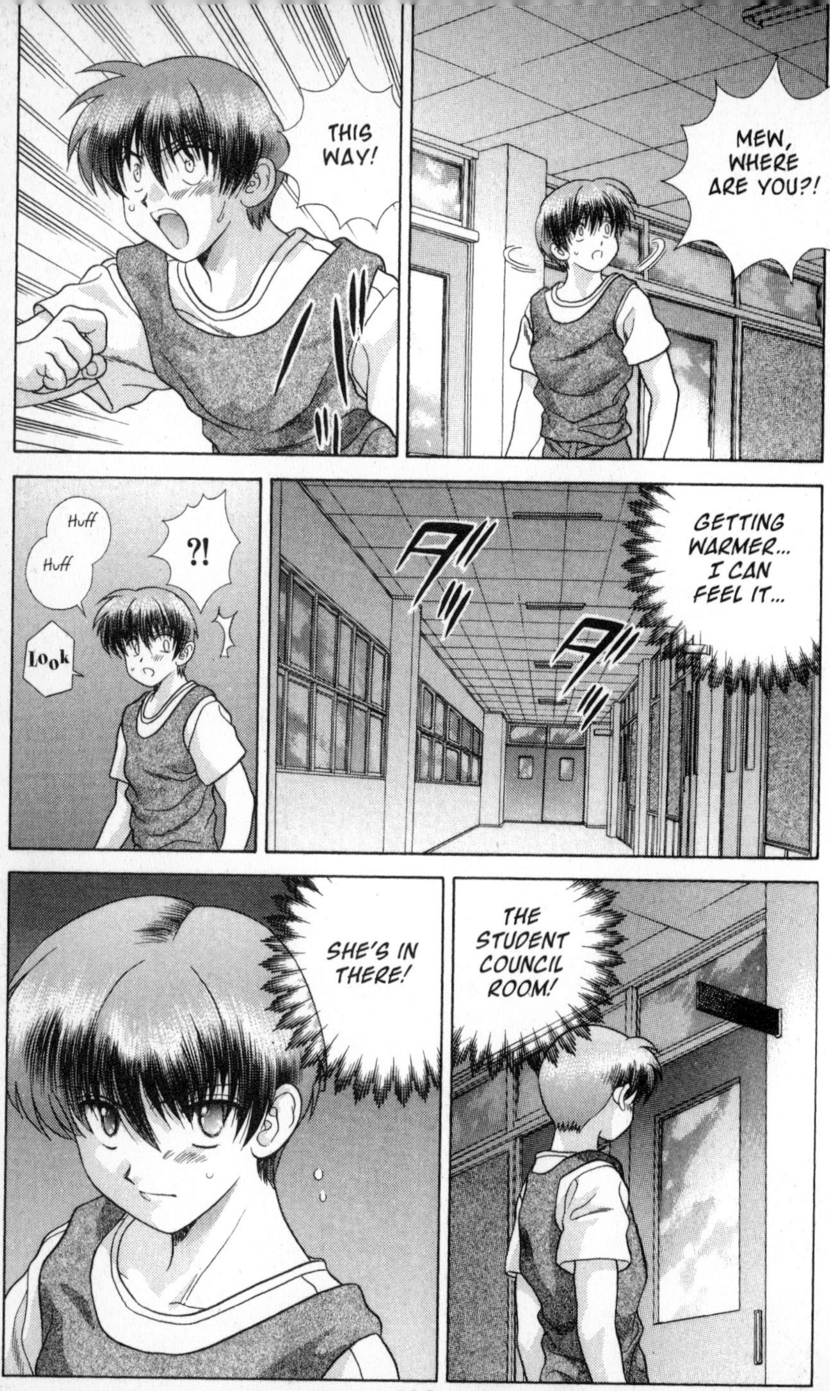
MEW, WHERE ARE YOU?!
THIS WAY!
GETTING WARMER... I CAN FEEL IT...
?!
Huff
Huff
Look
THE STUDENT COUNCIL ROOM!
SHE'S IN THERE!

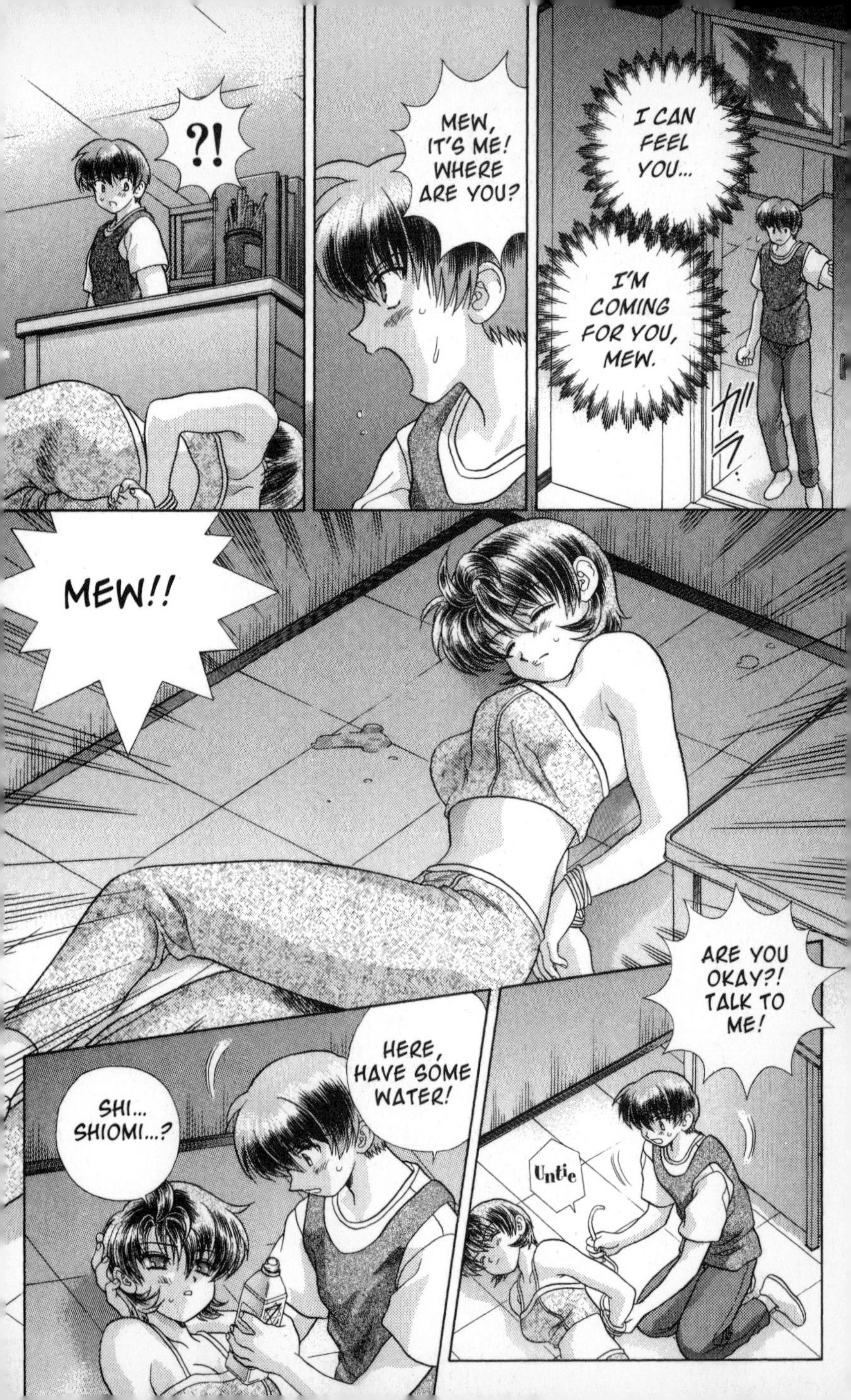
I CAN FEEL YOU...
I'M COMING FOR YOU, MEW.
ガラ
MEW, IT'S ME! WHERE ARE YOU?
?!
MEW!!
ARE YOU OKAY?! TALK TO ME!
Untie
HERE, HAVE SOME WATER!
SHI... SHIOMI...?

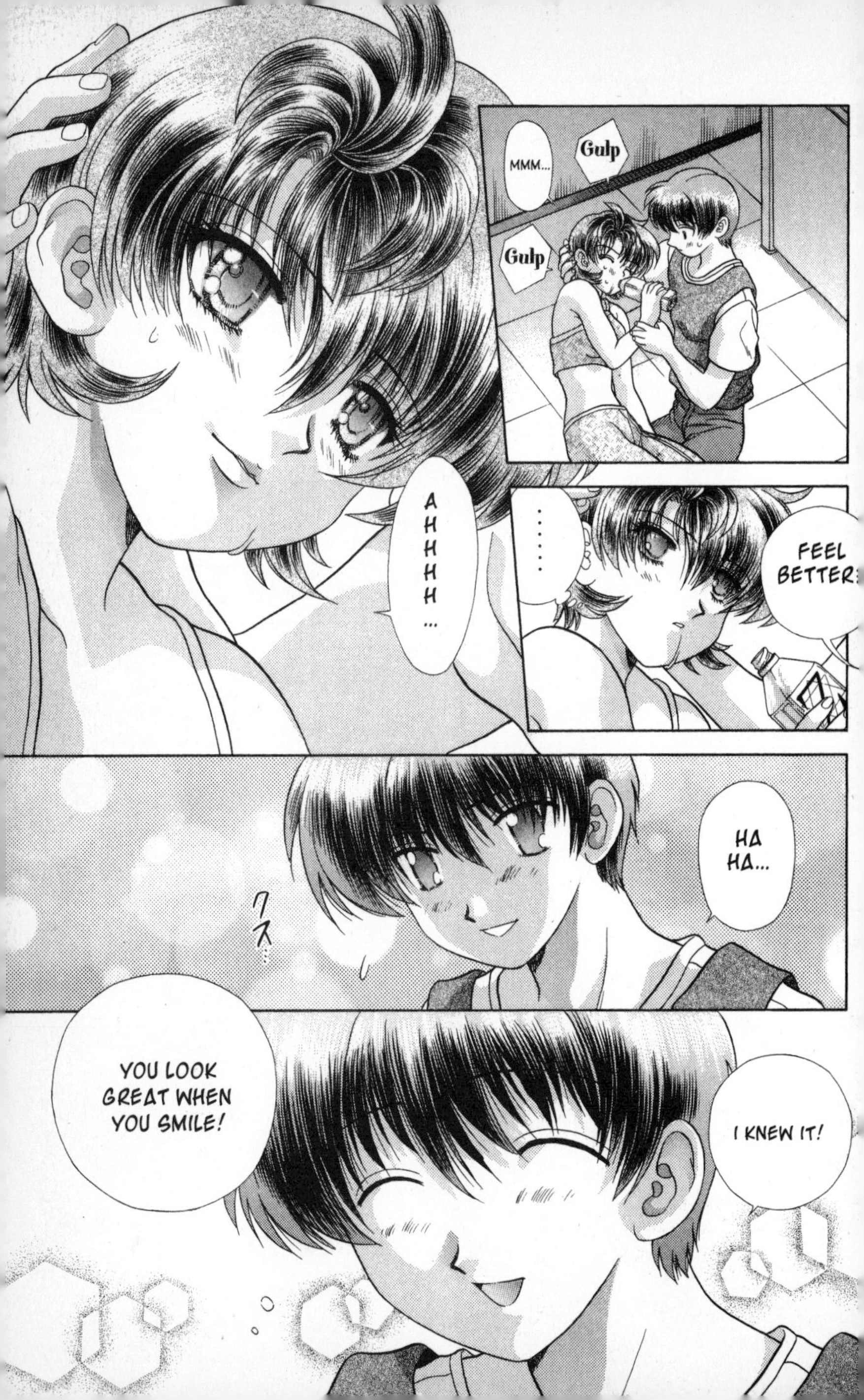
Gulp
MMM...
Gulp
FEEL BETTER
......
AHHHHH...
HA HA...
クス...
I KNEW IT!
YOU LOOK GREAT WHEN YOU SMILE!

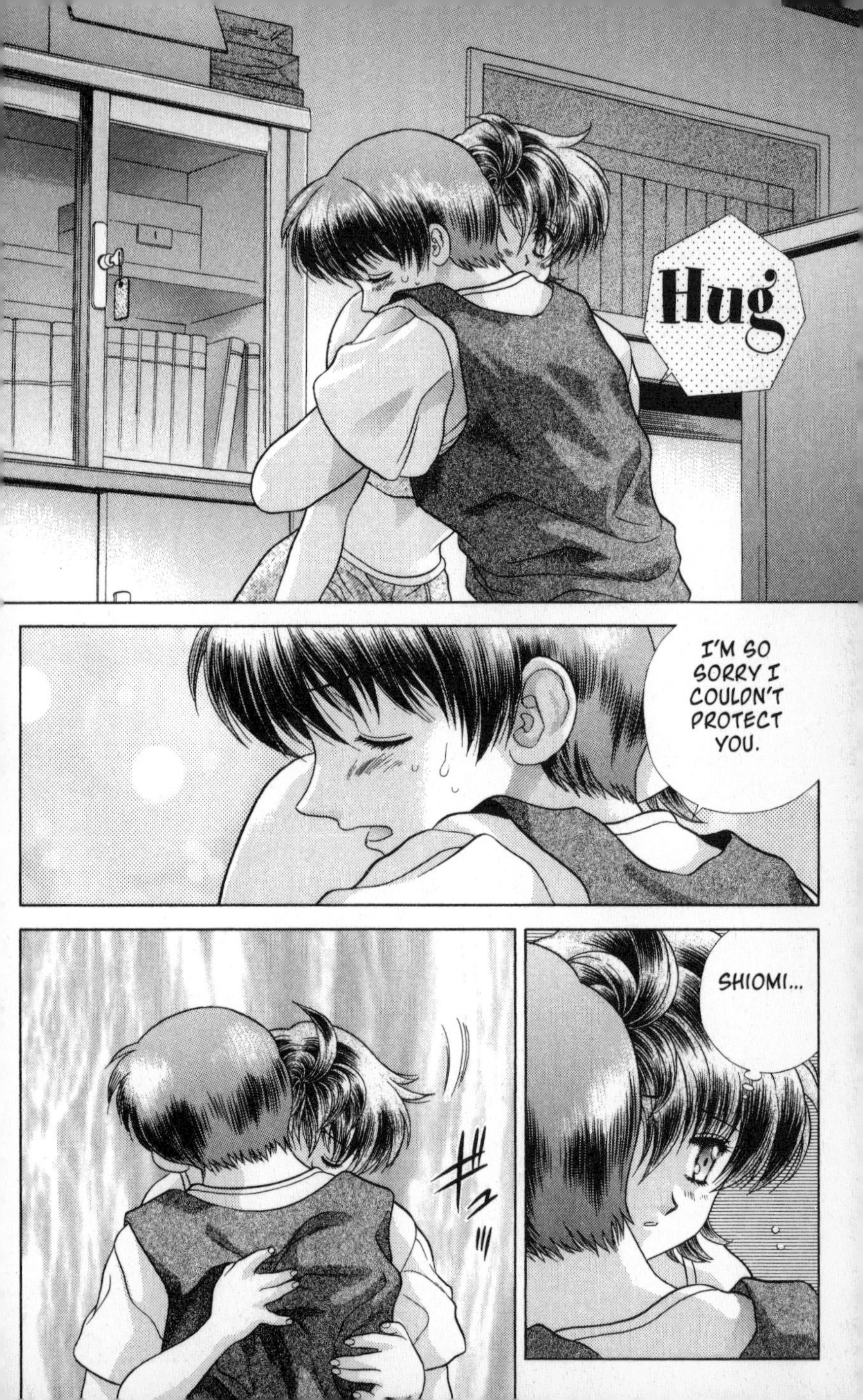
Hug
I'M SO SORRY I COULDN'T PROTECT YOU.
SHIOMI...

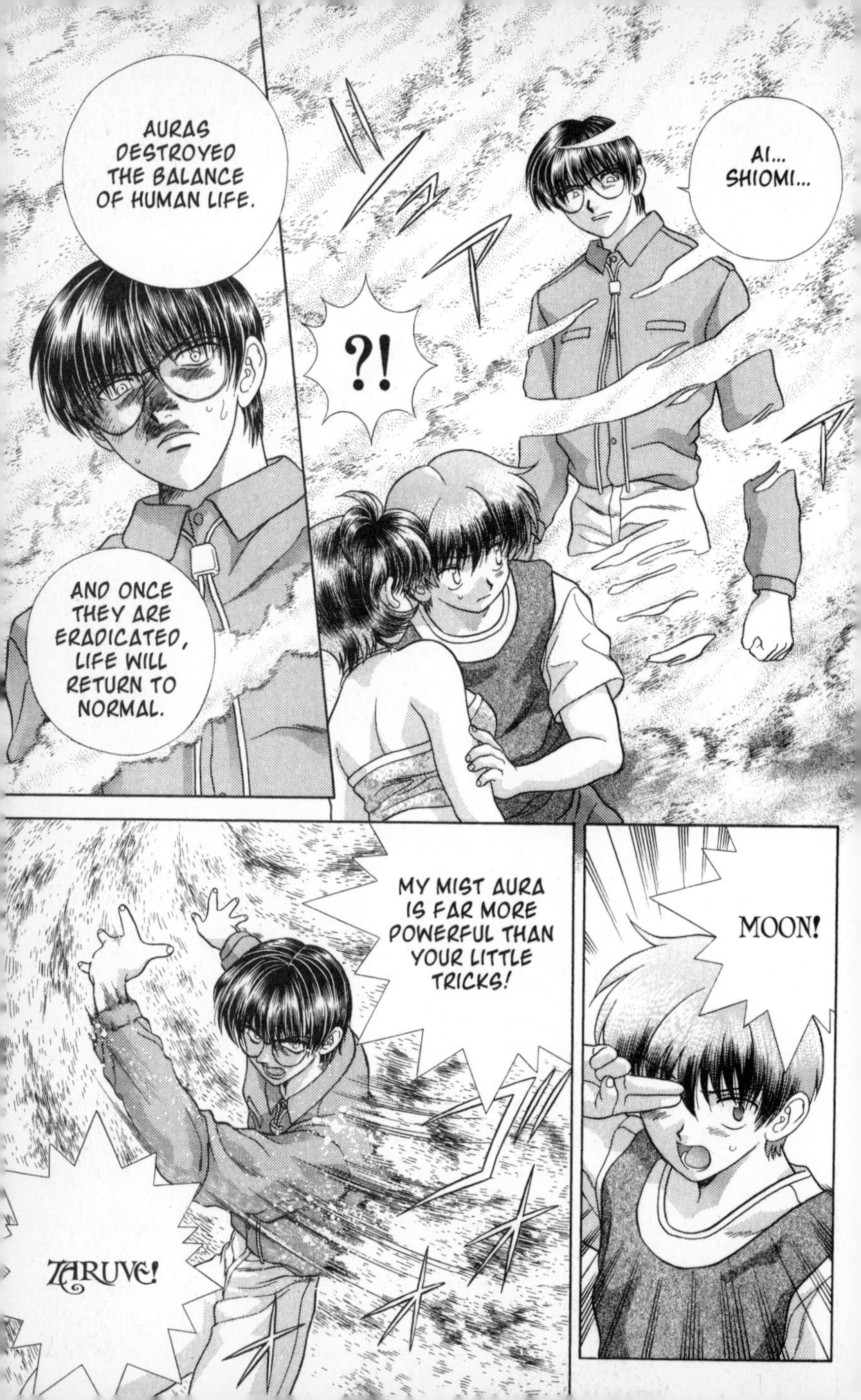
AI... SHIOMI...
?!
AURAS DESTROYED THE BALANCE OF HUMAN LIFE.
AND ONCE THEY ARE ERADICATED, LIFE WILL RETURN TO NORMAL.
MOON!
MY MIST AURA IS FAR MORE POWERFUL THAN YOUR LITTLE TRICKS!
TARUVE!

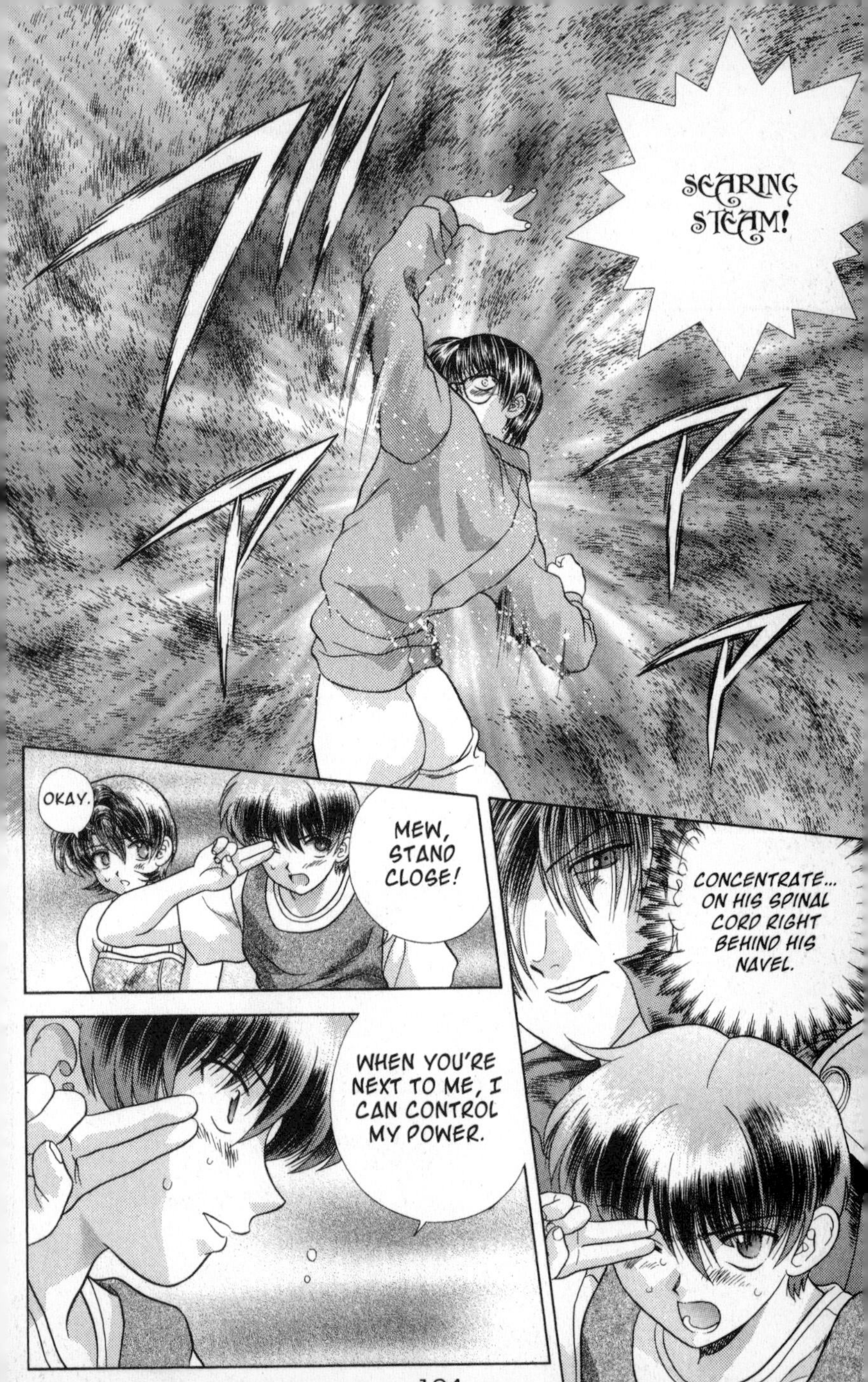
SEARING STEAM!
CONCENTRATE... ON HIS SPINAL CORD RIGHT BEHIND HIS NAVEL.
MEW, STAND CLOSE!
OKAY.
WHEN YOU'RE NEXT TO ME, I CAN CONTROL MY POWER.

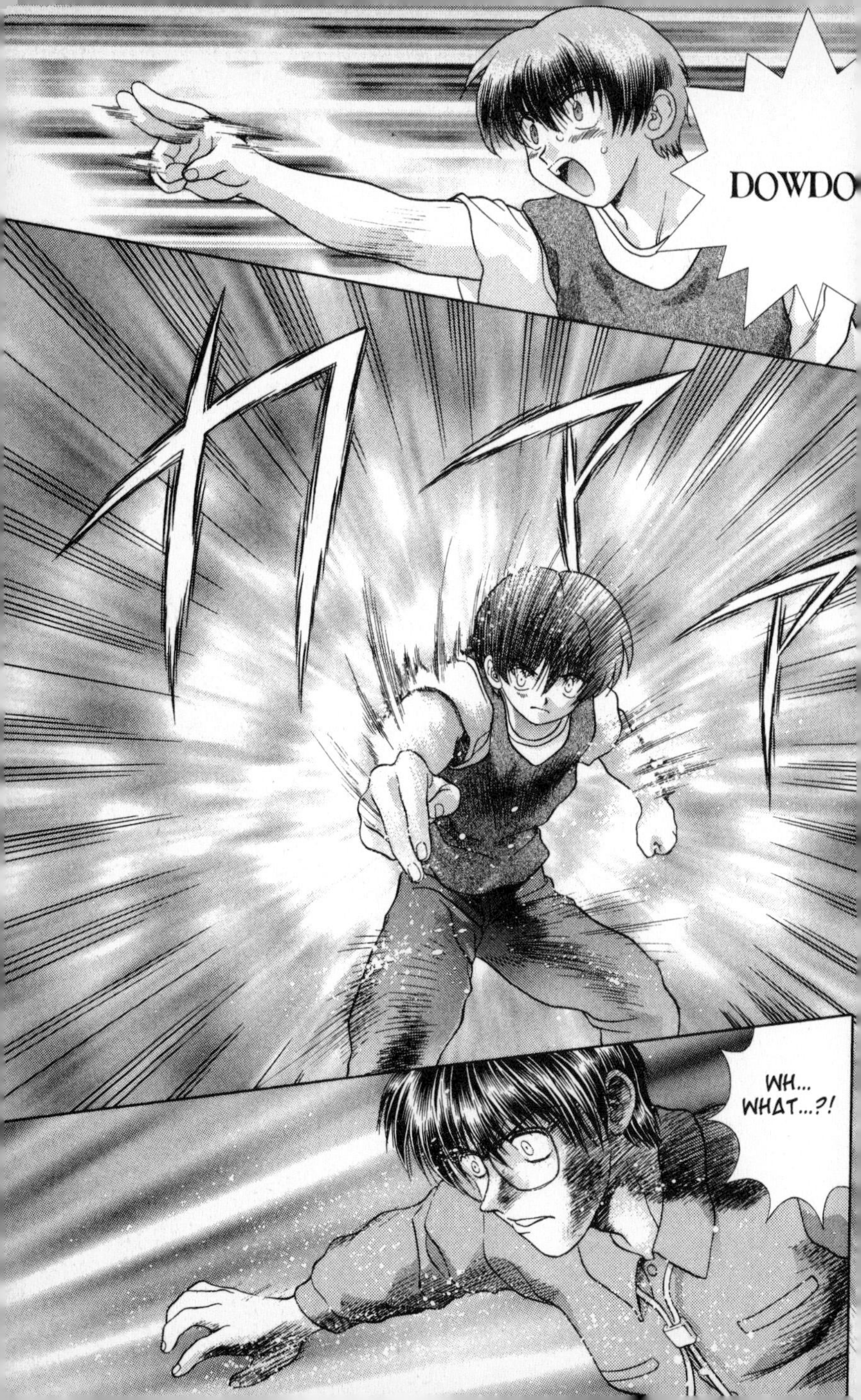
DOWDO
WH... WHAT...?!

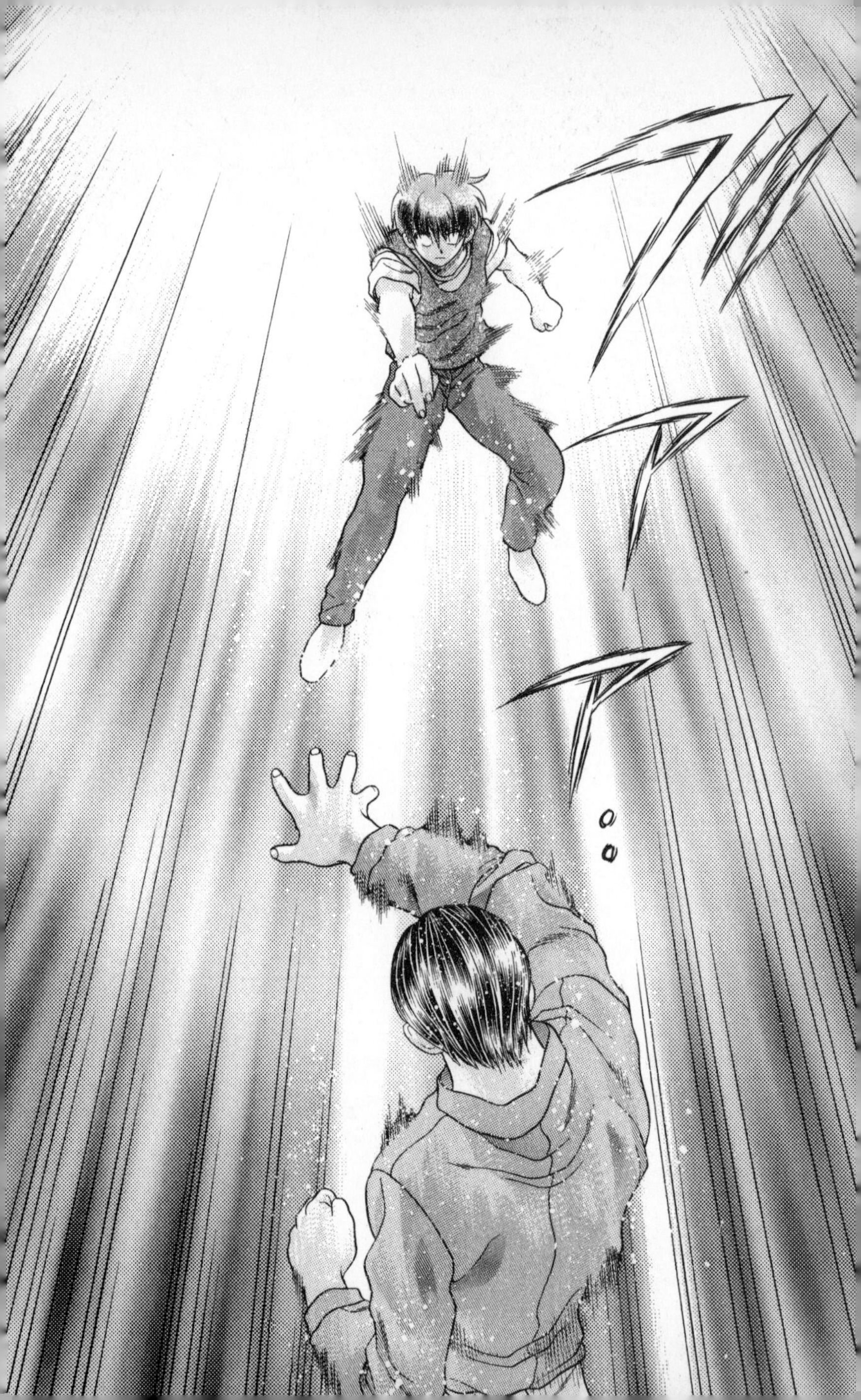

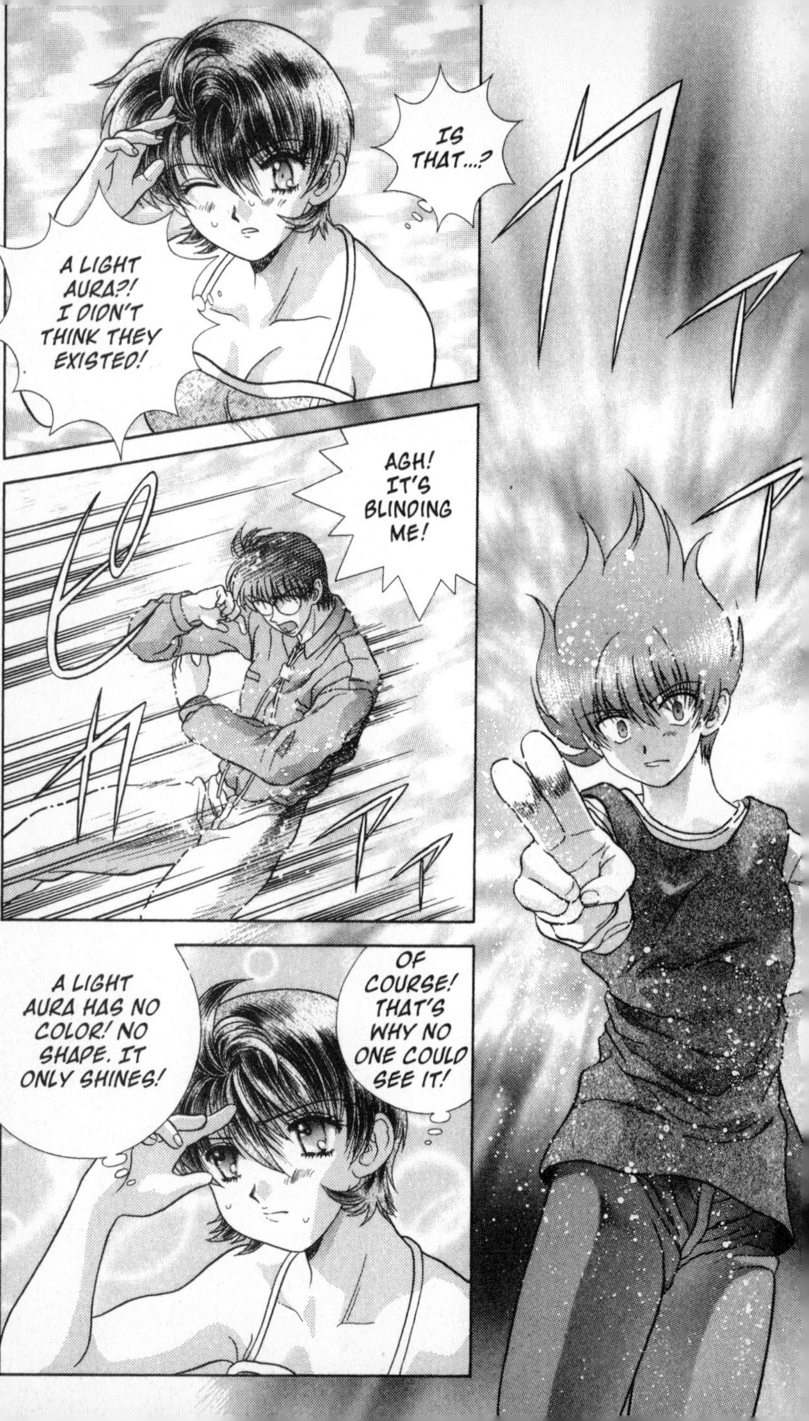
IS THAT...?
A LIGHT AURA?! I DIDN'T THINK THEY EXISTED!
AGH! IT'S BLINDING ME!
OF COURSE! THAT'S WHY NO ONE COULD SEE IT!
A LIGHT AURA HAS NO COLOR! NO SHAPE. IT ONLY SHINES!

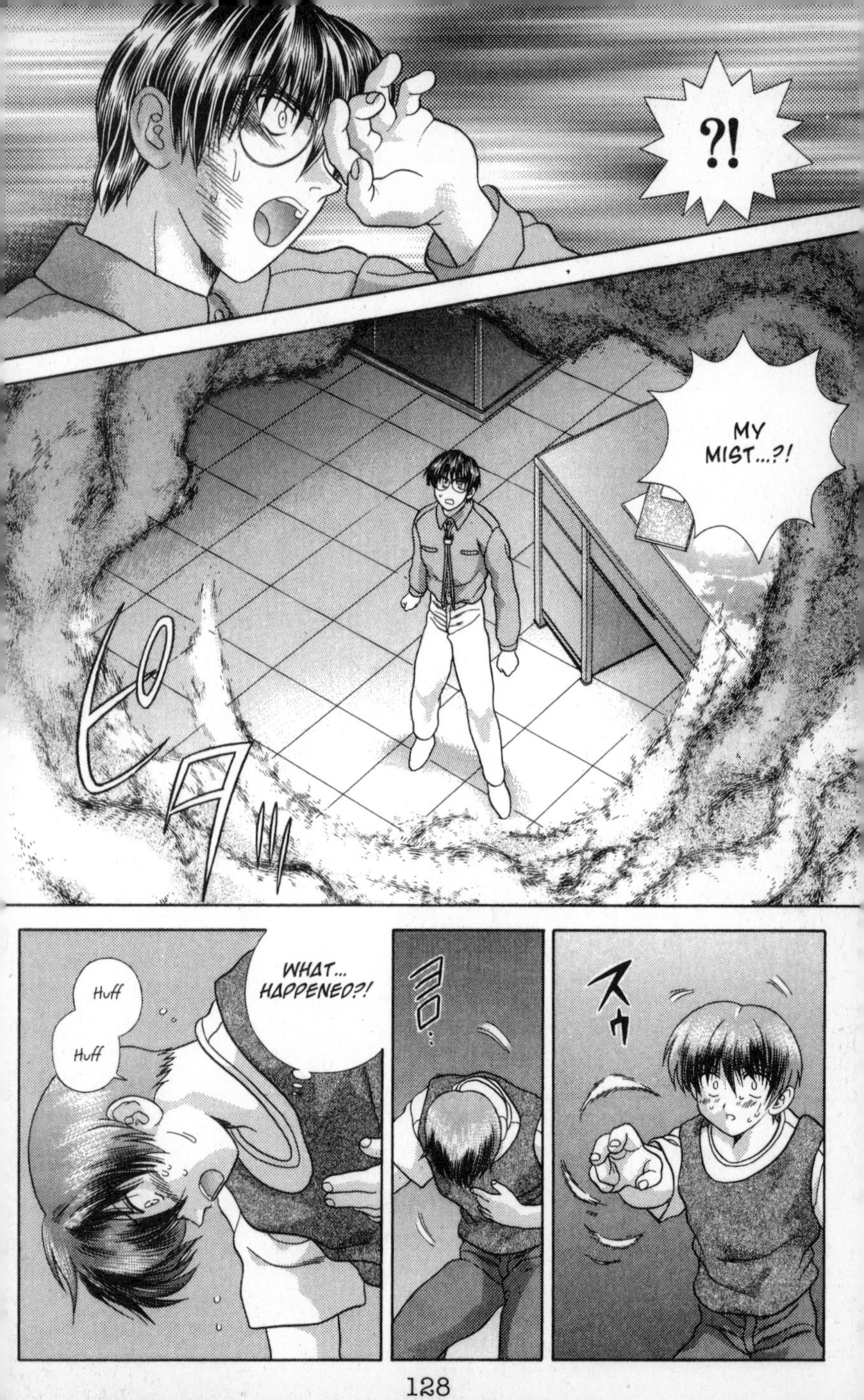
?!
MY MIST...?!
ピタ
スゥ
ヨロ…
WHAT... HAPPENED?!
Huff
Huff

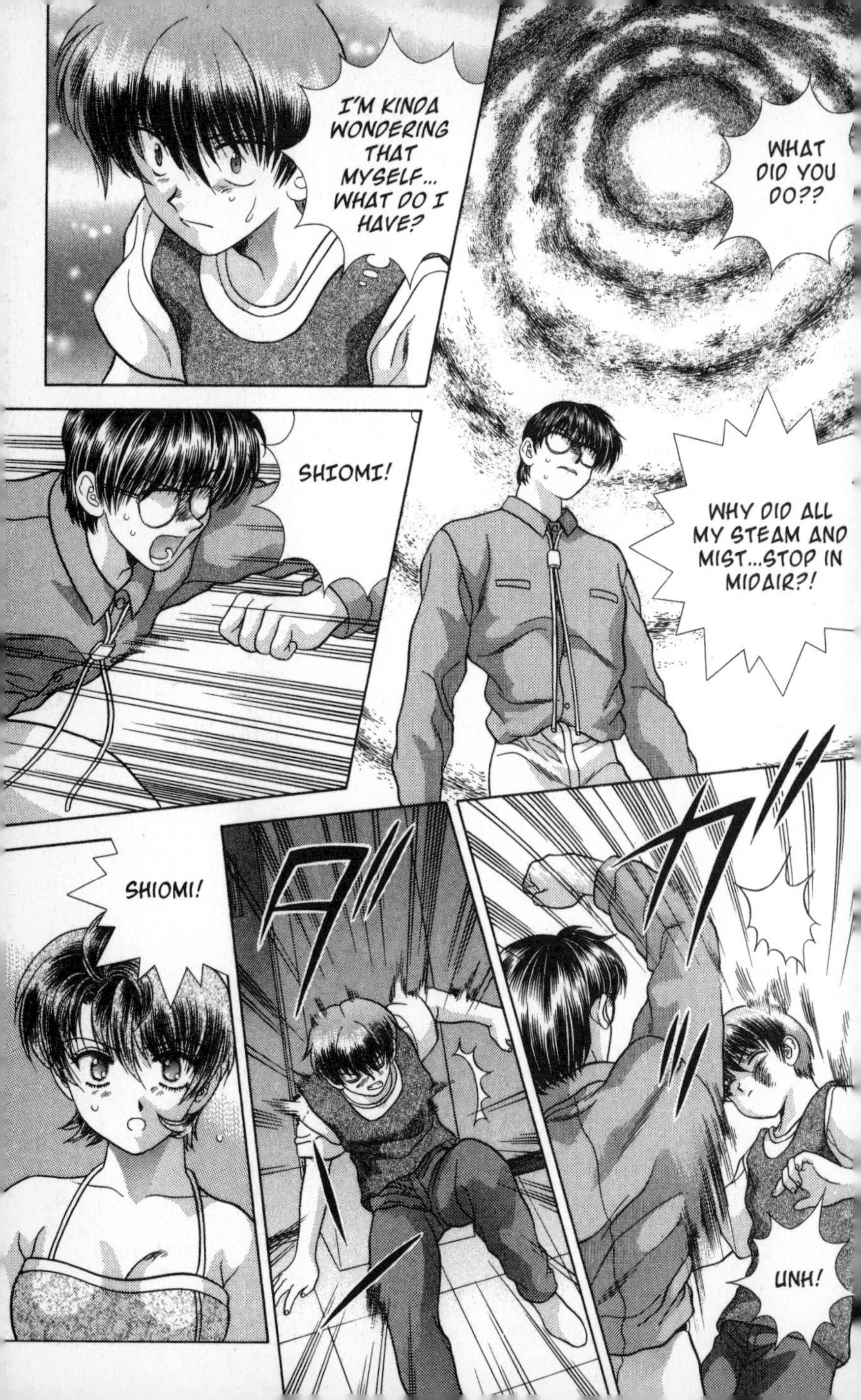
WHAT DID YOU DO??
I'M KINDA WONDERING THAT MYSELF... WHAT DO I HAVE?
WHY DID ALL MY STEAM AND MIST...STOP IN MIDAIR?!
SHIOMI!
ガ
UNH!
ダ
SHIOMI!

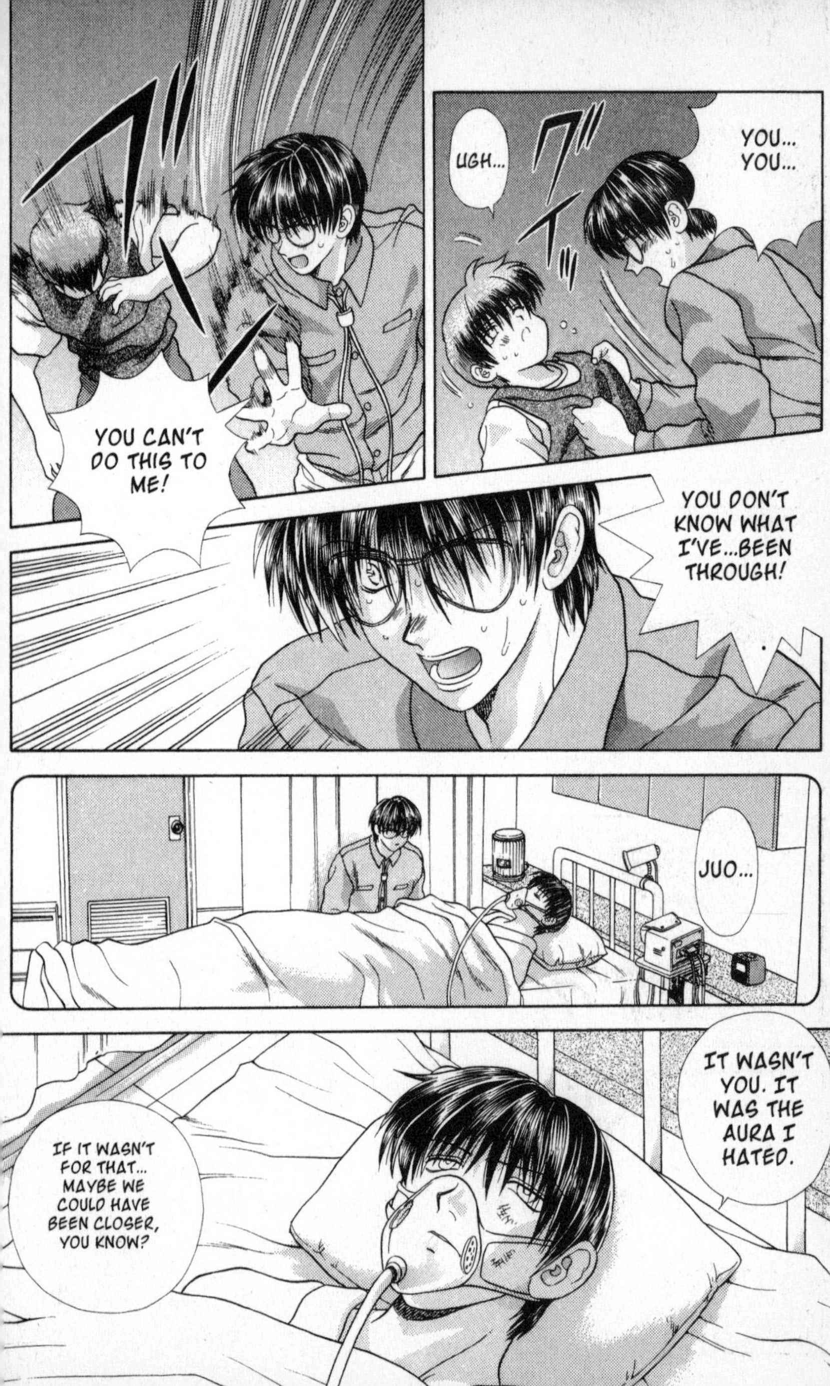
YOU... YOU...
UGH...
YOU CAN'T DO THIS TO ME!
YOU DON'T KNOW WHAT I'VE...BEEN THROUGH!
JUO...
IT WASN'T YOU. IT WAS THE AURA I HATED.
IF IT WASN'T FOR THAT... MAYBE WE COULD HAVE BEEN CLOSER, YOU KNOW?

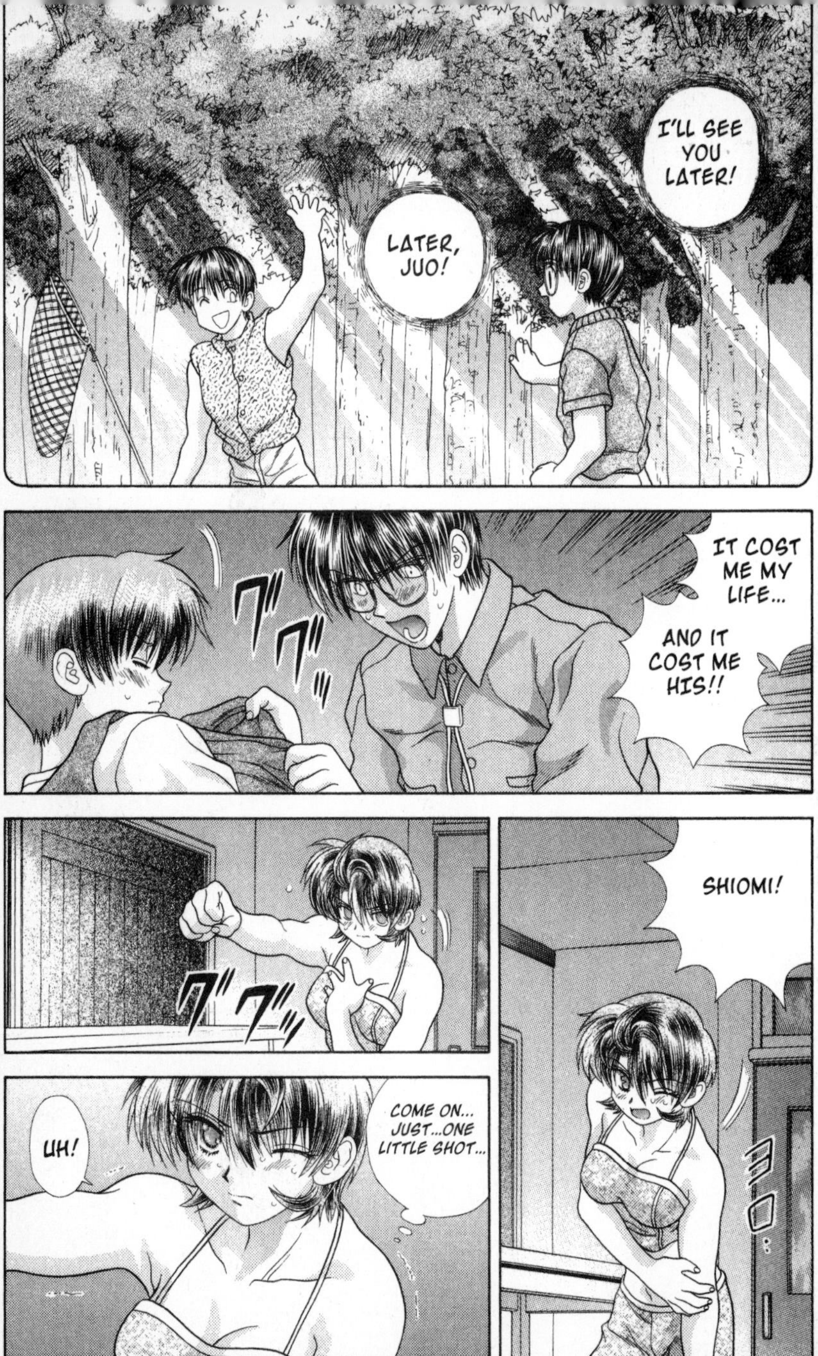
I'LL SEE YOU LATER!
LATER, JUO!
IT COST ME MY LIFE...
AND IT COST ME HIS!!
SHIOMI!
COME ON... JUST...ONE LITTLE SHOT...
UH!

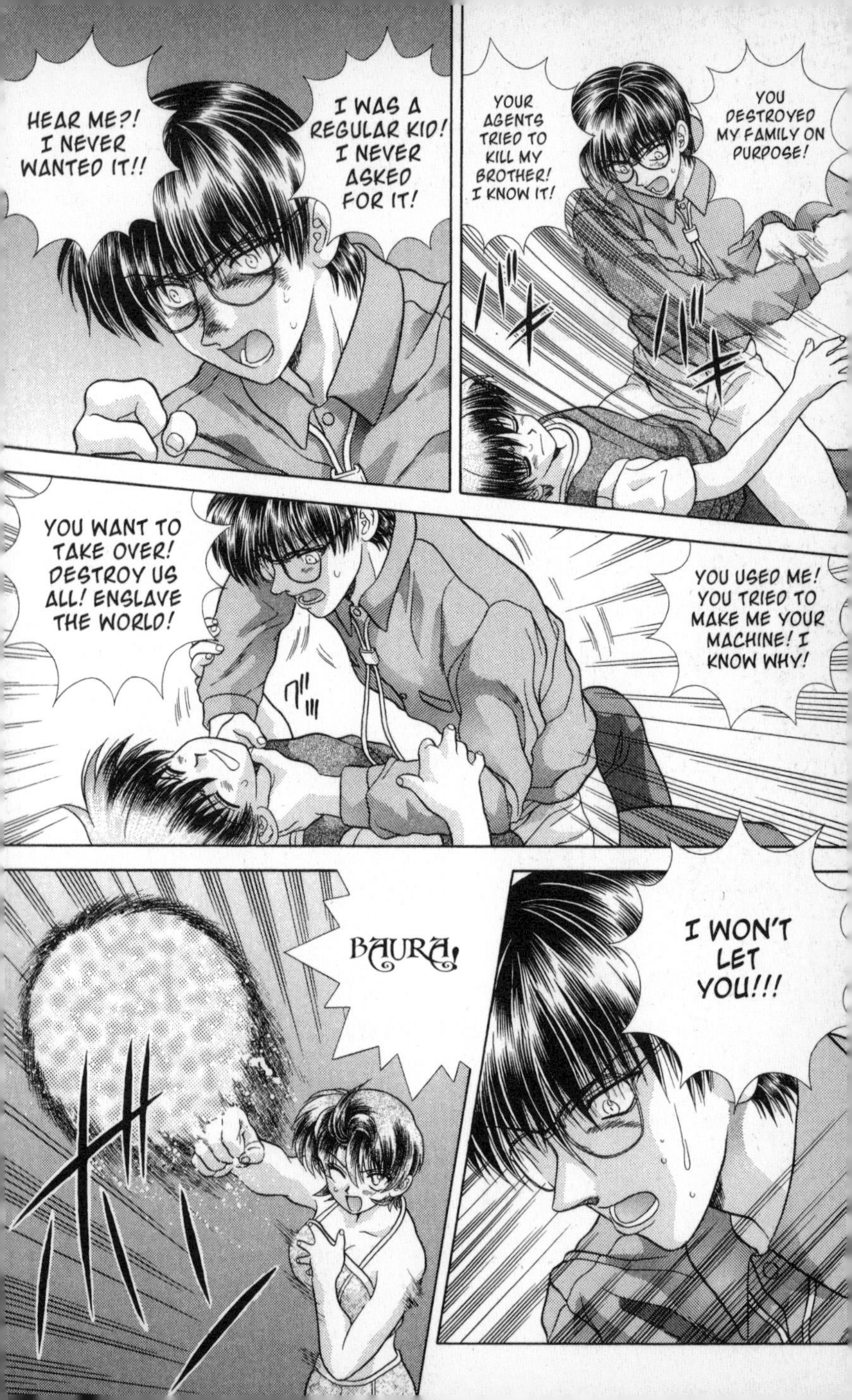
YOU DESTROYED MY FAMILY ON PURPOSE!
YOUR AGENTS TRIED TO KILL MY BROTHER! I KNOW IT!
I WAS A REGULAR KID! I NEVER ASKED FOR IT!
HEAR ME?! I NEVER WANTED IT!!
YOU USED ME! YOU TRIED TO MAKE ME YOUR MACHINE! I KNOW WHY!
YOU WANT TO TAKE OVER! DESTROY US ALL! ENSLAVE THE WORLD!
I WON'T LET YOU!!!
BAURA!

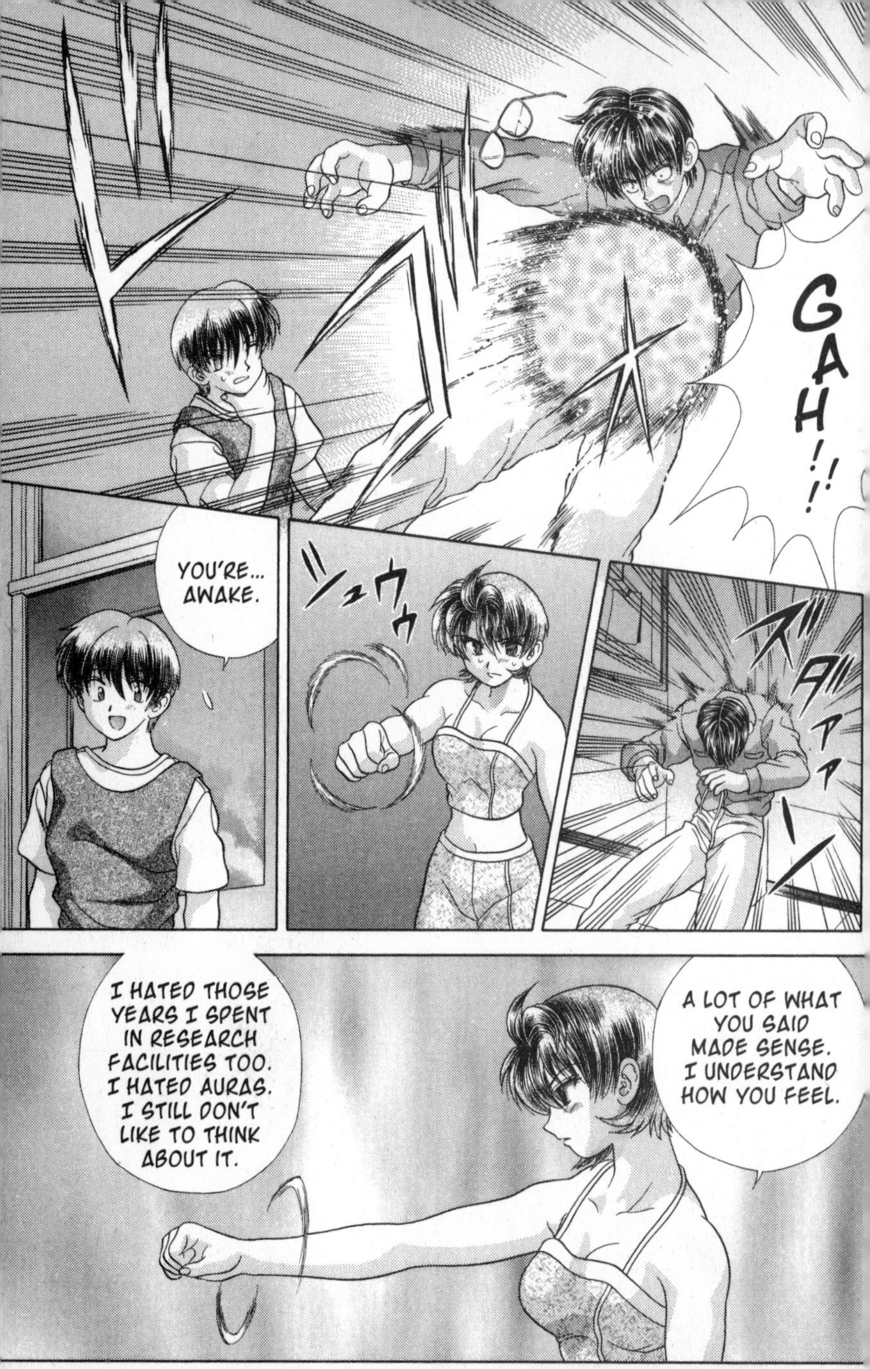
GAH!!!
YOU'RE... AWAKE.
A LOT OF WHAT YOU SAID MADE SENSE. I UNDERSTAND HOW YOU FEEL.
I HATED THOSE YEARS I SPENT IN RESEARCH FACILITIES TOO. I HATED AURAS. I STILL DON'T LIKE TO THINK ABOUT IT.

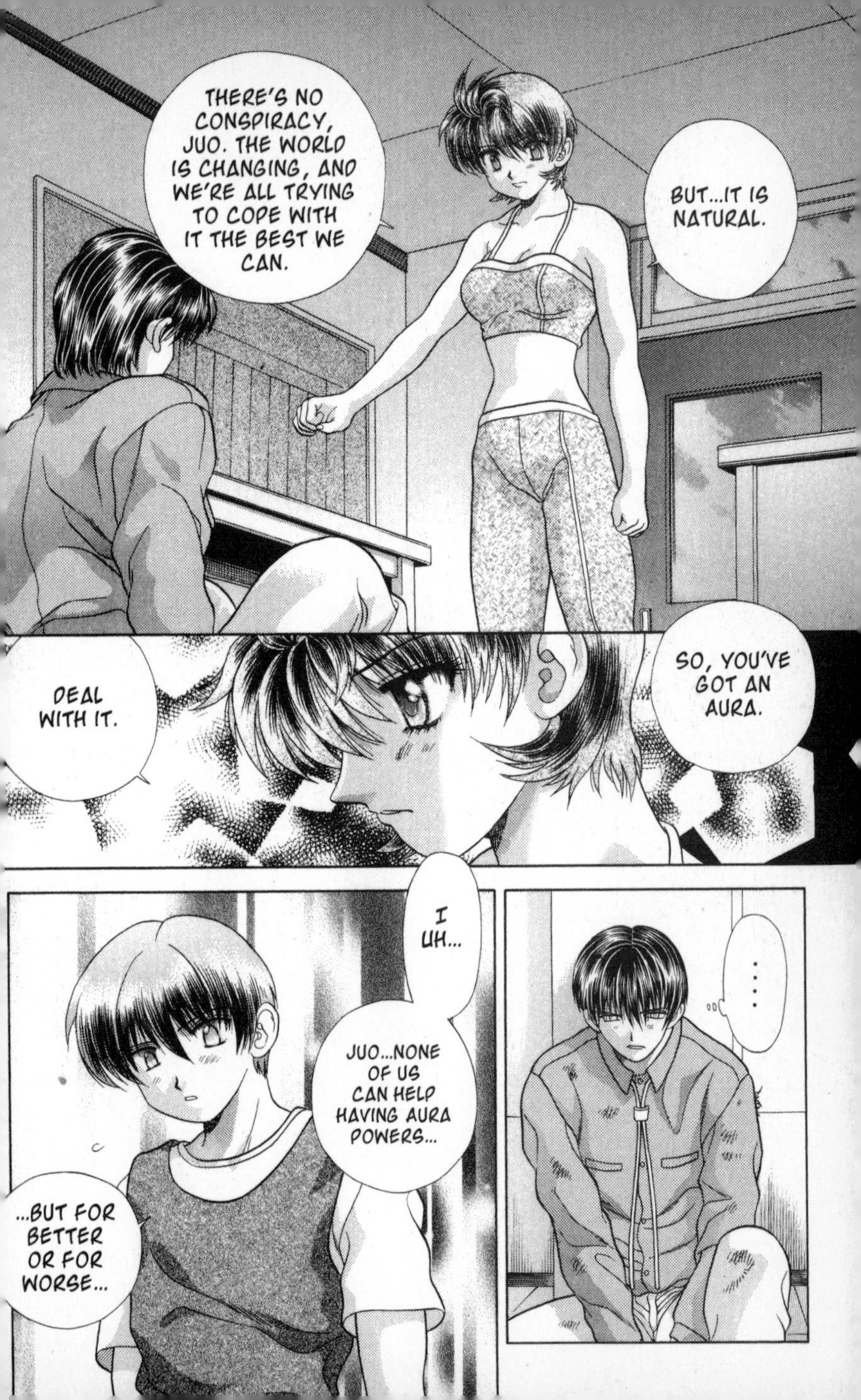
BUT...IT IS NATURAL.
THERE'S NO CONSPIRACY, JUO. THE WORLD IS CHANGING, AND WE'RE ALL TRYING TO COPE WITH IT THE BEST WE CAN.
SO, YOU'VE GOT AN AURA.
DEAL WITH IT.
....
I UH...
JUO...NONE OF US CAN HELP HAVING AURA POWERS...
...BUT FOR BETTER OR FOR WORSE...

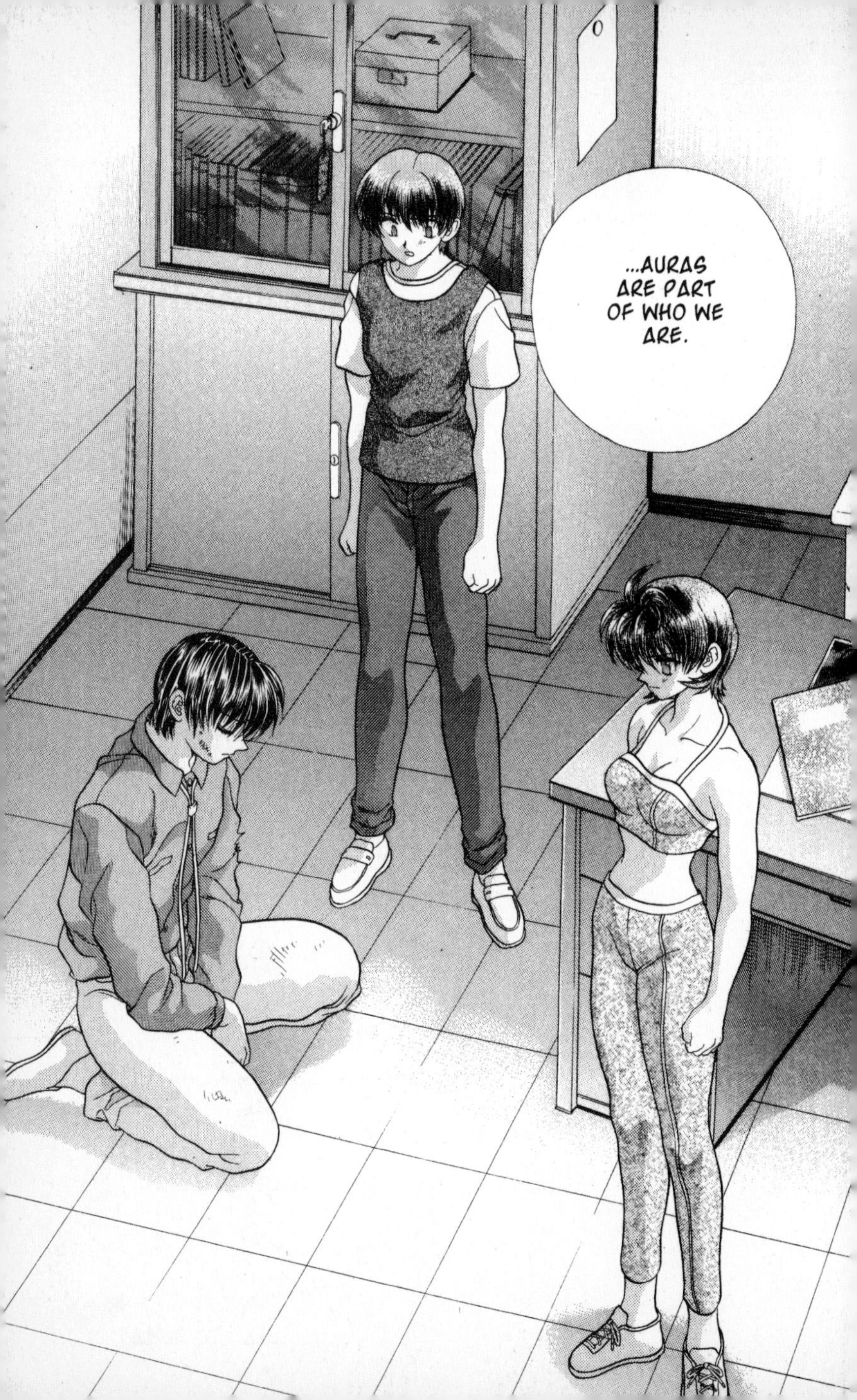
...AURAS ARE PART OF WHO WE ARE.

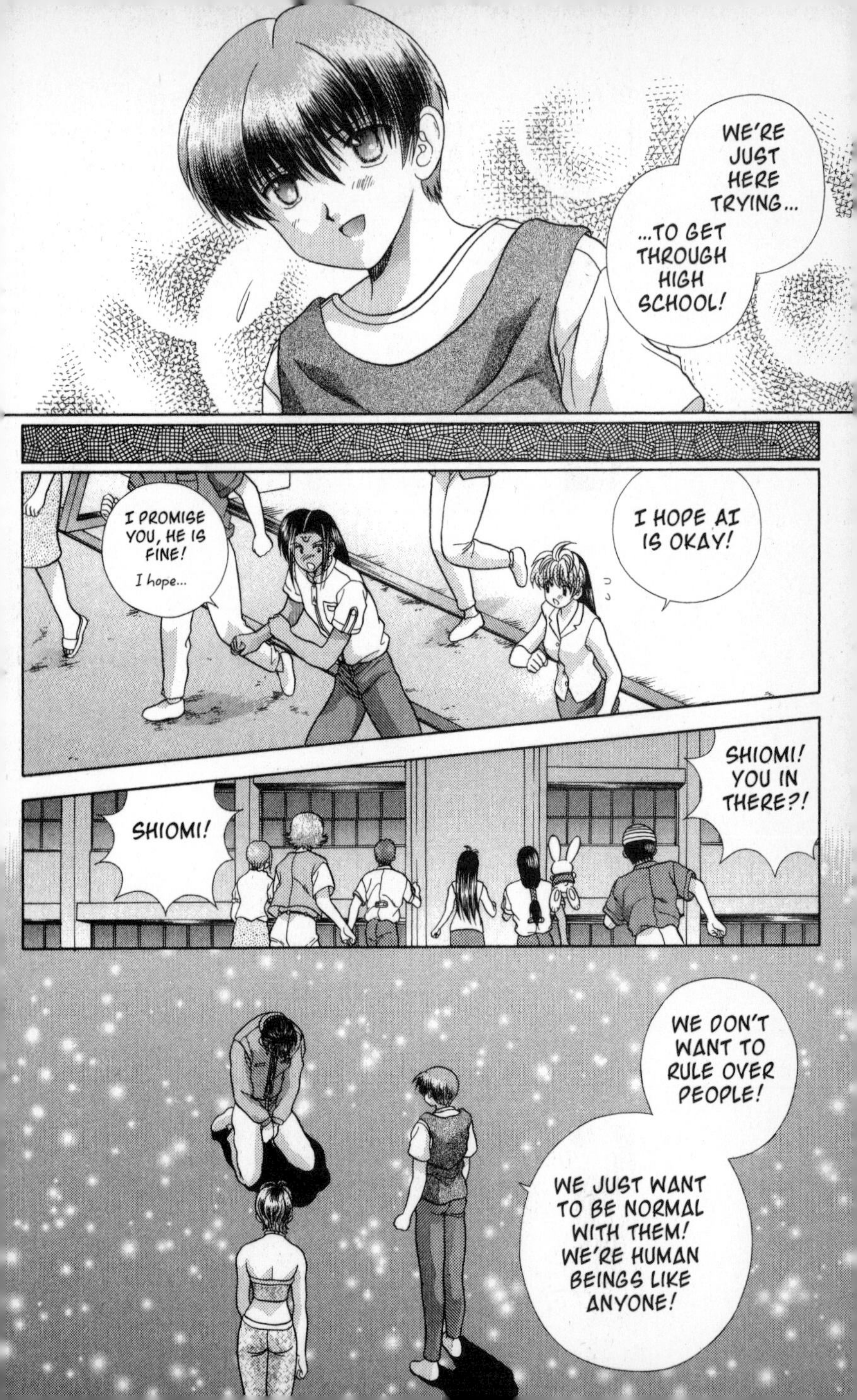
WE'RE JUST HERE TRYING...
...TO GET THROUGH HIGH SCHOOL!
I HOPE AI IS OKAY!
I PROMISE YOU, HE IS FINE!
I hope...
SHIOMI! YOU IN THERE?!
SHIOMI!
WE DON'T WANT TO RULE OVER PEOPLE!
WE JUST WANT TO BE NORMAL WITH THEM! WE'RE HUMAN BEINGS LIKE ANYONE!

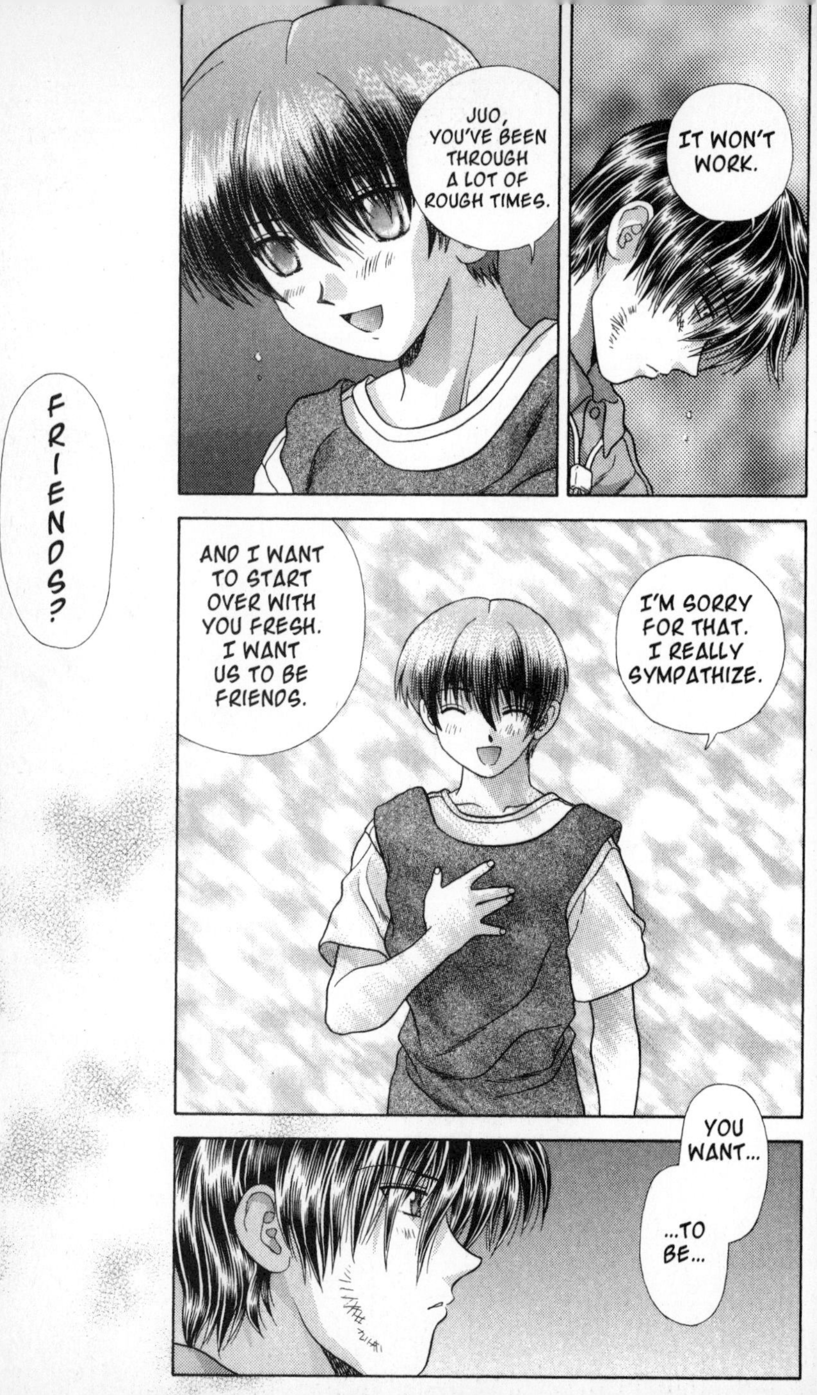
IT WON'T WORK.
JUO, YOU'VE BEEN THROUGH A LOT OF ROUGH TIMES.
I'M SORRY FOR THAT. I REALLY SYMPATHIZE.
AND I WANT TO START OVER WITH YOU FRESH. I WANT US TO BE FRIENDS.
YOU WANT...
...TO BE...
FRIENDS?

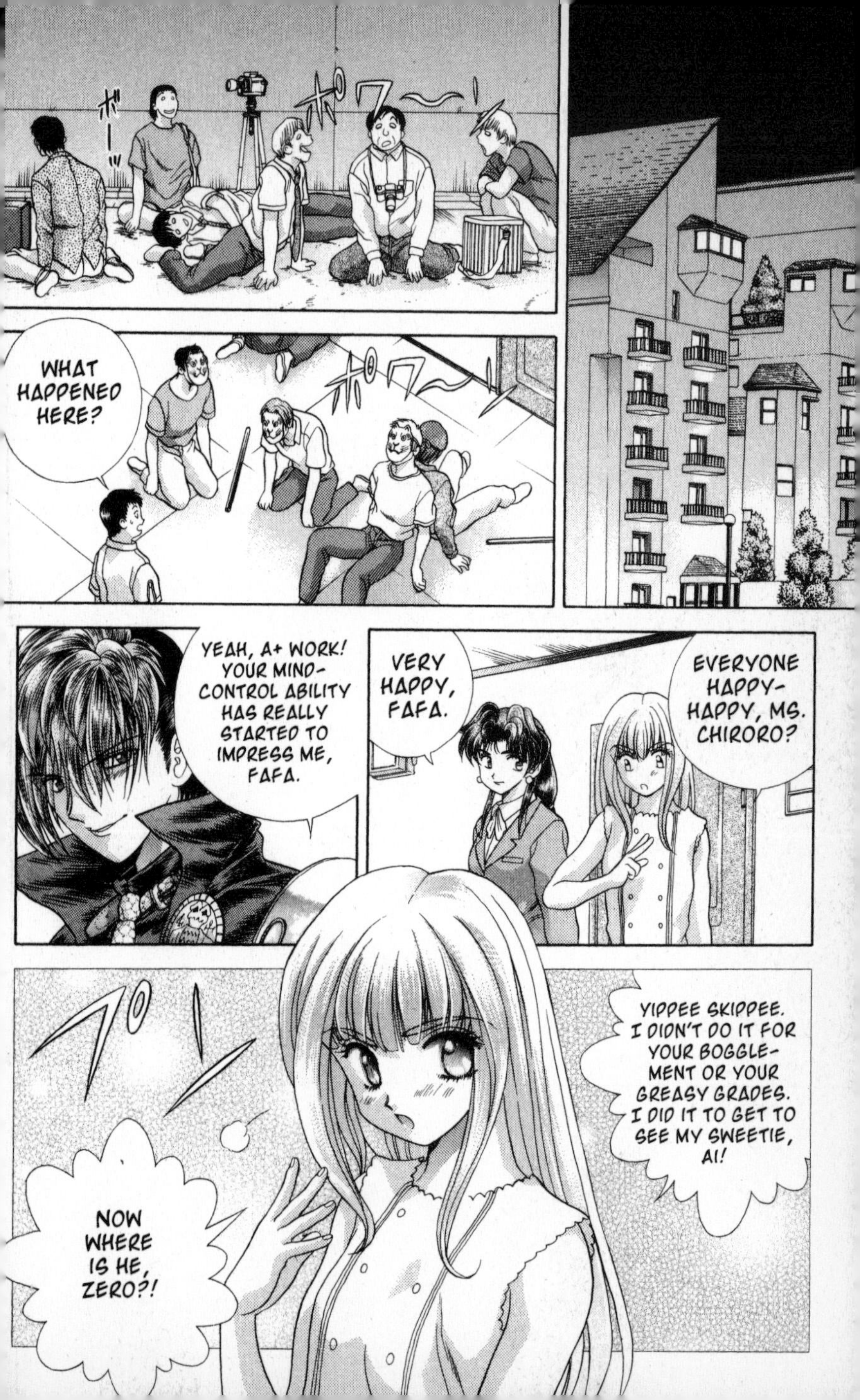
WHAT HAPPENED HERE?
EVERYONE HAPPY-HAPPY, MS. CHIRORO?
VERY HAPPY, FAFA.
YEAH, A+ WORK! YOUR MIND-CONTROL ABILITY HAS REALLY STARTED TO IMPRESS ME, FAFA.
YIPPEE SKIPPEE. I DIDN'T DO IT FOR YOUR BOGGLEMENT OR YOUR GREASY GRADES. I DID IT TO GET TO SEE MY SWEETIE, AI!
NOW WHERE IS HE, ZERO?!

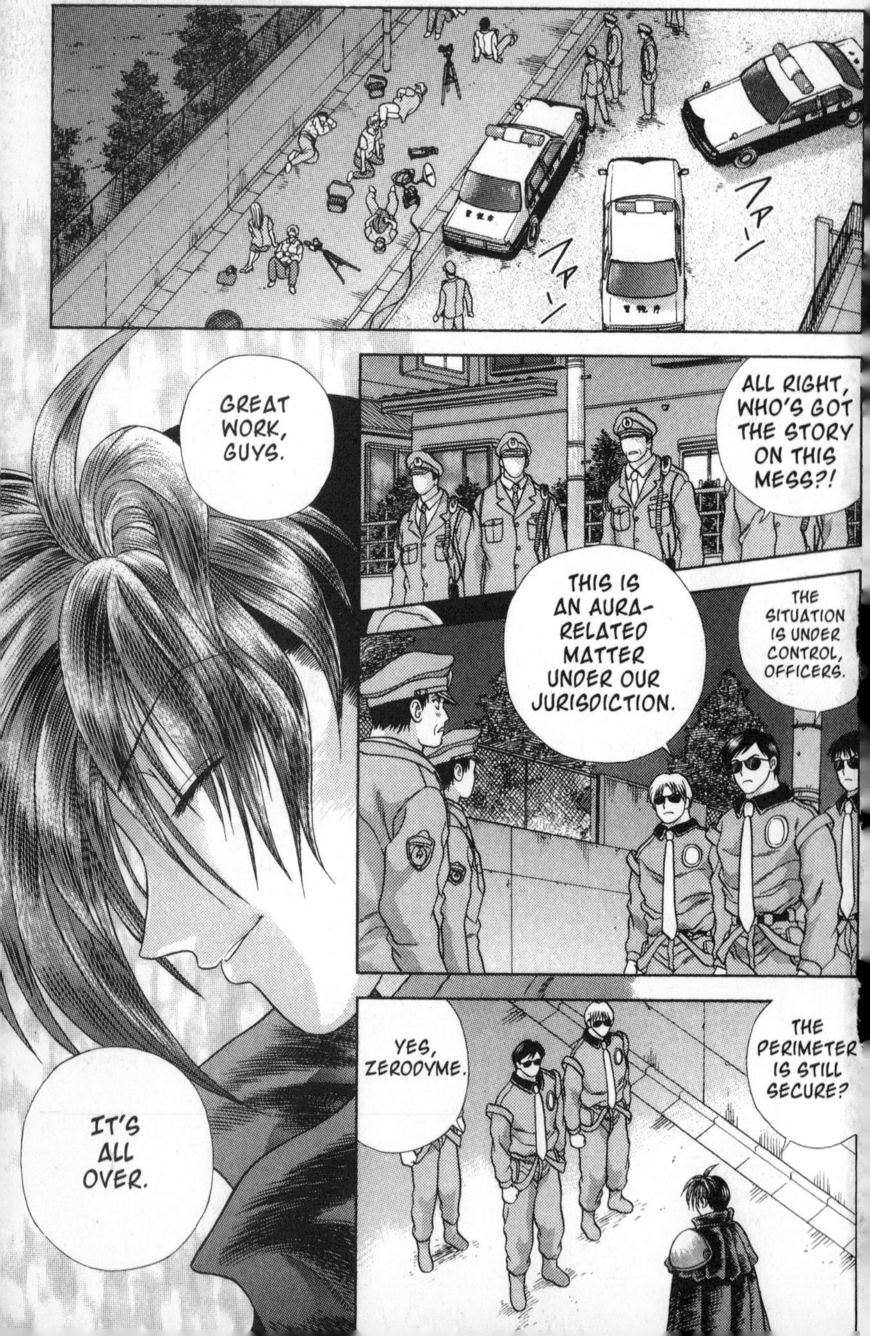
ファーン
ファーン
ALL RIGHT, WHO'S GOT THE STORY ON THIS MESS?!
THE SITUATION IS UNDER CONTROL, OFFICERS.
THIS IS AN AURA-RELATED MATTER UNDER OUR JURISDICTION.
THE PERIMETER IS STILL SECURE?
YES, ZERODYME.
GREAT WORK, GUYS.
IT'S ALL OVER.

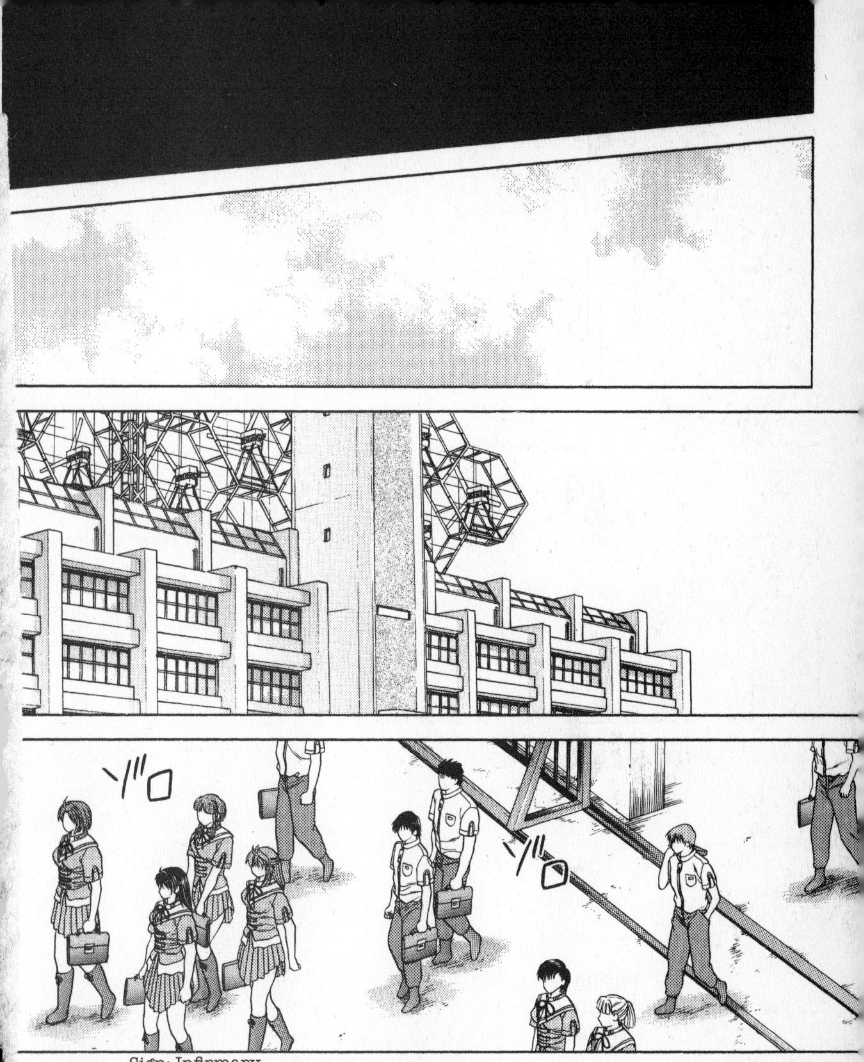
ゾロ
ゾロ

Sign: Infirmary

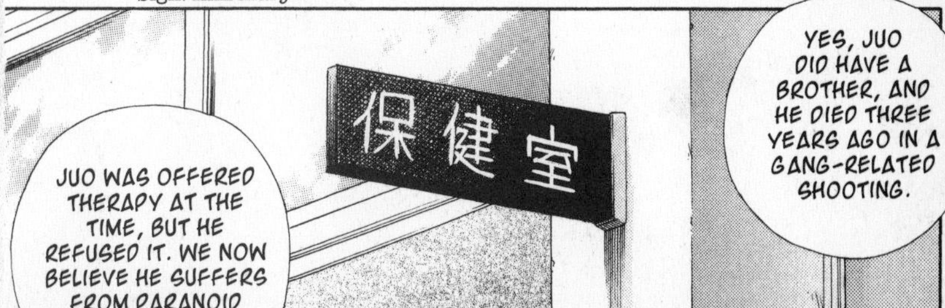
保健室
YES, JUO DID HAVE A BROTHER, AND HE DIED THREE YEARS AGO IN A GANG-RELATED SHOOTING.
JUO WAS OFFERED THERAPY AT THE TIME, BUT HE REFUSED IT. WE NOW BELIEVE HE SUFFERS FROM PARANOID SCHIZOPHRENIA.

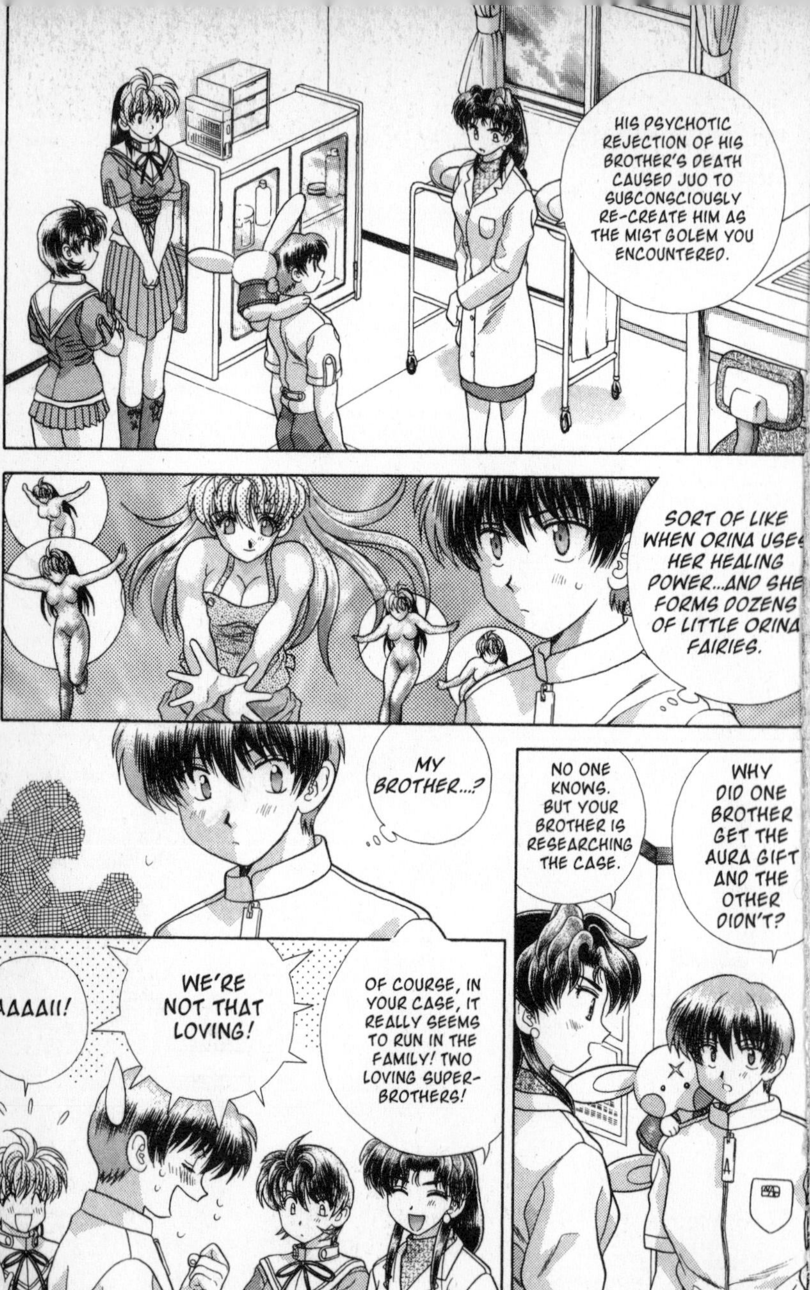

HIS PSYCHOTIC REJECTION OF HIS BROTHER'S DEATH CAUSED JUO TO SUBCONSCIOUSLY RE-CREATE HIM AS THE MIST GOLEM YOU ENCOUNTERED.
SORT OF LIKE WHEN ORINA USES HER HEALING POWER...AND SHE FORMS DOZENS OF LITTLE ORINA FAIRIES.
WHY DID ONE BROTHER GET THE AURA GIFT AND THE OTHER DIDN'T?
NO ONE KNOWS. BUT YOUR BROTHER IS RESEARCHING THE CASE.
MY BROTHER...?
OF COURSE, IN YOUR CASE, IT REALLY SEEMS TO RUN IN THE FAMILY! TWO LOVING SUPER-BROTHERS!
WE'RE NOT THAT LOVING!
AAAAII!

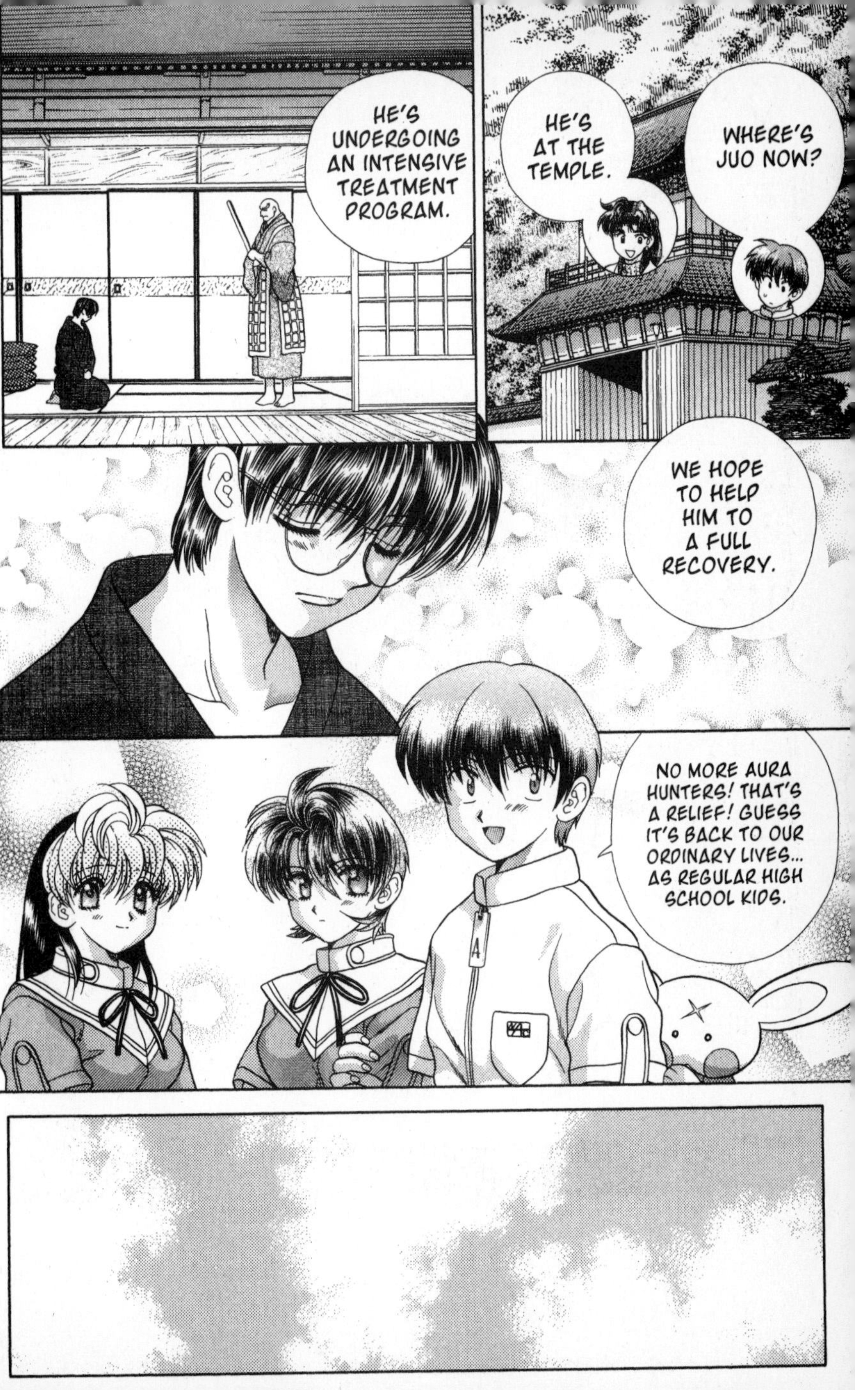
WHERE'S JUO NOW?
HE'S AT THE TEMPLE.
HE'S UNDERGOING AN INTENSIVE TREATMENT PROGRAM.
WE HOPE TO HELP HIM TO A FULL RECOVERY.
NO MORE AURA HUNTERS! THAT'S A RELIEF! GUESS IT'S BACK TO OUR ORDINARY LIVES... AS REGULAR HIGH SCHOOL KIDS.

The Aura Conspiracy END

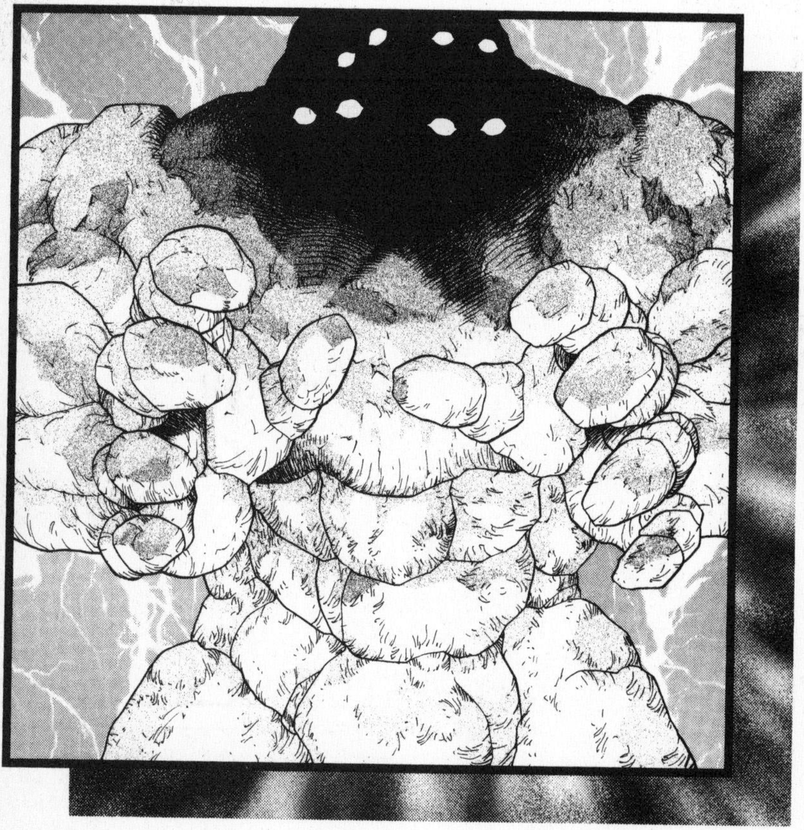

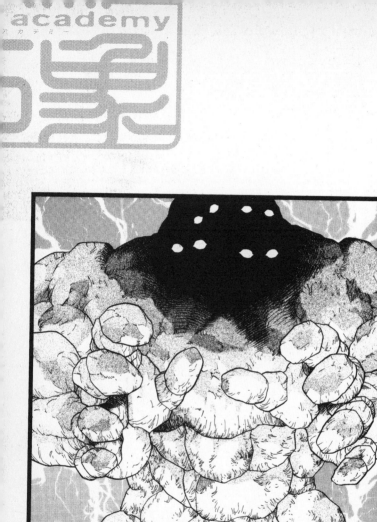

Chapter 13: Run to the Sun

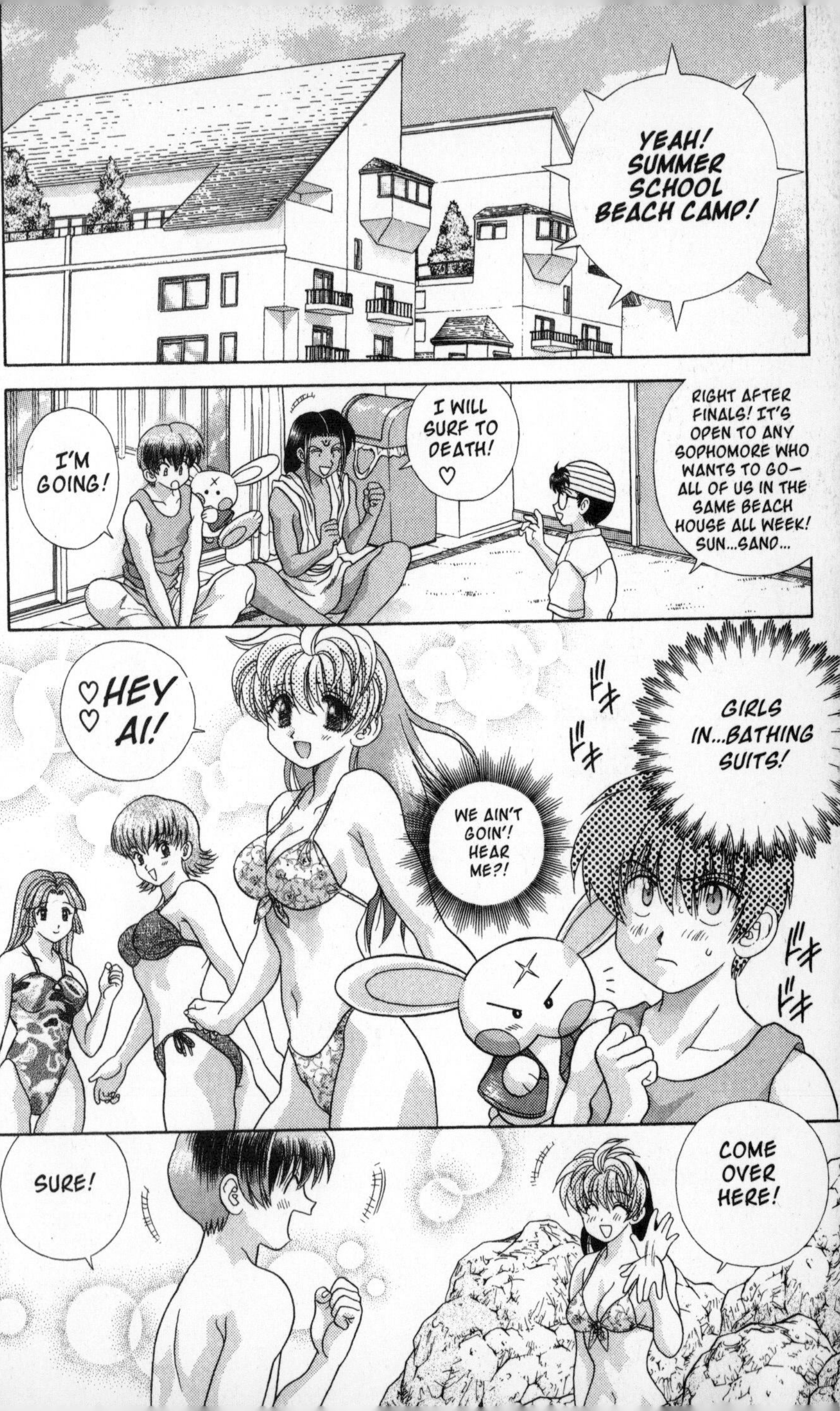
YEAH! SUMMER SCHOOL BEACH CAMP!
RIGHT AFTER FINALS! IT'S OPEN TO ANY SOPHOMORE WHO WANTS TO GO— ALL OF US IN THE SAME BEACH HOUSE ALL WEEK! SUN...SAND...
I WILL SURF TO DEATH! ♡
I'M GOING!
GIRLS IN...BATHING SUITS!
ドキ ドキ
WE AIN'T GOIN'! HEAR ME?!
♡HEY ♡AI!
ドキ ドキ
COME OVER HERE!
SURE!

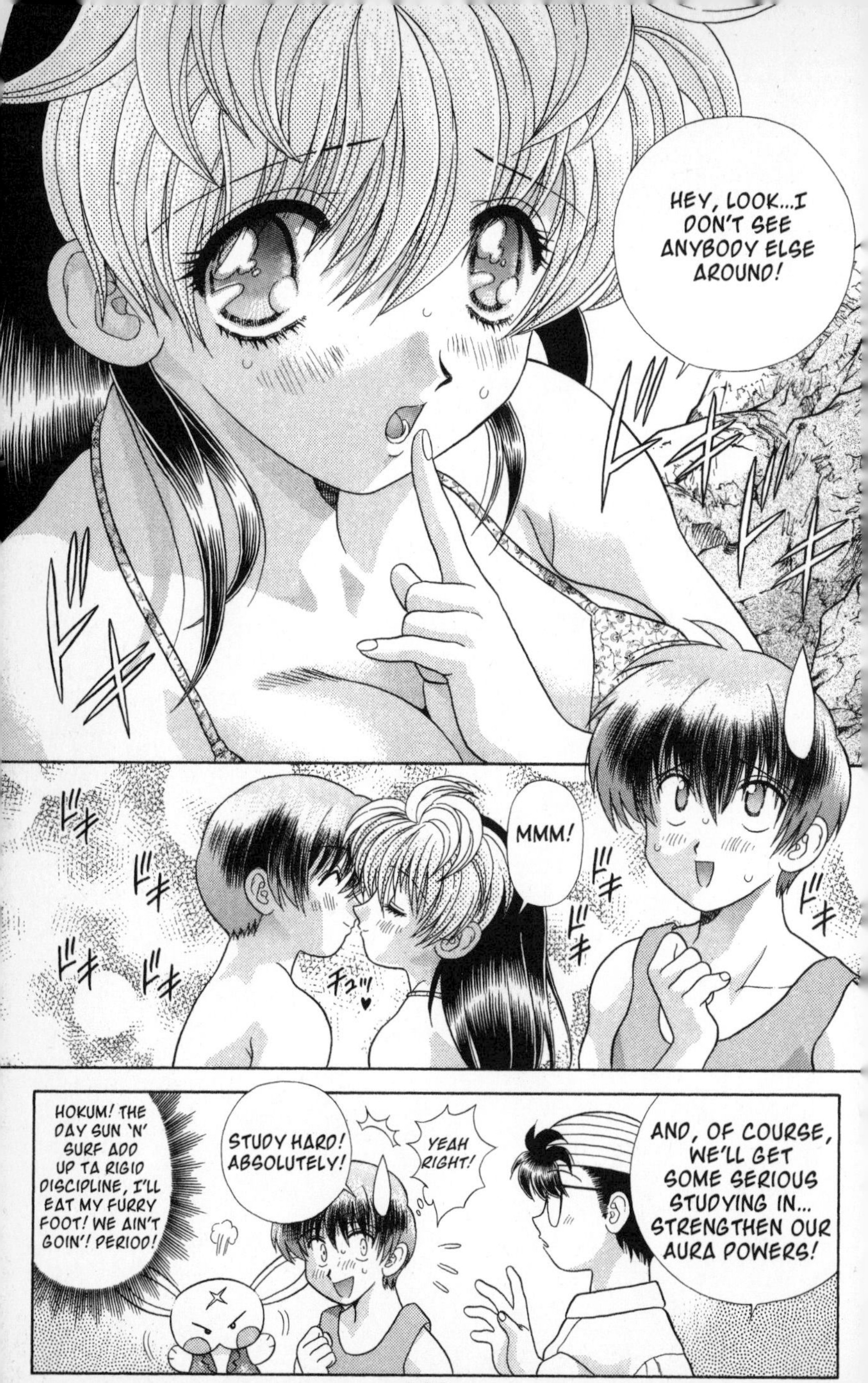
HEY, LOOK...I DON'T SEE ANYBODY ELSE AROUND!
ドキドキ
ドキドキ
MMM!
ドキ
ドキ
ドキ
ドキ
ドキ
ドキ
チュッ♥
AND, OF COURSE, WE'LL GET SOME SERIOUS STUDYING IN... STRENGTHEN OUR AURA POWERS!
YEAH RIGHT!
STUDY HARD! ABSOLUTELY!
HOKUM! THE DAY SUN 'N' SURF ADD UP TA RIGID DISCIPLINE, I'LL EAT MY FURRY FOOT! WE AIN'T GOIN'! PERIOD!

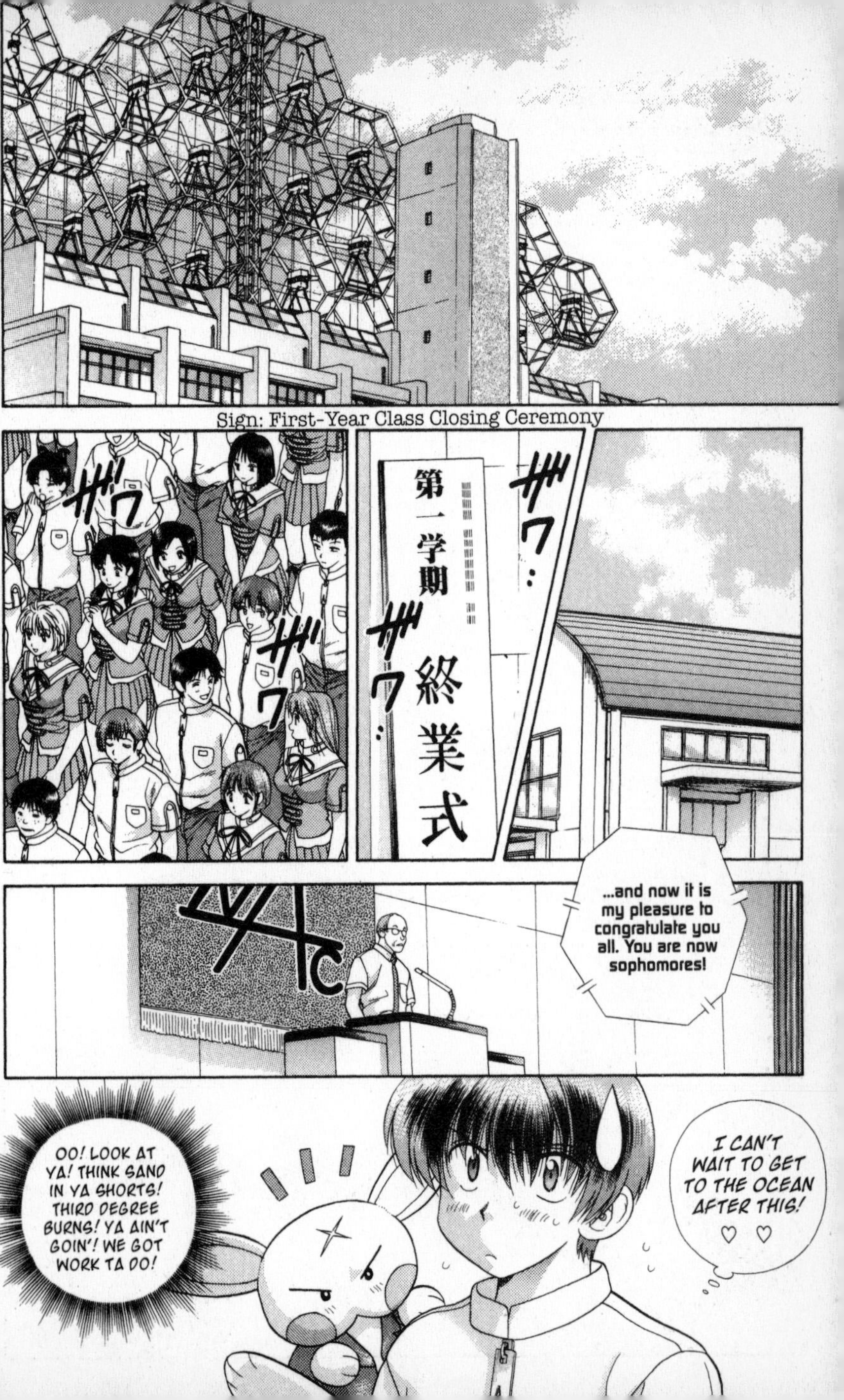
Sign: First-Year Class Closing Ceremony
ザワ…
第一学期 終業式
ザワ ザワ
…and now it is my pleasure to congratulate you all. You are now sophomores!
I CAN'T WAIT TO GET TO THE OCEAN AFTER THIS! ♡ ♡
OO! LOOK AT YA! THINK SAND IN YA SHORTS! THIRD DEGREE BURNS! YA AIN'T GOIN'! WE GOT WORK TA DO!

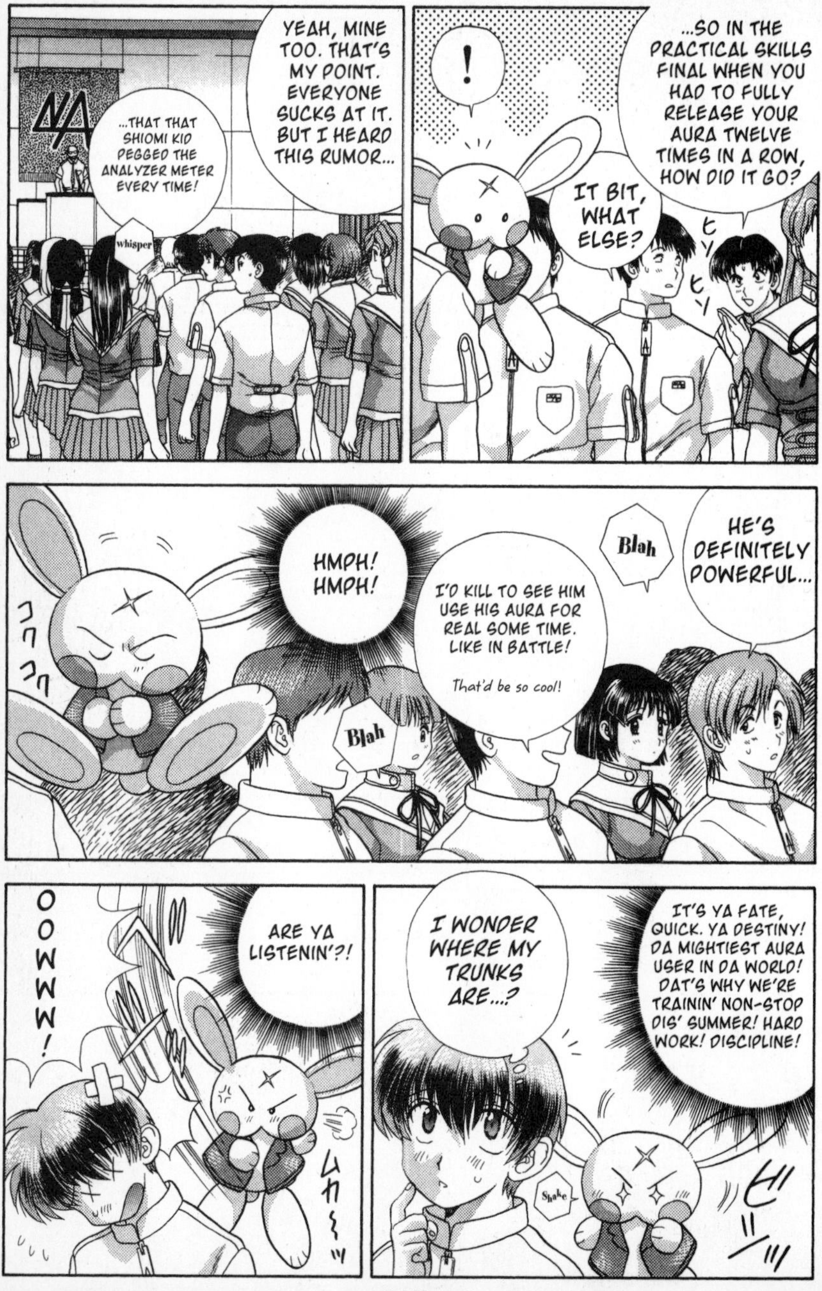
...SO IN THE PRACTICAL SKILLS FINAL WHEN YOU HAD TO FULLY RELEASE YOUR AURA TWELVE TIMES IN A ROW, HOW DID IT GO?
IT BIT, WHAT ELSE?
!
YEAH, MINE TOO. THAT'S MY POINT. EVERYONE SUCKS AT IT. BUT I HEARD THIS RUMOR...
...THAT THAT SHIOMI KID PEGGED THE ANALYZER METER EVERY TIME!
whisper
HE'S DEFINITELY POWERFUL...
Blah
I'D KILL TO SEE HIM USE HIS AURA FOR REAL SOME TIME. LIKE IN BATTLE!
That'd be so cool!
HMPH! HMPH!
Blah
IT'S YA FATE, QUICK. YA DESTINY! DA MIGHTIEST AURA USER IN DA WORLD! DAT'S WHY WE'RE TRAININ' NON-STOP DIS' SUMMER! HARD WORK! DISCIPLINE!
I WONDER WHERE MY TRUNKS ARE...?
Shake
ARE YA LISTENIN'?!
OOWWWW!

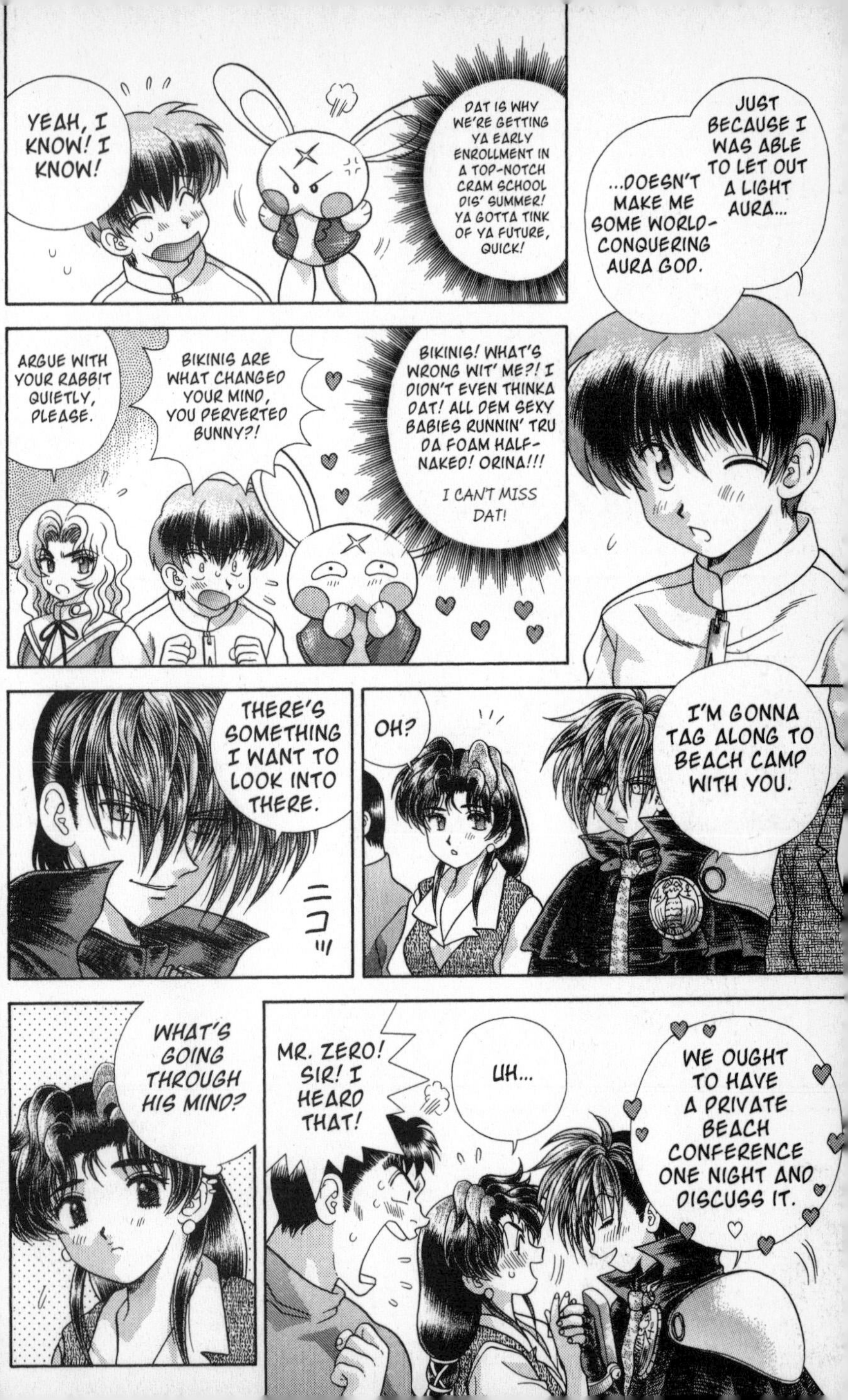
JUST BECAUSE I WAS ABLE TO LET OUT A LIGHT AURA...
...DOESN'T MAKE ME SOME WORLD-CONQUERING AURA GOD.
DAT IS WHY WE'RE GETTING YA EARLY ENROLLMENT IN A TOP-NOTCH CRAM SCHOOL DIS' SUMMER! YA GOTTA TINK OF YA FUTURE, QUICK!
YEAH, I KNOW! I KNOW!
BIKINIS! WHAT'S WRONG WIT' ME?! I DIDN'T EVEN THINKA DAT! ALL DEM SEXY BABIES RUNNIN' TRU DA FOAM HALF-NAKED! ORINA!!!
I CAN'T MISS DAT!
BIKINIS ARE WHAT CHANGED YOUR MIND, YOU PERVERTED BUNNY?!
ARGUE WITH YOUR RABBIT QUIETLY, PLEASE.
I'M GONNA TAG ALONG TO BEACH CAMP WITH YOU.
OH?
THERE'S SOMETHING I WANT TO LOOK INTO THERE.
ニコッ
WE OUGHT TO HAVE A PRIVATE BEACH CONFERENCE ONE NIGHT AND DISCUSS IT.
UH...
MR. ZERO! SIR! I HEARD THAT!
WHAT'S GOING THROUGH HIS MIND?

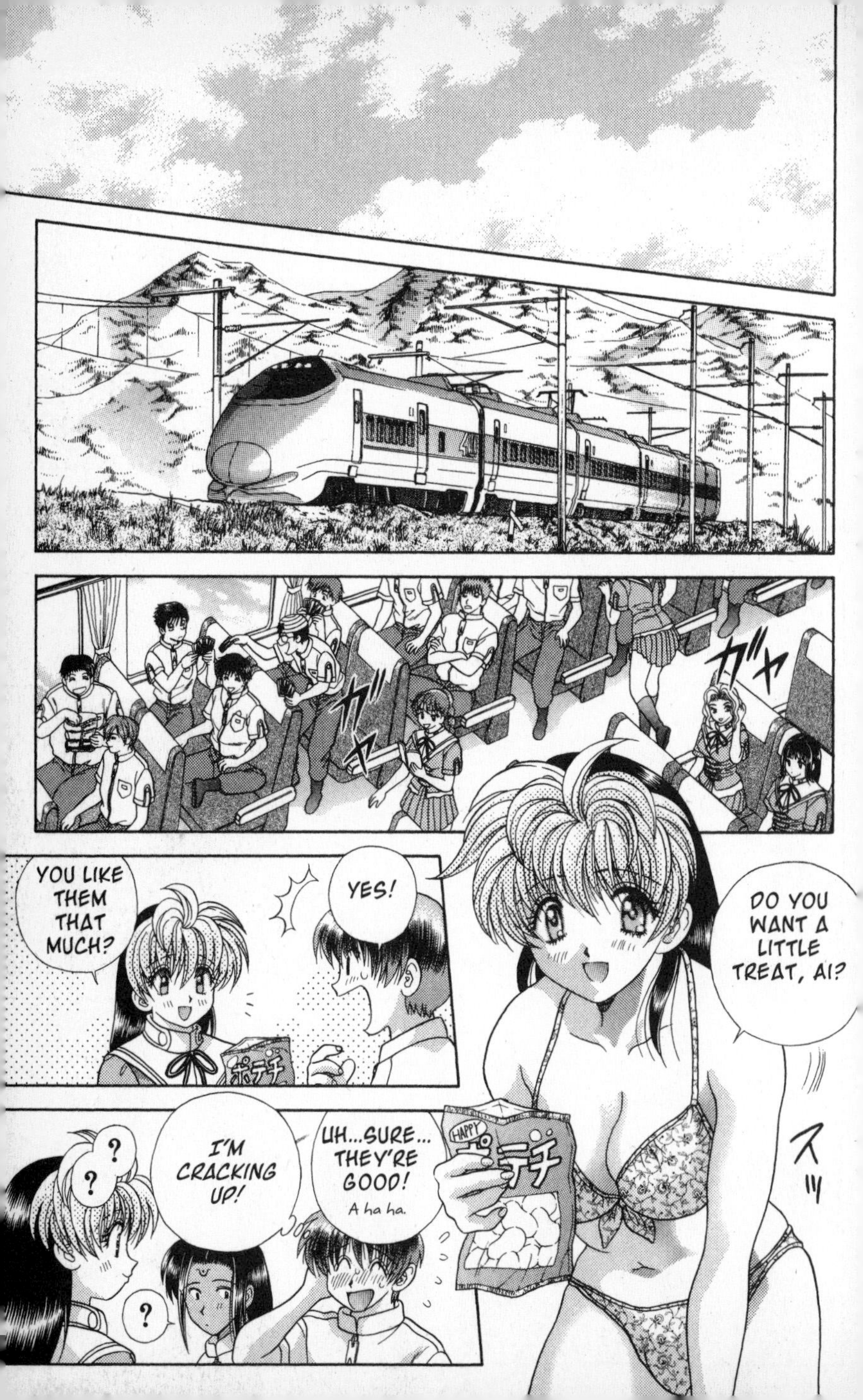
ガヤ
ガヤ
DO YOU WANT A LITTLE TREAT, AI?
スッ
YES!
YOU LIKE THEM THAT MUCH?
HAPPY
ポテチ
UH...SURE... THEY'RE GOOD!
A ha ha.
I'M CRACKING UP!
?
?
?

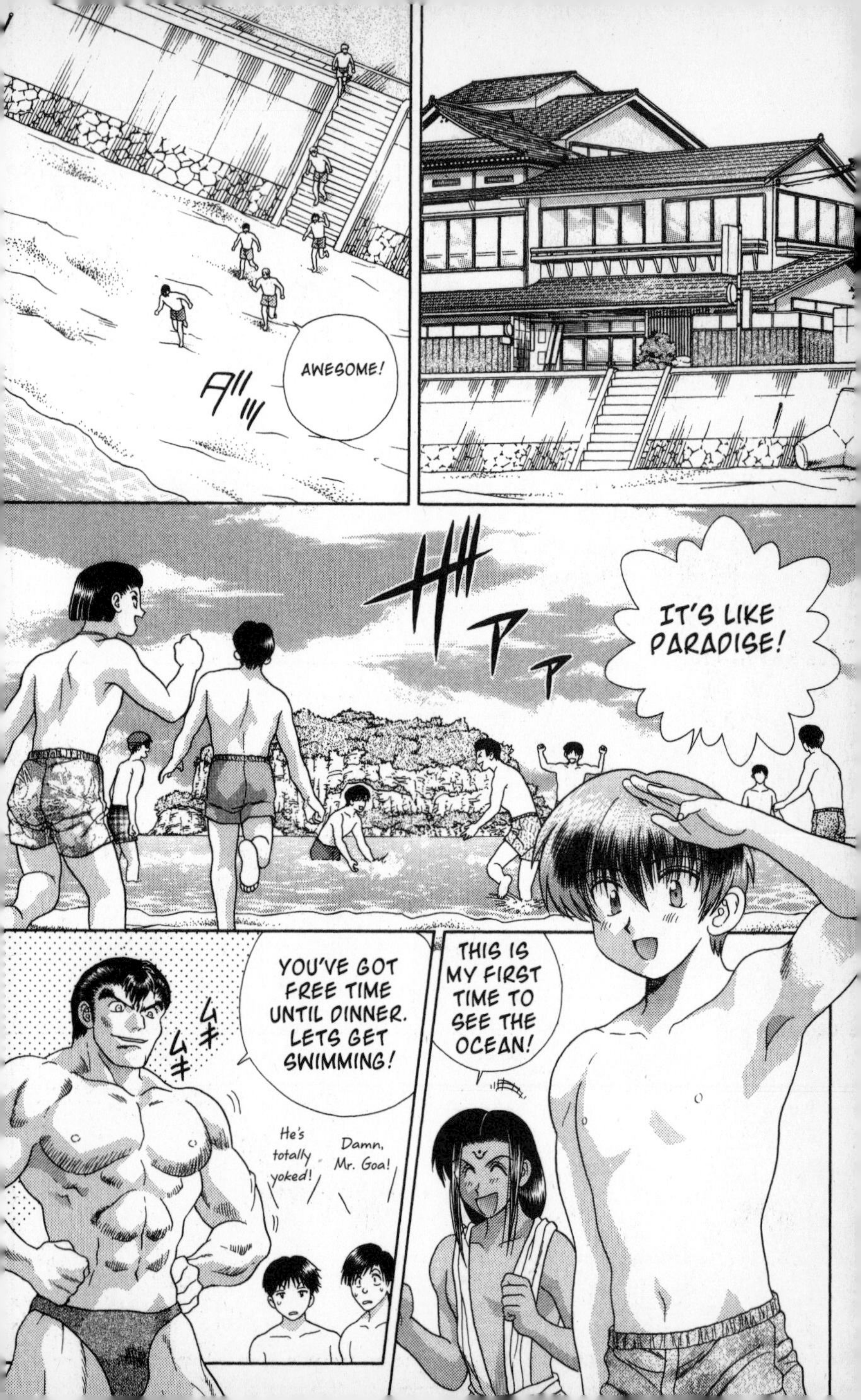
AWESOME!
IT'S LIKE PARADISE!
THIS IS MY FIRST TIME TO SEE THE OCEAN!
YOU'VE GOT FREE TIME UNTIL DINNER. LETS GET SWIMMING!
ムキ ムキ
Damn, Mr. Goa!
He's totally yoked!

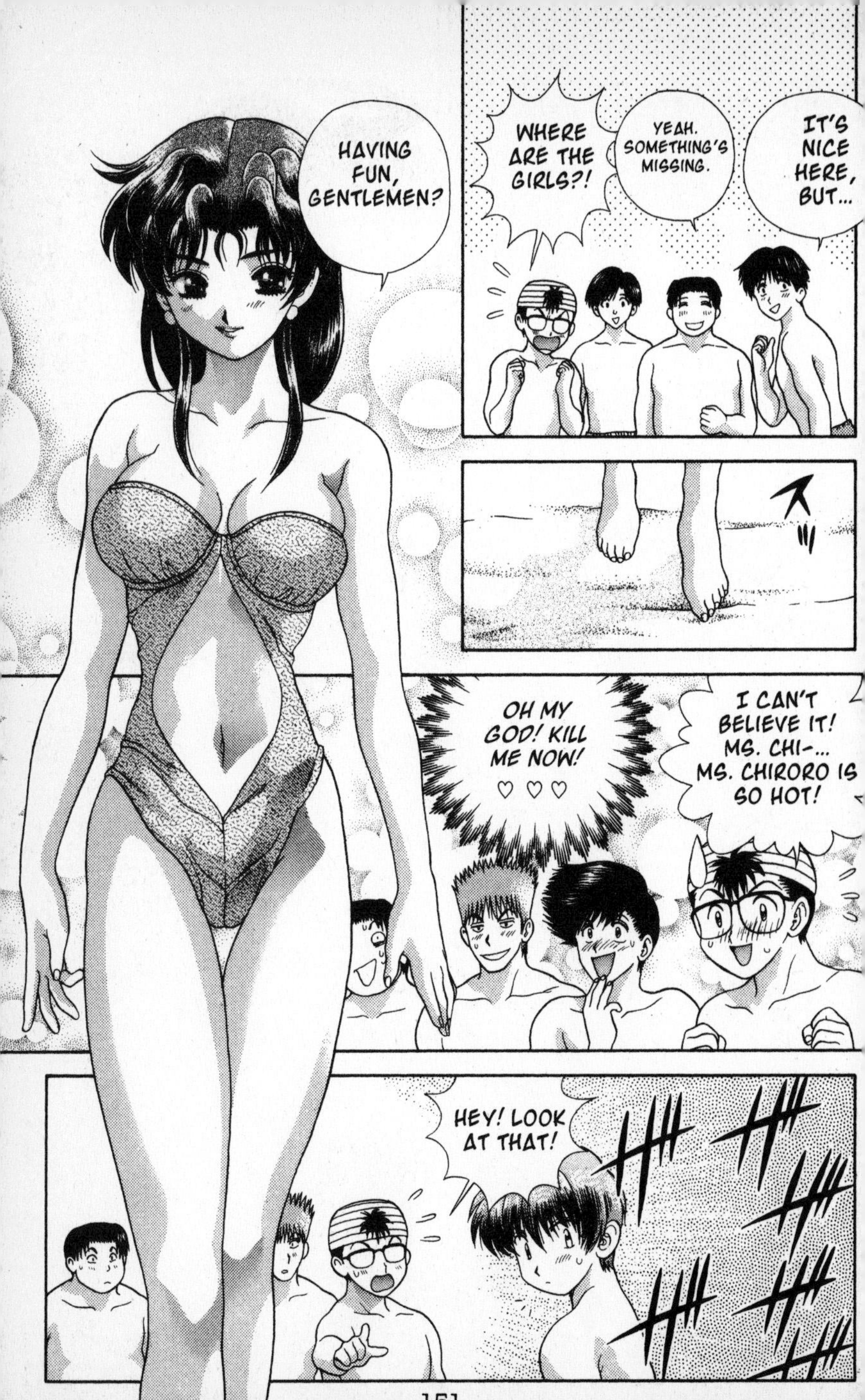
IT'S NICE HERE, BUT...
YEAH. SOMETHING'S MISSING.
WHERE ARE THE GIRLS?!
HAVING FUN, GENTLEMEN?
I CAN'T BELIEVE IT! MS. CHI-... MS. CHIRORO IS SO HOT!
OH MY GOD! KILL ME NOW! ♡ ♡ ♡
HEY! LOOK AT THAT!

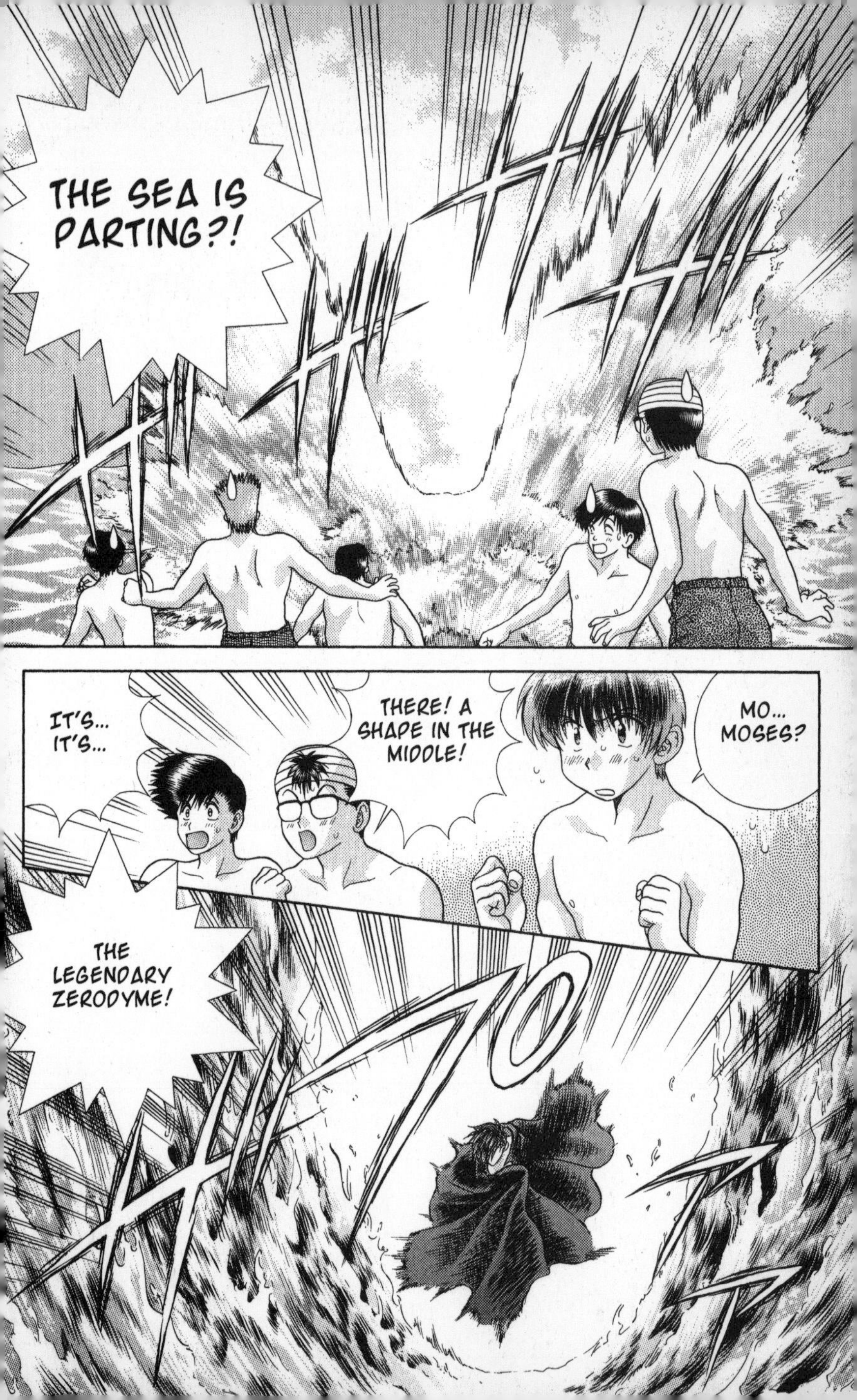
THE SEA IS PARTING?!
MO... MOSES?
THERE! A SHAPE IN THE MIDDLE!
IT'S... IT'S...
THE LEGENDARY ZERODYME!

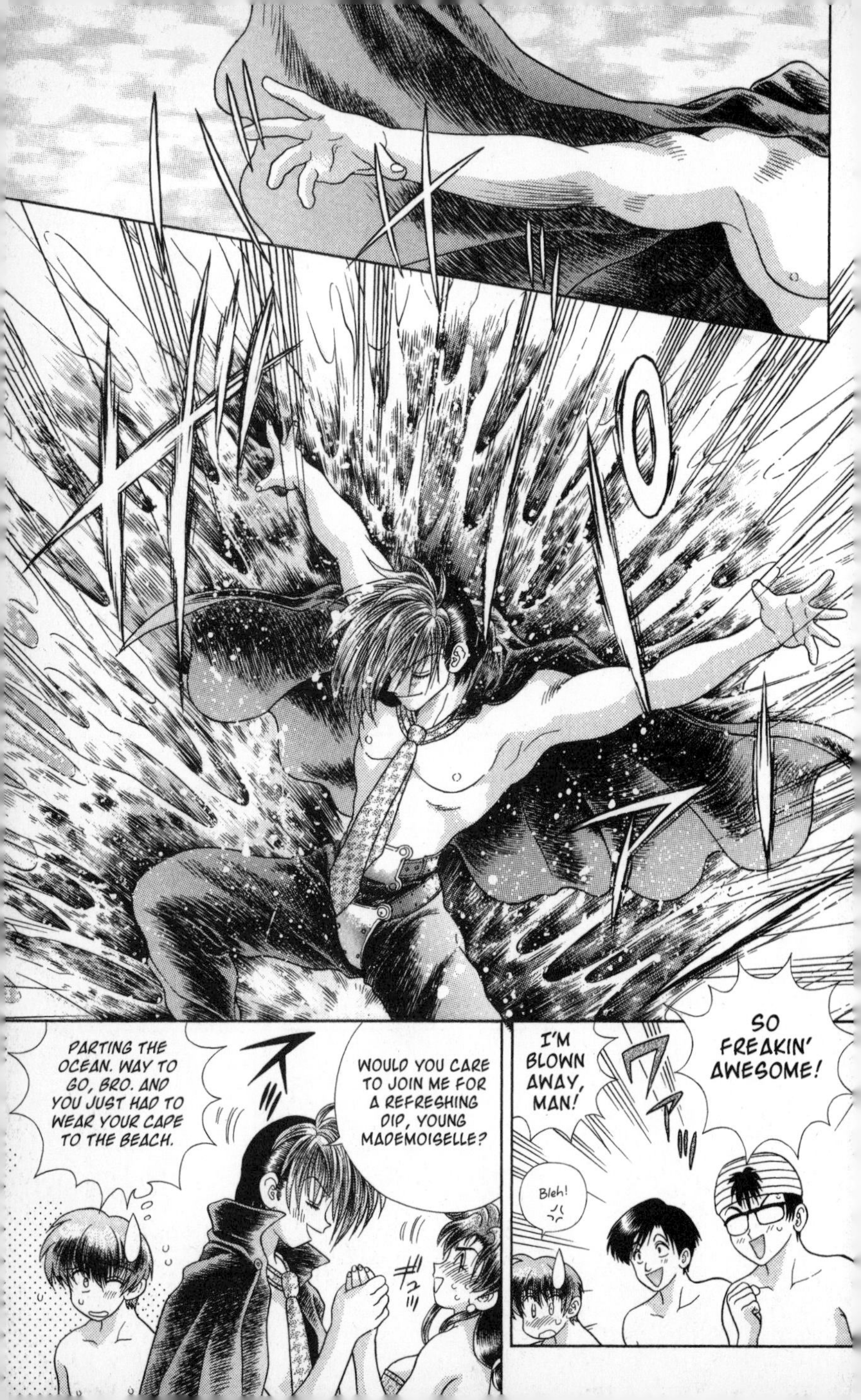
SO FREAKIN' AWESOME!
I'M BLOWN AWAY, MAN!
Bleh!
WOULD YOU CARE TO JOIN ME FOR A REFRESHING DIP, YOUNG MADEMOISELLE?
PARTING THE OCEAN. WAY TO GO, BRO. AND YOU JUST HAD TO WEAR YOUR CAPE TO THE BEACH.

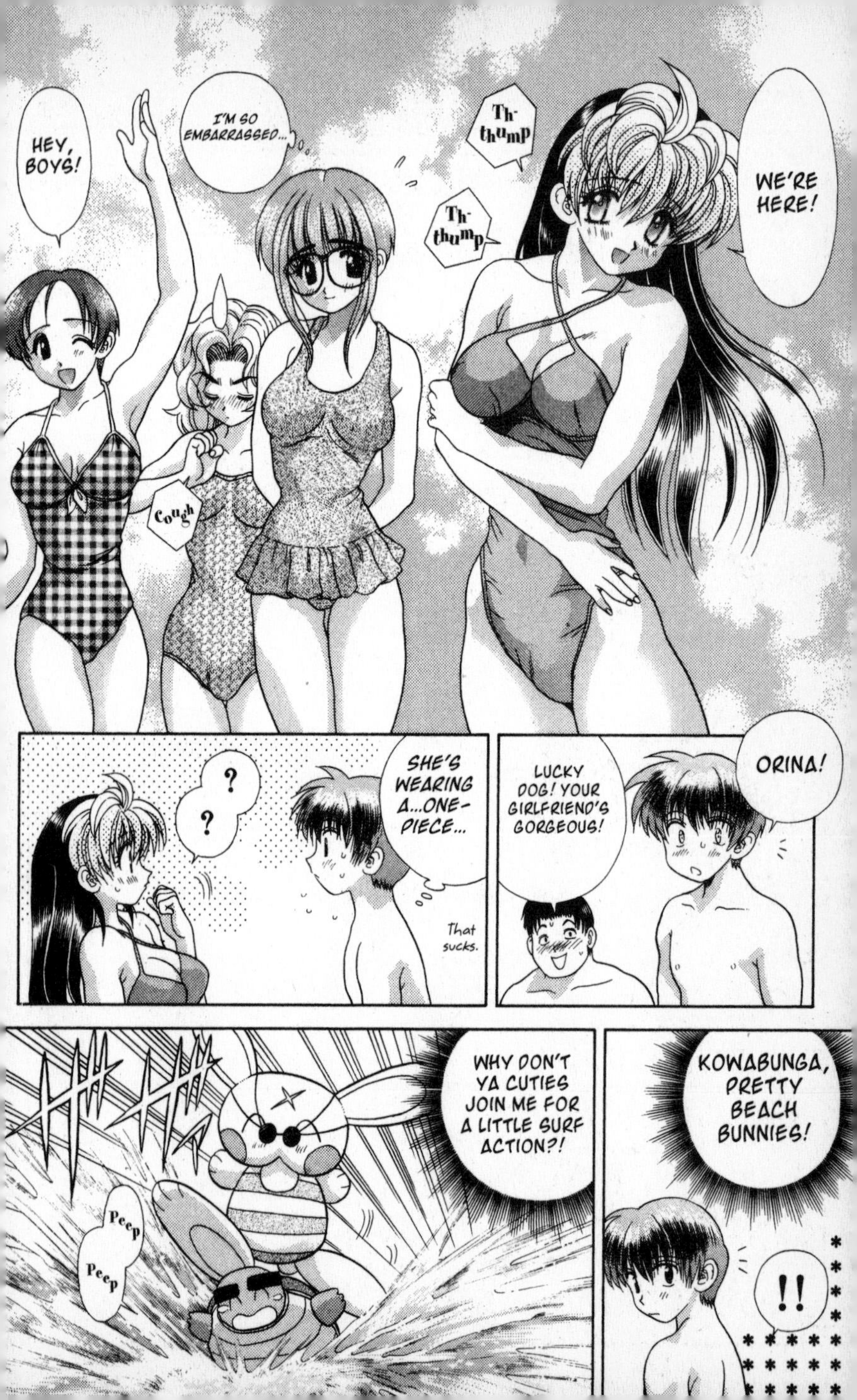
WE'RE HERE!
Th-thump
Th-thump
I'M SO EMBARRASSED...
Cough
HEY, BOYS!
ORINA!
LUCKY DOG! YOUR GIRLFRIEND'S GORGEOUS!
SHE'S WEARING A...ONE-PIECE...
That sucks.
?
?
KOWABUNGA, PRETTY BEACH BUNNIES!
!!
WHY DON'T YA CUTIES JOIN ME FOR A LITTLE SURF ACTION?!
Peep
Peep

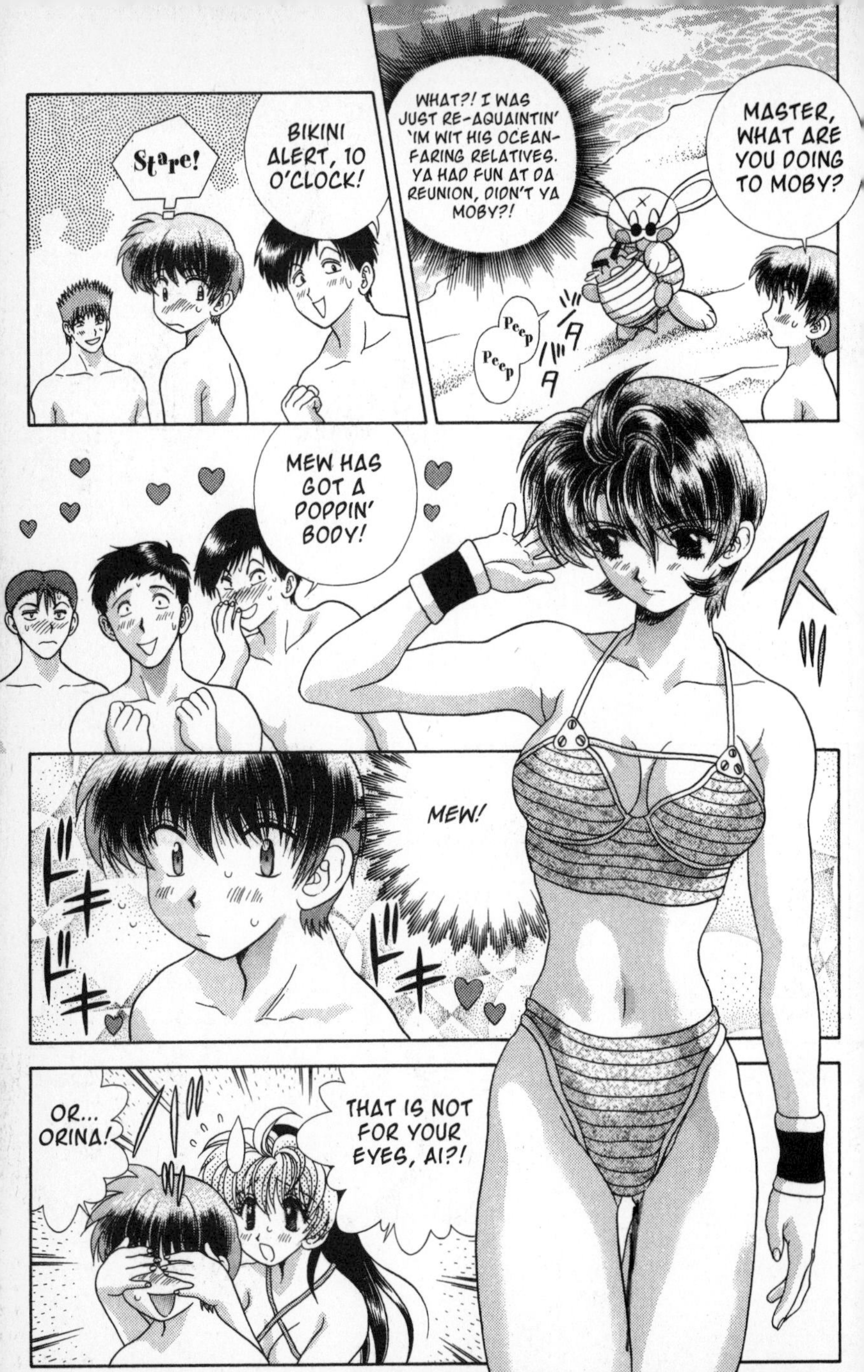
MASTER, WHAT ARE YOU DOING TO MOBY?
WHAT?! I WAS JUST RE-AQUAINTIN' 'IM WIT HIS OCEAN-FARING RELATIVES. YA HAD FUN AT DA REUNION, DIDN'T YA MOBY?!
Peep
Peep
BIKINI ALERT, 10 O'CLOCK!
Stare!
MEW HAS GOT A POPPIN' BODY!
MEW!
ドキ
ドキ
ドキ
THAT IS NOT FOR YOUR EYES, AI?!
OR... ORINA!

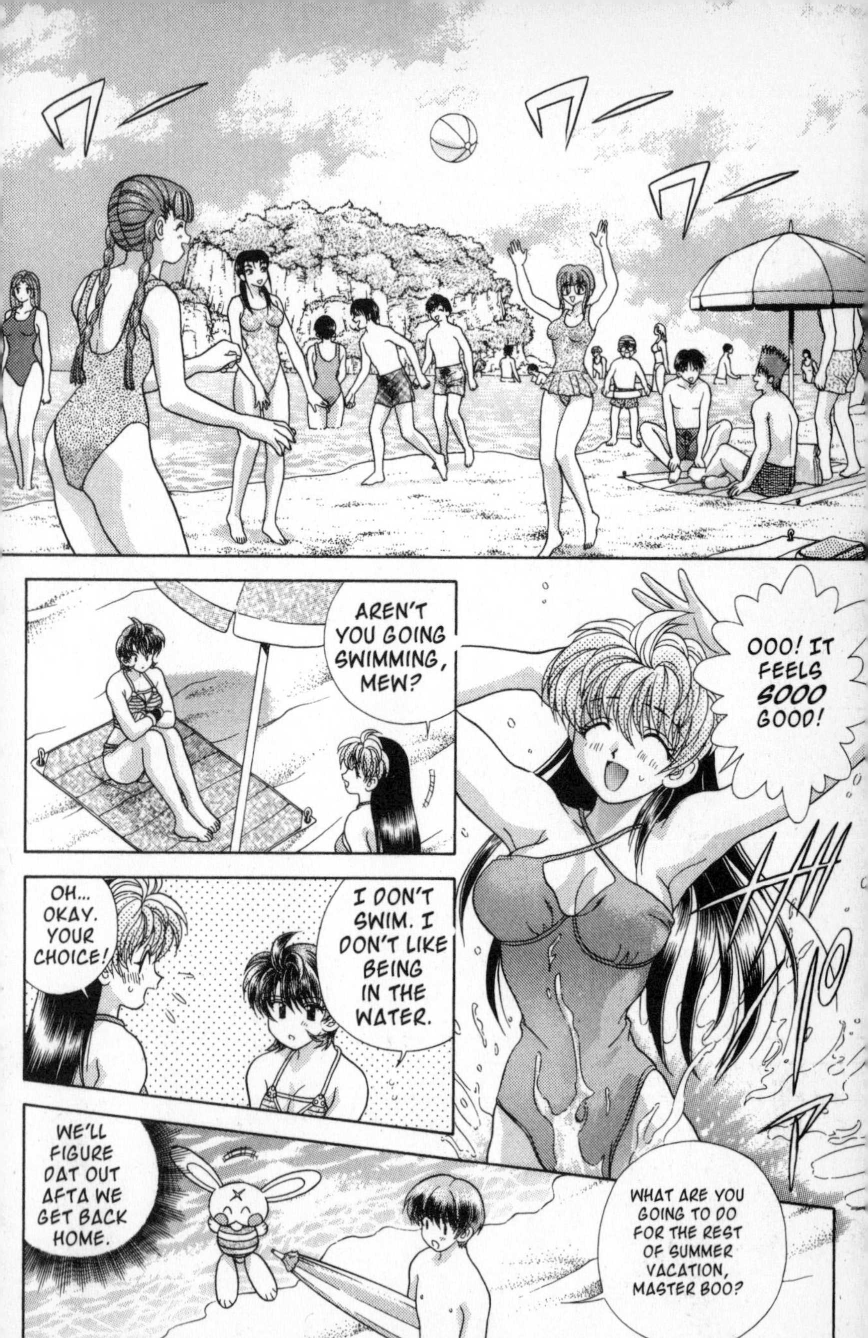
OOO! IT FEELS SOOO GOOD!
AREN'T YOU GOING SWIMMING, MEW?
I DON'T SWIM. I DON'T LIKE BEING IN THE WATER.
OH... OKAY. YOUR CHOICE!
WHAT ARE YOU GOING TO DO FOR THE REST OF SUMMER VACATION, MASTER BOO?
WE'LL FIGURE DAT OUT AFTA WE GET BACK HOME.

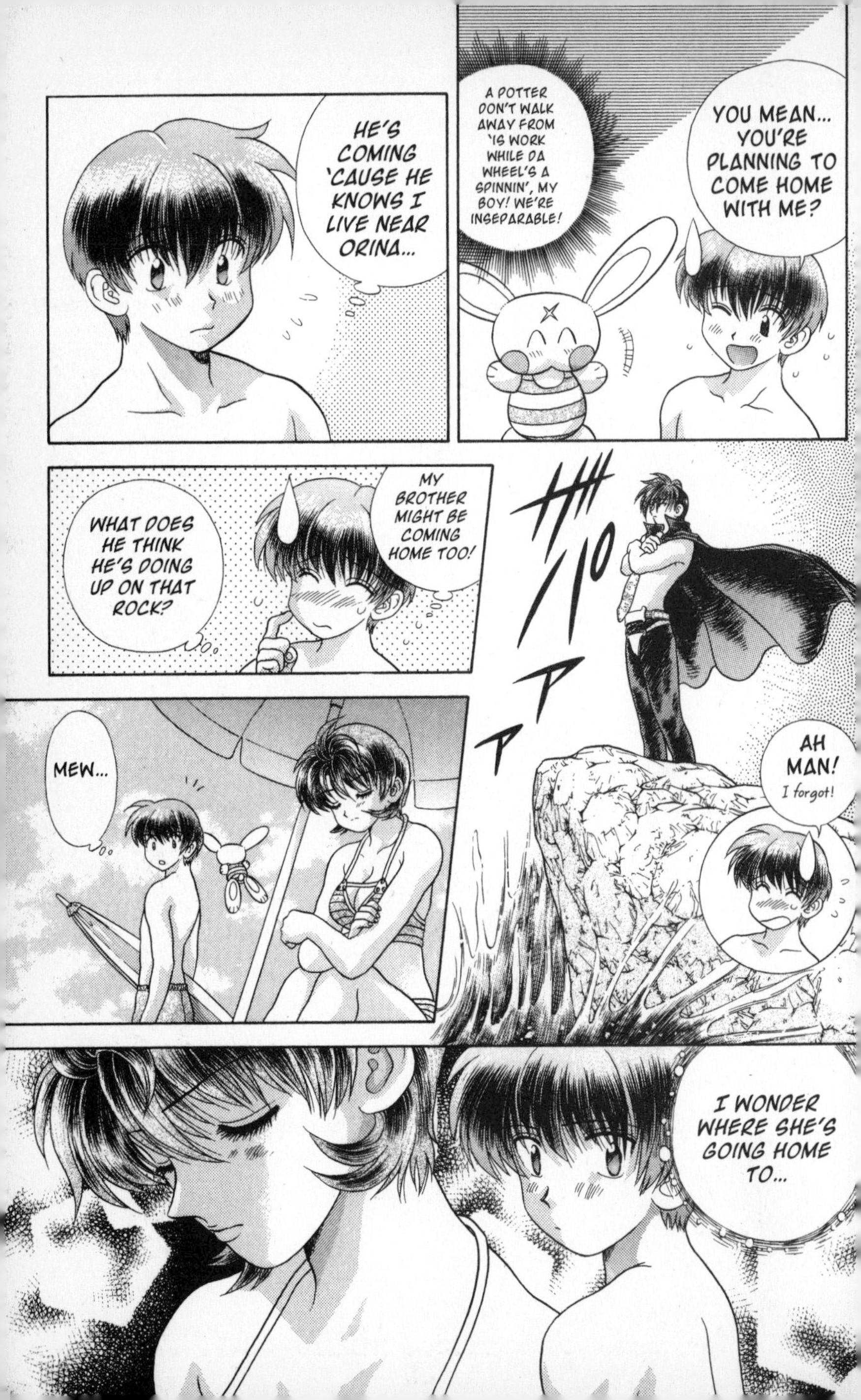
YOU MEAN... YOU'RE PLANNING TO COME HOME WITH ME?
A POTTER DON'T WALK AWAY FROM 'IS WORK WHILE DA WHEEL'S A SPINNIN', MY BOY! WE'RE INSEPARABLE!
HE'S COMING 'CAUSE HE KNOWS I LIVE NEAR ORINA...
AH MAN! I forgot!
MY BROTHER MIGHT BE COMING HOME TOO!
WHAT DOES HE THINK HE'S DOING UP ON THAT ROCK?
MEW...
I WONDER WHERE SHE'S GOING HOME TO...

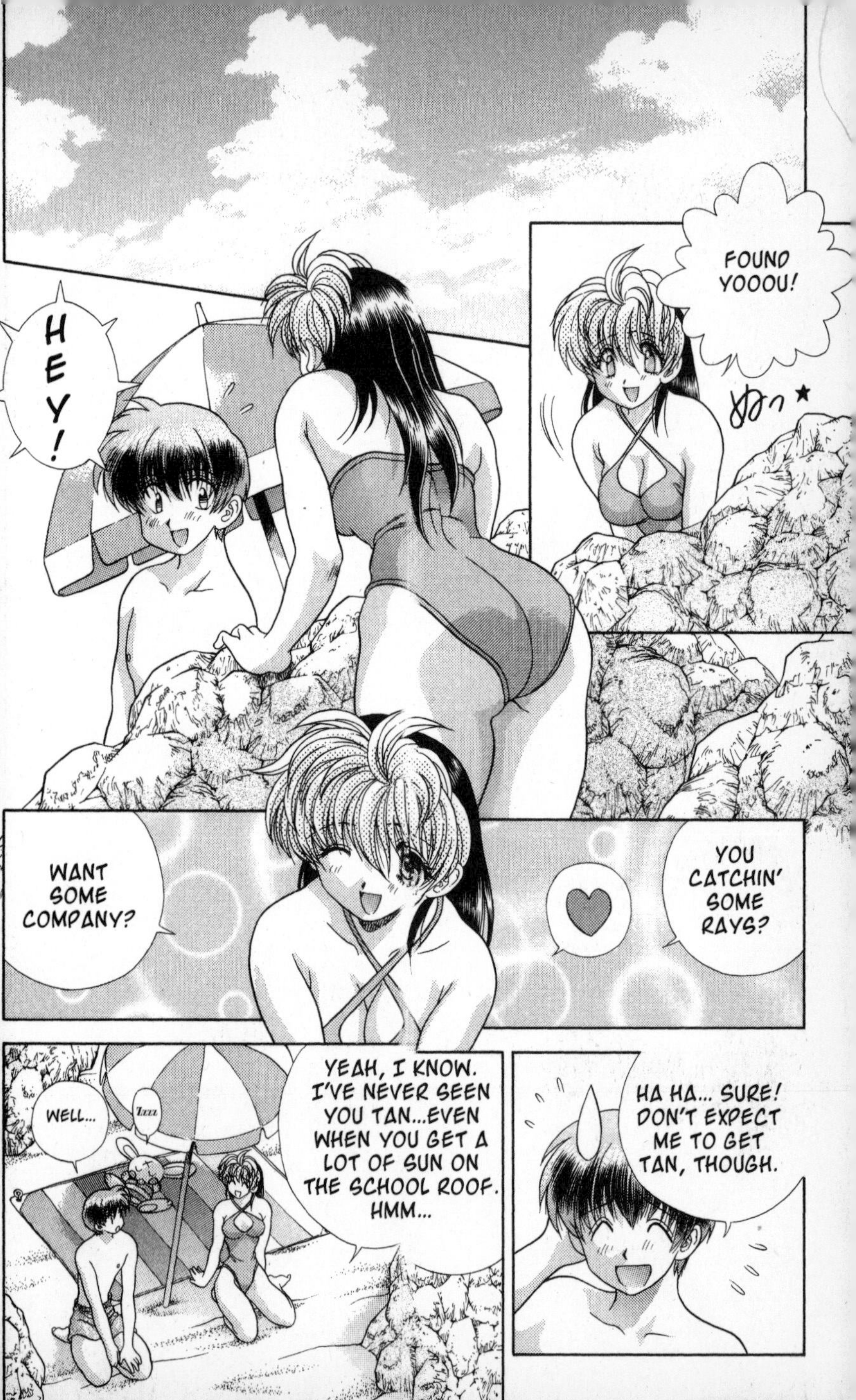
FOUND YOOOU!
ぬっ★
HEY!
YOU CATCHIN' SOME RAYS?
WANT SOME COMPANY?
HA HA... SURE! DON'T EXPECT ME TO GET TAN, THOUGH.
YEAH, I KNOW. I'VE NEVER SEEN YOU TAN...EVEN WHEN YOU GET A LOT OF SUN ON THE SCHOOL ROOF. HMM...
Zzzz
WELL...

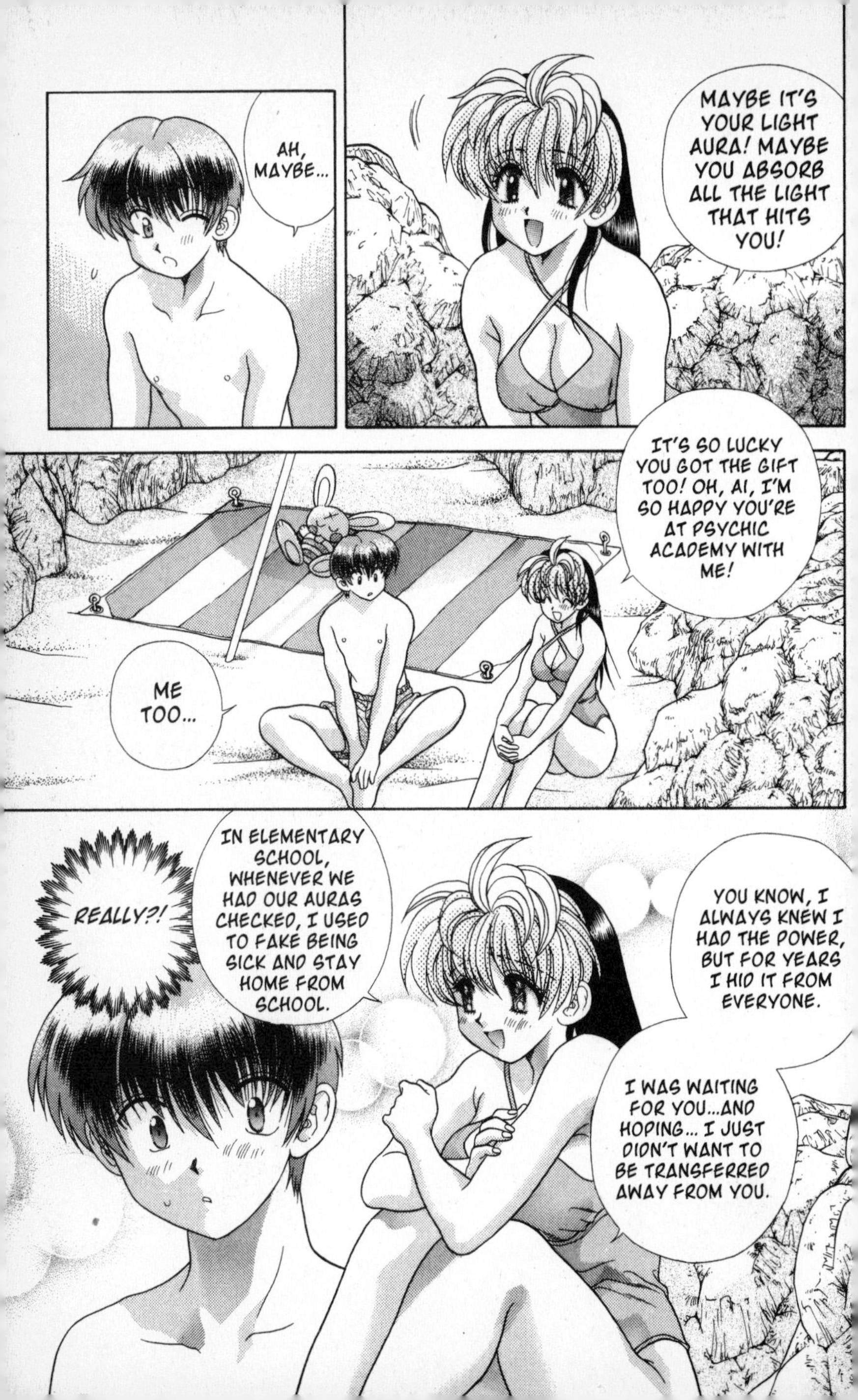
MAYBE IT'S YOUR LIGHT AURA! MAYBE YOU ABSORB ALL THE LIGHT THAT HITS YOU!
AH, MAYBE...
IT'S SO LUCKY YOU GOT THE GIFT TOO! OH, AI, I'M SO HAPPY YOU'RE AT PSYCHIC ACADEMY WITH ME!
ME TOO...
YOU KNOW, I ALWAYS KNEW I HAD THE POWER, BUT FOR YEARS I HID IT FROM EVERYONE.
IN ELEMENTARY SCHOOL, WHENEVER WE HAD OUR AURAS CHECKED, I USED TO FAKE BEING SICK AND STAY HOME FROM SCHOOL.
REALLY?!
I WAS WAITING FOR YOU...AND HOPING... I JUST DIDN'T WANT TO BE TRANSFERRED AWAY FROM YOU.

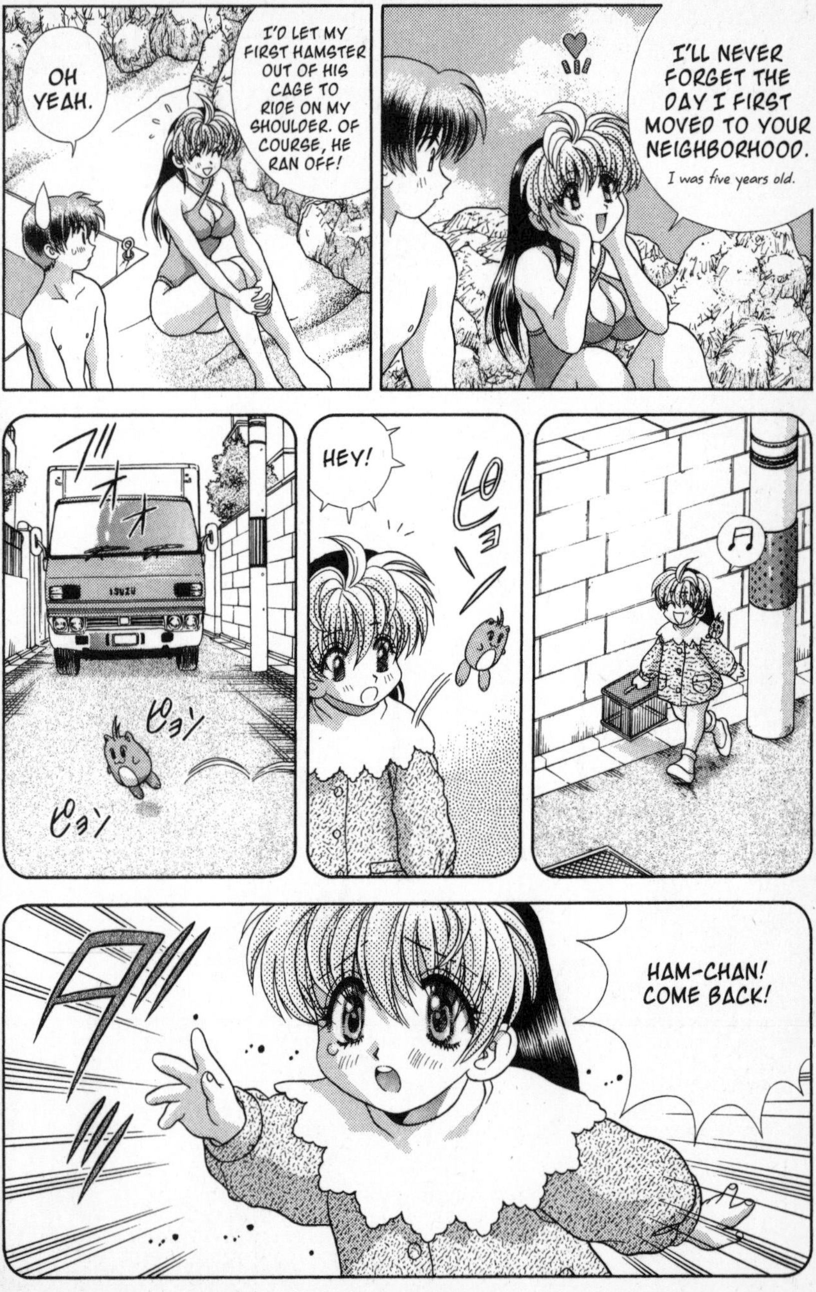
I'LL NEVER FORGET THE DAY I FIRST MOVED TO YOUR NEIGHBORHOOD.
I was five years old.
I'D LET MY FIRST HAMSTER OUT OF HIS CAGE TO RIDE ON MY SHOULDER. OF COURSE, HE RAN OFF!
OH YEAH.
♪
HEY!
ピョン
ブォオ
ピョン
ピョン
ダッ
HAM-CHAN! COME BACK!

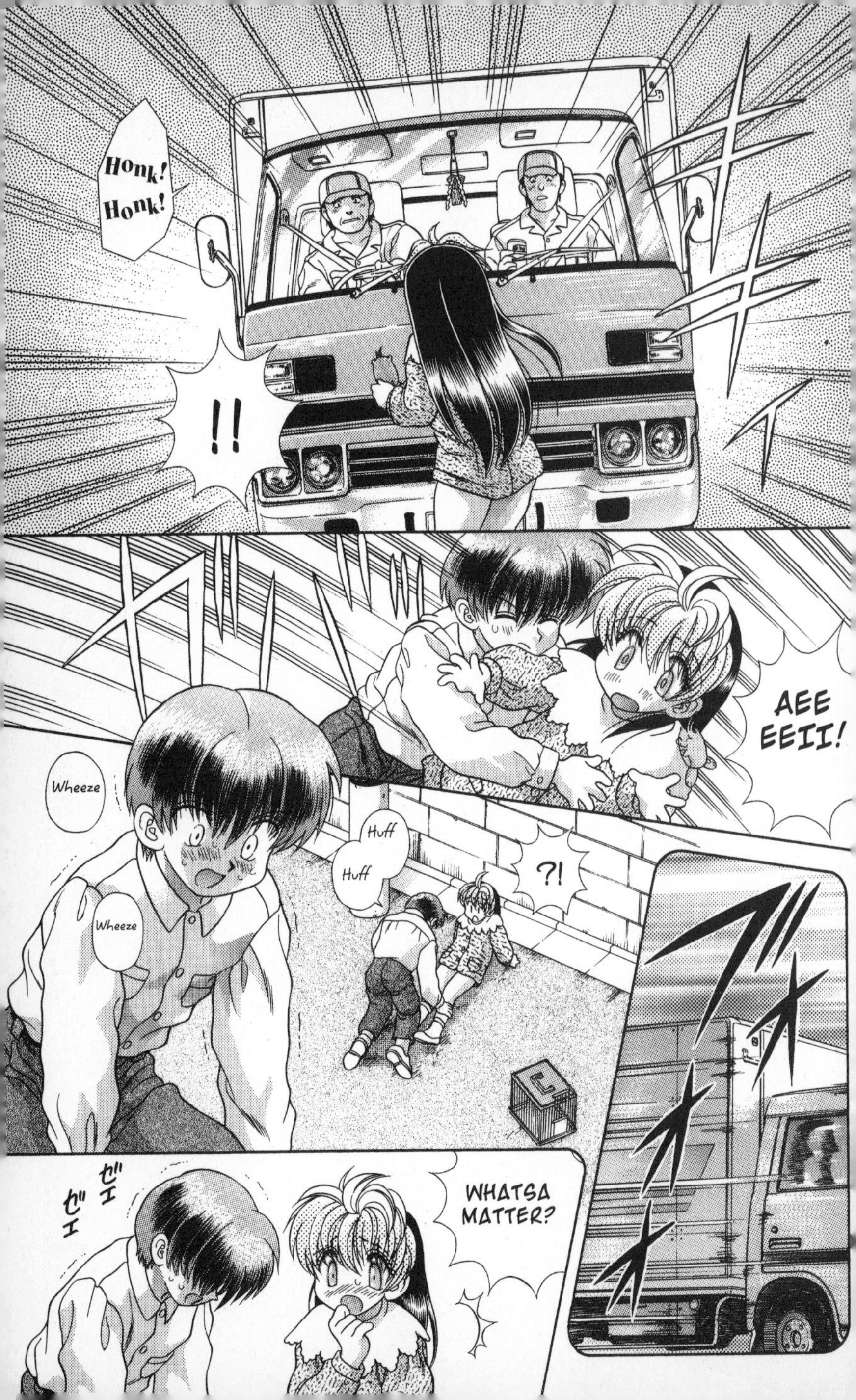
Honk! Honk!
!!
AEE EEII!
?!
Huff Huff
Wheeze
Wheeze
WHATSA MATTER?
ゼイ ゼイ

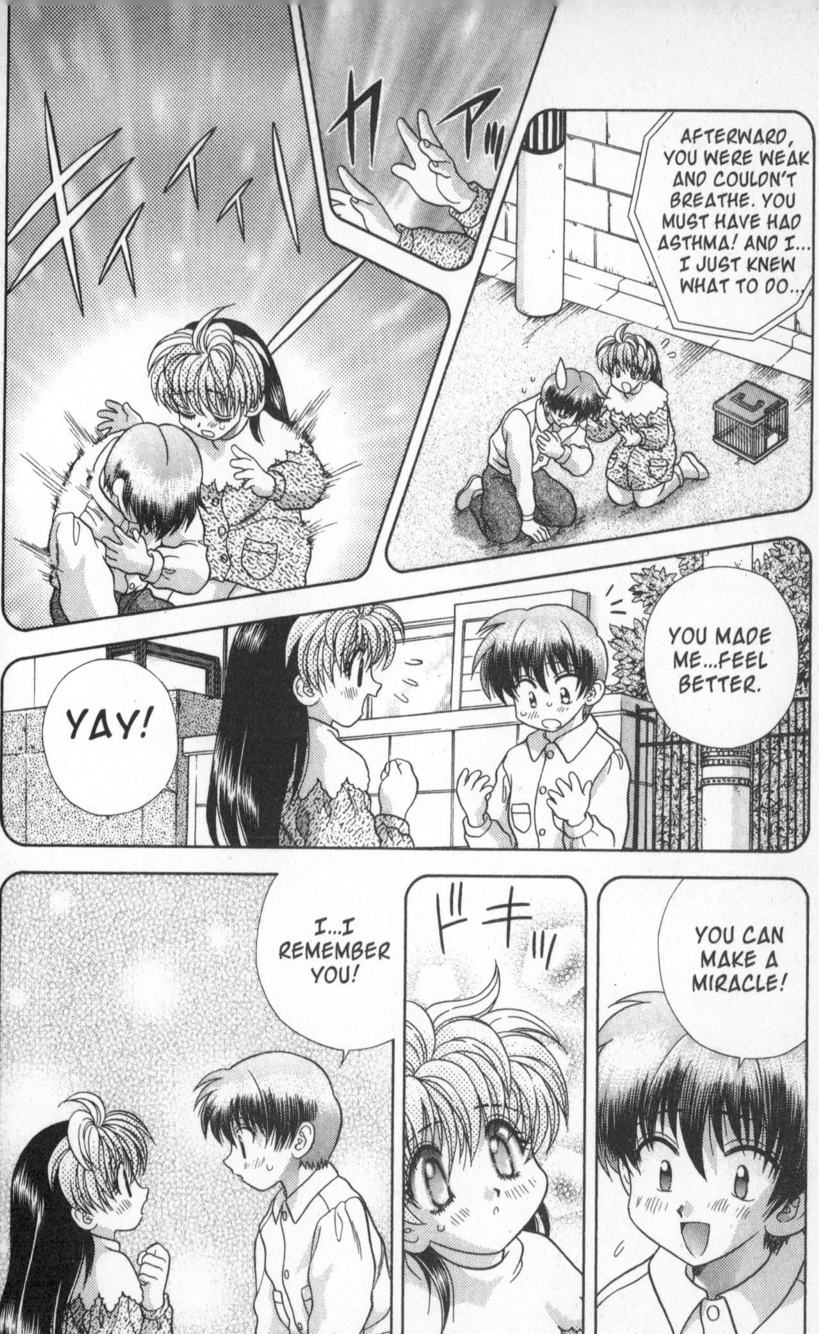
AFTERWARD, YOU WERE WEAK AND COULDN'T BREATHE. YOU MUST HAVE HAD ASTHMA! AND I... I JUST KNEW WHAT TO DO...
YOU MADE ME...FEEL BETTER.
YAY!
YOU CAN MAKE A MIRACLE!
ドキ
I...I REMEMBER YOU!

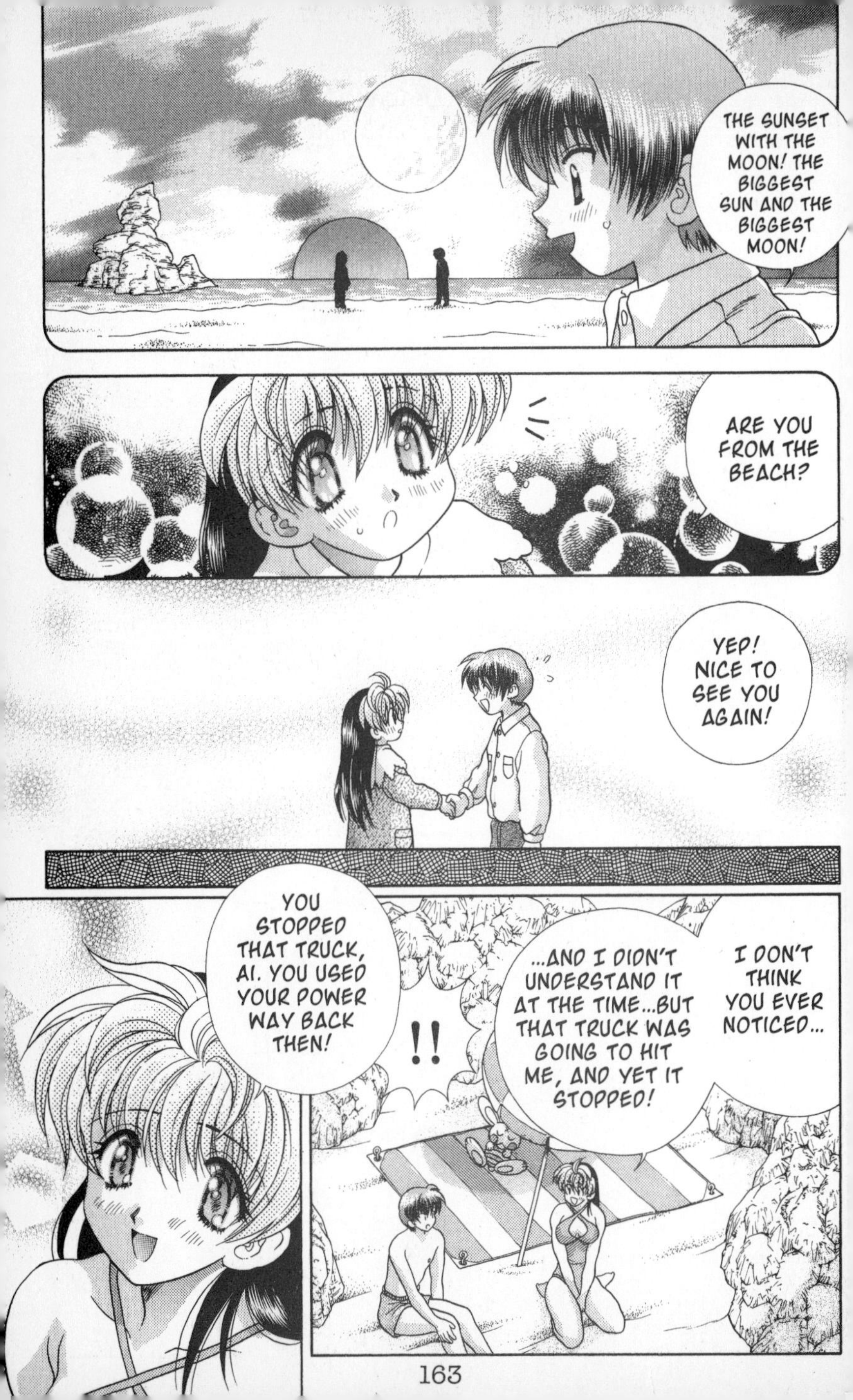
THE SUNSET WITH THE MOON! THE BIGGEST SUN AND THE BIGGEST MOON!
ARE YOU FROM THE BEACH?
YEP! NICE TO SEE YOU AGAIN!
I DON'T THINK YOU EVER NOTICED...
...AND I DIDN'T UNDERSTAND IT AT THE TIME...BUT THAT TRUCK WAS GOING TO HIT ME, AND YET IT STOPPED!
!!
YOU STOPPED THAT TRUCK, AI. YOU USED YOUR POWER WAY BACK THEN!

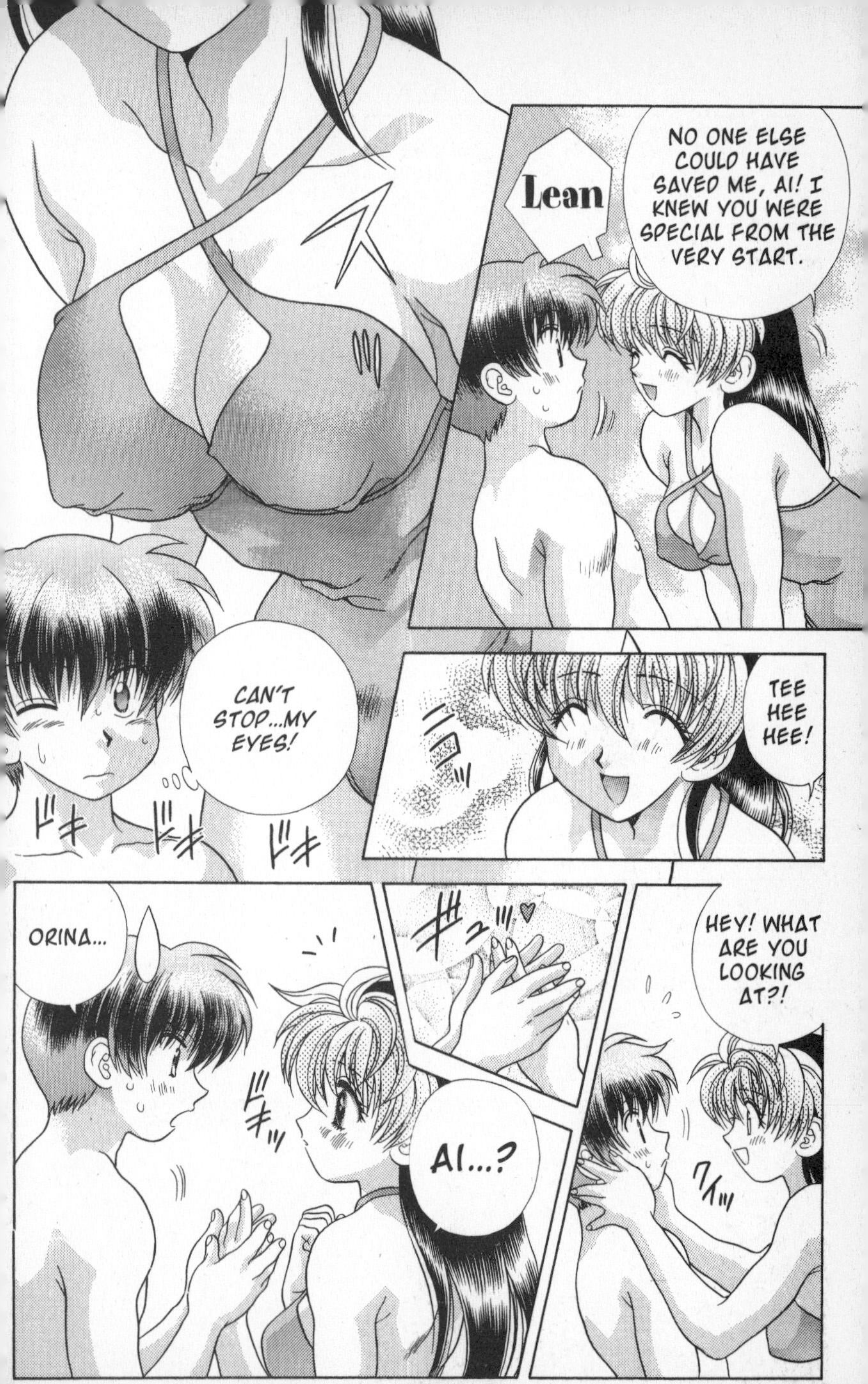
Lean
NO ONE ELSE COULD HAVE SAVED ME, AI! I KNEW YOU WERE SPECIAL FROM THE VERY START.
TEE HEE HEE!
CAN'T STOP...MY EYES!
HEY! WHAT ARE YOU LOOKING AT?!
ORINA...
AI...?

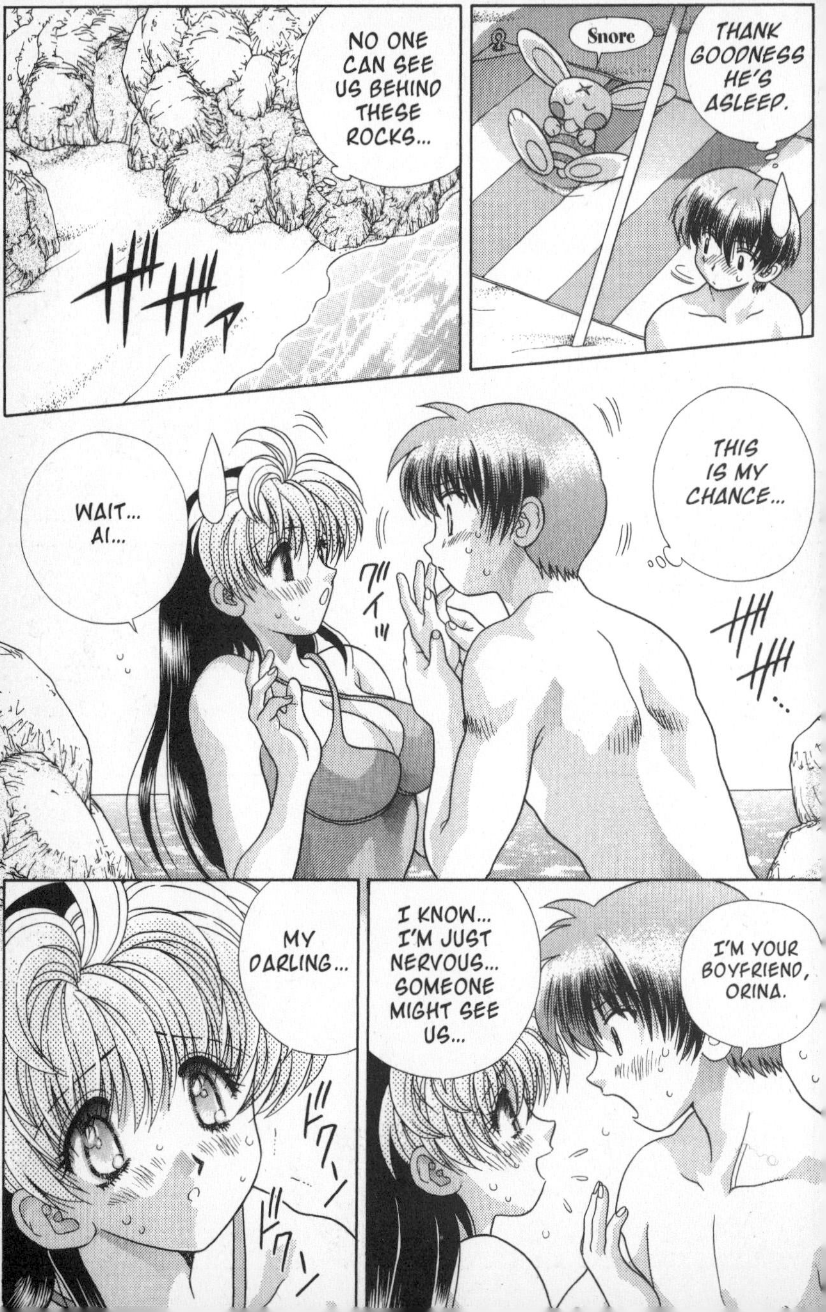
Snore
THANK GOODNESS HE'S ASLEEP.
NO ONE CAN SEE US BEHIND THESE ROCKS...
THIS IS MY CHANCE...
WAIT... AI...
I'M YOUR BOYFRIEND, ORINA.
I KNOW... I'M JUST NERVOUS... SOMEONE MIGHT SEE US...
MY DARLING...

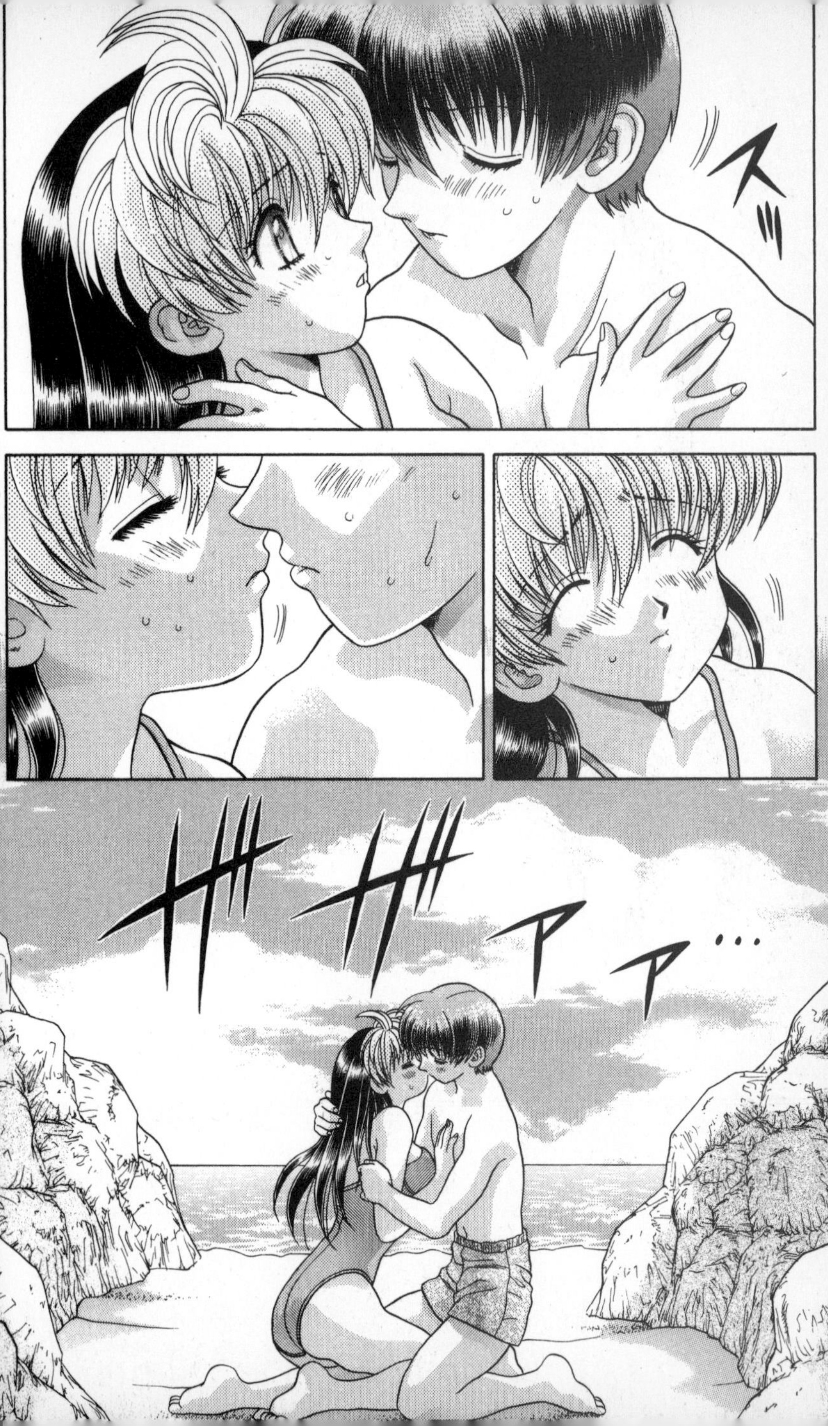
ス
ザザアア…

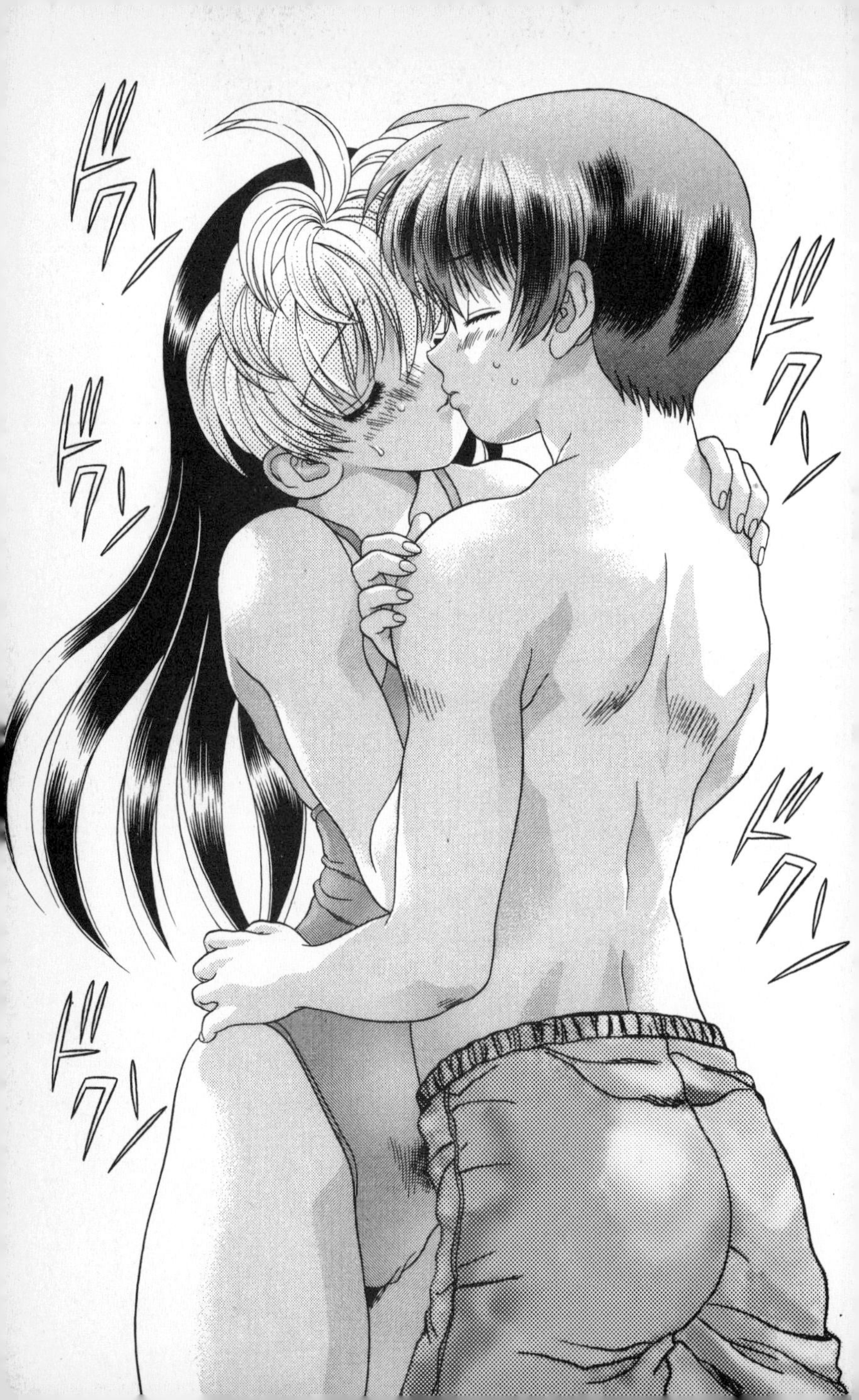
ドクン
ドクン
ドクン
ドクン
ドクン

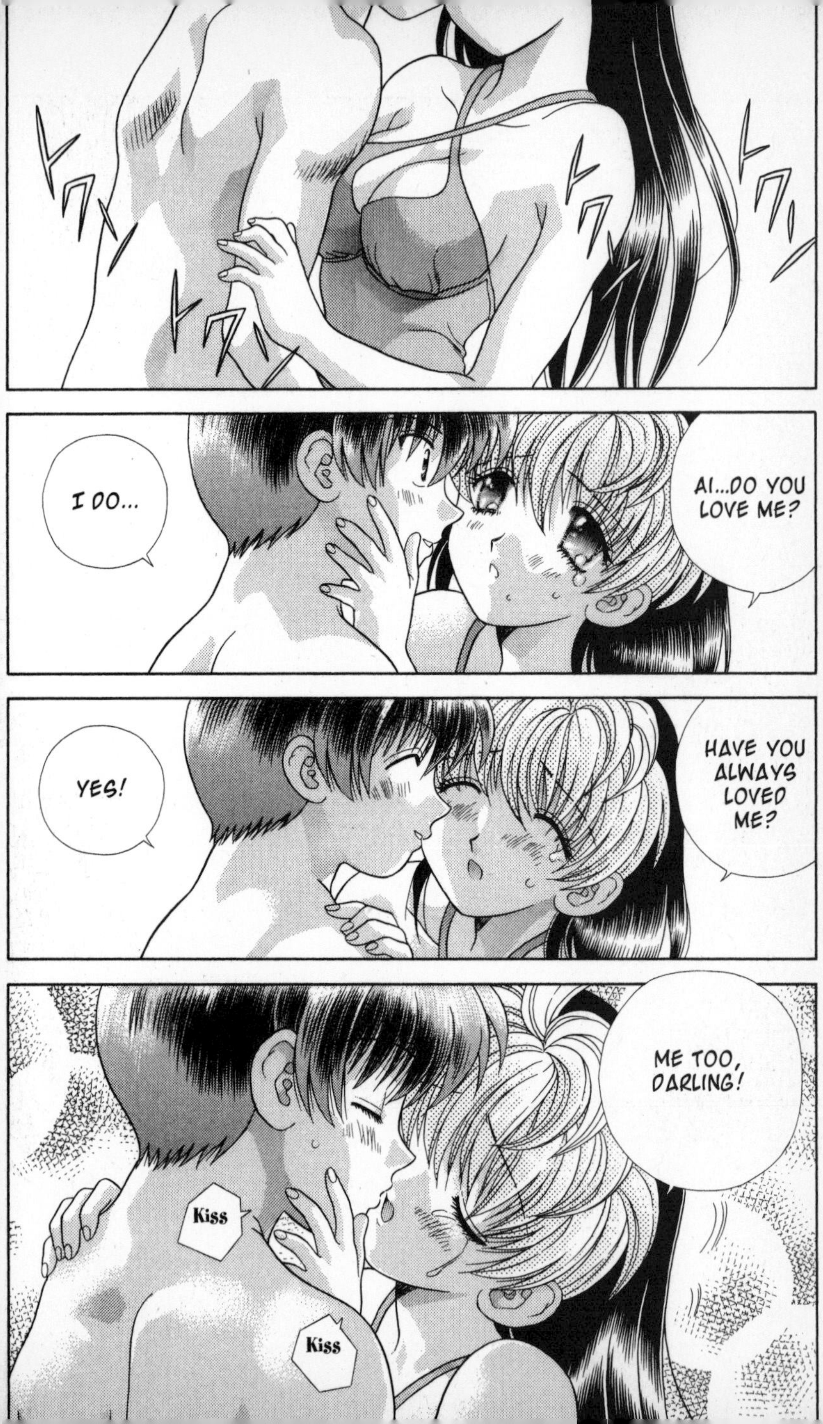
AI...DO YOU LOVE ME?
I DO...
HAVE YOU ALWAYS LOVED ME?
YES!
ME TOO, DARLING!
Kiss
Kiss

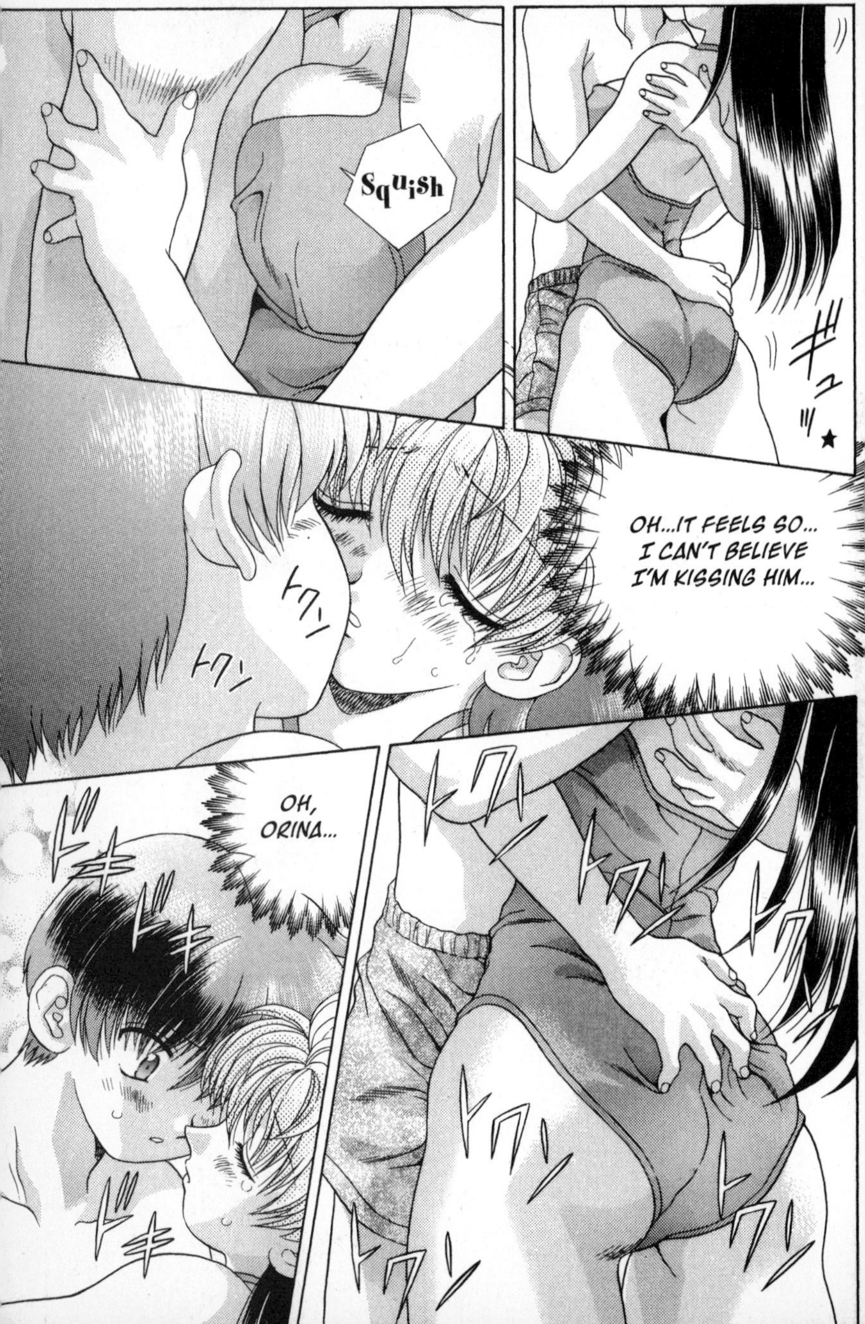

ギュッ★
Squish
トクン
トクン
OH...IT FEELS SO... I CAN'T BELIEVE I'M KISSING HIM...
トクン
トクン
トクン
トクン
トクン
トクン
OH, ORINA...
ドキドキ
ドキ

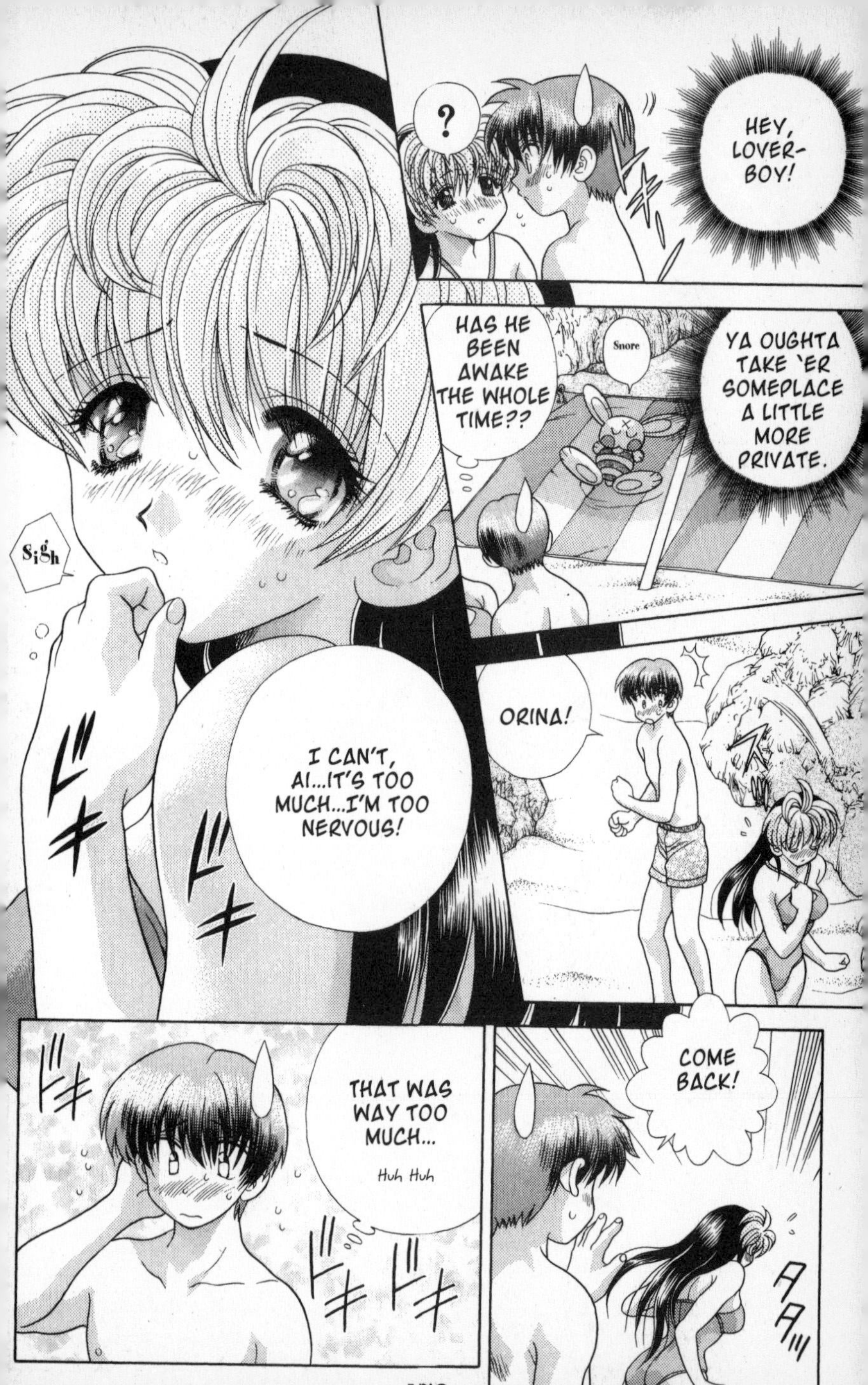
HEY, LOVER-BOY!
?
YA OUGHTA TAKE 'ER SOMEPLACE A LITTLE MORE PRIVATE.
HAS HE BEEN AWAKE THE WHOLE TIME??
Snore
ORINA!
Sigh
I CAN'T, AI...IT'S TOO MUCH...I'M TOO NERVOUS!
ドキ
ドキ
COME BACK!
タタ
THAT WAS WAY TOO MUCH...
Huh Huh
ドキ
ドキ
ドキ

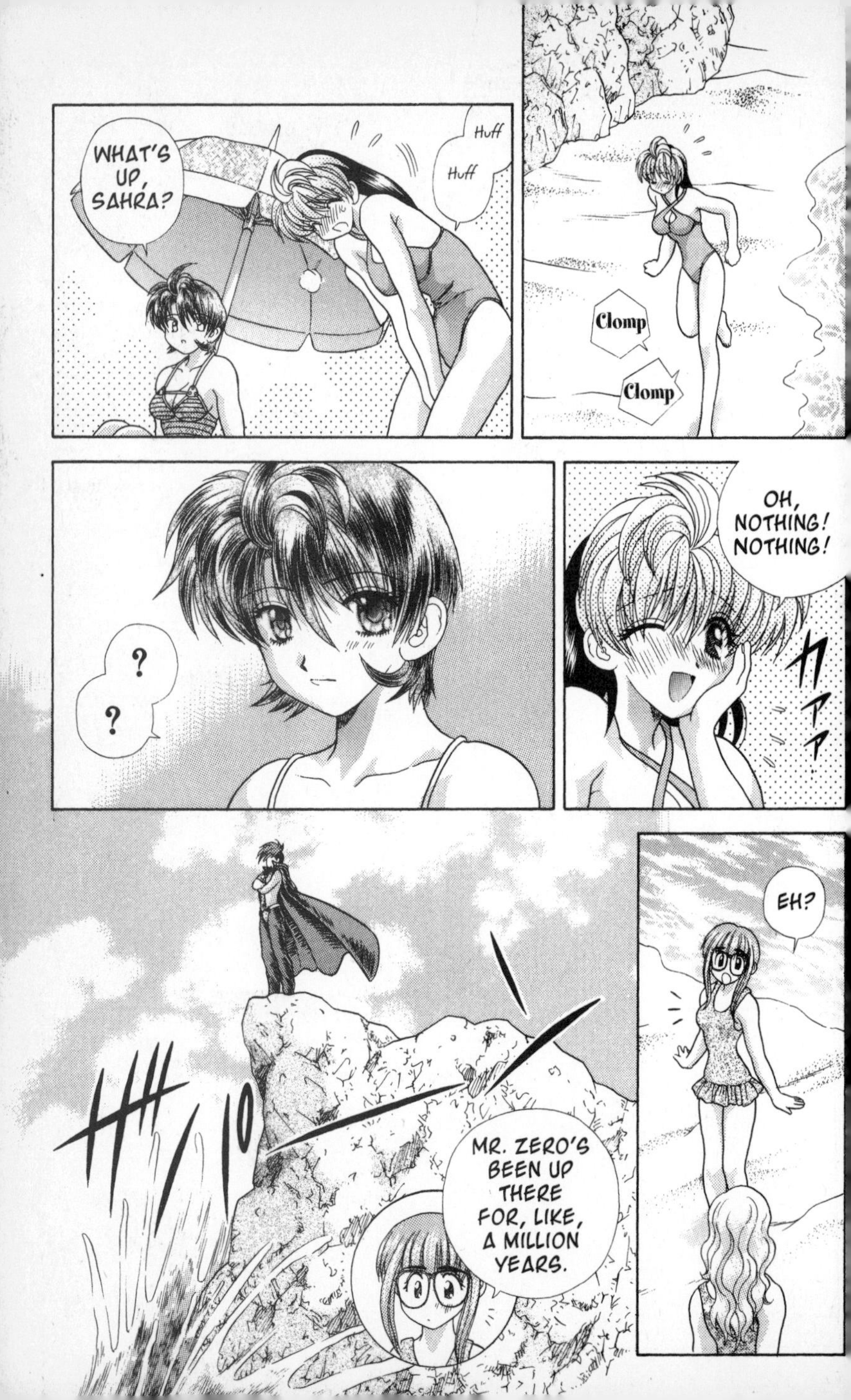
Clomp
Clomp
Huff
Huff
WHAT'S UP, SAHRA?
OH, NOTHING! NOTHING!
?
?
EH?
MR. ZERO'S BEEN UP THERE FOR, LIKE, A MILLION YEARS.

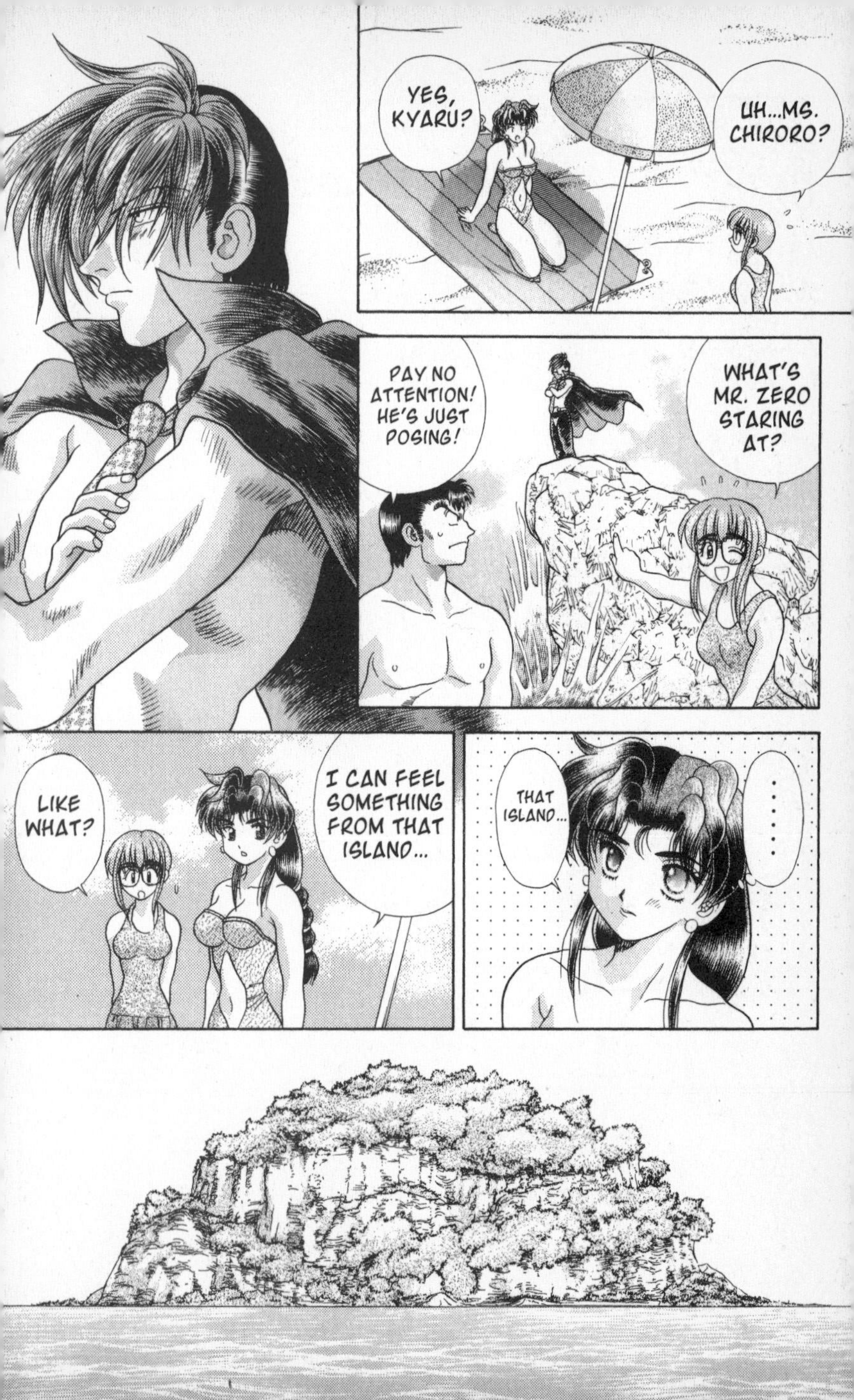
UH...MS. CHIRORO?
YES, KYARU?
WHAT'S MR. ZERO STARING AT?
PAY NO ATTENTION! HE'S JUST POSING!
......
THAT ISLAND...
I CAN FEEL SOMETHING FROM THAT ISLAND...
LIKE WHAT?

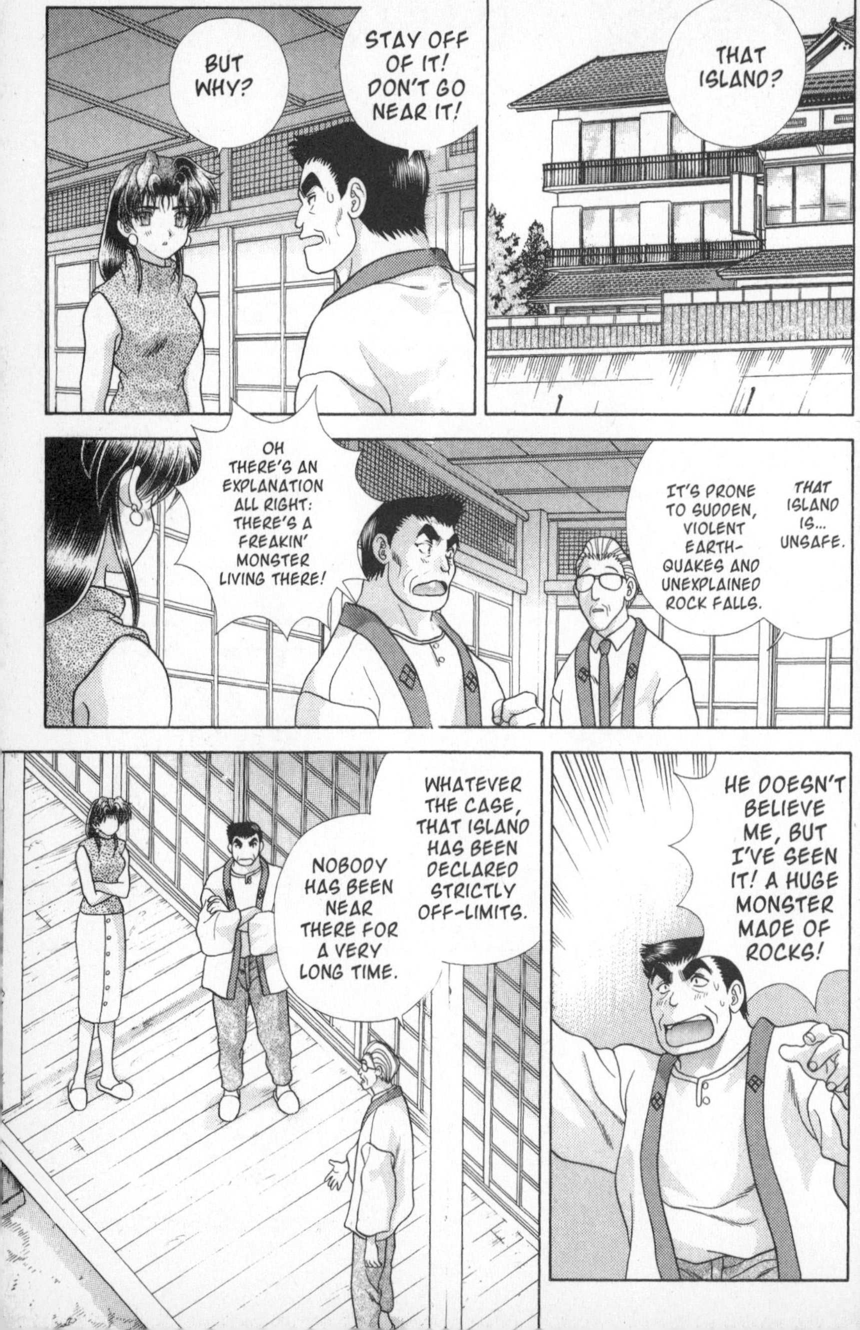
THAT ISLAND?
STAY OFF OF IT! DON'T GO NEAR IT!
BUT WHY?
THAT ISLAND IS... UNSAFE.
IT'S PRONE TO SUDDEN, VIOLENT EARTH-QUAKES AND UNEXPLAINED ROCK FALLS.
OH THERE'S AN EXPLANATION ALL RIGHT: THERE'S A FREAKIN' MONSTER LIVING THERE!
HE DOESN'T BELIEVE ME, BUT I'VE SEEN IT! A HUGE MONSTER MADE OF ROCKS!
WHATEVER THE CASE, THAT ISLAND HAS BEEN DECLARED STRICTLY OFF-LIMITS.
NOBODY HAS BEEN NEAR THERE FOR A VERY LONG TIME.

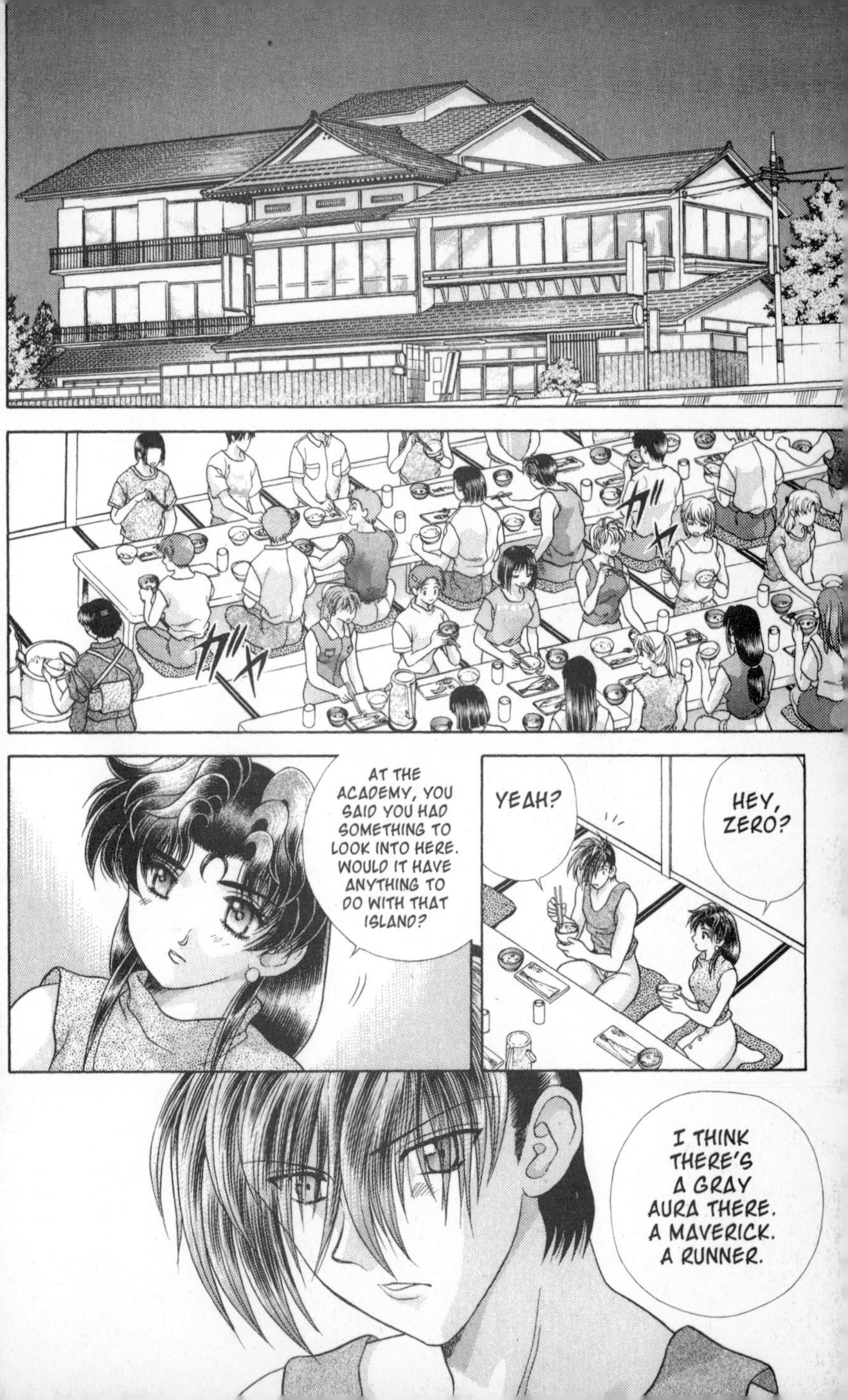
ガヤ
ガヤ
HEY, ZERO?
YEAH?
AT THE ACADEMY, YOU SAID YOU HAD SOMETHING TO LOOK INTO HERE. WOULD IT HAVE ANYTHING TO DO WITH THAT ISLAND?
I THINK THERE'S A GRAY AURA THERE. A MAVERICK. A RUNNER.

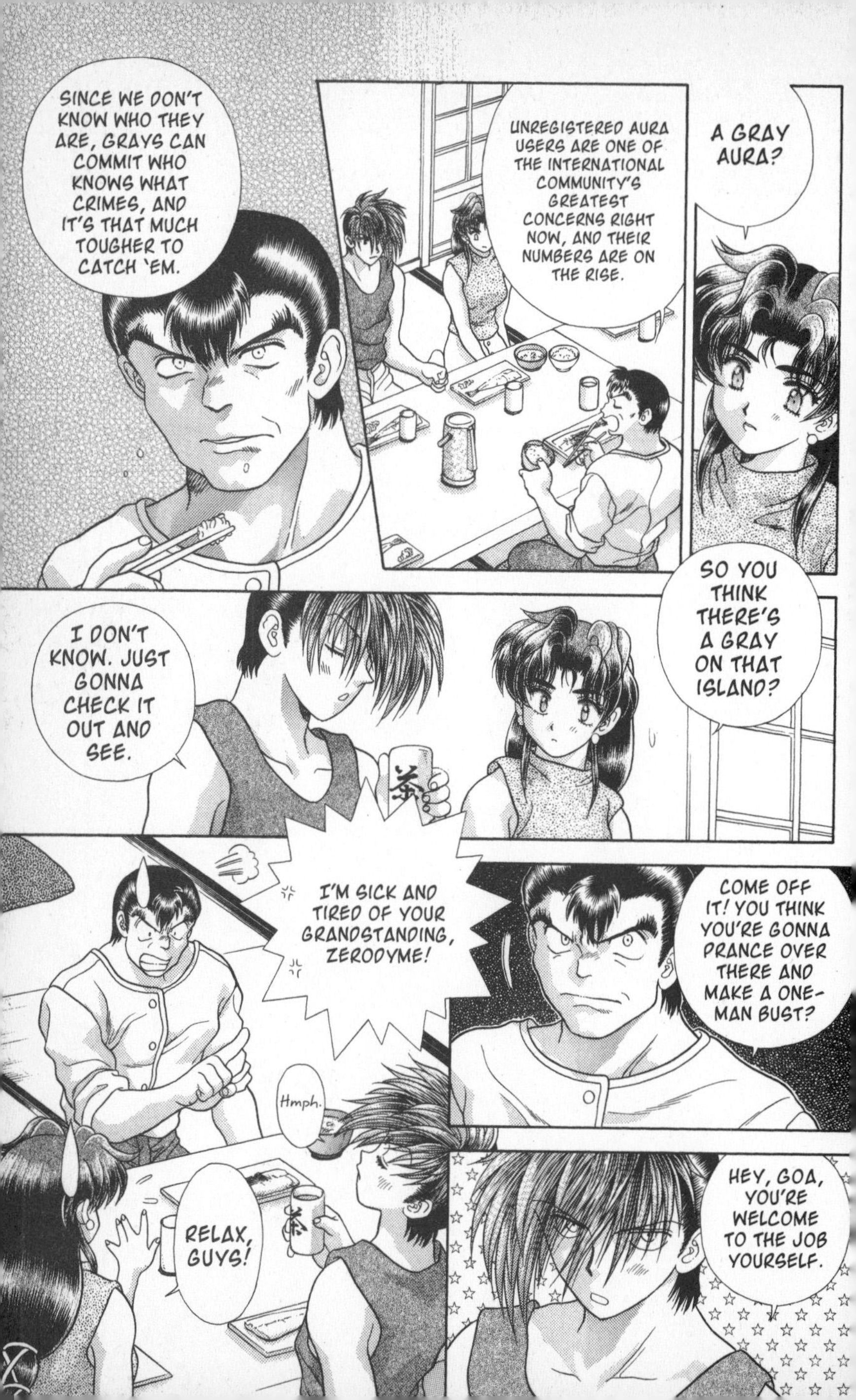
A GRAY AURA?
UNREGISTERED AURA USERS ARE ONE OF THE INTERNATIONAL COMMUNITY'S GREATEST CONCERNS RIGHT NOW, AND THEIR NUMBERS ARE ON THE RISE.
SINCE WE DON'T KNOW WHO THEY ARE, GRAYS CAN COMMIT WHO KNOWS WHAT CRIMES, AND IT'S THAT MUCH TOUGHER TO CATCH 'EM.
SO YOU THINK THERE'S A GRAY ON THAT ISLAND?
I DON'T KNOW. JUST GONNA CHECK IT OUT AND SEE.
I'M SICK AND TIRED OF YOUR GRANDSTANDING, ZERODYME!
COME OFF IT! YOU THINK YOU'RE GONNA PRANCE OVER THERE AND MAKE A ONE-MAN BUST?
HEY, GOA, YOU'RE WELCOME TO THE JOB YOURSELF.
Hmph.
RELAX, GUYS!

Sign: Inn - Sea of Japan (Nihonkai)

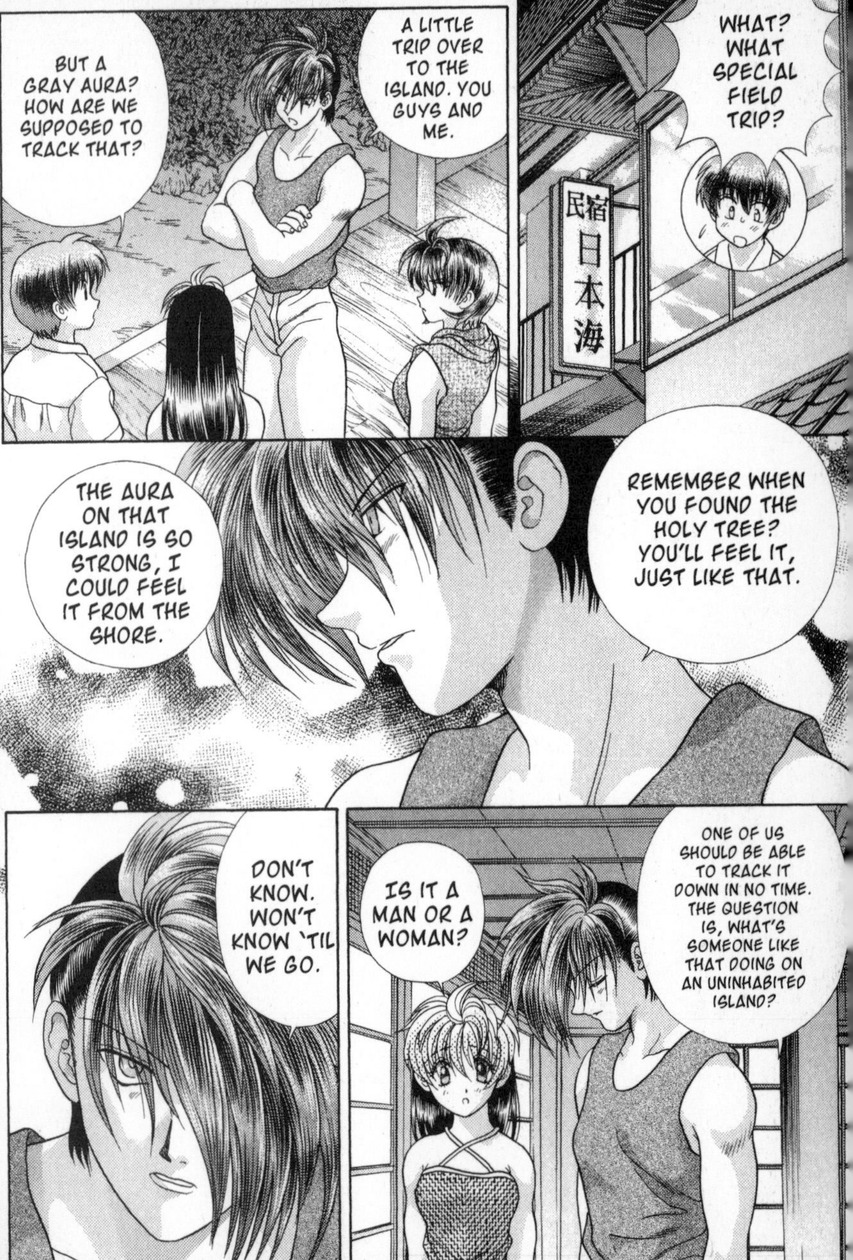

WHAT? WHAT SPECIAL FIELD TRIP?
民宿 日本海
A LITTLE TRIP OVER TO THE ISLAND. YOU GUYS AND ME.
BUT A GRAY AURA? HOW ARE WE SUPPOSED TO TRACK THAT?
REMEMBER WHEN YOU FOUND THE HOLY TREE? YOU'LL FEEL IT, JUST LIKE THAT.
THE AURA ON THAT ISLAND IS SO STRONG, I COULD FEEL IT FROM THE SHORE.
ONE OF US SHOULD BE ABLE TO TRACK IT DOWN IN NO TIME. THE QUESTION IS, WHAT'S SOMEONE LIKE THAT DOING ON AN UNINHABITED ISLAND?
IS IT A MAN OR A WOMAN?
DON'T KNOW. WON'T KNOW 'TIL WE GO.

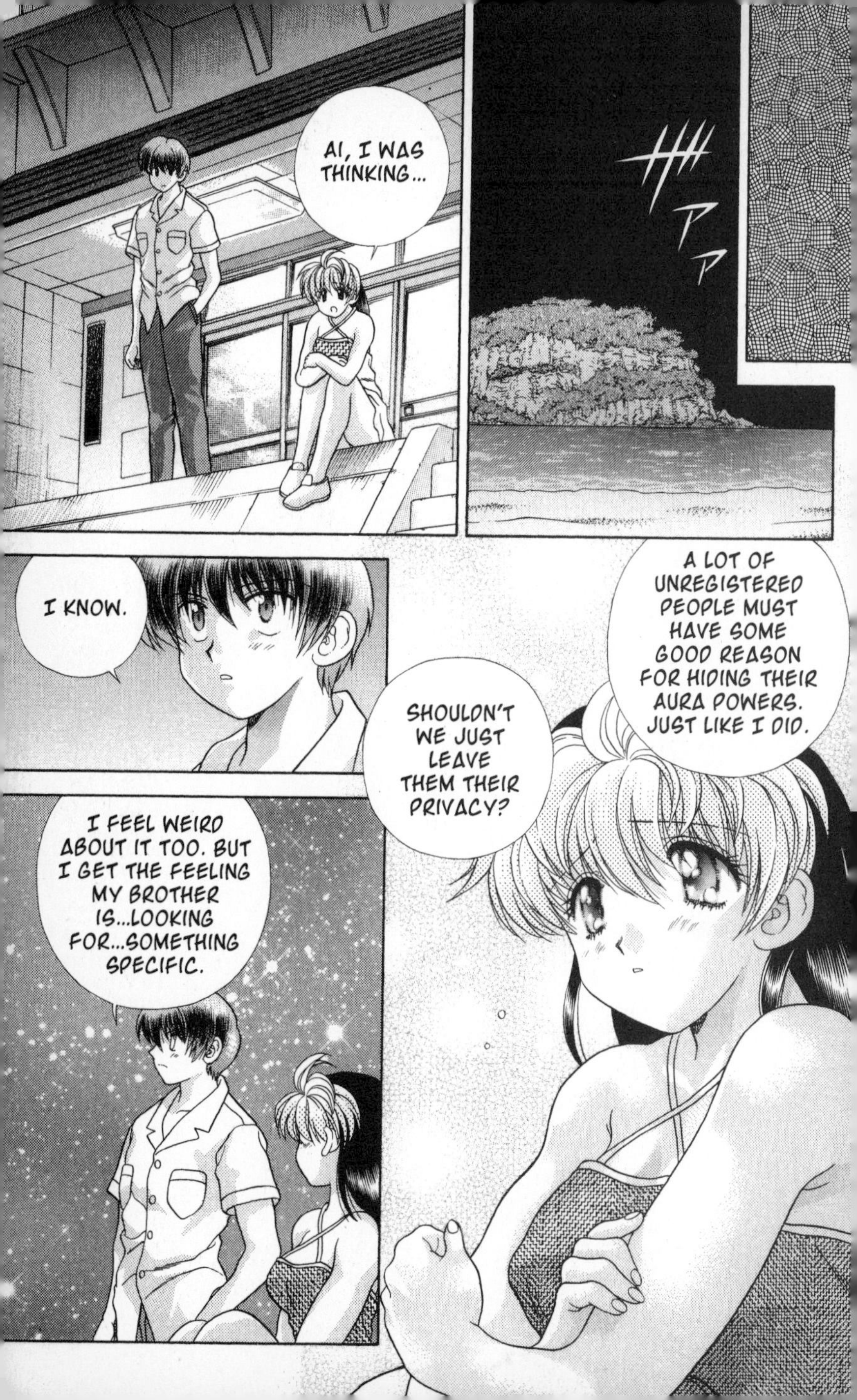
AI, I WAS THINKING...
A LOT OF UNREGISTERED PEOPLE MUST HAVE SOME GOOD REASON FOR HIDING THEIR AURA POWERS. JUST LIKE I DID.
SHOULDN'T WE JUST LEAVE THEM THEIR PRIVACY?
I KNOW.
I FEEL WEIRD ABOUT IT TOO. BUT I GET THE FEELING MY BROTHER IS...LOOKING FOR...SOMETHING SPECIFIC.

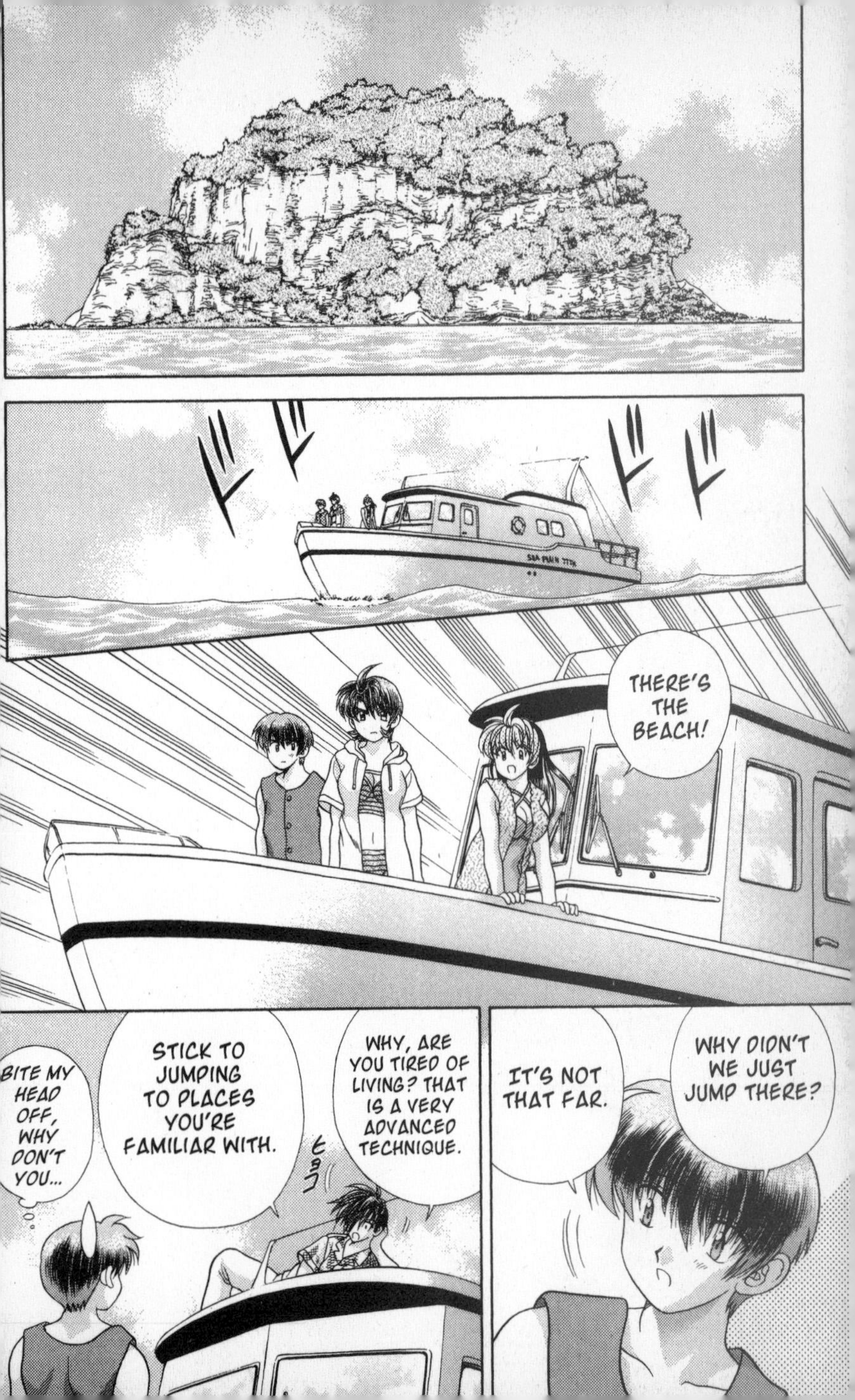
ドド
ドド
THERE'S THE BEACH!
WHY DIDN'T WE JUST JUMP THERE?
IT'S NOT THAT FAR.
WHY, ARE YOU TIRED OF LIVING? THAT IS A VERY ADVANCED TECHNIQUE.
ヒョコ
STICK TO JUMPING TO PLACES YOU'RE FAMILIAR WITH.
BITE MY HEAD OFF, WHY DON'T YOU...

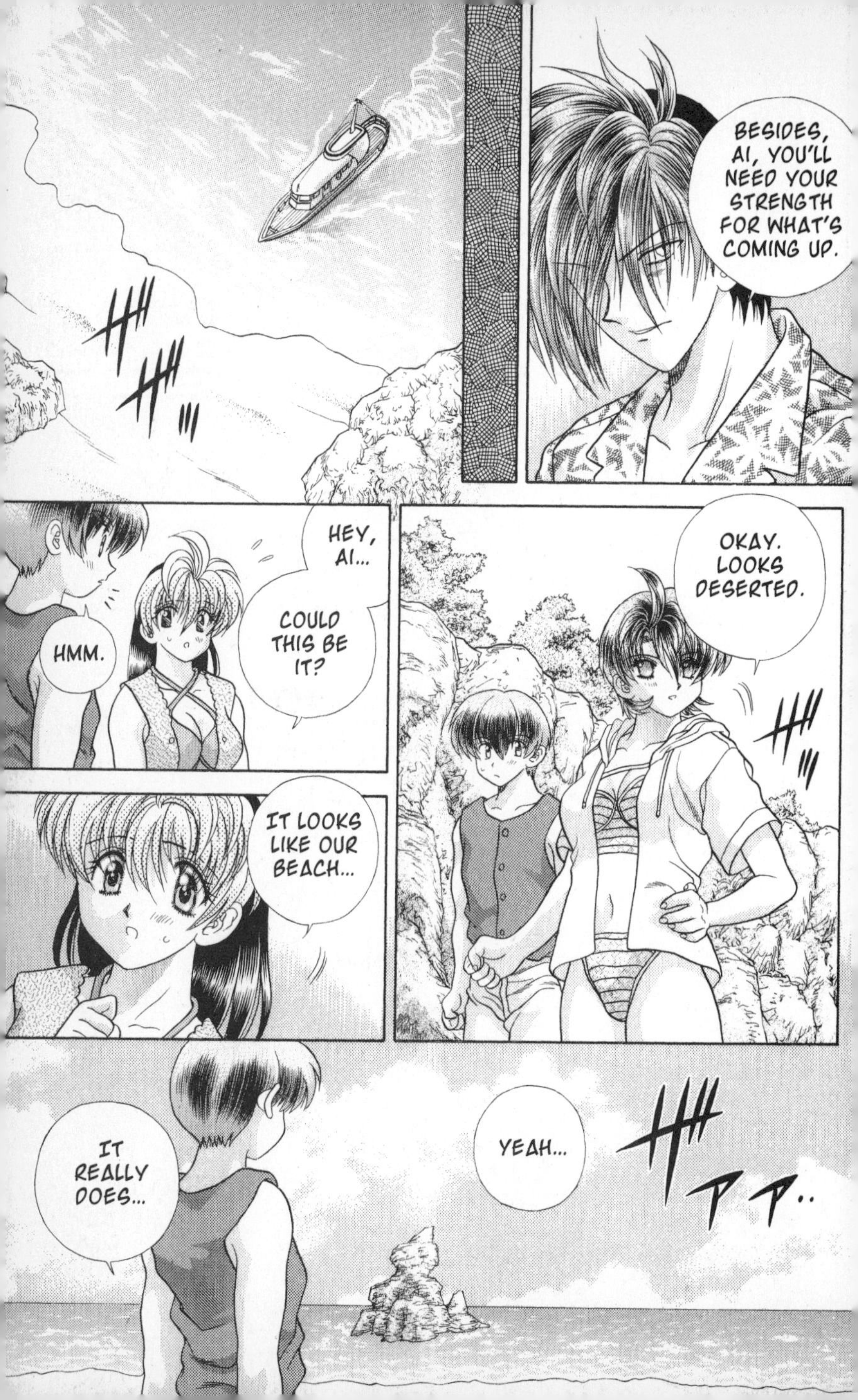
BESIDES, AI, YOU'LL NEED YOUR STRENGTH FOR WHAT'S COMING UP.
OKAY. LOOKS DESERTED.
HEY, AI...
COULD THIS BE IT?
HMM.
IT LOOKS LIKE OUR BEACH...
YEAH...
IT REALLY DOES...

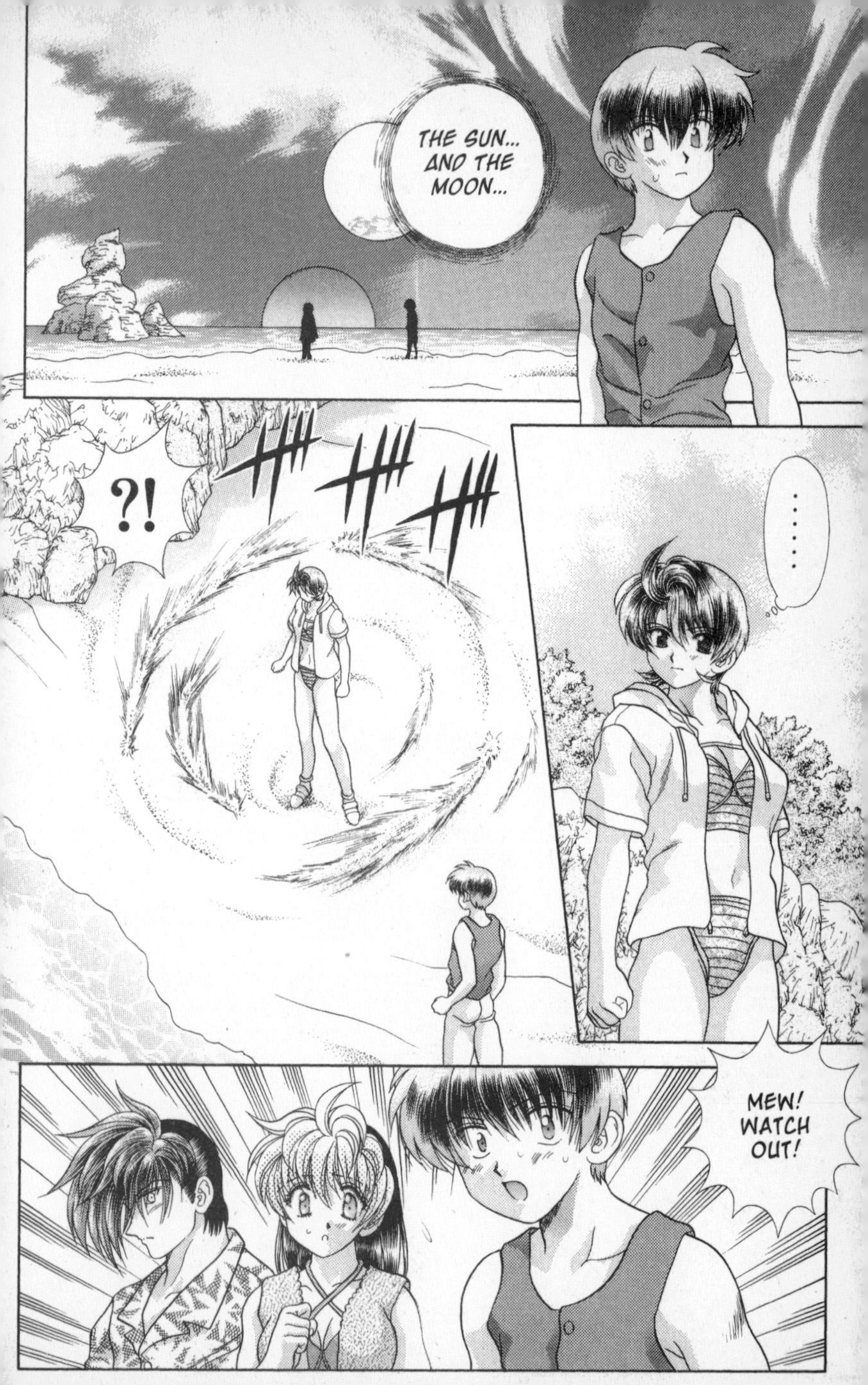
THE SUN... AND THE MOON...
......
?!
MEW! WATCH OUT!

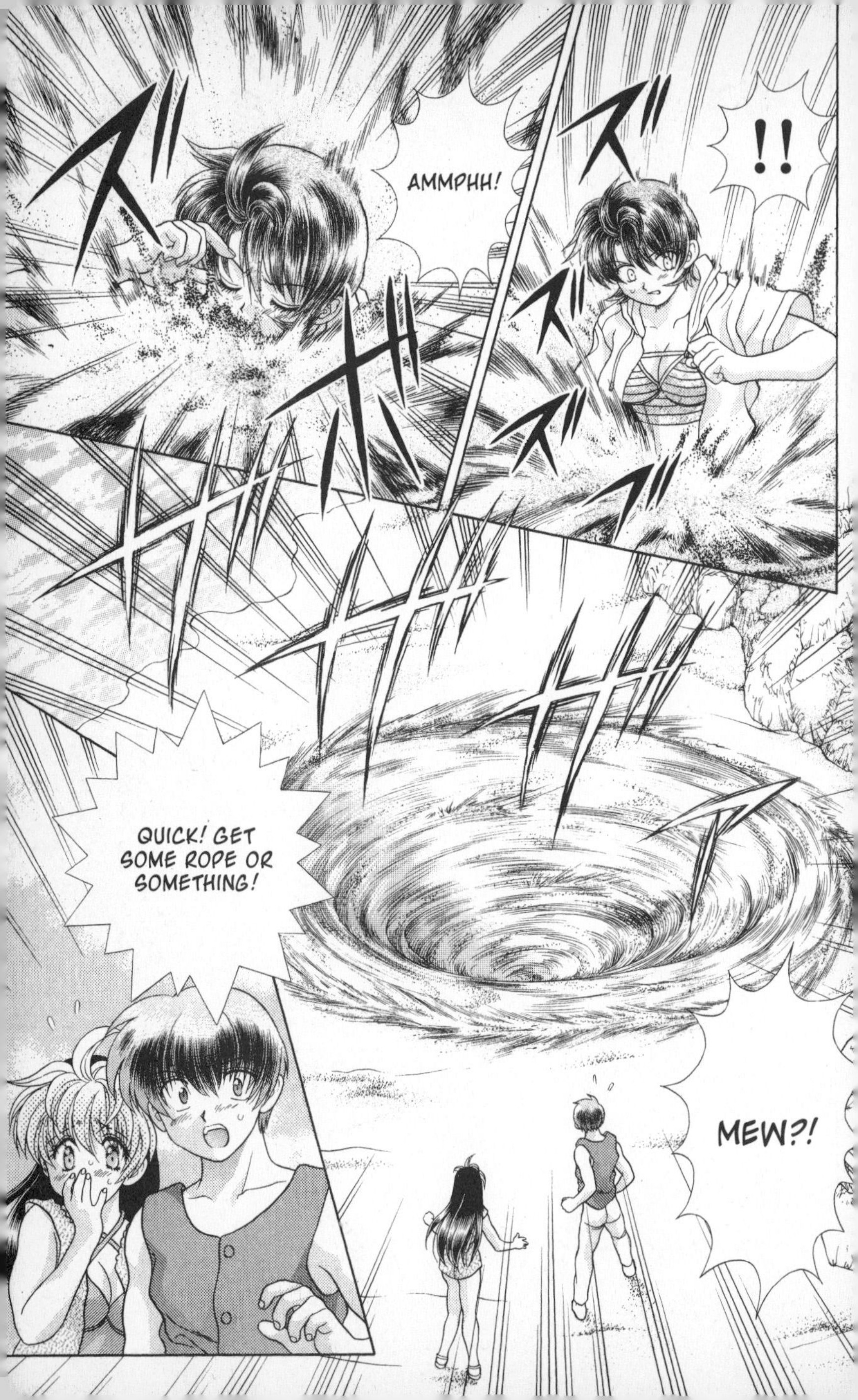
!!
AMMPHH!
MEW?!
QUICK! GET SOME ROPE OR SOMETHING!

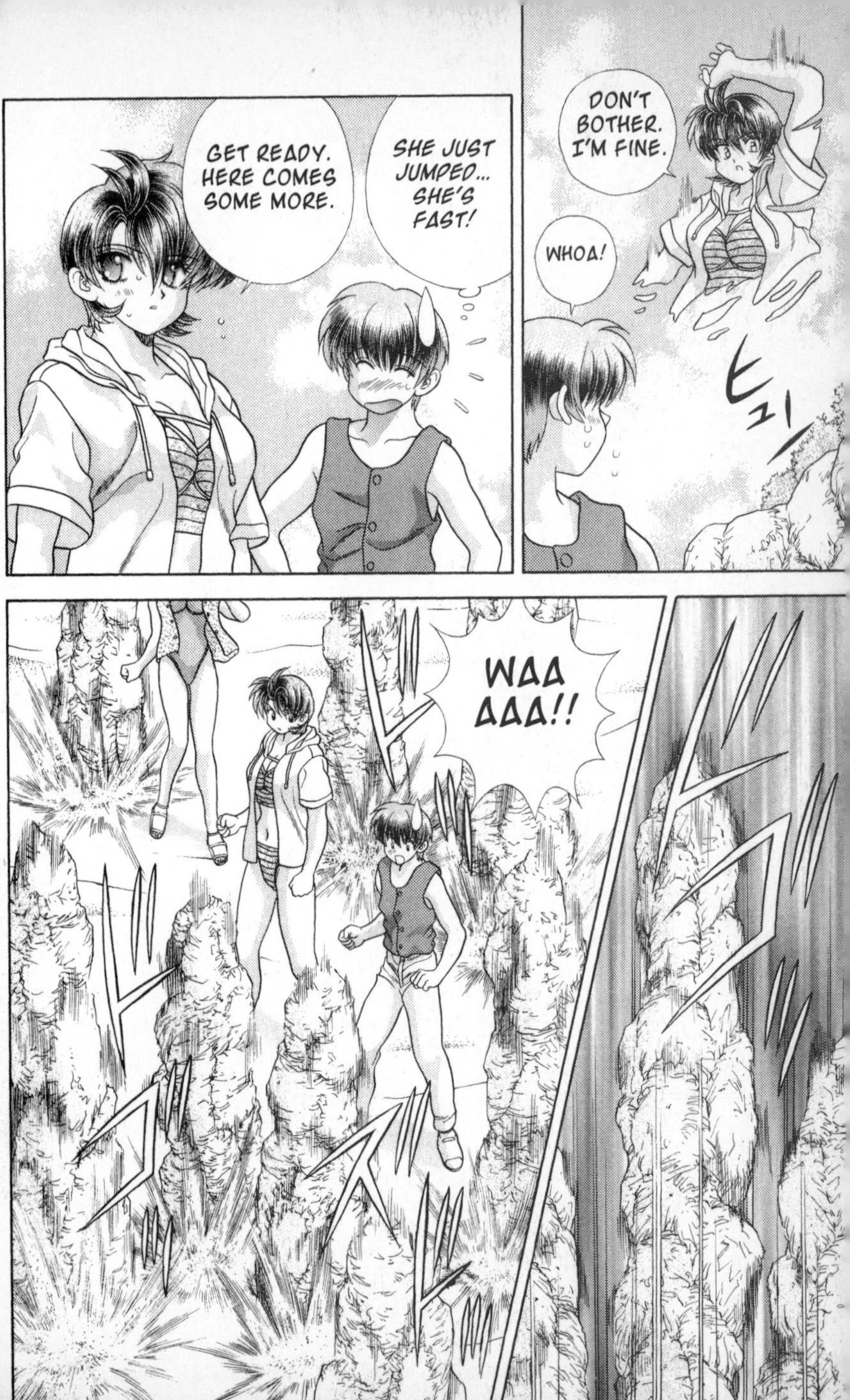
DON'T BOTHER. I'M FINE.
WHOA!
SHE JUST JUMPED... SHE'S FAST!
GET READY. HERE COMES SOME MORE.
WAA AAA!!

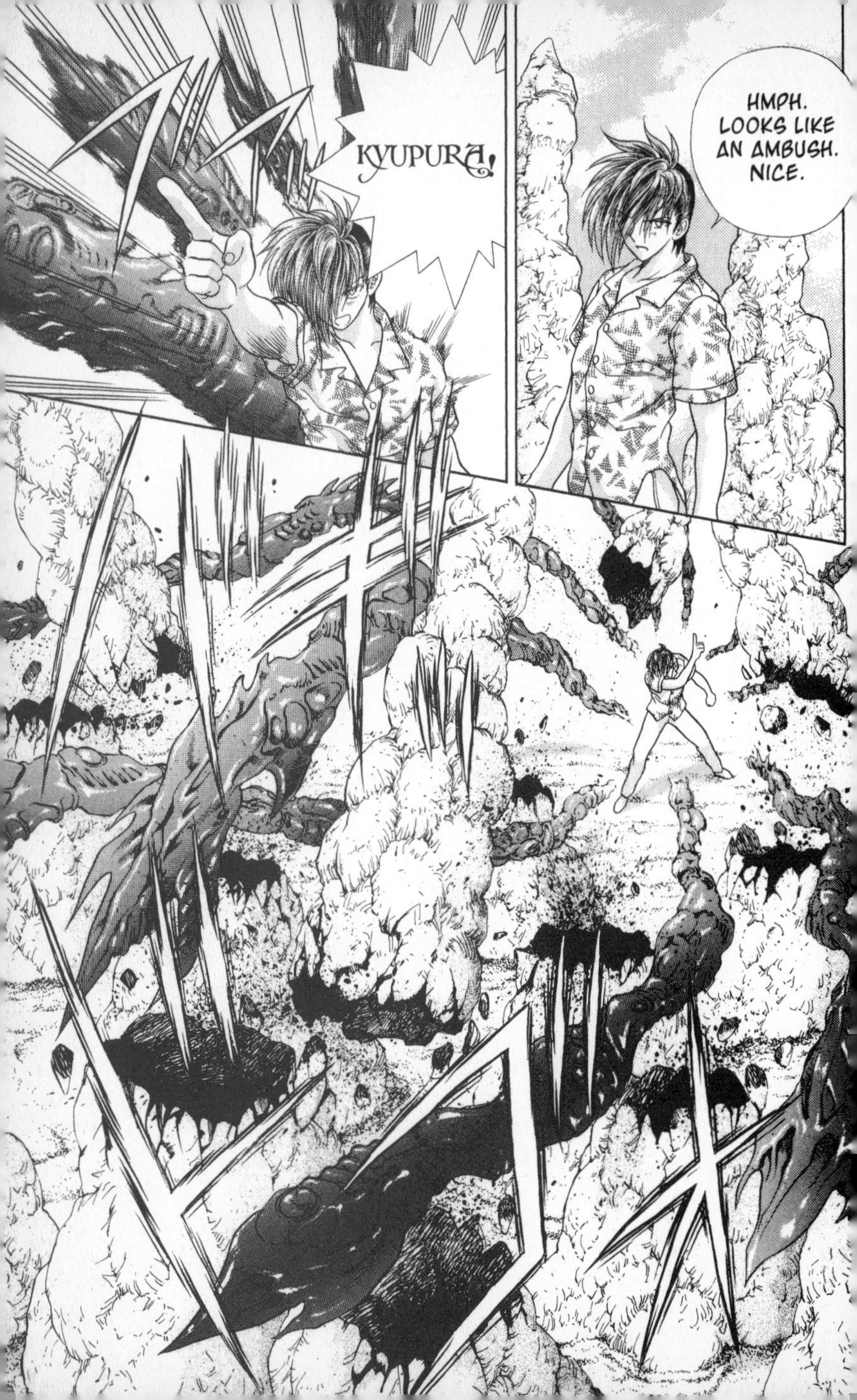
HMPH. LOOKS LIKE AN AMBUSH. NICE.
KYUPURA!

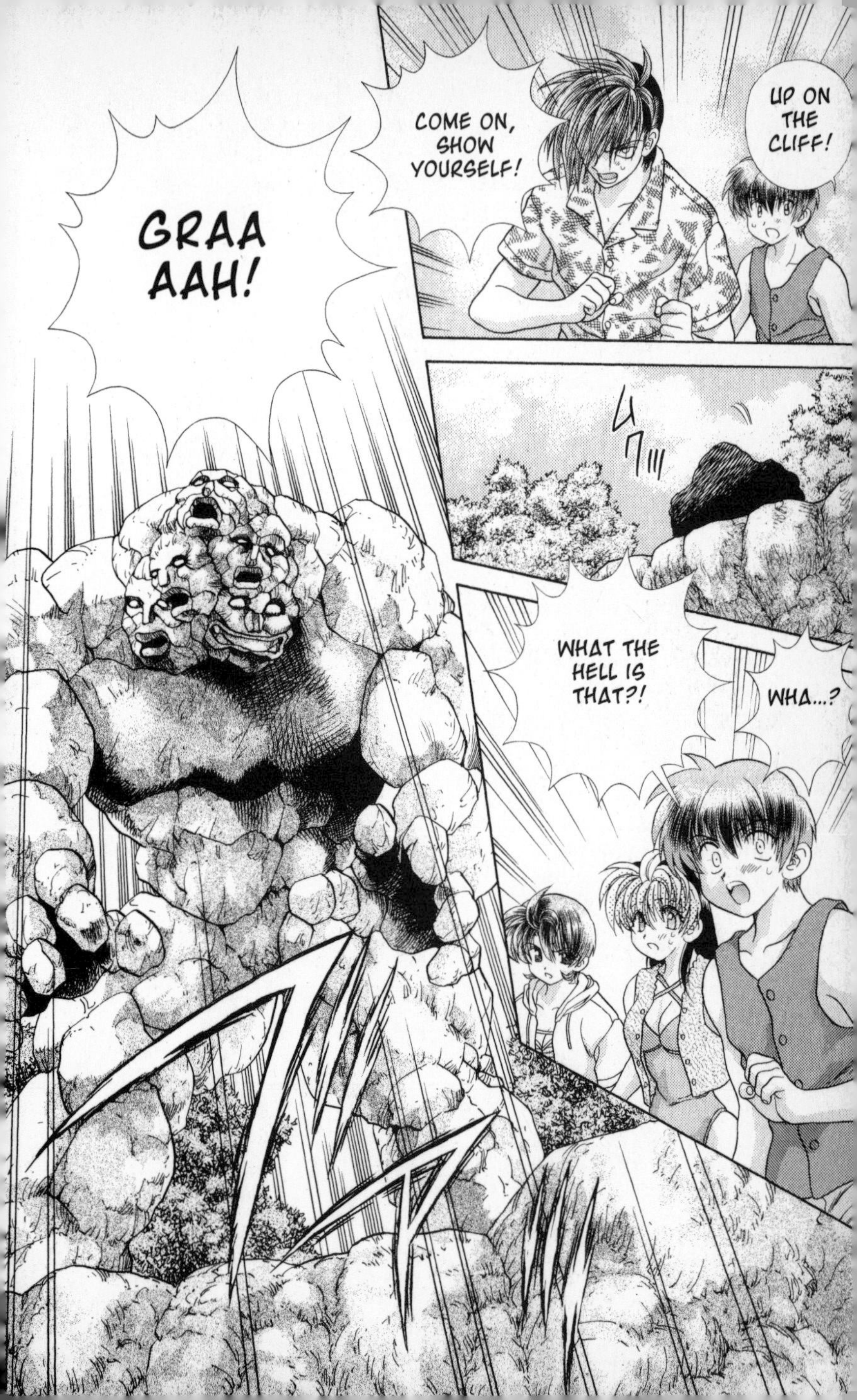
UP ON THE CLIFF!
COME ON, SHOW YOURSELF!
WHA...?
WHAT THE HELL IS THAT?!
GRAA AAH!

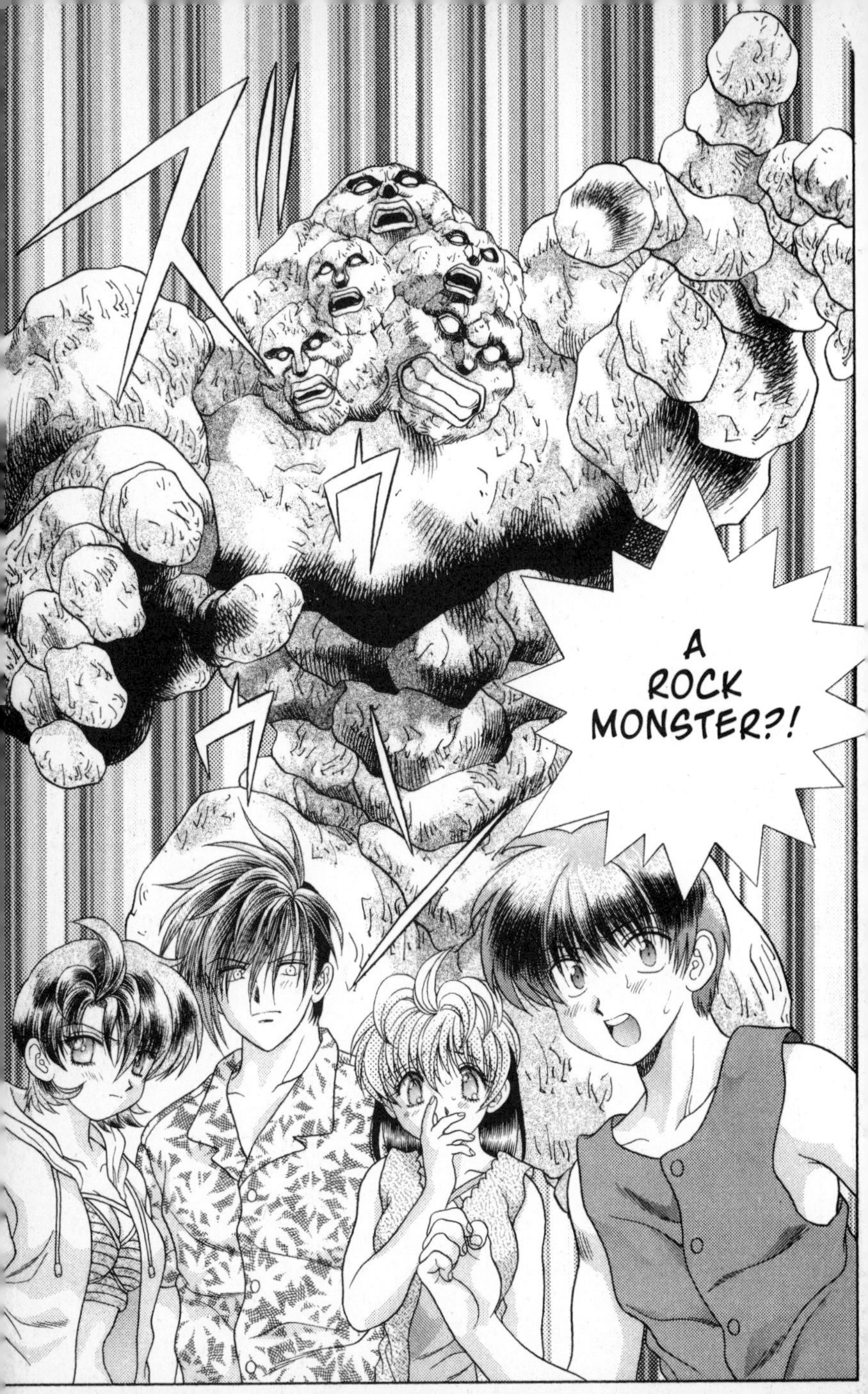
A ROCK MONSTER?!

Psychic Academy Volume 4 END

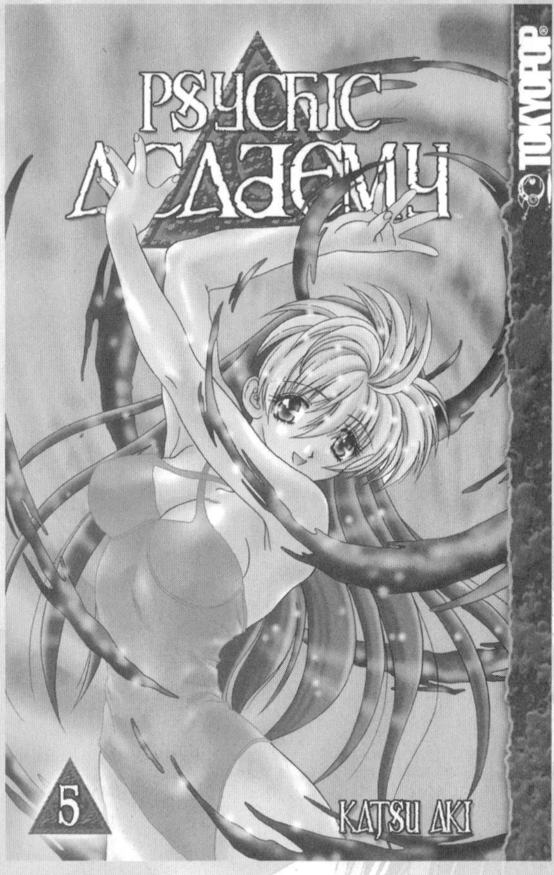
TOKYOPOP
PSYCHIC ACADEMY
5
KATSU AKI

In the next volume...

The secret behind the rock monster and the mysterious gray aura rumored to exist on the island will be revealed in the next thrilling volume of Psychic Academy...as will the reason Sahra can't face her love with Ai, and the reason Mew can't handle it either. But when members of the A.D.C. show up interested in Ai, the young boy will have to prove mastery over his powers or else face being sent off to California, where his abilities, both constructive and destructive, can be monitored.

ALSO AVAILABLE FROM 🔷TOKYOPOP®

ALSO AVAILABLE FROM TOKYOPOP®

MANGA

.HACK//LEGEND OF THE TWILIGHT
@LARGE
ABENOBASHI: MAGICAL SHOPPING ARCADE
A.I. LOVE YOU
AI YORI AOSHI
ANGELIC LAYER
ARM OF KANNON
BABY BIRTH
BATTLE ROYALE
BATTLE VIXENS
BRAIN POWERED
BRIGADOON
B'TX
CANDIDATE FOR GODDESS, THE
CARDCAPTOR SAKURA
CARDCAPTOR SAKURA - MASTER OF THE CLOW
CHOBITS
CHRONICLES OF THE CURSED SWORD
CLAMP SCHOOL DETECTIVES
CLOVER
COMIC PARTY
CONFIDENTIAL CONFESSIONS
CORRECTOR YUI
COWBOY BEBOP
COWBOY BEBOP: SHOOTING STAR
CRAZY LOVE STORY
CRESCENT MOON
CROSS
CULDCEPT
CYBORG 009
D•N•ANGEL
DEMON DIARY
DEMON ORORON, THE
DEUS VITAE
DIABOLO
DIGIMON
DIGIMON TAMERS
DIGIMON ZERO TWO
DOLL
DRAGON HUNTER
DRAGON KNIGHTS
DRAGON VOICE
DREAM SAGA
DUKLYON: CLAMP SCHOOL DEFENDERS
EERIE QUEERIE!
ERICA SAKURAZAWA: COLLECTED WORKS
ET CETERA
ETERNITY
EVIL'S RETURN
FAERIES' LANDING
FAKE
FLCL
FLOWER OF THE DEEP SLEEP
FORBIDDEN DANCE
FRUITS BASKET
G GUNDAM

GATEKEEPERS
GETBACKERS
GIRL GOT GAME
GIRLS EDUCATIONAL CHARTER
GRAVITATION
GTO
GUNDAM BLUE DESTINY
GUNDAM SEED ASTRAY
GUNDAM WING
GUNDAM WING: BATTLEFIELD OF PACIFISTS
GUNDAM WING: ENDLESS WALTZ
GUNDAM WING: THE LAST OUTPOST (G-UNIT)
GUYS' GUIDE TO GIRLS
HANDS OFF!
HAPPY MANIA
HARLEM BEAT
HYPER RUNE
I.N.V.U.
IMMORTAL RAIN
INITIAL D
INSTANT TEEN: JUST ADD NUTS
ISLAND
JING: KING OF BANDITS
JING: KING OF BANDITS - TWILIGHT TALES
JULINE
KARE KANO
KILL ME, KISS ME
KINDAICHI CASE FILES, THE
KING OF HELL
KODOCHA: SANA'S STAGE
LAMENT OF THE LAMB
LEGAL DRUG
LEGEND OF CHUN HYANG, THE
LES BIJOUX
LOVE HINA
LUPIN III
LUPIN III: WORLD'S MOST WANTED
MAGIC KNIGHT RAYEARTH I
MAGIC KNIGHT RAYEARTH II
MAHOROMATIC: AUTOMATIC MAIDEN
MAN OF MANY FACES
MARMALADE BOY
MARS
MARS: HORSE WITH NO NAME
MINK
MIRACLE GIRLS
MIYUKI-CHAN IN WONDERLAND
MODEL
MOURYOU KIDEN
MY LOVE
NECK AND NECK
ONE
ONE I LOVE, THE
PARADISE KISS
PARASYTE
PASSION FRUIT
PEACH GIRL
PEACH GIRL: CHANGE OF HEART

05.26.04T

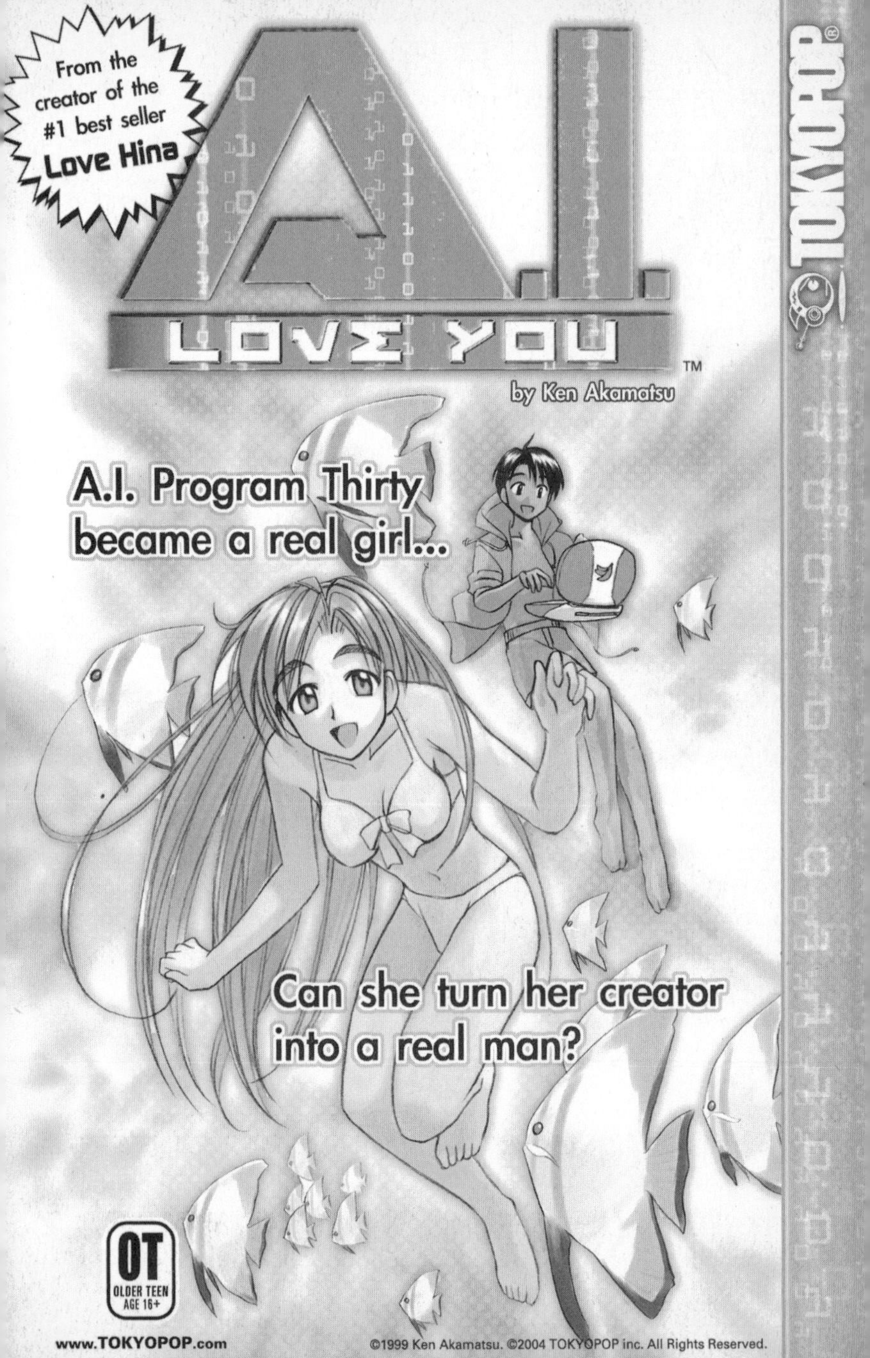

From the creator of the #1 best seller Love Hina
A.I. LOVE YOU™
by Ken Akamatsu
TOKYOPOP®
A.I. Program Thirty became a real girl...
Can she turn her creator into a real man?
OT
OLDER TEEN AGE 16+

SGT FROG WANTS YOU!

SGT⊕FROG
KERORO GUNSOU

A WACKY MANGA OF ALIEN FROGS & WORLD DOMINATION BY MINE YOSHIZAKI

T
TEEN
AGE 13+

STOP!

This is the back of the book.
You wouldn't want to spoil a great ending!

This book is printed "manga-style," in the authentic Japanese right-to-left format. Since none of the artwork has been flipped or altered, readers get to experience the story just as the creator intended. You've been asking for it, so TOKYOPOP® delivered: authentic, hot-off-the-press, and far more fun!

DIRECTIONS

If this is your first time reading manga-style, here's a quick guide to help you understand how it works.

It's easy... just start in the top right panel and follow the numbers. Have fun, and look for more 100% authentic manga from TOKYOPOP®!

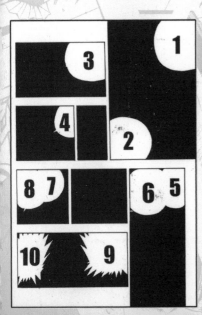